THE REBUKE
OF HISTORY

The Rebuke of

HISTORY

The Southern
Agrarians and
American
Conservative
Thought

PAUL V. MURPHY

THE UNIVERSITY OF NORTH CAROLINA PRESS
Chapel Hill and London

© 2001 The University
of North Carolina Press
All rights reserved

Set in Janson Type by
Tseng Information Systems, Inc.

Manufactured in the United
States of America

The paper in this book meets
the guidelines for permanence
and durability of the Committee
on Production Guidelines
for Book Longevity of the
Council on Library Resources.

Library of Congress
Cataloging-in-Publication Data
Murphy, Paul V.
The rebuke of history: the
Southern Agrarians and
American conservative
thought / Paul V. Murphy.
   p. cm.
Includes bibliographical
references and index.
ISBN 0-8078-2630-8
(cloth: alk. paper)—
ISBN 0-8078-4960-X
(pbk.: alk. paper)
1. Conservatism—United States—
History—20th century.
2. Agrarians (Group of writers)
3. Southern States—Intellectual
life—20th century.   I. Title.
JC573.2.U6 M87   2001
320.52'0973'0904—dc21
2001027128

05
04
03
02
01
5
4
3
2
1

FOR
MY MOTHER
AND
IN MEMORY OF
MY FATHER

CONTENTS

ILLUSTRATIONS

ACKNOWLEDGMENTS

I am indebted to the staffs of the libraries and archives where I conducted my research, particularly to Marice Wolfe, Michael Sims, Suellen Stringer-High, and Strawberry Luck at the Special Collections Department of Heard Library at Vanderbilt University; Margaret Sherry and Alice Clark at the Princeton Rare Book and Manuscript Library; Margaret Kulis at the Newberry Library; William Massa at the Sterling Memorial Library at Yale University; and Tony Wappel at the Special Collections Department of the University Libraries at the University of Arkansas. I especially thank Bill Cooper of the King Library at the University of Kentucky for his assistance in acquiring material on Richard Weaver. My thanks also to Richard Coughlin, director of the Pickler Memorial Library at Truman State University, for extending interlibrary loan privileges to me in the summer of 1998. I thank William F. Buckley Jr. for permission to examine his papers at Sterling Memorial Library, Francis Cheney for permission to examine the Brainard Cheney Papers at Vanderbilt University, and Robert Cowley for permission to microfilm the correspondence between Allen Tate and Malcolm Cowley at the Newberry Library and for entrusting me with valuable photographs from his family's collection. I am grateful to Wendell Berry, Thomas Fleming, Eugene D. Genovese, John Shelton Reed, the late C. Vann Woodward, and Clyde N. Wilson, who consented to be interviewed or to speak to me about my study, even as they had no guarantees about the nature of the final product. I am especially thankful to the late Russell Kirk, who gave me permission to examine his papers both at the Clarke Historical Library and at his home in Mecosta, Michigan, and to both him and Annette Kirk for their gracious hospitality in hosting me at their home.

I thank all those who assisted me in the research and writing of this book or who granted me permission to print quotations from published and unpublished materials. The judgments and opinions expressed in the following, as well as all faults and errors, are mine alone. In particular, I thank the family of Donald Davidson for graciously permitting me to quote extensively from his unpublished papers. Their permission to do so should in no way be construed as agreement with my interpretations or conclusions or endorsement of any of the particular opinions expressed in this book.

This book began as a dissertation. My research was supported, in part, by the Indiana University College of Arts and Sciences, the Indiana University Graduate School, and the History Department at Indiana University. I must also acknowledge Mrs. Anna Maners, my landlady in Bloomington for several years, whose exceedingly generous rental terms amounted to an indirect subsidy of my work. I owe a great debt to the members of my dissertation committee, which included Casey Blake, Steven Stowe, Michael McGerr, and David Nordloh. They sharpened my analysis at all points. In particular, Steven Stowe infused me with enthusiasm for the project many times over the years and guided me along the complex paths of southern history. Casey Blake served as an ideal mentor and a unflagging supporter in my years of contingent employment after graduate school. He has made my thinking and writing immeasurably clearer and has provided me with an invaluable model for the practice of intellectual history. For all this and more, I am extremely grateful. Along the way, many others have provided assistance in large ways and small, including the anonymous reviewers of this manuscript, Robert Cummings, George M. Curtis, Michael O'Brien (who encouraged me early in the project), David Thelen, James J. Thompson, and Bernard Sheehan. I am grateful for their assistance, especially as I know many will disagree strongly with parts of the resulting book. I also thank J. J. Pionke, my high-spirited research assistant at Truman State University, and Lewis Bateman, David Perry, and Grace Buonocore, my editors.

Much of this was written and revised while teaching on an adjunct and temporary basis; I am grateful for my colleagues at the various institutions that have housed me, including my colleagues in the History Department at Grand Valley State University, where I have ended up. I owe my greatest debts to my graduate school colleagues, whose intellectual camaraderie, friendship, and hospitality were sustaining over this period. Debbie Gershenowitz, Lisa Orr, Meg Meneghel, Richard Pierce, Matt Vosmeier, and Sarah McNair Vosmeier suffered through early drafts of this study as members of my dissertation group. They and John Borsos, John Chappell, Emilye Crosby, John Dichtl, Carol Engelhardt, Patrick Ettinger, Andy Evans, Nancy Godleski, Stuart Little, Jeff Matlak, Lydia Murdoch, Paul Schadewald, Liann Tsoukas, and Alex Urbiel provided gifts of good humor, encouragement, and wise advice that cannot easily be repaid.

Above all, I thank my family, who made this enterprise possible. This work is dedicated to my mother, whose love and support was ever present and always appreciated, and to the memory of my father, whose constitutional skepticism and unwillingness to leave any idea or opinion unexamined inform every line.

THE REBUKE
OF HISTORY

The Rebuke of History

The past is always a rebuke to the present. . . . It's a better rebuke than any dream of the future. It's a better rebuke because you can see what some of the costs were, what frail virtues were achieved in the past by frail men.

Robert Penn Warren at the Fugitives' reunion, May 1956

In November 1980 the prophets returned to Nashville, Tennessee, to be honored. Vanderbilt University hosted a symposium honoring the Southern Agrarians on the fiftieth anniversary of the publication of *I'll Take My Stand: The South and the Agrarian Tradition* (1930). *I'll Take My Stand* was an indictment of the industrial civilization of modern America. The authors hoped to preserve the manners and culture of the rural South as a healthy alternative. The book was the inspiration of two Vanderbilt English professors and poets, John Crowe Ransom and Donald Davidson, and their former student, the poet Allen Tate. It was composed of twelve essays written by twelve separate individuals, the title page declaring them to be Twelve Southerners.

In 1980, the three surviving contributors, novelists Robert Penn Warren and Andrew Nelson Lytle and psychologist Lyle Lanier, attended the Vanderbilt symposium to listen to papers analyzing their achievement and to participate in their own discussion of the book moderated by literary critic Cleanth Brooks, a longtime associate of the Agrarians. An essayist in *Time* magazine, claiming that 150 doctoral theses had been written about the book, remarked on the appeal of Agrarianism to modern-day environmentalists and theorists of the "zero-sum" society. "Why do the Agrarians, with their crusty prophecies and affirmations, still sound so pertinent, half a very non-agrarian century later?" he asked. The answer, he felt, lay in the power of Agrarianism as a poetic metaphor. This was a view shared by the organizers of the event, who, in a volume derived from it, argued that *I'll Take My Stand* was a prophetic book. Once dismissed as a nostalgic, backward-looking defense of a romanticized Old South, the book was rather "an affirmation of universal values" and a defense of the "religious, aesthetic, and moral foundations of the old European civilization."[1]

The book appeared at the end of a decade that had seen numerous anthologies of original essays designed to assess the state of modern civilization. Yet this collection stood out and continues to fascinate because of the sheer intransigence of its stance. Industrial society devalues human labor by replacing it with machines, argued the Twelve Southerners. Machine society undercut the dignity of labor and left modern man bereft of vocation and in an attenuated state of "satiety and aimlessness," glutted with the surfeit of consumer goods produced by the industrial economy. Industrialism, they argued, was inimical to religion, the arts, and the elements of a good life—leisure, conversation, hospitality. Modern Americans, Donald Davidson declared elsewhere, live a scattered life, condemned to follow a "thousand highly specialized pursuits" and consumed by "bits of urban piece-work." "In civilization," he argued, "time is measured in tiny units held in delicate synchronization to the central master-clock, which jerks with it, minute to minute, second to second, the servile movements of men." The critic Stark Young, who scathingly attacked the austere banalities of former president Calvin Coolidge in his contribution, imagined the boast of a modern booster: "In our town we've got twenty thousand miles of concrete walks." "And where do they lead?" was his retort.[2]

The Twelve Southerners were frankly reactionary and seriously proposed returning to an economy dominated by subsistence agriculture. The best terms to represent the opposition between southern and American ways of living, they argued, were agrarian versus industrial. The theory of agrarianism, they declared, "is that the culture of the soil is the best and most sensitive of vocations, and that therefore it should have the economic preference and enlist the maximum number of workers." Why, they asked, should modern men accept a social system so manifestly inferior to what had gone before? "If a community, or a section, or a race, or an age, is groaning under industrialism, and well aware that it is an evil dispensation," the Twelve Southerners declared, "it must find the way to throw it off. To think that this cannot be done is pusillanimous." They infused their antimodernism with southern bravado and a declared willingness to live within the narrow bounds of a traditional life. As was evident in the title's reference to "Dixie," *I'll Take My Stand* was a self-conscious defense of the South, undertaken sixty-five years after Robert E. Lee surrendered at Appomattox Court House. The Twelve Southerners were "reconstructed but unregenerate," John Crowe Ransom suggested. In confronting the forces of modernity, the Southern Agrarians adopted the strategy of the quintessential traditionalist described in John Donald Wade's essay, a man who "went about fortifying himself by his knowledge of history and of ancient fable, telling himself that man had immemorially drawn his best strength from the earth that mothered him."[3]

The passage of years revealed an almost protean quality to Agrarianism. It came to mean very different things to a variety of different thinkers. Indeed, the contributors themselves, over the years, interpreted and reinterpreted their original impulse in light of changing convictions and interests. In 1930, *I'll Take My Stand* was an indictment of industrial capitalism and a warning of its potential to destroy what the Agrarians considered a more humane and leisurely social order. For some, it later came to be a statement of Christian humanism. For others, it was a rousing defense of the southern heritage and southern culture, which, in turn, meant a defense of the Western tradition. For others, Agrarianism was merely a metaphor for the simple life—one not consumed with materialism. For others still, the symposium was part of a traditional southern political discourse, which warned against centralized power and a strong state and which stood against bourgeois liberalism. After World War II, the nascent conservative movement—poised against what it perceived to be an unwise liberal elite and in defense of traditional values and American capitalism—subsumed the Agrarians within its intellectual tradition. The Agrarians became respected, if quixotic, dissenters from the main trend of American progressivism.

The question asked by the *Time* essayist in 1980 remains, however: Why do the Agrarians remain so pertinent years after *I'll Take My Stand* was first published? In 1980 Robert Penn Warren and Lyle Lanier did not dwell on the metaphorical implications of Agrarianism. At the symposium, they commented on the problems of contemporary American society. In an interview a few months before the symposium, Warren argued that technology was destroying the "human personality" and threatening the very basis of democracy. Earlier in the year, Lanier, anticipating the Vanderbilt conference, confided his doubts about the value of his own thoughts to Warren. "I don't feel overly confident now that I can have anything worthwhile to say then about what I stand *for* in these dismal times," he wrote. "As in 1930, what to stand *against* seems much easier to identify."[4] Lanier had plenty to say by the following November, listing the ills of modern America, from the condition of the environment to the prevalence of ghettos to the southward movement of midwestern industries in order to exploit cheap labor (a new kind of carpetbagger, in Lanier's view).[5] While Warren and Cleanth Brooks fretted about the social effects of machines and high technology, Lanier cited Barry Commoner on the decentralization of electric power and speculated about the nationalization of some multinational corporations.[6] Brooks cited the historian Christopher Lasch's pessimistic analysis of American culture, *The Culture of Narcissism* (1979), in support of the arguments in *I'll Take My Stand*, and Lanier confessed to checking the *Wall Street Journal* periodically, "just to keep up with what the enemy is up to"![7] Agrarianism had been, and remained, more than a metaphor to these men. It was a program of action, and the enemy was still industrial capitalism.

Since the founding of the nation, southerners had sought a way to reconcile modernity and tradition, to participate in the modern market economy while retaining the shockingly premodern (yet profitable) system of slave labor. Slaveholders were alternately beguiled by the riches of the capitalist marketplace and appalled at the prospect of a society based on the pecuniary impulse and the self-interest, chicanery, and competitiveness of the market.[8] *I'll Take My Stand* and Agrarianism were rooted, in part, in this older southern desire to reconcile tradition and progress, to become reconstructed but unregenerate. But the Agrarians were also shaped by the modernist trends in European and American thought in the late nineteenth and early twentieth centuries—by the Darwinism, relativism, naturalism, and empiricism that had shaken all orthodoxies about God, history, and human nature. Their immediate context was the somewhat somnolent South of the 1920s, but these intellectuals, poets, and social scientists eagerly confronted the intellectual trends of the time: bohemianism and cultural radicalism, literary modernism, socialism, cultural nationalism, liberal Protestantism, and the cult of science and efficiency. The 1920s offered a richer discourse on the crises of faith, morals, and science produced by modernity than any decade since. Agrarianism was an attempt to respond to questions being asked by others besides southerners: Is it possible to satisfy the felt needs for community, leisure, and stability in the dizzying whirl of modern life? How do we validate values in a disenchanted and secular age?

The Twelve Southerners' response was both radical and conservative. In large part, the participation of figures such as Ransom and Tate (and also Davidson) was motivated by concerns resulting from cultural modernism. Tate and Ransom were conservative modernists themselves; both were concerned with the decline of religious authority in modern life. In some ways, the Agrarians sought to preserve the values and structure of Victorian society, as it was known in the South prior to the 1920s, from the solvent of modernist culture. But *I'll Take My Stand* was also a response to modernization, the sweeping economic and social changes that were reshaping the South at the time the symposium was written. The Agrarians did not preach a blanket resistance to modernity; nor, although far from taking a pluralist stance, did they desire to scapegoat ethnic minorities or conspiratorial elites for the ills of modernity. They did not simply retreat into a disengaged advocacy of the Great Books and moral absolutes, nor did they call for the reestablishment of a patriarchal Christian order (although Allen Tate, for one, would seem to have welcomed such an event). Instead, they rejected industrial capitalism and the culture it produced. In *I'll Take My Stand* they called for a return to the small-scale economy of rural America as a means to preserve the cultural amenities of the society they knew. Ransom and Tate believed that only by arresting the progress of industrial capitalism and its imperatives of science and efficiency could a social order capable of fostering and validating humane values and traditional religious faith be preserved. Skeptical and unorthodox themselves, they admired the capacity of orthodox religion to provide surety in life.

For Ransom and Tate, the two things—the modernist challenge to Victorian values and the industrial challenge to the agrarian economy—were related. Later conservatives would not see this as the case. In 1930, agrarianism as an economic program was at the heart of the Agrarian movement; by the 1950s, practical agrarianism had been displaced from this position. Rather, the South as a symbolic marker of both traditional society and Western civilization became the central element of the Agrarian discourse. Modernism and modernization were no longer deeply related; what was a radical conservatism was now southern traditionalism. This bifurcation of economic and cultural analysis, which the Agrarians had originally resisted, reflects a distinctive attribute of the conservative movement that was emerging in the 1950s and transforming the leadership of the American Right.

Three distinct groups of intellectuals have preserved the memory of the Agrarians since 1930. Students of southern culture have long been fascinated by *I'll Take My Stand*, not only because of its volatile mix of sharp-edged modernist critics like Ransom, Tate, and Warren and heartfelt, southern nationalists such as Davidson and the historian Frank L. Owsley but also because of its role in formulating the idea of the South in modern culture. Richard H. Gray, Fred Hobson, Richard H. King, Michael Kreyling, Michael O'Brien, and Daniel Joseph Singal illuminate the contours of the white southern mentality. They place *I'll Take My Stand* in the long tradition of southern apologetics and stress the ways in which the culturally constructed idea of the South served the personal intellectual needs and political purposes of particular southern writers, including the Agrarians.[9] Historians Michael O'Brien and Daniel Joseph Singal have pointed to the role this concept played in mediating between the fading values of Victorianism and the emerging ethos of modernism for a generation of southerners.[10] Literary scholar Michael Kreyling has recently emphasized the role that the Agrarians played in constructing the southern literary tradition, arguing that they created an image of the South to function as a conservative cultural center for their society and to buttress their own cultural authority.[11]

At the same time, generations of southern literary academics have nurtured the reputation of the Agrarians because of their role in creating and promoting the extraordinarily rich tradition of the literary arts in the modern South. For many of these scholars, the Agrarians were both vital figures in the mid-twentieth-century southern literary renascence and much respected role models. Following Allen Tate, who was, for them, perhaps the most influential southern intellectual in the mid-twentieth century, they interpreted Agrarianism as a defense of the humanistic tradition of the West. In this, they tended to depoliticize *I'll Take My Stand;* the book, as O'Brien observed, was "edited into a metaphor." According to Louis D. Rubin Jr., Agrarianism was not a practical program but an "extended metaphor," akin to Jefferson's pastoral myth of the sturdy yeoman, for the importance of the arts, family relations, and religious faith to the southern mind.[12] In a 1967 study of southern writers, he stated his position more forcefully: "Neither a treatise on economics, nor a guide to political action, nor yet a sociological blueprint, the Agrarian symposium was an image of what the good life could be."[13] Lewis Simpson shared this view. Agrarianism, Simpson pointedly declared, "although it has been widely misinterpreted as a political movement—a misunderstanding promoted by the Agrarians' own misinterpretation of their basic motives—was a literary movement."[14] C. Hugh Holman characterized Agrarianism as a "mythic embodiment" of such values as individual integrity, a religious and moral view of life, and family.[15]

In contrast, this study treats Agrarianism as a tradition of social thought and traces its transmutation and splintering in the years after 1930 in order to illuminate often overlooked trends in American intellectual life as well as the development of American conservative thought in this century. Intellectual historians usually relegate the Agrarians to the role of colorful, if compelling, exponents of regionalism.[16] Similarly, historians of the conservative movement have studied the conservative thinker Richard M. Weaver, an important interpreter of Agrarianism, in the context of postwar traditionalism but have not fully explored his intellectual roots in Agrarianism.[17] Later conservative thinkers—even many of the Agrarians themselves

—walked away from the radical implications of Agrarianism.[18] Conservatives, southern and otherwise, constitute the final group to preserve the memory of the Agrarians. Conservatives have proudly honored the Agrarians as perceptive forefathers and tend to present them as southern traditionalists—proponents of a social order based on religion, opponents of a godless and untraditional leviathan state, critics of a rootless individualism, and, above all, stout defenders of the South, which necessarily entails a defense of southern tradition, culture, and values. The late literary scholar M. E. Bradford and the historian Eugene D. Genovese have argued that the Agrarians were part of a long tradition of southern conservatism. This tradition of antistatist conservatism was, for Bradford, patriarchal and republican in nature and is, in Genovese's eyes, the most convincing American critique of bourgeois individualism.[19] Mark G. Malvasi has published a recent study in this vein.[20]

The modernist anxiety over religious faith, which profoundly shaped Ransom and Tate, has faded among these conservatives. Postwar inheritors of the Agrarian tradition, such as Weaver and Bradford or some of the writers published in the conservative magazine *Chronicles*, exhibited no doubt in the absolute authority of Christian revelation. (As a consequence, their ability to appeal to the secular and the skeptical has been limited.) Tate almost immediately began to argue that Agrarianism was really a mode of Christian humanism. Weaver, too, sought to universalize Agrarianism. He made of it an antiliberal philosophy of order, one suitable to the needs of an anxious America after World War II. This study is, in part, an explanation of the way figures such as Davidson, Weaver, and Bradford converged with the Right and how the Right, in turn, was reshaped into a postwar "conservative movement" by individuals such as William F. Buckley Jr. and his associates at the *National Review*. Buckley and his colleagues were, in their support of a strong military state and their faith in free-market capitalism, in some ways antithetical to the Old Right that existed prior to the 1950s. Their ability to seize control of and redirect the Right is a phenomenon in need of fuller analysis—a task for which this study provides some beginnings.

A final element of the study is an attempt to understand the role of the past in Agrarian thought. If the modernists Ransom and Tate believed in 1930 that a radical restructuring of the social economy of the nation might lead to the renewal of Christian faith, Davidson saw in Agrarianism a simpler route to faith. For Davidson, southern history itself proved sufficient to validate values. In submission to the past, Davidson found who he was. Agrarianism became for him a form of white southern identity politics. "Identity" is a relatively recent concept in American culture. As historian Philip Gleason observed, the term became popular among social psychologists and sociologists because it fit the concerns of post–World War II America. Whether used to describe the process of socialization (as Erik Erikson intended when speaking of the "identity crisis") or the role of ethnicity or race in social relations, the concept enabled intellectuals to talk about the relationship between the individual and the larger collectivity, particularly the way in which individual personality and a sense of selfhood were engendered by the larger society through cultural norms, status requirements, and role-playing.[21] Ironically, it is Davidson, the most reactionary of the original Agrarians, who is, in many ways, the most relevant of the Agrarians to contemporary concerns. He was a harbinger of identity politics, the Agrarian for whom history and heritage formed the core of personal meaning and self-esteem.

Looked at from a broader perspective, Davidson emerges as a pivotal figure in the Agrarian tradition. It was Davidson, along with neo-Agrarians such as Weaver, who was crucial to transforming Agrarianism into a form of traditionalist conservatism after World War II. Davidson and others came to see the South as a synecdoche for Western civilization. The impetus for *I'll Take My Stand* had been two sets of concerns—one raised by modernism's challenge to Victorian values and the other by modernization's challenge to the agrarian economy. For Davidson, these two challenges resolved into one: the challenge that proponents of the new order—whether modernists critics of traditional culture or progressive advocates of the regulatory and social welfare state—posed to the South. Davidson shifted his focus from the effects of progress to the progressives who seemed to favor them. Long treated as a rather narrow and somewhat simple representative of Agrarianism because of his hardy romanticism and his overt racism and white supremacy, it was Davidson who most influenced contemporary neo-Agrarianism. He most shaped many conservative postwar interpretations of Agrarianism. It was his ideas and instincts that were most predictive of future trends in the South and the nation.

The authors of *I'll Take My Stand* evoked the mythology of the Lost Cause; the anthology was consciously underwritten by an explicit appeal to southern nationalism. To be southern and of the Agrarians' generation was, in some ways, to feel as inheritors of a noble but failed tradition. The Agrarians felt social tradition in the form of the pressure of the past. A culture is inherited. It is communicated as history, which is a master narrative of society's development but also a set of cultural myths, assumptions, and values that intercut in complex ways with one's own personal development. Part of the reason that the original Agrarian project failed lay in this connection between the social and the personal as well as in the announced intention of Agrarianism to return to an older form of social organization. Not only was the historical validity of the Agrarians' reconstruction of the antebellum social order open to dispute, but the projected loyalty to the southern past became entirely too demanding for many of the Agrarians. The psychological toll of deep historical introspection would evidence itself in striking ways. Caroline Gordon exhibited a southern nostalgia as strong as any member of the group, including Davidson, the most unreconstructed of the Agrarians. Married to Tate and relegated to the margins of the cultural agitation of the Nashville "brethren" as she wrote her own filiopietist books on the South, Gordon wrote the young aesthete and future impresario of the New York City Ballet Lincoln Kirstein in 1931 of her "regret for the lost cause." "It would have been better, I think, if our grandfathers had been carried off the field dead," she declared. "The South that exists today has little of the Old South in it—we have sold out, certainly." [22] Gordon's comment, if taken seriously, suggests the level of guilt that a contemporary southerner might have faced. He or she lived with the ceaseless rebuke of the honored dead fathers—the men whose sacrifice on the battlefields of the Civil War was in vain if their posterity allowed the precious cultural heritage of the South to slip through their fingers. Gordon's belief that her contemporaries betrayed the past for mere material satisfactions suggests an even greater level of culpability. The paradox for southerners of the Agrarians' generation—to change but to remain loyal to history—remained a continuing source of division for the Agrarians and undercut the radical conservatism of *I'll Take My Stand*.

At a reunion of the Fugitive poets in May 1956, Warren confessed that for many years he had shut Agrarianism from his mind, being more preoccupied with the cataclysmic social and political forces that played forth in Europe and Asia. Agrarian discussions—"a sort of quarreling over the third highball"—seemed irrelevant, a sentimental product of his long-ago student homesickness. But he now believed that his old Agrarian enthusiasms were an attempt "to recapture, to reassess." Rather than being irrelevant, they were tied into the major problems of the age. The growth of great nation-states, even if democratic, had marginalized the individual. Indeed, the individual was reduced to meaninglessness, with no sense of responsibility, no sense of past and place. In this context, the Agrarian image of a better antebellum South came to represent for Warren a potential source of spiritual revitalization.[23] The past recalled not as a mythical "golden age" but "imaginatively conceived and historically conceived in the strictest readings of the researchers" could be a "rebuke to the present." [24]

In the end, the history of the Agrarian tradition was shaped by the pressure of the past on this group of southern intellectuals—a past whose legacy included segregation and white supremacy. The pressure of the past pitted Warren against his friend and former teacher Davidson. In the 1950s and 1960s, Davidson played a leading role in the attempt to preserve the system of segregation. Warren took his stand against it. Loyalty to the southern past and the ambiguous lessons of Agrarianism led both men in very different directions. The southerner, Ransom wrote in *I'll Take My Stand*, "identifies himself with a spot of ground, and this ground carries a good deal of meaning; it defines itself for him as nature."[25] This may be so, but the interpretation of this meaning has been the subject of much conflict among southerners, white and black, throughout the century. At the heart of Agrarianism was the question not only of where do I stand, but also, who belongs? And it was not the ground that provided the answers but the human beings who took their stands upon it.

CHAPTER ONE

The Radical Conservatism of
I'll Take My Stand

*It is strange, of course, that a majority of men anywhere could even
as with one mind become enamored of industrialism: a system that
has so little regard for individual wants.*

Twelve Southerners, *I'll Take My Stand*

"The great worth of the Agrarian group was the society we made,"
Agrarian Andrew Nelson Lytle recalled years later. "We liked one
another. We were the same kind of people, and we usually met socially as well as for discussion. Sometimes for a party, or set-back
or a little poker."[1] The Agrarian circle originated at Vanderbilt University in Nashville, Tennessee, in the years between 1910 and 1930,
at a time when most faculty members lived on campus and relations
between faculty and students extended well beyond the classroom.
John Crowe Ransom, who began teaching at his alma mater in 1914,
shared quarters in Kissam Hall with eight other bachelor instructors.
Their rooms became a haven for students. It was natural for Donald
Davidson, a student, to invite Ransom, his Shakespeare teacher, to
join a group of friends who discussed philosophy and shared ideas.
The group usually met off campus, often in the company of Sidney
Hirsch, a Nashville aesthete whose special gift seems to have been to
spark conversation. "Out on the Hirsches' porch, with the cigar ends
glowing occasionally, a debate always insured from the nature of the
company, it is *The* Happiness," one member of the group wrote to an
absent friend.[2]

The membership in this circle varied over time, as faculty, students,
and friends came and went, but its members shared a close bond, often
referring to themselves collectively as the "brethren." World War I
intervened, but many in the group reassembled at Vanderbilt after the
war. Their interests eventually turned to poetry, and from 1922 to

1925 they published a magazine of verse entitled the *Fugitive*, which attracted notice in both New York and England. Allen Tate, a brilliant undergraduate, became a member of the Fugitive group in 1921; in 1923 he met Robert Penn ("Red") Warren, a tall, red-haired, and ungainly sixteen-year-old sophomore from Kentucky. They shared a room in the Vanderbilt Divinity School. It "was filled with dirty shirts, cigarette butts, filth to the waist, and empty bottles," Warren later recalled. "Gangs of people would come there to argue poetry and read aloud." Warren contributed wall illustrations depicting scenes from literary works, including T. S. Eliot's *The Waste Land*.[3]

Ransom's house was a "second home" to Warren, a place of leisure and camaraderie. Ransom enjoyed tennis, excelled at golf, and would sometimes play bridge or poker for an entire weekend. He once rented a bankrupt country club for a year so that he and his friends could use the tennis courts and billiard tables. The Agrarians, friends from Vanderbilt and Nashville, visiting writers—all would socialize together, whether at a camp in the country; at the farm in Guntersville, Alabama, of Lytle's father; or at Benfolly, the house Tate's older brother purchased for him, which overlooked the Cumberland River. The Agrarian movement, Warren suggested, was a "menagerie," held together by "a common shared history as Southerners."[4]

By the 1920s, the South was in the throes of modernization, a process only fitfully managed by southerners. After the end of Reconstruction, "New South" boosters—businessmen and urban-based professionals and publicists—enthusiastically sponsored the building of railroads and encouraged industrial development and the expansion of cities, as well as the spread of the Yankee ideas of hard work and material success. They defined progress as increasing prosperity and economic opportunity for the average southerner. The rapid modernization of the South promoted by these New South businessmen bred profound social and cultural changes. The locus of southern society moved from the country to the city, resulting in a destabilization of southern agricultural life and the disruption of many of its distinctive features, including the age-old symbiotic relationship between planter and yeoman (and the newer, post–Civil War paternalism of the credit-making rural storeowner and the sharecropper); the reciprocity and exchange of rural and small-town living; and the ritualized trips of country folk to the county seat, whether to socialize, shop, engage in legal or business transactions, or listen to an orator. After the 1880s, the rate of urban growth in the South doubled the national average. Plantations decayed as southerners moved to a city or left the South entirely. While villages and towns grew in population by 5 million people between 1880 and 1910, the South as a whole experienced a net drain exceeding 1.2 million whites and 500,000 blacks.[5]

The city of Nashville was no exception to these larger trends. Between 1880 and 1930, the city's population increased three and one-half times, reaching a level just below 154,000 by the latter date. Led by an aggressive entrepreneurial class, Nashville was a city on the make in the late nineteenth century, becoming a regional leader in railroads, industry, commerce, and education. Although lagging behind such cities as Atlanta, Birmingham, and Memphis in growth, Nashville possessed milling and storage facilities for grain that were unmatched in the South after the turn of the century. Rural emigrants who streamed into the city during World War I and the postwar agricultural depression discovered a city divided into distinct residential and commercial zones and possessing sizable suburban development, segregated, of course, by race and class. By the 1920s, Nashville boasted a diversified economy and was a regional center in banking, insurance, and securities trading. (Local boosters nicknamed Union Street the "Wall Street of the South.") Its leadership in education was undisputed; the city was home to the George Peabody School of Teachers and two black schools—Fisk University and Meharry Medical College—as well as Vanderbilt.[6]

Some southerners resisted the new dispensation, lamenting the loss of distinctive southern traditions and social practices. "I ask in Heaven's name," one southerner wrote after reading an article by a spokesman for the New South, "is it essential that a southern man must eat dirt or wallow therein, denounce his ancestry or ridicule their foibles, or otherwise degrade himself to prove his newborn loyalty and devotion to the new order of things?" The vociferous testimonials to the New South creed by figures such as Atlanta newspaperman Henry Grady were met by equally strong denunciations. The South, critics charged, was selling itself cheaply to northern capitalists.[7] Commenting on the rise of the textile industry at the turn of the century, historian Edward L. Ayers noted the "pervasive sense of decline of Southern rural life," which created "a sense of dissatisfaction and desperation" driving white families into "public work," meaning the textile mills. "The demographic pressure on the land, the decline of cotton prices, the growing percentage of women to men in the older regions, the mobility of blacks, the disaffection of the young for rural life—all these dislocations made it easier to undergo the powerful dislocation of leaving home to work in a textile mill." In Nashville, National Life and Accident, carrying its advertising to a new medium, established radio station WSM in 1925 and soon inaugurated the Saturday night Barn Dance, dubbed the "Grand Ole

Opry." The showcase for hillbilly music was immensely appealing to an audience of southern rural folk, whether living in the countryside or displaced to the city. Its popular brand of instant nostalgia for rural life reflected southerners' ambivalence toward the changes produced by modernization.[8]

Historically, the South was a closed, rigid society, founded on an assumed orthodoxy with regard to social norms, particularly those concerning race. A veneer of genteel custom, often centered on ritualized, public deference to authority and an exaggerated emphasis on manners, decorum, and civility, covered the hard expectations of conformity to this orthodoxy. White southern society demanded of its members, white and black, not only conformity to written and unwritten rules but also loyalty to an often informal but clearly defined social hierarchy. In return, the white southerner gained a deep sense of community, identity, and familial connection. Black southerners gained quite a bit less.

The great dilemma posed by modernization was the balancing of change and tradition: How could the South both modernize and remain its essential self? Many southerners contemplated modernity with an uneasiness at the prospect of losing special southern customs and ways of life. For the white elite, modern life threatened an established power structure and social leadership. For whites in general, the issue was retaining white supremacy, particularly as cities introduced new and more threatening possibilities for the intermingling of the races. The white majority retained power by means of segregation, disenfranchisement, and the use of terror, particularly lynching. Between 1889 and 1915, white southern society experienced a paroxysm of radical race hatred and racial terrorism, with the result that the system of white supremacy was reaffirmed.[9] Southern whites succeeded in making blacks invisible in their society. By the 1920s, the earlier radicalism had subsided, and, enjoying a period of relative racial peace, white southerners allowed the "negro problem" to recede from the forefront of their consciousness.[10] The southern white vision of a solid, organic South, buttressed by the civil religion of the Lost Cause, was reflected in such works as Wilbur J. Cash's *Mind of the South* (1941), a critical analysis of the overpowering and oppressive unity—the "savage ideal"—of southern life. "In the popular mind of the white South in the decades after World War I," historian Joel Williamson writes, "there was no race problem, no black history, and no history of race relations if the Yankees and Communists, Catholics and Jews, outsiders and aliens would simply leave black people alone." Southerners of the period, Williamson argues, were comfortably out of step with the nation. "The South was a fine spun living dream, and, in the decades of the 1920s and 1930s, the dream waxed rosy, romantic, and unreal."[11]

The large social and economic forces transforming the South affected Vanderbilt University no less than Nashville. The university originated in 1872 as Central University of the Methodist Episcopal Church, South. Bishop Holland N. McTyeire gave the institution decisive shape and form—and a new identity—when he secured the financial backing of the aging New York shipping and railroad magnate Cornelius Vanderbilt in 1873.[12] As Paul K. Conkin observed, the university, "like most other private universities, was born of an unholy alliance of piety and plutocracy." The rechristened Vanderbilt University opened its doors in 1875, eventually garnering almost $1.2 million from Commodore Vanderbilt and his son.[13] After a protracted and bitter conflict, the university won its autonomy from the Methodists in 1914, and Chancellor James H. Kirkland subsequently oversaw a revision of the curriculum, which included reducing the requirements in Latin and Greek, and kicked off a major fund-raising drive. An institutional symbol of sectional reunion and convergence, Vanderbilt raised more than $20 million from northern benefactors (specifically, the Vanderbilt family, the Carnegie corporation, and various Rockefeller charities) between 1915 and 1930. It was the upper South's foremost university in the 1920s despite the fact that, owing to the generally narrow and restrictive cultural climate of the South and the tendency of the university's administration to hire like-minded and deferential faculty, its faculty was somewhat disengaged from the major trends of national intellectual life. The school's homogeneous student body was drawn primarily from central and western Tennessee and Kentucky, northern Georgia, Alabama, and Mississippi and parts of Arkansas and Texas.[14]

All the same, the culture of Vanderbilt and the closeness of the community were conducive to the development of the Fugitive writers. There was something of a literary ferment at Vanderbilt in the 1920s. Even a football player, Warren liked to recount later in life, attempted to write poetry.[15] Ransom, Davidson, Tate, and other of the Fugitive poets were all members of the Calumet Club, an honorary society of Vanderbilt journalists and would-be writers. Davidson and Jesse Wills, another Fugitive poet, were both members of the Old Oak and Coffee House, two distinguished Nashville literary clubs.[16] By the late 1920s, the interests of the key members of this Nashville circle turned toward the South as a whole. The New Yorker William S. Knickerbocker, recently arrived in Monteagle, Tennessee, as professor of English at Sewanee and editor of the *Sewanee Review*, claimed to play a role in the origins of Agrarianism. Sometime between 1926 and 1928, Knickerbocker arranged to have Ransom speak at Sewanee before the EQB (*ecce quam bonam*) club. Ransom's chosen topic was a recent series of articles on the South written by Bruce Bliven, editor of the *New Republic.* After touring the southern states, Bliven was convinced that the South was becoming indistinguishable, in mores, industry, and labor, from the rest of the nation. Knickerbocker later remembered that Ransom made seemingly offhanded challenges to various passages in Bliven's articles. "He indulged in pure lyric, the celebration of The South and its Tradition. In his own rare mind, something like a catalysis had happened," Knickerbocker recalled. Ransom's remarks were published in the *Sewanee Review* in the spring of 1928 and contained the entire basis of Southern Agrarianism.[17] "The impression is being given out," Ransom began, "that the Old South—seat of an antiquated culture whose persistence has been such an anomaly in these longitudes—is being industrialized, and brought into line with our forward-looking and hundred-percent Americanism." Ransom denied that this was true.[18]

The first efflorescence of southern fervor among Davidson, Ransom, and Tate—and the first talk of a collective work on the South— had occurred in the spring of 1927, when Tate suggested a symposium on southern literature.[19] Tate's 1927 proposal is not extant, but it set off a flurry of excitement. Davidson welcomed Tate's animus against the boosterism of the pro-business, progressive New South propagandists. Davidson was already impassioned on these issues. "I feel so strongly on these points that I can hardly trust myself to write," he declared. He expressed enthusiasm for Tate's idea, writing to John Gould Fletcher, "We have maybe found a Cause of a sort; we may be able, as you say, to 'do something for the South.'"[20] The idea of a symposium flagged in 1927 but was revived in 1929, this time as a symposium on southern matters in general. Serious discussion about a collection of essays began in earnest late that summer.[21] The impetus seems to have come from Davidson and was in part a response to plans under way for a symposium to be organized by Howard Mumford Jones, a professor of English at the University of North Carolina.

I'll Take My Stand: The South and the Agrarian Tradition appeared on November 12, 1930.[22] Although most of the contributors to the *Fugitive* did not contribute to *I'll Take My Stand*, Agrarianism developed out of the same social milieu—one marked by deep camaraderie as well as intellectual commitment. Ten of the twelve contributors were associated with Vanderbilt at one time or another: Ransom, Davidson, and John Donald Wade taught in the English Department; Frank L. Owsley and Herman Clarence Nixon taught in the History Department; Lyle Lanier taught in the Psychology Deparment; and Tate, Warren, Andrew Nelson Lytle, and Henry Blue Kline were former students. The two remaining contributors were acquaintances of Tate: Stark Young, an established critic in New York; and John Gould Fletcher, an expatriate southern poet.

Ransom drafted the book's introduction, entitled a "Statement of Principles," but all the contributors subscribed to it. It contains a coherent critical analysis of the South and the nation. The Twelve Southerners rejected the systematic application of scientific expertise to the system of production in society because, they argued, such an enterprise failed to provide the good life it promised, degraded the concept of labor, and introduced a meretricious consumerism into American life. Moreover, the Agrarians resisted the modern socio-logical tendency to analyze society as a whole and ascribe primary im-portance to broad and abstract social forces, which are often defined in terms of statistical measures. They insisted that life be analyzed in terms of the individual. The southerners encapsulated their criticism, programmatically and metaphorically, in the opposition between the agrarian and industrial orders (xxxvii).[23]

The underlying core of the "Statement of Principles" was a rejec-tion of the hollow blandishments of science and the industrial econ-omy that translated the scientific ethos into the system of production and, inevitably, into society as a whole. "The capitalization of the ap-plied sciences has now become extravagant and uncritical; it has en-slaved our human energies to a degree now felt to be burdensome," the Agrarians wrote (xxxix). Science simply does not deliver what it prom-ises. It is supposed to ease labor but it does not: the modern worker's "labor is hard, its tempo is fierce, and his employment is insecure" (xl). Labor is to be enjoyed, but the modern scientific attitude, with its emphasis on labor-saving machines, ensures that it is seen as onerous and below one's dignity (xl–xli). Moreover, the entire industrial sys-tem breeds overproduction, unemployment, and growing inequality in the distribution of wealth (xli). The Agrarians warned of techno-logical unemployment. "A fresh labor-saving device introduced into an industry," they argued, "does not emancipate the laborers in that industry so much as it evicts them" (xlv).

Proponents of industrialism promised greater consumption, but, in the eyes of the Agrarians, the effects of industrialization were uni-formly deleterious. "We have more time in which to consume, and many more products to be consumed," they allowed. "But the tempo of our labors communicates itself to our satisfactions, and these also become brutal and hurried" (xlii). The "strictly-business or industrial civilization" is subtly corrosive of religion because it undercuts the humble submission to nature that is the essence of religion. The arts, in turn, decay because of a decline in sensibility and the loss of leisure necessary to observe nature with disinterest. And, finally, the social amenities—manners, conversation, hospitality, sympathy, family life, romantic love—suffer (xlii–xliii). In the end, Americans are saddled with the continuous pressure of advertising, with its salesmen who desperately "coerce and wheedle" the modern consumer into maintaining the habits necessary to feed the insatiable engine of the economy (xlv–xlvi).

"It is strange, of course, that a majority of men anywhere could even as with one mind become enamored of industrialism: a system that has so little regard for individual wants," the Agrarians declared. Ultimately, their opposition to industrial capitalism led them to a consideration of the individual rather than the group. This essential distrust of the sociological or socialist viewpoint underlying all progressive or social democratic policy making and politics provided the motivating conservative core of *I'll Take My Stand*: "Men are prepared to sacrifice their private dignity and happiness to an abstract social ideal, and without asking whether the social ideal produces the welfare of any individual man whatsoever. But this is absurd. The responsibility of men is for their own welfare and that of their neighbors; not for the hypothetical welfare of some fabulous creature called society" (xlvi).

The southerners' proposed response was a return to the society oriented around the hardy individualism and self-sufficiency of the agrarian life, and, in one way or another, the twelve essays in the volume were designed to explain the possibilities of a return to such a life. John Crowe Ransom began the lead essay with a call to "look backward rather than forward" (1). His specific aim was to articulate the modern southerner's desire to accept change but not what he considered the deficiencies of northern culture. The southerner desired to be, in Ransom's words, "reconstructed but unregenerate." Progressives reject the attachment to the past, but Ransom declared nostalgia to be a healthy symptom of resistance to deracination (6). His essay was a defense of the situated and enduring community— the life of establishment, one that does not sacrifice the "free activity of the mind" to personal advancement but instead allows for leisure, which Ransom saw as the wellspring of the "good life" (10, 8–11). Such a life, Ransom argued, is European in conception and style. It is constantly endangered by the American pioneering spirit. Ransom's model of the leisured culture was the antebellum South, which, he argued, ignoring the conditions of poor whites and enslaved blacks, achieved a "rural sort of establishment":

> The arts of the section, such as they were, were not immensely passionate, creative, and romantic; they were the eighteenth-century social arts of dress, conversation, manners, the table, the hunt, poli-

tics, oratory, the pulpit. These were arts of living and not arts of escape; they were also community arts, in which every class of society could participate after its kind. The South took life easy, which is itself a tolerably comprehensive art. (12)

The Civil War shattered this establishment, and the impoverished South, Ransom observed, had refused to return to the pioneering task, which, in modern times, means industrialization (15). Met by persecution from the North, the South retreated into itself in rage, with adverse consequences to both regions. Unrestrained industrialism rampaged across the North while the South sank into desuetude (15–17). Thus Ransom criticized southerners for allowing themselves to be dominated by the North and for not industrializing on their own terms, which would mean creating an economy nicely balanced between agriculture and industry (21–22). "Unregenerate southerners," he wrote, "were trying to live the good life on a shabby equipment, and they were grotesque in their effort to make an art of living when they were not decently making the living." Nevertheless, the South retained its superior perception of the conditions of a good, established life. "In the country districts great numbers of these broken-down Southerners are still to be seen in patched blue-jeans, sitting on ancestral fences, shotguns across their laps and hound-dogs at their feet, surveying their unkempt acres while they comment shrewdly on the ways of God" (16).

The question Ransom addressed was whether the South would be able to look backward and forward at the same time, whether it could industrialize to a limited extent while resisting the "Great Progressive Principle" and somehow retaining the secrets of southern culture and the southern philosophy of the establishment (20–22). At the same time, he was conveying a particularly aesthetic conception of the good life. To live in balance with nature and to live leisurely is to treat one's life as a work of art. The factories that were producing clouds of coal smoke, which left Nashville with soot-marked buildings, were aesthetically unpleasing.[24] Donald Davidson treated aesthetics more explicitly, arguing that meaningful art grows out of the region and society into which the artist is born and is not created by the artist alienated from his or her home territory but rather by one chiefly connected to it. "What is a picture for, if not to put on one's wall?" Davidson exclaimed. The habit of confining art to museums symbolized a dissociation of the modern individual from the deep spiritual sources of culture. "The truly artistic life is surely that in which the aesthetic experience is not curtained off but is mixed up with all sorts of instruments and occupations pertaining to the round of daily life. It ranges all the way from pots and pans, chairs and rugs, clothing and

houses, up to dramas publicly performed and government buildings"
(39–40).

The artist, Davidson argued, can and must speak in the voice of
his or her native place. Industrial civilization, he believed, undercut
the artist's ability to do this. The root of the contemporary malad-
justments among artists lay in the industrial and democratic revolutions of the eighteenth century. Artists, understandably, became disillusioned with the new order and expressed their contempt through
romanticism. The romantic artist adopted the pose of the "noble
exile." This self-imposed social exile, however, cut off any possibility
for an authentic use of tradition in art, depriving society of effective
traditional art (32). In the South, however, one could still protect the
type of culture that is a mirror for artists, a culture that fosters the
identification of the artist with society rather than subverts it. In this
type of culture, artists would see themselves in their region's pasts
and could live "an integrated life," Davidson believed (53).

The Agrarian indictment of industrial capitalism articulated by
Ransom and Davidson and in the "Statement of Principles" was bol-
stered with the appeal to southern history. Laid open for all to see in
the history books was the corruption and destruction attendant when
relations between people were based on money, not on respect or custom. The near-fatal blow that the agrarian culture of the South received, in the Agrarians' view, came from an aggrandizing and greedy
North. The Civil War was most definitely not about human bondage.
"Slavery was a feature monstrous enough in theory," Ransom coolly
observed, "but, more often that not, humane in practice; and it is impossible to believe that its abolition alone would have effected any
great revolution in society" (14).

The actual history of the South was treated by historian Frank L.
Owsley. In Owsley's view planters and yeomen alike partook of a
common culture. They were bound by shared rituals and a shared
faith:

> The amusements might be the fine balls and house parties of the
> planter or the three-day break-down dances which David Crock-
> ett loved, or horse races, foot races, cock and dog fights, boxing,
> wrestling, shooting, fighting, log-rolling, house raising, or corn-
> shucking. It might be crude or genteel, but it everywhere was
> fundamentally alike and natural. The houses were homes, where
> families lived sufficient and complete within themselves, working
> together and fighting together. And when death came, they were
> buried in their own lovely peaceful graveyards, to await doomsday
> together. (71–72)

The North—expansive and aggressive, built on centralization and standardization—was, by nature, antipathetic to the South. The conflict between them was "irrepressible." Owsley upheld the Confederacy as an example of unbridled individualism and sturdy independence and yet, at the same time, presented it as a culture governed by order and respect for common values. States' rights was an argument used to defend against an encroaching North, but it also accurately reflected the governing principle of southern life: the fostering of individual freedom through the absence of strong central governance. The Confederacy, in Owsley's view, maximized personal freedom, yet this entailed no strong desire on the people's part for democracy. Owsley's antebellum South was quasi-feudal, even prepolitical: it constituted a multitude of self-sustaining regions governed by local economic interests. Such a society possessed a disorderly and fractious system of government, Owsley argued, but it fostered social and economic freedom (88–89).

Slavery, Owsley declared, "was no simple question of ethics; it cut across the categories of human thought like a giant question mark. It was a moral, an economic, a religious, a social, a philosophical, and above all a political question." It was, however, "no essential part of the agrarian civilization of the South," according to Owsley (76). It was, he argued, foisted upon the South by England. "Negroes had come into the Southern Colonies in such numbers that people feared for the integrity of the white race," Owsley wrote. "For the negroes were cannibals and barbarians, and therefore dangerous. No white man who had any contact with slavery was willing to free the slaves and allow them to dwell among the whites." Two races cannot live together in a condition of equality, Owsley declared. One will always seek to dominate the other. The white southerner determined that blacks "must either rule or be ruled." If blacks ruled, white civilization would wither and die (77, 82).

No other contribution to the symposium reached the levels of ugliness of Owsley's essay. (The postbellum South, Owsley wrote vituperatively, "was turned over to the three millions of former slaves, some of whom could still remember the taste of human flesh and the bulk of them hardly three generations from cannibalism.") Yet it made explicit what was unstated throughout the book: southern society was the model of a nonmarket social economy, but it was, historically, completely intertwined with a system of exploitation and slavery based on race (62).

John Gould Fletcher used a historical analysis of southern schooling to address the issue of education in the South. Modern education, he held, subordinates the goals of scholarship and character formation to the inferior goal of training to make a living (120). High school has become, Fletcher argued, "nothing more than a mass-production factory, with the essential aim of making as many graduates as possible with as little trouble to either teacher or pupil as possible" (118). The real purpose of education should be, he felt, "to produce the balanced character—the man of the world in the true sense, who is also the man with spiritual roots in his own community in the local sense" (111). Fletcher's prescription for the public school system included the institution of a more regularized curriculum, the founding of manual training and agricultural schools for students, both black and white, who do not need extended academic education, and the development of mechanisms to distinguish the promising students who could form an intellectual and well-trained elite in society from those less gifted in this way (120–21).

Lyle Lanier's contribution was ostensibly a philosophical assessment of the concept of "progress." He included a discussion of the historical evolution of the idea of progress in Western culture since the time of the Greeks as well as an explanation of the relationship between American pragmatism and progress, with an extended treatment of the social philosophy of John Dewey. But Lanier's actual focus was an issue more germane to social psychology—the use of the term "progress" as a "super-slogan" and "magic word" to promote industrial capitalism (123, 131–32). In the process, he delivered a scathing indictment of industrial capitalism. The benighted Dewey, Lanier believed, hoped that the forces of industrialization would create a new corporate existence, which would lead to a higher level of human fulfillment (137–38, 141–42). Lanier emphatically rejected Dewey's socialist impulses and asserted, instead, the essential individualism of Americans, declaring it to be a part of human nature, an innate function of human "neuro-muscular-glandular systems" (142–43). Lanier saw no communion created by industrialism, and he denounced corporate capitalism as "economic anarchy" (using a phrase of Dewey's), exploitative to an unprecedented degree and leading to concentrated wealth and power and corrupted politics. It produced a labor system that was, he believed, akin to slavery (140–42, 145). Industrialism would, he thought, produce "personal isolation, and a fractionation of life functions into an ever-expanding and differentiating system of formalized institutions" (148). He pointed ominously to the ways in which social agencies assumed some of the moral and educational functions of the family. He also highlighted the permanent unemployment created by technological improvements, which left a deracinated proletariat subject to the "convulsions of a predatory and decadent capitalism" (146, 149–51). "Progress" had come to be a catchword for the idea that "the greater part of a nation's energies should be directed toward an endless process of increasing the production and consumption of goods" (148). Lanier's antidote, of course, lay in an effort to reestablish an individualistic, agrarian economy.

Allen Tate composed the most difficult and, in some ways, discordant essay in the collection.[25] His premise was that a vibrant and popularly received religion must form the basis of a sound, agrarian social order—and that the South had, in fact, been deficient in this. Tate began the essay by favorably contrasting a "whole" vision with the abstract vision of the scientific, or utilitarian, mind. The abstract mind reduced objects to their use value rather than appreciating them as things in themselves. It devalued key cultural institutions, thereby sapping their power. "Abstraction is the death of religion no less than the death of anything else," he declared. When we look at the past with the abstracting half vision of science, history appears to be the product of large social forces in which all the variety and richness are left out. Thus, Tate argued, abstraction was the "cosmopolitan destroyer of Tradition" (156–58, 160–63).

Tate claimed that the South was really no different than the rest of America in this regard. It had allowed its tradition to slip away. In his essay, Tate tended to use "tradition" and "religion" interchangeably. Historically, Tate argued, the South had failed to develop the "Dogma" of a true religion. It had never possessed the unity of mind that the critic T. S. Eliot, for one, claimed had characterized premodern Europe. The development of a feudal social system in the South was an anomaly resulting from the particular climactic conditions found in America. Those who saw the South as embodying precapitalist values were deceived, Tate believed. In fact, the South had developed a feudal socioeconomic system without the concomitant feudal structure of beliefs. Instead of a feudal religion, the South had only the "non-agrarian and trading religion" of Protestantism, which Tate scorned. "The South would not have been defeated had she possessed a sufficient faith in her own kind of God," Tate wrote. "She would not have been defeated, in other words, had she been able to bring out a body of doctrine setting forth her true conviction that the ends of man require more for their realization than politics. The setback of the war was of itself a very trivial one" (166–68, 174).

Tate mused on the burden of history for modern southerners. He realized the hold that history had on all people; it was the "concrete fact" to which all must be loyal, he observed. But southerners did not actually inherit a viable religion. They only inherited the "secular image of religious conviction"—the economic structure. In the case of the South, this consisted of the vestiges of a feudal socioeconomic structure (174–75). The southern model of abstract thinking was Thomas Jefferson. Tate saw Jefferson's political legacy as the South's only hope—albeit a paradoxical one—for regaining its tradition. Jefferson the Deist was, of course, the great southern symbol of the secular intellect and champion of the separation of church and state. Jefferson's formula, Tate argued, was simple: "The ends of man are sufficiently contained in his political destiny" (173). Most southerners may never have believed this dictum, and it went against the grain of "tradition" and "religion" as Tate defined those concepts, yet Jeffersonian rationalism and naturalism were all the modern southerner had left.

Tate's essay in *I'll Take My Stand* was a very ambivalent endorsement of political radicalism. The southerner, Tate argued, may only take hold of tradition by "violence," that is, with politics. Southerners, in other words, must desperately attempt to make a political order do the work of a spiritual one. In order to retain a society feudal in spirit, Tate was suggesting, Americans must reverse the natural process of historical development. If the economy is the "secular image" of religion, then perhaps altering the political economy would create an alternate religious conviction. The only hope for re-creating a spiritually whole life was to roll back the socioeconomic transformation of capitalism and return to the society and economy that feudal religion had encouraged. "Reaction is the most radical of programs; it aims at cutting away the overgrowth and getting back to the roots," Tate wrote. "A forward-looking radicalism is a contradiction; it aims at rearranging the foliage." This was the paradox of the modern southerner (and all moderns), Tate believed: "He must use an instrument, which is political, and so unrealistic and pretentious that he cannot believe in it, to re-establish a private, self-contained, and essentially spiritual life" (174–75).

Herman Clarence Nixon provided a survey of the southern economy, arguing that the South still retained a "fairly even balance" between agriculture and industry (178). Moreover, Nixon provided a historical analysis of the region's economy, suggesting that the Old South elites were carefully and gradually moving toward an economy that balanced agriculture and industry. The Civil War displaced these moderate agrarians, however. After the war, southern crop diversification and industrial development were delayed owing to lack of capital, and the South was vulnerable to a northeastern financial elite (188–89). Nixon was critical of New South propagandists. The call for industrialization was not new to the South, he believed, but the New South boosters were novel in their craven capitulation to the spirit of industrialism (193–94, 176–78). Excessive industrialization creates an "idle urban proletariat," Nixon argued; it is unstable, breeds socialism, and (Nixon cited the British thinkers John Maynard Keynes and John A. Hobson and the American Parker T. Moon on this point) breeds imperialism (195–97). Southerners, he concluded, should pursue a program of moderate industrialization and resist selling their soul for a "mess of industrial pottage" (199).

If Nixon provided a dispassionate analysis of the history and strengths of the southern economy, Andrew Nelson Lytle contributed a more lyrical and pointed treatment of the same subject. His essay, entitled "The Hind Tit," was divided into three parts. Lytle first traced the decline of the independent farmer in the South historically. He then presented an almost absurdly idyllic portrait of life on a small farm and concluded with a description of how modern forces destroyed this farm life. His thesis was contained in the title's piquant metaphor: the farmer, weak and defensive, was now like the runt of the sow's litter. "Squeezed and tricked out of the best places at the side," Lytle wrote, "he is forced to take the little hind tit for nourishment; and here, struggling between the sow's back legs, he has to work with every bit of strength to keep it from being a dry hind one, and all because the suck of the others is so unreservedly gluttonous" (245).

For Lytle, a strong and superior culture existed on southern farms, and he attempted to convey the details of this life: the reassuring and regular routine of chores, never bound too tightly by any schedule; the small omens and signs the farmer reads in nature, never dependent on science to instruct his husbandry; the raucous celebrations of postharvest play-parties, where the patterns of courtship and pairing are both modeled and enacted. Poverty, disease, enervating monotony, back-breaking labor, the isolation of farm life—no negatives mar Lytle's portrait of agrarian organicism. Nor does hunger intrude at the midday repast, which even Lytle admitted may not match his description in every region of the South:

> The midday meal, like all meals in the country, has a great deal of form. It is, in the first place, unhurried. Diners accustomed to the mad, bolting pace of cafeterias will grow nervous at the slow performance of a country table. To be late is a very grave matter, since it is not served until everybody is present. But only some accident, or unusual occurrence, will detain any member of the family, for dinner is a social event of the first importance. The family are together with their experiences of the morning to relate; and merriment rises up from the hot, steaming vegetables, all set about the table, small hills around the mountains of meat at the ends, a heaping plate of fried chicken, a turkey, a plate of guineas, or a one-year

ham, spiced, and if company is there, baked in wine. A plate of
bread is at each end of the table; a bowl of chitterlings has been set
at the father's elbow; and pigs' feet for those that like them. (226)

Lytle's vivid depiction of the rural South—simple, wholesome, un-
governed by the mechanical timepiece, self-sufficient, organic, sturdy
—was the South as the Agrarians wanted to see it.

The Civil War, according to Lytle, had turned "an agrarian Union"
into "an industrial empire" with an empire's concomitant need for
expansion and the aggressive competition for markets. The pursuit
of happiness, Lytle argued, had become the pursuit of wealth, with
any higher purpose in life forgotten by the vast majority. The pursuit had become "a nervous running-around . . . without the logic,
even, of a dog chasing its tail" (202, 216). The money economy was
destroying farming as a way of life. "What industrialism counts as
the goods and riches of the earth the agrarian South does not, nor
ever did," he declared (208). Modern farmers were told to industrialize, to increase their yields, to adopt scientific management. Lytle's
reply evoked all the mythology of the yeoman ideal: "A farm is not a
place to grow wealthy; it is a place to grow corn" (204–5). Lytle's (and
the Agrarians') ultimate solution was a rejection of the "machine-
facture" goods of industry and a return to the untainted folk manu-
factures of the rural culture. "Do what we did after the war and the
Reconstruction: return to our looms, our hand crafts, our reproduc-
ing stock. Throw out the radio and take down the fiddle from the wall"
(244).

Robert Penn Warren treated the South's most distinctive institution—segregation—in an essay entitled "The Briar Patch." Warren suggested means to minimize conflict between white and black
laborers. Blacks were unfit to make their own way in society after the
abolition of slavery, Warren argued. They fell victim to manipulation
by uncaring whites and thus lost a most precious commodity (and one
that was central to maintaining peace in the South): the confidence
of the white man in the black. "The rehabilitation of the white man's
confidence for the negro is part of the Southern white man's story
since 1880," Warren wrote (248).

Warren argued for equal protection of blacks under the law and,
following Booker T. Washington, advised blacks to educate themselves to improve their economic status. They needed vocational education before higher education. Warren's essay was, on the whole, a
rather moderate defense of segregation. Part of his aim was to define
a place for the black in the South. The black professional might be
disgusted at discrimination, but he must ask himself what it is that
truly upsets him, Warren suggested. "Does he simply want to spend

the night in a hotel as comfortable as the one from which he is turned away, or does he want to spend the night in the same hotel?" Warren asked rhetorically. Segregation, Warren argued, will not end for a long time, and it was merely radicals who insisted on attacking it. The radical will not be satisfied with separate but equal:

> The negro radical, or the white radical in considering the race problem, would say that he wants the second thing—he wants to go to the same hotel, or he wants the right to go to the same hotel. The millennium which he contemplates would come to pass when the white man and the black man regularly sat down to the same table and when the white woman filed her divorce action through a negro attorney with no thought in the mind of any party to these various transactions that the business was, to say the least, a little eccentric.

In addressing the black man, however, Warren could only appropriate the words of Washington: "We can be as separate as the fingers, yet one as the hand in all things essential to human progress" (254, 249-52, 260).

Two of the volume's essays took the form of fictionalized character sketches. John Donald Wade's concerned Cousin Lucius, a small-town teacher, farmer, peach orchard entrepreneur, and, eventually, bank president. Although his life charted the course of industrialization in the South, Cousin Lucius remained a model of agrarian virtue, committed to his community and to the values for which it stood—hard work, thrift, humility, and the making of a good but modest life. In the essay, Wade described the gradual obsolescence of such a character. Cousin Lucius had attempted to forge a "master compromise" between agriculture and commercialization, placing his faith in the hope that "an agricultural community could fare well in a dance where the fiddles were all buzz-saws and the horns all steam-whistles" (284). But, as time progressed, the compromise proved illusory; his neighbors, in fact, lost sight of tradition, lusted after money and easy credit, and, generally, succumbed to the allures of the boom-and-bust capitalist economy, ultimately forsaking small-town values and community (284-98).

Cousin Lucius believed that a youthful critic of his leadership of the bank wanted, "without effort, things that have immemorially come as the result of effort only," his goal being to "go faster and faster on less and less" (292). Henry Blue Kline's sketch attempted to probe the psychology of William Remington, a young southern man from this generation. In it, Kline attacked the sterility of the Jazz Age "culture of aimless flux" and the banality of consumer capitalism (325). His protagonist, a young college graduate, was alienated and disconnected, in part because of his immersion in literature, history, music, and art and in part because of his highly individualistic temperament, both characteristics that were fostered by his college professors but that had, in fact, unfitted him for the world (302–3). Remington moved to the North but disdained the superficial social swirl of the metropolis and dithered on his choice of career (304–16). The onset of the Great Depression served to open Remington's eyes to the shallowness of the current economic order, with its ceaseless injunctions to "buy to the limit" in order to end the current crisis (317). Remington rejected the "progressivist fetich," retreating to an unspecified border region between North and South and establishing a congenial company of countercultural outcasts from the consumer order who sought to convince others to "give more of themselves to being something and less to a perpetual becoming something else, more to the social arts and graces and less to going places and doing things, more to such strenuous activity as writing verses—no matter how bad ones—and less to such passive business as globe-trotting with one's sensations" (325, 322–27).

Stark Young, who, with Fletcher, was the most established of the Twelve Southerners, wrote the volume's final essay, "Not in Memoriam, but in Defense." Ransom began the symposium with the injunction to look backward. Young began his essay, a direct address to southerners intended to rally their desire to defend southern culture, by declaring, "We can never go back" (328). Young did not object to southerners' zealous pursuit of industrialization, but he called on them to use their cultural inheritance to resist the mentality of industrialism (353, 355). "We can accept the machine, but create our own attitude toward it," he argued (355). Writing in the haughty tones of the aristocrat, Young assailed the "flatness, excitement, and sterility" of American life as well as the "chapel-going" piety of the narrow-minded, self-righteous, and dull middle class (333, 337–38). He unabashedly identified southern culture with the white, antebellum, slaveholding elite (328, 336–37). The essence of this cultural inheritance was a provincial attachment to the place of one's youth, a culture of manners and decorum, and "Southern family sense" (or the habitual southern obsession with parentage, bloodlines, and extended kin relations) (344–48).

The aristocratic ideal in southern culture was, Young admitted, superficial in some ways—being characterized by mere acquaintance with the classics, only the "whiff of poets," a taste for social polish and oratory—but it was founded on a profound sense of self and deep social commitments. The characteristics of the southern aristocrat included honor, *amour propre*, mutuality, obligation, and self-control. Young understood the South as a cultural essence, which could be maintained even with a drastically changing socioeconomic reality. His essay did not make a necessary association between southernness and agrarianism. His primary concern was to bolster southerners' pride in their past by, for example, dismissing the outsiders' scorn for southern hospitality as insincere gush (345–46). Even if only three Virginia families could be traced to nobility in England, even if southern estates were modest compared with those of other lands, even if one resorts to believing lies about one's heritage, Young insisted on maintaining the old faith:

> Is it not better that I should believe lies, believe in my family, desiring its luster for myself, shamed by its ideals and my own unworthiness, touched by the past of its affections and its standards, than to believe another special sort of modern American lie, such a one, for instance as believes Mr. Henry Ford's opinion on art to be of any importance, merely because of his success with wheels in a mechanical system that makes men constantly dryer, more thwarted and less exercised, and Mr. Ford richer and richer? (351)

Young ended the symposium with an expression of faith in the South's ability to modernize and yet retain its distinctiveness. He articulated a conception of change as a mysterious relation between the individual and a "new order," one governed by the "god" of "Mutability" and in which, in an "almost mystical sense," "so long as we are alive, we are not the same and yet remain ourselves" (359). Paul K. Conkin has emphasized the lack of unity in *I'll Take My Stand*. "It still defies full understanding unless one is willing to probe deeply into the background of each essay," he writes. "Few people ever read all the book, and well-insulated from its diverse and elusive content almost everyone has some oversimplified view of what it is all about. The trouble is that, in some place or another, it was about almost everything."[26] Conkin's statement is accurate. However, *I'll Take My Stand* was a much more cohesive volume than he allows, not least of all in the authors' concern for the god of Mutability. The Agrarians, like many other southerners in the 1920s, sought both to change and to remain themselves, to preserve what they considered a valuable cultural inheritance endangered by social and economic change yet still play an important role in twentieth-century America.

The unity of their program was deeper, however. The Agrarians' radical conservatism called for a return to the roots of the social economy of the South. The authors uniformly scorned industrial capitalism, not only for the sterile and desiccated consumerism that they believed it produced but also for the immiseration and insecurity that it offered the average worker. They all dismissed the modern cult of progress, so rampant in America in the 1920s, and considered a surfeit of cheap consumer goods to be a poor trade for time and leisure. They refused to conceive society in sociological terms, and, although they tended toward an organic conception of a tradition-directed society, they thought of themselves as principled defenders of individualism, which they defined in terms of character rather than self-fulfillment or the satisfaction of desires. They celebrated individualism but not in terms of personal freedom. They believed the Agrarian economy— bound as it was by limits, modest expectations, and tradition—promised the widest range of opportunity for the development of individual character.

At root, *I'll Take My Stand* was an attack on the "business civilization" of America; and, in this, the Agrarians were very much in the mainstream of social criticism. A dissatisfaction with the callow hedonism, crass consumerism, and spiritual shallowness of the years between 1910 and 1930 was articulated by a variety of thinkers, whether conservatives, such as Irving Babbitt, Paul Elmer More, and George Santayana; radicals, such as the "Young Intellectuals" Randolph Bourne, Van Wyck Brooks, Lewis Mumford, and Waldo Frank; or independent critics such as H. L. Mencken. Departing from the cultural Left, however, the Agrarians rejected what they considered romantic notions of individualism. Critics such as Van Wyck Brooks and Lewis Mumford emphasized the ways in which bourgeois culture inhibited the free growth of personality. They dreamed of a society wherein human life lived richly in community would produce a more fulfilled individual. Other modernists embraced free love and bohemianism as an antidote to bourgeois repression or looked to art, psychoanalysis, and primitivism as a means of cultural revolution. The Agrarians, however, rejected any program of cultural liberation as firmly as they did the shallow and destructive capitalist culture such a program was designed to negate. They proposed, instead, the preservation of the cultural tradition of leisure and order that they believed characterized the South. This they considered a radical idea, for it entailed going to the roots of American culture and restructuring the American economy.[27]

There were indeed deep divisions between the Agrarians that were both implicit and explicit in *I'll Take My Stand.* And the Agrarians' dream of an integrated industrial-agrarian order remained vague and undeveloped. But the symposium itself was unified in its call to preserve a traditional social order as an alternative to industrial capitalism. The divided mind of Agrarianism was there, indeed, to be seen throughout the volume, but it did not rise into full view until after the publication of the founding statement.

CHAPTER TWO

Humanism and Southernism
The Intellectual Origins of Agrarianism

As you say, it is a great mistake to suppose that Humanism is a real substitute for religion, and while Nietzsche or Arnold may ripen our minds with partial insights (i.e. cultivate us), only God can give the affair a genuine purpose. What I mean is, that the church contains the only body of doctrine already latent in us as feeling: Nietzsche or Kant brings no feeling. That is the fallacy of men like [Gorham] Munson—they expect a set of abstractions to create the equivalent emotion out of the air.

Allen Tate to John Crowe Ransom, 27 July 1929

To understand the failure of a radically conservative Agrarianism, it is necessary to understand the contradictions of its origins. The radical conservatism of *I'll Take My Stand* was quickly eclipsed for two reasons. It was, in one sense, crushed between two differing viewpoints, best represented by the contrasting figures of Allen Tate and Donald Davidson. Put simply, these two key originators of Agrarianism envisioned it in fundamentally different ways. Davidson saw Agrarianism as an obdurate and romantic immersion in southern culture, which, conceived as a source of direction and values, was an alternative to more abstract political theory and philosophical speculation; Tate, as an almost ironic and self-consciously quixotic foray into cultural debate. Davidson considered Agrarianism to be a defensive statement of faith and a source of identity; for Tate, it was more an emblem of the paradoxical condition of moderns—they knew of a previous age that provided spiritual wholeness but were unable to return to that older spiritual homeland.

The differences between the two men illuminate the dynamic that both drove the organization of *I'll Take My Stand* and, eventually, divided the contributors. Reading through the letters of Ransom and

Tate, one sees that religious faith was an obsession for both, as, to be sure, it was for many intellectuals emerging from a culture of orthodoxy into one of disbelief. They perceived, like their contemporaries Walter Lippmann and Joseph Wood Krutch, a crisis of morals in modern America. Agrarianism was their attempt at a solution. Ransom and Tate did not reassert the Christian doctrines or orthodox moral values. They were skeptics themselves, and they scorned the New Humanists—the other major conservative intellectuals of the day. Rather, their concern with the validation of values led to an interest in the ways in which the socioeconomic structure of society conditioned religious faith. They began to believe that the crisis in faith was less a matter of the intellect and more a problem in traditional life. In this Davidson could agree. But, as Ransom and Tate theorized about the matrix of religious faith, Davidson found a secular alternative in a steadfast and devoted faith in the southern past, which provided him with both values and, even more precious, identity.

John Orley Allen Tate, the youngest of three sons, was born in 1899. His youth was peripatetic. "We sometimes moved two or three times a year, moving *away* from something my mother didn't like; or perhaps withdrawing would be a better word; for my mother gradually withdrew from the world, and withdrew me also, gradually, from the time I was a small boy; so that we might as well have been living, and I been born, in a tavern at a crossroads," Tate recalled in a memoir. His education was erratic and varied, spread among schools in Nashville; Ashland and Louisville, Kentucky; Evansville, Indiana; and Cincinnati, Ohio.[1] Tate's formidable mother, Eleanor Parke Custis Varnell, was the overwhelming influence of his youth. She was descended from the Virginia gentry, and her family owned a farm in Prince William County, Virginia, called Chestnut Hill, which Tate remembered from his childhood. During the Civil War, an older family home, built on the same land, was burned by Union troops on their way to the first battle at Bull Run. Tate remembered being taken to see the ruins of Pleasant Hill, "overrun with honeysuckle and poisonous jimson weed," as a child.[2]

Eleanor Varnell married below her class, at least in her own mind. Her husband, John Orley Tate, came from Scotch-Irish ancestors who had settled in Kentucky and Tennessee. In fact, she, too, was of Scotch-Irish descent, and John had forebears from Virginia. A condition of their marriage was that John manage the Varnell family lumber business in Mount Vernon, Illinois. Personally volatile and prone to drinking, philandering, and occasional violence, the elder Tate was an ineffectual manager, and the business failed. The family had to sell property to support itself. Furthermore, John Tate disgraced the

Allen Tate, 1920.
(Courtesy Photographic Archives,
Vanderbilt University)

family, giving his mother, Tate believed, grounds for divorce. For the
young Tate, summering with his mother in Washington, Virginia,
or the mountain resorts of Tennessee, the failure of his father must
have been palpable, the power of his mother suffocating. Growing up,
then, Tate imbibed the ragged dreams of fading prestige and a familial
history marked by male ineptitude and shame. Andrew Nelson Lytle
recalled a chance meeting he had with Tate, Caroline Gordon (Tate's
wife), and Tate's mother in Monteagle, Tennessee, in the summer of
1928. When Tate spotted his mother, he turned pale and exclaimed,
"My God! There's Mama." Throughout the ensuing visit, Tate continually repeated, "Mama, we got to go now."[3]

Precocious and arrogant, Tate entered Vanderbilt University in
1918. The self-assured Tate thrived in the undergraduate setting and

collected friends with a taste for literature, such as Robert Penn Warren. In 1921 Davidson invited Tate to join the Fugitive group, which Tate proceeded to dazzle with his brilliant mind and unwavering advocacy of modern poetics. Tate and Davidson were lifelong friends and shared a fascination with the southern past. In personality, however, they were quite unlike: Tate was brash, impetuous, and intensely social; Davidson, retiring, wracked with self-doubt, and inclined to avoid conflict. Ultimately, too, their intellectual paths diverged.[4]

After a short stint teaching high school in order to earn money, Tate embarked on a career as an independent writer. In the spring of 1924 he visited New York City and insinuated himself into the avant-garde literary scene that had coalesced there just a few years earlier. He befriended such young literary figures as Hart Crane (with whom he had corresponded); the poets Malcolm Cowley and E. E. Cummings; Walter Slater Brown, who had been imprisoned in France with Cummings while both were ambulance drivers in World War I; Mark Van Doren, who taught English at Columbia University; Gorham Munson, the founder and editor of *Secession;* and Matthew Josephson, who founded and edited *Broom.* "I'm greatly thrilled by the mere *physique* of this great city!" he wrote Davidson. "The subway is simply marvellous. Fancy going under a huge river at the rate of 40 miles an hour!" Tate, who had chafed under the strict social rules governing Vanderbilt, reveled in the freedom. "I didn't come to New York to conquer it; merely to live as a civilized being in a place where it isn't important whether you drink liquor or are a virgin, and to see a few congenial people when I care to," exulted Tate.[5]

In New York City Tate worked as an assistant to Susan Jenkins Brown (Walter Slater Brown's wife), who edited the pulp magazine *Telling Tales.* The Browns, Kenneth Burke, Cowley, Crane, Josephson, and Tate met often at the offices of *Telling Tales* or for drinks at the Poncino Palace, a speakeasy in the Village. Once or twice a week, and usually every Saturday, the group would share dinner at a favorite Italian restaurant run by John Squarcialupi. In general festive and rowdy, the small circle combined high literary discussion with mischievous antics.[6]

Before beginning his life in New York in the fall of 1924, however, Tate returned to the South in the summer, in part because he wanted to spend time with Warren, who was recovering from depression, which was so severe that it had led to a suicide attempt.[7] Tate visited Warren at his home in Guthrie, Kentucky, and it was there that he met Caroline, an aspiring writer who lived with her family nearby. Gordon, four years older than Tate, was, according to a biographer, overwhelmed by his attentions, not having attracted serious suitors previously. Tate seduced her in a churchyard, and she followed him back to New York. They saw each other for two months, but she did not become a member of his social circle; they broke up at Christmas, although by that time she was pregnant with their daughter, Nancy. Tate reluctantly agreed to a wedding, which was a rather gloomy affair at City Hall.[8]

Even while a student in Nashville, Tate had written Hart Crane of his desire to escape "the malignant, personal sentimentalism of Nashville," comparing life in Nashville to "intellectual castration." In New York, Tate grew scornful of his Fugitive colleagues, dismissing their unfavorable criticisms of his work as irrelevant. "I knew my own business, good or bad, better than anybody else. Actually I only submitted my work to meetings as part of the duty of a member; I never got much out of it, either of grief or joy," he wrote Davidson from New York. Nashville was artificial and jejune, and Tate had escaped it.[9]

Throughout the 1920s, Tate honed a modernist outlook, through critical reviews, essays, and informal discussion, as well as in his poetry. He affirmed the worth of regionalist writing, arguing in a letter to Malcolm Cowley in 1928 that what is of value in any poetry is of "provincial origin," and criticized the expatriate T. S. Eliot for his Anglophilia — "he has dried up his native roots and expects to renew them with the urine of St. Thomas."[10] All the same, Eliot, whom Tate championed while a student at Vanderbilt, was an intellectual guide for Tate. Tate affirmed the classical modernism of Eliot his entire life. Classical modernism was defined by a rejection of Victorian moralism and pieties, a devotion to recondite symbolism and formalist technique in literature, a reverence for tradition, and an anxious search for spiritual certainty in what was regarded to be a hopelessly fragmented and disunified civilization. Eliot hailed the neglected Metaphysical and Elizabethan poets of England. Their world, he asserted, allowed for intellectual and emotional unity; objects were perceived by the conscious and unconscious simultaneously. Since the eighteenth century, however, a "dissociation of sensibility" had set in with the result that, by the twentieth century, the flux of sensation was being walled off from the workaday world of intellectual abstractions in which men and women increasingly lived. When Davidson reacted positively to Eliot's poetry, Tate wrote him that Eliot was the "most intelligent man alive, and there's no possibility of doubting it." ("*I* have known it all along!" he could not resist adding.) Tate accepted Eliot's dictum that all art is a development of tradition and argued further that literature should be grounded in just that unity of mind that Eliot claimed to see in premodern Europe. Tate suggested that myths were the embodiments of such a unified mind-set. Thus, poetry, if ultimately successful, must be rooted in common myths and beliefs. But as early as his *Fugitive* writings, Tate had stated his pessimistic opinion that, in fact, such culturally unifying myths no longer existed in modern society. He conceived of himself as a spiritual exile. A tradition, once possessed by his society, was now forever gone. The "disappearance of themes" preoccupied Tate and constituted, he wrote his friend Cowley in November 1926, the "literary aspect of modernism." [11]

Although Tate was a committed modernist, his friendships in the bohemian and expatriate communities of New York and Paris pushed him deeper into both a southern and reactionary self-identification. He became interested in the Catholic Revival, a movement of Roman Catholic lay intellectuals and clergy aspiring to integrate traditional doctrine with modern trends in thought in order to form an effective Christian humanism. The Catholic Revival began in Europe in the late nineteenth century but reached its peak, in both Europe and the United States, in the years between World War I and the Second Vatican Council in the 1960s. It was based in England and France and had a strong literary component. A number of major writers and thinkers were Catholic converts, including Jacques Maritain and Christopher Dawson, both leading Revival writers, as well as G. K. Chesterton, Evelyn Waugh, Ronald Knox, Graham Greene, and Paul Claudel. (Much later, Tate and Maritain became close friends, and, on Tate's baptism into the Catholic Church in 1950, Maritain became his godfather.) Other influential Revival thinkers included Georges Bernanos, Léon Bloy, Etienne Gilson, François Mauriac, Charles Péguy, Emmanuel Mounier, Julian Greene, Hilaire Belloc, Eric Gill, Christopher Hollis, and Martin D'Arcy. The Anglican converts W. H. Auden, C. S. Lewis, and Eliot shared a sensibility with the Catholic intellectuals. The Revival had its greatest impact in the United States in the 1940s and boasted a list of noted literary converts as well, including Tate, Gordon (who preceded her husband into the church by three years), Katherine Anne Porter, Ernest Hemingway, Dorothy Day, Thomas Merton, Clare Booth Luce, Jean Stafford, Robert Lowell, Tennessee Williams, Wallace Stevens, and Walker Percy.[12]

The Catholic Revival had both right-wing manifestations, such as the French royalist group Action Française, led by Charles Maurras, and the lay organization Opus Dei, and left-wing manifestations, such as Dorothy Day's Catholic Worker movement in the United States. (Maritain was associated with Action Française for fifteen years.) Its outlook was decidedly medieval, looking to the world before the sixteenth century as a model of social and intellectual unity. "Informed by a distinctive philosophy of historical decline," historian Peter Huff observed, "negating the popular Enlightenment notion of inevitable progress, the Catholic Revival produced a rather bleak portrait of the modern world. To the writers of the Revival, modernity

was the result of vast cultural disintegration, the massive fragmentation and distortion of vital institutions stretching back to Christian and classical antiquity." The Revival coincided with a renewed
interest in and reverence for Thomas Aquinas and the scholastics,
or medieval "schoolmen." Deriving from the debates that preceded
the First Vatican Council (1869–70), neo-Scholasticism, or Thomism, was given a distinctive shape in the interwar period by Maritain
and Gilson. Thomism was enormously influential among the Catholic hierarchy and within Catholic intellectual circles. Rooted in Aristotelian metaphysics, Thomists aimed to define an intellectual stance
that would unite the assorted disciplines in which moderns pursued
knowledge. They aimed at the understanding of God and divine revelation through the use of reason; the supernatural, they argued, is
complementary to nature, and humans could, through the use of reason and the senses, trace the operation of God in the universe.[13]

Neo-Scholasticism provided Catholics with a philosophy of life
rooted in the purported unity of spirit and intellect achieved in the
Middle Ages. It was driven both by the felt imperative to restore the
centrality of God in Western culture and by a deep spiritual longing,
which was manifested in various devotional movements, including a
liturgical arts movement; Catholic novels and memoirs; and a mystical theology centered around Christ's body. Revivalists such as Maritain did not, historian Philip Gleason argued, "wish to reproduce the
medieval past but to create its modern analogue—a society animated
and ordered by the Christian religion as Catholics understood it."[14]

Tate read some of the French intellectuals of the Catholic Revival
while in France in 1928 and 1929, as well as Christopher Hollis's *The
American Heresy*, a book critical of American secularism. He observed
Action Française with interest and toyed with the idea of converting to Catholicism. Commenting on a recent bout of depression that
Davidson had described in a letter, Tate revealed his own spiritual
self-absorption at the time. "We are all at present doomed to live a
harrowing life," he wrote, "and it may or may not be more harrowing
than the lives of all men everywhere who have tried to find some ultimate discipline of the soul." It was perhaps harder to find salvation in
the thirteenth century, Tate suggested, but the literary fruits of the
quest were "grander and more coherent." "That was largely because
salvation was common, not personal," Tate concluded.[15]

Tate's embrace of the South was more than an intellectual flirta-
tion. He confided to Cowley in 1929 that he had suppressed his intense
views and emotions concerning "the late War between the States"
from the age of eighteen to twenty-five, but they had lately come
forth. "I have given in to them simply because they are mine, and I
can't pretend to believe in any others," he observed. Yet his southern

identity was fraught with ambivalence, as was evidenced in his lyric poem "Ode to the Confederate Dead," what Warren referred to as his "Confederate morgue piece," which he began to compose in 1926.[16]

Tate's well-known "Ode" is often interpreted as a meditation on the modern person's disconnection from the past, which ends with no resolution. No means to wholeness, no epiphany, was vouchsafed. But, in addition to presenting a portrait of modernist alienation, Tate's poem portrayed a man living very uncomfortably with his own past, in a culture very much obsessed with history. Many years later, in 1938, Tate declared that the "Ode" was " 'about' solipsism or Narcissism, or any other *ism* that denotes the failure of the human personality to function properly in nature and society." The linking of narcissism and the Confederate dead, he argued, was not historical or logical but enacted in the poem itself and in the dramatic situation he wrote about: the ruminations of a man as he stands at the edge of a Confederate graveyard at dusk, looking obsessively for his own reflection in his people's past. The poem, then, was "a certain section of history made into experience, but only on this occasion, and on these terms."[17]

In the poem, the protagonist, standing in a Confederate cemetery, staring at "row after row" of tombstones, is haunted by the past. Such was the common experience of all moderns, Tate suggested:

> You know, who have waited by the wall,
> The twilit certainty of an animal,
> Those midnight restitutions of the blood
> You know, the immitigable pines, the smoky frieze
> Of the sky, the sudden call; you know the rage
> Of Heraclitus and Parmenides. (33)[18]

The relationship between past and present was one of alienation, Tate believed. The dead are truly dead; the modern is a spiritual exile from his or her own heritage. The reference to pre-Socratic philosophers of mutability accentuated the point. For Tate the modern narcissist sees not the dead but only himself. In the poem, the protagonist is haunted by the bravery of the dead Confederate soldiers and the frustration of their sacrifice, ticking off bloody battles: Shiloh, Antietam, Malvern Hill, Bull Run. He is in no way sure that he would have made the sacrifice that the Confederate soldiers did and does not know what to make of these men, who were sent to their death, "Rank upon rank, hurried beyond decision" (34).

The South as a whole, Tate believed, was imbued with a sense of defeat. This separated southern intellectuals from such critics as the New Englander Van Wyck Brooks. The South knew that it had lost its heritage at Appomattox; New Englanders did not yet realize that all moderns are fatally dissociated. "We cannot, doubtless, be too smug; our self-knowledge has been forced upon us at the point of bayonets that now rust in museums," he wrote fellow southerner and poet John Gould Fletcher.[19] The second-to-the-last stanza of the "Ode" carries the questions posed to a protagonist burdened with such knowledge, in whom it is an emotional truth:

> What shall we say who have knowledge
> Carried to the heart? Shall we take the act
> To the grave? Shall we, more hopeful, set up the grave
> In the house? The ravenous grave? (35)

The past is often entwined with guilt, resentment, bittersweet regret. It often demands "midnight restitutions" and is quite capable of opening the door wide to one's most self-destructive tendencies. An embrace of the past, Tate seemed to be warning, invites fruitless self-absorption—defeat. Visiting graves was a potentially dangerous occupation.

Tate left the South as a youth and circulated in the bohemian circles of Hart Crane and Malcolm Cowley, struggling to make a living as an independent writer. Donald Davidson's personal and professional life was more quiet, orderly, and self-contained, and he achieved neither the fame nor the stature that Tate later did. Davidson was born in Campbellsville, Tennessee, near Pulaski, in 1893. His father was a schoolteacher, eventually becoming co-principal of a southern academy; his mother was a music and elocution teacher. The elder Davidson schooled him in the classics but also imparted a keen interest in American folk songs and stories. But it was his paternal grandmother, a young woman during the Civil War, who made the deepest impression on Davidson as a child. He slept in her room, with its oval-framed pictures, old rocking chair, and relics of the past, and he learned the story of his people. "I yield to nobody in my love of the South, and my loyalty to its best traditions," Davidson wrote in 1925. "My blood-kin fought at Shiloh and Murfreesboro, and I claim a personal affinity with the soil of Middle Tennessee." While attending preparatory school, he would sit on a bench outside a country store, talking for hours with two Confederate veterans.[20]

Davidson was educated at home until the age of eight, when he entered the Lynnville Academy in Tennessee and was placed in the fifth grade. At the age of twelve he enrolled in a well-regarded preparatory school, Branham and Hughes, in Spring Hill, Tennessee. Davidson excelled and by 1909 was thoroughly steeped in a rigorous classical curriculum. From this point until he began graduate work in English, Davidson's education was marked by interruptions due to

financial hardship. After a year at Vanderbilt University financed by
a family friend, he was forced to withdraw owing to lack of funds. He
returned only after spending four years teaching school in small Tennessee towns. Davidson left again in 1916 to teach school in Pulaski;
his final credit was earned when he enlisted in the army in 1917. It was
on his return to Vanderbilt after teaching school that Davidson and
the circle of like-minded friends, which included John Crowe Ransom, began to meet regularly to discuss ideas. For the next twenty
years, through the Fugitive and Agrarian periods, this loose association of men became the center of Davidson's intellectual life in Nashville.[21]

Davidson saw combat briefly in World War I. Before leaving for
Europe he married Theresa Scherrer, a native of Ohio whom he had
met while she was teaching at Martin College in Pulaski. A daughter was born to them while Davidson was in France. Returning from
Europe, he struggled to find work. He applied for jobs in Cleveland—
at an advertising agency, in the public schools, at the *Plain Dealer*—
but he wanted to pursue graduate studies at Vanderbilt. Although his
wife's family wanted her to stay in Ohio at least temporarily, Davidson
wrote his father early in 1919, "I do not think that anything can keep
me long away from the South. It is my country." Davidson was initially
unable to secure a teaching appointment, but at the last minute he
received a teaching job at Kentucky Wesleyan College for the 1919–
20 year. The next year he received an instructorship from Vanderbilt, yet he continued to work outside jobs to earn extra money. For
a while he was a reporter for the *Nashville Tennessean;* another summer he wandered the cotton-mill towns of Alabama selling wall maps
of the United States and the state of Alabama.[22] Throughout the
1920s Davidson taught at Vanderbilt. In addition, in 1924 he began
to edit the *Nashville Tennessean*'s book page, which he did until it became a victim of the Great Depression in November 1930. Davidson
also wrote poetry, publishing his first volume, *The Outland Piper,* in
1924.[23]

Like Tate, Davidson reacted against modernization. But he was not
deeply influenced by modernism or the Catholic Revival, as Tate was.
Davidson's intellectual inspiration lay in the widespread movement
of romantic nationalism that dominated cultural debate in America
from 1900 to 1945. A broad stream of nineteenth-century European romanticism (found in Lessing, Herder, Taine, Coleridge, and
Wordsworth) informed a rising urge by Americans to define a national art, to articulate, in Charles C. Alexander's words, "a vision of
a genuinely native, nationally representative artistic expression."[24] As
early as 1881 Walt Whitman, the great American romantic nationalist,
predicted the rise of a native, "autochthonous" American art.[25]

Much of the cultural nationalism of the interwar years fed into an efflorescence of regionalist thinking, which took diverse forms, including the regional planning of southern sociologist Howard Odum and like-minded scholars at the University of North Carolina, the thriving artistic colonies in Taos and Santa Fe, the western writings of Mary Austin, Mari Sandoz, and Walter Prescott Webb, the pioneering folk collecting of B. A. Botkin and his *Folk-Say* anthologies, and the national regional planning efforts of thinkers such as Lewis Mumford. These regionalists were attempting, Robert L. Dorman argued, to refashion the organic communities of their memories; regionalism was a cultural product of the provinces and derived from Americans' efforts to work through their resistance to modernity. Many regionalists shared the opinion of the midwestern muralist Thomas Hart Benton, who declared that cities "offer nothing but coffins for living and thinking." The genuine American culture, regionalists argued, was rooted in the organic traditions of the folk, who enjoyed a firm sense of place.[26]

Davidson's regionalism was linked to a deep identification with the South, and his cultural criticism (as was all the Agrarians' to a degree) reflected a specifically southern mode of rhetoric. Davidson's allegiance to the Lost Cause mythology of the South, however, was among the strongest of the group. The southern worship of the Lost Cause in the fifty years after the Civil War amounted to a civil religion. The Confederate nation, Charles Reagan Wilson declared in his study of the religion of the Lost Cause, "survived as a sacred presence, a holy ghost haunting the spirits and actions of post–Civil War Southerners." Even before the Civil War, southerners believed that their civilization embodied agrarian and spiritual values absent from the North. Southern romanticism, including the cult of male chivalry and the peculiar love for the novels of Sir Walter Scott, predated Confederate nationalism, but the suffering of the war—the "baptism of blood," in the staple rhetoric of Confederate oratory—created a new, cultural conception of southern identity. Southern ministers tended this cultural nationalism, often turning it to their own moralistic purposes, well into the twentieth century. "The cultural dream replaced the political dream: the South's kingdom was to be of culture, not of politics," Wilson wrote.[27] The southern religion of the Lost Cause, which was embodied in numerous ceremonies commemorating the sacrifices of the Confederate warriors, stressed the need to preserve the Christian character of southern culture over and against the shallow, materialistic culture of the victorious North. The South had been redeemed by its bloody sacrifice, the ministers preached, in the traditional rhetoric of Anglo-American evangelicalism. The Lost Cause religion, Wilson concluded, served as a type of revitalization movement, helping to give meaning to the lives of a defeated people in order to build a sense of common identity and mobilize society for recovery and reconstruction.[28]

While Tate was gleefully shedding the burdens of southern culture, then, Davidson turned his attention more seriously to his southern heritage. In 1925, he argued that the success of a southern writer is measured by the degree to which the author is "genuinely autochthonous," or speaks from native traditions. Certain artists, like Robert Frost and Thomas Hardy, were genuinely autochthonous, Davidson argued. "They are literally speaking," he wrote, "of the same time and place with their generation and section, and, whatever their superiority as geniuses, they are not detached from men's fundamental thoughts and feelings." Such artists, although using local materials, could, Davidson believed, more aptly speak to universal themes.[29]

Something of a New South liberal in the mid-1920s, Davidson became more socially conservative as the decade progressed. In an April 1928 column, Davidson artfully combined a strong defense of folk wisdom and American diversity with an equally strong rejection of cosmopolitanism and social tolerance. Cosmopolitanism and mass culture, he argued, eroded the strength of localistic subcultures. In place of an education in their region's history, modern Americans were bombarded from all sides with appeals to false ideals and sham values. "Cosmopolitanism is the virtue of an industrial age," Davidson argued, "but it is also a defect, so far as it destroys diversity." A diversity of vibrant regional cultures was good, but a promiscuous cosmopolitanism, as classical models attested, sapped the character of a nation. Rome, in spite of its republican government, succumbed to the defect of cosmopolitanism. It "rapidly lost its sturdiness, falling a fairly easy prey to decadence, partly because it was too comfortably tolerant. It consolidated and selected, but it did not originate." Provincialism, then, was the only basis for a healthy cultural diversity as well as a bar against industrial standardization.[30]

For Davidson memory was a source of strength, holding out hope of transformation. Tate's "Ode" exposed inner tension and irresolution, but Davidson's major work, *The Tall Men*, published in 1927, was marked by spiritual openness and a quasi-sacramental faith in the rituals of social memory. *The Tall Men* was, Davidson wrote John Gould Fletcher, "in many ways, prefatory; it is a self-orientation, after which I may go on with a feeling that I know where I am headed." His goal, he wrote his editor, R. N. Linscott, was to "re-state deep sources of racial experience" to counteract the disillusionment of the modern world. He explicitly contrasted his efforts with Eliot's: "The idea is to arrive at some basis for an attitude of acceptance, which, while resting on the past, would not wholly reject the present—a

Donald Davidson, 1928.
(Courtesy Photographic Archives,
Vanderbilt University)

mood of positiveness rather than the gesture of defeat to be found, say, in The Waste Land."[31]

When published in 1927, *The Tall Men* consisted of ten separate poems. (The ninth part, "Resurrection," was omitted on reissue in 1938.) It is an account of the process of remembrance in one man, the quasi-autobiographical narrator of the poem. Separate sections treat, in turn, the pioneer past of the Tennessee frontier, the cultural memory of the Civil War, the perplexities shared by the disillusioned generation coming to maturity at the time of World War I, the experience of young Americans fighting in that war, and the religious questioning of the returning veterans. Near the end, Davidson inserted a love poem honoring the narrator's Ohio-born wife and celebrating the healing powers of love. The penultimate poem in the 1927 edition, "Resurrection," explicitly substitutes the presence of historical memory for the presence of a risen Christ. The final poem, "Fire on Belmont Street" serves as an epilogue. In it, a rampaging fire serves as metaphor for the spiritual and social decay of modern society. An actual fire in a house arouses great alarm, but the metaphorical fire of corruption and decay, which is raging all around moderns so destructively, goes unnoticed.[32]

In the second section of the long poem, Davidson delivered a paean to the hardy pioneers of old Tennessee, whose "words were bullets" and who "Talked with their rifles bluntly and sang to the hills / With a whet of axes" (65).[33] They serve, by contrast, to underscore the effete nature of modern men. As the narrator paces the "long street," a central metaphor in Davidson's work for the poet's journey into the past, he is struck by the enervation caused by modern technology. In the interdependent modern world, the narrator merely exists, facing life passively. Davidson deliberately identified modern rootlessness with the habits of the city:

> Assisted to a chair (Grand Rapids) by
> Two slippers (from St. Louis) bites cigar
> (Perhaps Havana) strikes a match (Bellefonte)
> Unwrinkles trousers (Massachusetts) leafs
> The *New York Times* (by U.S. Postal Service). (84)

Despite the banality of life, Davidson's Tennessean nevertheless has a bond with the rough, violent pioneers, for they comprise his own racial stock. "Tallness is not in what you eat or drink," the narrator observes, "But in the seed of man" (67).[34]

Davidson's *Tall Men* was, in effect, an effort to translate the Lost Cause ideology into a form compatible with the modernist sensibility. The poem was romantic and lyrical but also centrally concerned with alienation, ennui, and emotional upheaval. Moreover, Davidson rejected the evangelical piety at the core of the conventional southern exposition of the Lost Cause religion. The poem portrays the act of remembrance as sacramental in and of itself. As Michael M. Jordan observed, "Davidson seeks to achieve purification and rebirth by means of a declared sacrament of history remembered, a secular memorial of the heroism and valor of the Confederate dead." By rejecting conventional Christianity, Jordan argued, Davidson rejected a "transcendent solution to modern man's spiritual crisis." Instead, *The Tall Men*'s narrator propounds a generalized life worship, identifying with the vitality present in the seed passed from generation to generation. "Oh, come away, death!" the narrator says, "I who have had no ending cannot know / What it is to end" (123). The unification of man with his racial past, not with a transcendent Being, is the essence of the sacrament of history. The conventional image of God is only a product of the "rumors of men," his name "repeated as a charm / for comfort's sake when wind blows cold and death / Stands at the road's edge, a shadow beckoning *Stop*" (123). The soul, which is man's racial seed, will not be contained in the broken mold that is conventional religion (123–24).[35]

Davidson presented an even more secularized version of the south-ern civil religion of the Lost Cause, if such a thing was possible. As Davidson wrote his editor in 1927, the South, in order to "retain its spiritual entity," must not repudiate but instead become more con-scious of the past.[36] In *The Tall Men*, he repeatedly presented the re-membrance of the past as an interweaving of the narrator's present self with memory. The past is in the soil, which contains the dead, not in a museum.

> I have trod old floors,
> Tiptoed through musty rooms and glanced at letters
> Spread under glass and signed *Yr Obt Servant*,
> And wistfully conned old platitudes in stone. (73)

Confined to this sort of remembrance only, the past is dead. Rather, the narrator weaves the past into his own soul through an active re-living of it in memory, symbolically partaking of the past by picking a flower from the soil where the dead still reside, asking himself if he will forget

> The dead young men whose flesh will not reflower
> But in this single bloom which now I pluck,
> Weaving it into my spirit as victors weave
> A chaplet, gathered from mould, for honor's sake? (81)

The narrator's words echo those of the Eucharistic prayer at the Ro-man Catholic mass:

> This is my body, woven from the dead and living,
> Given over again to the quick lustration
> Of a new moment. This is my body and spirit,
> Broken but never tamed, risen from the bloody sod,
> Walking suddenly alive in a new morning. (81–82)

The remembering is a form of spiritual purification, a ritual built upon the graves of the Confederate dead. Whereas the dead serve no life-giving function in Tate's barren graveyard, for Davidson the earth encasing the dead yields the possibility of redemption.

In "Resurrection," the sacramental theme is given full expression. Instead of a risen Christ, the narrator encounters (and is reborn through) the remembered sacrifices of his ancestors. He is able to face the modern world with a renewed sense of his historical inheritance.

> Beneath us tier on tier are locked in mould
> The bones of those who fought and loved here once
> Like us who fight and love.
> . . . .

The tall men, lie within the land they won.

.   .   .   .

Out of their death
Leaps now our life, out of decay the flash
Of this high moment, out of the shadow, light.[37]

Not only are the Confederate dead the fathers of those who came
after, but their Christ-like sacrifices secured the land on which the
modern Tennesseans have made their lives. To fail to nurture one's
history and fulfill the obligation to ancestors who sacrificed their lives
was to risk the loss of one's identity, one's strength, and perhaps one's
claim to justice or power in society, as well. The losers in Davidson's
poem—those whom the Tall Men defeated, the American Indians—
cannot speak from their burial mounds because there is nobody to
speak for them. Their sacrifice was for nothing in Davidson's view:
no one claims their heritage (136–37).

Tate and Davidson were writing their respective southern "morgue
pieces" concurrently, and, when Tate read a draft of Davidson's work
in the spring 1926, his criticism was, to use Davidson's own word, astringent. "You are really trying to write a history of your mind," Tate
argued, "but this mind is not so simple as you think."[38] Although Tate
admired much of the verse, he argued that the epic was disordered and
repetitive. Nor did it meet the modernist aesthetic Tate had so carefully formulated since his student days at Vanderbilt. He counseled
Davidson against publishing it. The fact that the poem failed, Tate
argued, was evidence that the materials were inadequate, for Davidson's expertise as a poet was evident throughout. "This is identical
with something I wrote you long before I saw the poems, to the effect
that our past is buried so deep that is is all but irrecoverable," Tate
wrote Davidson. "The result of this remote stratification of the material is that you offer a product which is neither bird, nor beast, nor
fowl: it is not poetry, it is not philosophy, it is not sociology: it is a
little of all three, and none."[39] Tate could not see southern history as
a source of identity.

The essential critical differences related to Davidson's beliefs about
the past, and Davidson elucidated these differences by criticizing
Tate's "Ode," a final copy of which Tate had forwarded at about the
same time to Davidson. Davidson lauded Tate's brilliance as a poet
but argued that his astringency, his acidlike sensibility, prevented a
rich treatment of any subject. "When you deal with *things themselves*,
the things become a ruin and crackle like broken shards under your
feet," Davidson wrote. Tate, he believed, made no true effort to recover the past—an effort that was central to Davidson's entire project

as a poet and thinker. The Confederate dead were a "peg" on which to hang Tate's own pessimistic musings on his own dead emotions. The poem, from Davidson's perspective and as Tate later affirmed, was an exercise in bitter solipsism. Indeed, Tate's poem presented a modern man's confrontation with the graves of the dead as a scene of utter disconnection and frustrated understanding. The beauty of the poem is cold, Davidson wrote. "And where, O Allen Tate, are the dead? You have buried them completely out of sight—with them yourself and me." Tate's belief in a sharp break between the modern person and the values and emotions of the past abrogated the possibility of the spiritual resurrection portrayed in Davidson's poem. "You keep whittling your art to a finer point," Davidson warned Tate, "but are you also not whittling yourself." [40]

In April 1927, shortly after Tate and Davidson's critical exchange on the "Ode" and *The Tall Men*, Tate's own southern revival entered its most intense phase. He contracted with Earle Balch, a New York publisher, to write a history of the Confederate general Stonewall Jackson.[41] At about the same time, he proposed a collective project on the South to Ransom.[42] By the middle of 1928, he was reviewing books on Civil War history for the *New Republic*.[43] In the summers of 1927 and 1928, Tate would, with either Caroline, their daughter Nancy, or his good friend Andrew Lytle, travel through Virginia and Tennessee to visit old battle sites. "Our interest was divided all the way between battlefields and cousins, and it would be hard to decide which savored more of antiquity," Tate wrote to Davidson after his visit to Virginia. He followed the trail of Stonewall Jackson through the Shenandoah Valley, still discernible despite the passage of years. When he found the widow of one of Jackson's captains, she displayed a treasured lock of hair from Jackson's horse. When he stooped to the ground, Tate found crushed minié balls. On a visit to Gettysburg, Tate was fascinated by the closeness of the opposing battle lines—"from the back of Seminary Ridge one could distinguish the features of people on Cemetery." [44]

When Tate's respectful *Stonewall Jackson: The Good Soldier* (1928) appeared, Davidson must have been pleasantly astonished. "Somewhere he has found that the past is not only possible of recovery," Davidson wrote in a review of the book for *Nashville Tennessean* book page, pointedly echoing Tate's own dismissive analysis of *The Tall Men*. "It must be recovered, else we are lost in a wilderness of a million barren novelties, the shouting, staring wilderness of bizarre frenzies and outlandish jollities, left without trace of footsteps backward or forward. The genius of place and the quiet guiding daemon of the artist will not be denied. With their help the past will be recovered." Describing Tate's biography, Davidson reiterated what was to become his essential contention about southern life: "We must recover the past, or at least in some way realize it, in order that we may bring the most genuine and essential parts of our tradition forward in contact with the inevitable new tradition now in process of formation. Only thus can we achieve vital continuity in the national life."[45]

Neither Davidson's romantic sacramentalism of southern identity nor Tate's ambivalent modernism decisively shaped *I'll Take My Stand*, which began to take form in 1929. Rather, the Agrarian symposium articulated a distinct viewpoint, one founded on a socioeconomic critique of northern industrial capitalism, a cultural critique of consumer culture, and an appeal to the southern past. The book's intransigent tone and bid to preserve a specifically southern heritage did, however, provide a crucial emotional element. From the beginning, Tate was less fervently committed to the southernism of the symposium than some of the other contributors. For Tate, attuned to the politics of the cosmopolis, the volume was something of an intellectual gambit. His initial plans for the Agrarian project included the formation of an academy of southern intellectuals (of "Southern *positive* reactionaries"). Tactically, Tate intended, by announcing a strident and authoritarian social program, to "*create an intellectual situation interior to the South.*" Presumably, in the intellectual stir created, a well-disciplined group like his projected academy would be in a position to dominate the southern intellectual scene. Once this was accomplished, the South would represent a standing challenge to northern progressivism:

> The advantages of this program are the advantages of all extreme positions. It would immediately define the muddling and *unorganized* opposition (*intellectually* unorganized) of the Progressives: they have no *philosophical* program, only an emotional acquiescence to the drift of the age, and we should force them to rationalize into absurdity an intellectually untenable position. Secondly, it would crystallize into opposition or complete allegiance the vaguely pro-Southern opinions of the time.

Tate, an intellectual Robert E. Lee, planned to take a cultural war to the opponents' territory and outflank them. This time the South would not fail.[46]

After considering Tate's radical program, Davidson wrote back in October 1929 to point out a key weakness. Tate was being too abstract. "The Southern people are not actually united on anything these days—except the Negro question, and they do not know each other as well as they used to," he wrote. "How are they going to be attracted to a Cause unless it is linked up to something very concrete and of an importance that overwhelms all else—it can't be a mere intellectual issue or pure sentiment. It must be as important as Food, Money, Sex, before real work can be done." Tate agreed; an issue and money, he replied, were the group's prime requisites.[47]

It was only in late 1929 or early 1930 that the group actually began to think in terms of a defense of the *agrarian* South. By January 1930, Davidson, Ransom, and Lytle—after much "confabbing," in Ransom's phrase—had arrived at a master idea, one that would unite a concrete economic program with an appeal to sentiment. Together, they decided to preface the symposium with a manifesto of sorts. "We have decided to push things to a rapid conclusion," Davidson wrote. Lytle, Davidson, and Ransom worked out the "issue" around which to build the symposium: the opposition of agrarian versus industrial civilization. "The discussions with Ransom and Lytle have given the book (in our minds, at least) a slightly different turn, but I think that it will harmonize, rather than otherwise, with what you have probably been thinking," Davidson wrote Tate. With the agrarian-versus-industrial opposition, the Vanderbilt group obtained an economic critique that went to the base of American life and simultaneously appealed to the historical tradition of southerners. By adopting agrarianism as their unifying principle, they gained a vehicle for a cogent critique of industrial civilization, which they abhorred; and by invoking the mystical southern past, they were able to appeal to the emotions of southerners.[48]

After Ransom, Davidson, and Lytle hit on the organizing idea of agrarianism, work on the symposium proceeded apace. The three had bandied about names of possible contributors the previous summer and fall, and they solicited essays throughout the early months of 1930. Only at one point, in mid-February, did serious problems arise. The contributors bogged down in arguing over the manifesto that was to open the book, and their assorted obligations outside the symposium caused their commitment to flag. The introduction to the volume eventually became less a manifesto and more a loose statement of broad principles. But by the end of the month, Tate secured a contract with Harper and Brothers to publish the symposium; finished essays began arriving in Nashville by June.[49]

The leading Agrarians took the socioeconomic elements of *I'll Take My Stand*—the *agrarianism*, considered literally—very seriously. Their opposition to industrial capitalism reflected not only an age-old southern skepticism toward capitalism and the voguish criticism of American intellectuals in the 1920s but also the stark contrast they sought to make with the group of intellectuals with whom most American readers were likely to associate them: the New Humanists.

The Humanists were a loose-knit group of conservative intellectuals led by Irving Babbitt and Paul Elmer More. Charismatic and controversial, Babbitt was a fixture at Harvard University from 1894 onward. Bewailing the aridity and pedantry of the academy (he received a master's from Harvard but no further degree), Babbitt nevertheless was a maverick faculty member at Harvard for many years. More met Babbitt while doing graduate work at Harvard in Oriental and classical languages. Shy and withdrawn, he made his mark as a literary critic, serving for a time as literary editor of the *Nation*. In the 1920s, More taught at Princeton. During that decade, he alone of the Humanists began to interweave a defense of the Christian tradition into the Humanist philosophy. Humanism, which had percolated throughout American culture since the first decade of the century, reached its pinnacle of influence in 1929–30, the time when *I'll Take My Stand* was being planned: Seward Collins, who purchased the *Bookman* in 1927, made that venerable literary review a Humanist organ after he assumed the editorship in 1928; a Humanist symposium, edited by Norman Foerster, a professor of English at the University of Iowa, appeared in 1930; and a spate of essays in journals of all kinds made Humanism the center of literary controversy.[50]

The Humanists were not mere throwbacks to the "genteel tradition" in American culture that Randolph Bourne, Van Wyck Brooks, and others scathingly criticized, but they shared the older culture's insistence that art be judged by its moral content. They hoped for a recovery of manners and morals in American society and decried the decline of authority and tradition. The Humanists firmly rejected the post-Enlightenment worldview that trusted only human reason and scientific technique to know the world. Disregarding the lack of empirical evidence, they suggested that a core of stability and certainty existed within the human being. Part of a person, the flux, was constantly changing, Humanists argued; but another part, the higher self, was set against the flux of change and constituted the personal citadel of individuality and identity in each human being. This essence of personal identity was also the essence of humanness; it constituted an "inner check" on the base, natural self. "This center to which humanism refers everything, this centripetal energy which counteracts the multifarious centrifugal impulses, this magnetic will which draws the flux of our sensations toward it while itself remaining at rest, is the reality that gives rise to religion," wrote Norman Foerster in *American Criticism* (1928). The Humanists' dualistic psychology constituted the underpinning of a human-centered and nonreligious value system. The new source of identity lay in the ethical will of the individual, and the map of this ethical will was the great tradition of letters, especially the classical heritage.[51]

In addition to rejecting naturalism, the Humanists vehemently rejected romanticism and the celebration of the individual, which they believed pandered to the elemental, appetitive self common to all living things. They therefore rejected much of contemporary art, believing that art should elevate the human spirit and, ultimately, be didactic in purpose. Art, as Matthew Arnold phrased it, should be the "criticism of life." J. David Hoeveler summarized their criticism of modern culture in his study of the New Humanists: "The cult of emotion at the good life, the retreat to the personal as the single measure of truth, the escape from standards and norms by the appeal to the immediacy of the present—these were the symptoms of the hedonistic aesthetics that underlay the confusion of standards and the chaos that plagued the creative life in the modern world."[52]

The Humanists inveighed against modern education, believing education's proper role to be the passing on of a cultural past in order to mold modern values. They advocated a classical curriculum and deprecated trends toward the democratization of education, academic specialization, and the increasing focus on research in universities. Babbitt and More scorned democracy, placing their faith not in the unrestrained masses but in a cultural elite. They likewise rejected all strains of liberal thought, including the environmentalist approach to social problems and the humanitarian sensibility. Individuals are responsible for their own fate, the Humanists argued.[53]

Ransom, Tate, and Davidson had little patience for the Humanists. The reasons this was so are revealing, and in many ways they envisaged Agrarianism as an alternative, and more effective, Humanism—a southern humanism. The Humanists were, in fact, logical models for the three men as they contemplated a symposium on southern affairs in the spring and summer of 1929. Indeed, Gorham B. Munson, a New York critic and former editor of the avant-garde literary journal *Secession*, who was sympathetic to the Humanists, was a potential link between the Nashville group and the New Humanists. Davidson ran into Munson at the Yaddo writer's retreat in upstate New York. Munson was deeply immersed at the time in the cultural wars over Humanism; the following year he published an examination of Humanism entitled *The Dilemma of the Liberated*. He suggested that Davidson and Ransom forge an alliance with the Humanists and was so enthusiastic about the prospect that he wrote a memorandum, which Davidson forwarded to Ransom. Munson pointed out, Davidson wrote to Ransom in July 1929, that the Humanists' flaw was "their failure to have intimate touch, to be really a coherent body. They can only write and hope vaguely, whereas we, though constituting a group of less majestic proportions, really form a unit of mutual understanding and actively are in touch with a specific Cause."[54]

By this point, Allen Tate was already well versed in Humanist doctrine. That same month, July 1929, he published a polemic, entitled
"The Fallacy of Humanism," which T. S. Eliot had solicited for the
Criterion. A troubled religious skeptic, Tate flailed Humanism for
pretending to a type of religious authority to which it had no right.
As early as October 1928, Tate wrote to John Gould Fletcher of the
need to "go beyond the moral plane to the philosophical support beneath it." Until the age of John Milton, he declared, a "moral system might be identical with the attitude of the mind holding it." Tate
wrote: "We have got to find out what underlies our ideas; we have
got to *create* the attitude that will be really their equivalent." As ethical theory, Humanism is adequate, Tate believed, but sound theory
was not enough: "We have got to make it good as an attitude." The
problem was not that society lacked sound values and the makings of
a humanistic culture. The defect was in the hold these values had on
the minds of Americans.[55]

In a February 1929 letter to Davidson, Tate observed that Humanism was no advance over the naturalism that it ostensibly repudiated.
"I can never capitulate to naturalism," Tate declared to Davidson.
There can be no break with a monistic view of nature (one that did not
recognize a spiritual realm apart from the temporal one), he argued,
unless one accepts religion. "There is no dualism without religion,
and there is no religion without a Church; nor can there be a Church
without dogma," Tate wrote. "Protestantism is virtually naturalism;
when morality lacks the authority of dogma, it becomes private and
irresponsible, and from this it is only a step to naturalism." The cast of
Tate's mind, his reading in Catholic philosophers, and his immersion
in the study of the antebellum South and its social structures led him
to view religion in rather formal terms—as the church and its teaching magisterium. The lone individual moral will seemed completely
without efficacy.[56]

Tate criticized Humanism for being *merely* a body of ideas: there
was nothing to make this perfectly satisfactory moral theory a viable
force in modern life. Tate wanted an *authoritative* source for guidance,
something that could set dissociated minds right by reaching beneath
the surface and gripping the emotions. A truly humanistic society, he
wrote William S. Knickerbocker, would be one in which "humanism
is spontaneously possible." What the Humanists lack, Tate argued in
"The Fallacy of Humanism," is "technique," by which he meant the
means that convince a person that a particular body of belief is better
than another, that a set of propositions is certainly true. The friendly
reader of Humanist writings—a "believer in reason, tradition, and authority," as Tate himself professed to be—will have got "no specific
ideas about values—that is to say, they will have gained no technique

for acquiring them; and such a technique, they will reflect, is morally identical with the values themselves." Literature cannot substitute for religion, Tate declared. It was a felt religious faith that Tate wanted, and any social philosophy that fell short of this was, in fact, bound to merit his disapproval.[57]

Using Norman Foerster's *American Criticism* as an example, Tate scorned the specious reasoning that lay behind the Humanists' psychological dualism of higher and lower selves. This dualism did not hold, Tate argued. Any part of the human mind or person is inescapably a part of nature. Foerster's appeal to an "ethical imagination" in men, supposedly intuitively informed of verities beyond nature, was the desperate ploy (the "super-faith") of an overmatched mind. Reason, the ultimate arbiter of this "supernatural intuition," remained only reason—and to lay one's faith in this was to advance no further than the eighteenth-century *philosophes*. If they intended to present a viable ethics, the Humanists must specify what Tate called the "conditions" upon which that ethics rests. "These conditions are by no means fulfilled by a recourse to Sophocles, to Vergil, to Augustine, or to a mixture of these writers taken alone. You cannot get out of them a 'philosophy' or a 'religion'; literature is no substitute for religion, or for its defence, philosophy."[58]

Unlike religious dogma, the Humanists appealed to nothing beyond human nature to support their moral choices. When Tate forwarded Ransom his Humanism essay in the early summer of 1929, Ransom was impressed by the agreement between the two men. He agreed that Humanism had no binding appeal, considering Babbitt a "100% schoolmaster." "I have never found him making an effective appeal to such a public as the collegiate; his doctrine hasn't any blood in it, and is bound to go down against any competing doctrine," Ransom observed. "I have seen that he had no reason, no authority, for his position, though he referred much to Aristotle."[59]

Ransom was particularly impressed with the ending of Tate's essay. In the final five pages, Tate addressed the issue of the definition of values in a postreligious, disenchanted civilization. For Tate religion was the "sole technique for the validating of values." This is so because of religion's "successful representation of the problem of evil." Tate made his argument concrete through a metaphorical encounter between man and a snake. An American zoologist when confronted with a Philippine cobra would see a *"Naja samaransis"*—that is, he would apprehend the snake through the genus and species of abstract scientific language. But the primitive—or "head-hunter" in Tate's phrasing—"has a vivider feeling for the unique possibilities of the particular cobra; it may bite him; it may give him the evil eye—both richly qualitative experiences."[60]

In other words, the primitive may recognize the presence of evil, which the scientific modern would miss. Moderns had lost this ability to think religiously, to see the snake in the garden as the presence of evil in the world. Without an appreciation of evil, and thus a full apprehension of nature, one cannot have religion. While science quantifies and categorizes the snake, religion represents the human encounter with the snake. When the primitive recoils from the snake, he is supported by a religious tradition that has transmuted the ultimate mystery of humanity's encounter with nature into intelligible terms by way of myth. Tate's position almost amounted, somewhat tentatively and obliquely in 1929, to the suggestion that myth making and storytelling—literature—serve as the modern means by which humans define and validate values. It is no wonder that Ransom found Tate's article appealing, for this is the position Ransom himself would more forthrightly stake out in the coming year.[61]

Tate's philosophizing reinforced Ransom's own thinking about religion and myth. He particularly liked the snake image. John Crowe Ransom was, in many ways, the intellectual leader of the Agrarians. A soft-spoken poet, Ransom had taught English at Vanderbilt since 1914. He was born in Pulaski, Tennessee, in 1888, and his father and grandfather before him were Methodist ministers. His father, John James Ransom, spent time as a missionary in Brazil. His mother's family, the Crowes, were well established in middle Tennessee; her forebears had taken part in the formation of the Ku Klux Klan during Reconstruction. A gifted scholar, the young Ransom attended Vanderbilt and, on a Rhodes scholarship from 1910 to 1913, Oxford University, where he took the course in the "Greats," studying classical philosophy and history in the original Greek and Latin.[62] Despite his ministerial heritage, however, Ransom was a religious doubter even as he followed the rituals of organized Methodism. In a nineweek burst in 1929 Ransom composed "Giants for Gods," an examination of religion that was published in 1930 as *God without Thunder: An Unorthodox Defense of Orthodoxy*. It was indeed an unorthodox defense, especially coming from the son of two generations of Methodist ministers. Ransom defended a religion that was, as Paul Conkin observed, technically Unitarian; indeed, Ransom referred to his faith as Unitarian. He believed neither in the concept of religious revelation, the divinity of Christ, nor the idea of an afterlife. His defense of religion was, more forthrightly than Tate's, an instrumental defense: religion was a "necessary myth," as Kieran Quinlan observed in his study of Ransom's religious thought. "It is my idea," Ransom declared in *God without Thunder*, "that the myth should be defined for the modern unbeliever in terms of its psychic necessity—by a sort of natural history of supernaturalism."[63]

John Crowe Ransom, 1930.
(Courtesy Photographic Archives,
Vanderbilt University)

In the book, Ransom expressed his preference for the fire-eating gods of the Old Testament (Gods *with* thunder) as opposed to the Westernized man-god he thought characteristic of Christianity. Anticipating later neo-orthodox arguments, Ransom wanted a God who was the "author of evil as well as of good." "We wanted a God who wouldn't hurt us; who would let us understand him; who would agree to scrap all the wicked thunderbolts in his armament," Ransom wrote. "And this is just the God that has developed popularly out of the Christ of the New Testament: the embodiment mostly of the principle of social benevolence and of physical welfare." But, Ransom warned, such a God is not truly binding in the affairs of humans. "Gods are not Gods except when they are treated as Gods," Ransom declared, "and myths do not work in human civilization except when they are dogmas, tolerably hard, and exceedingly jealous of their rivals."[64]

Ransom believed that Tate's defense of religion and his own views were essentially the same. Submission to religion and tradition was a needed antidote to human pride and was at the heart of the thought of both men as they worked together to publish *I'll Take My Stand*. The importance they placed on religion is striking. As Ransom explained to Tate in a 4 July letter: "It is just as you say: Religion is fundamental and prior to intelligent (or human) conduct on any plane. . . . Religion is the only effective defense against Progress, & our vicious economic system; against empire and against socialism, or any other political foolishness." Referring to "Giants for Gods," Ransom argued that Western cultures tend to promulgate mythic giants (Prometheus, Satan/Lucifer, Jesus) whom they then mistake for gods. "Little by little the God of the Jews has been whittled down into the Spirit of Science, or the Spirit of Love, or the Spirit of Rotary; *and now religion is not religion at all, but a purely secular experience, like Y.M.C.A. and Boy Scouts,*" Ransom declared. "Humanism in religion means pretending that Man is God."[65] Tate concurred in a letter written later in the same month: "As you say, it is a great mistake to suppose that Humanism is a real substitute for religion, and while Nietzsche or Arnold may ripen our minds with partial insights (i.e. cultivate us), only God can give the affair a genuine purpose. What I mean is, that the church contains the only body of doctrine already latent in us as feeling: Nietzsche or Kant brings no feeling." Men like Munson, Tate declared, "expect a set of abstractions to create the equivalent emotion out of the air." Religion "is the crux of our Southern agitation— if we shall agitate," Tate wrote. "There is no doubt but that Southern nationalism would have survived a couple of centuries if Southern religion had been more in accord with Southern politics and society (vide Ireland)."[66]

The major role that religion played in the thought of Ransom and Tate in the summer of 1929 is all the more striking when considering its veritable absence from *I'll Take My Stand*. Tate's essay was, of course, an indictment of the inadequacies of the southern "trading religion" of Protestantism to serve as the basis of a social order. But the symposium as a whole held that it was the agrarian social economy, not medieval Catholicism or orthodox Calvinism, that underlay the leisured culture of the South. All the same, for Tate and Ransom, *I'll Take My Stand* was designed to be a corrective to the New Humanism. The two men scorned Humanism as a paltry effort to reform American culture. The Humanists were mere schoolteachers, in Ransom's image, importuning their unruly pupils to behave. They did not know how to appeal to people's emotions. As early as April 1929, Tate was dreaming of a southern "counter movement" to Humanism in a letter to James Southall Wilson, editor of the *Virginia Quarterly Review:* "We are historically much closer to its true meaning than a man in the New England tradition can ever be."[67]

It was in this context that Ransom forwarded to Tate Davidson's letter from Yaddo describing a possible alliance with the Humanists brokered by Gorham Munson. Munson had compared the southerners and their proposal to Action Française. Tate appreciated the comparison but pointed to a key difference: "Maurras had a body of ready-made, near-secular doctrine at hand for re-interpretation to the needs of his time. This point deserves full discussion: all I can do here is to point out that I do not see any of us as the founder of a religion." Tate alluded to the theme of his eventual essay in *I'll Take My Stand:*

> The remote source of the old Southern mind was undoubtedly Catholicism or at least High Church-ism—in spite of the Methodist and Baptist zeal of the Old South—and perhaps something could be done towards showing that the old Southerners were historically Catholics all the time. If that could be done, we have a starting point. For, as Munson says, we need a "master-idea." I cannot agree with his implication that we must manufacture the idea ourselves.[68]

This was the intellectual root of his deep differences with Davidson, for Davidson was content that southern history and folk tradition play the value-making role that Tate had designated for the church. Davidson tended to expect history to function as a religion, much in the manner of the southern religion of the Lost Cause. Tate never saw Agrarianism as a secular substitute for religion, and insofar as it became one, he scorned it. He worried that the symposium would attempt to assert some sort of ersatz religion, just as the Humanists did. He was skeptical of Munson's proposal to the same degree that he was skeptical of the Humanists' attempt to provide a list of recommended writings and values that could serve as the ethical center of American society.

Most important, Tate's response to Munson reveals the standard by which Tate was later to judge the Agrarian effort a failure. The symposium needed a "master-idea," an appeal to its audience equivalent to religion. Such a "master-idea" already had to be present in the lives of the people the symposium meant to address. As Tate wrote in *I'll Take My Stand* the following year: "Tradition must . . . be automatically operative before it can be called tradition."[69] But, poignantly, Tate believed that religion no longer was "automatically operative" in Western civilization in the 1920s. Nor, he realized, did the kind of "High Churchism" he favored ever really hold sway in the South.

It was Ransom, it seems, who pushed Agrarianism away from an exclusive concern with the dilemmas posed by the southern religious tradition—a theme that might well have been overpowering had Tate been the guiding force behind the symposium. But Tate was in France on his Guggenheim grant through much of the planning of the volume, while Ransom was at the center of things in Nashville. Ransom moved the critique of the Humanists beyond its "naturalistic" fallacies, in Tate's words, and toward a more overt southernism, which Tate later deprecated. It was Ransom, Davidson, and Lytle who, late in 1929, hit on the organizing idea of agrarianism. Ransom's own analysis of Humanism is instructive on this point.

As Tate drew fire from the Humanist Robert Shafer, dean of the University of Cincinnati, Ransom wrote an article, "Humanists and Schoolmasters," in Tate's defense, which, despite his best efforts, remained unpublished.[70] Ransom's defense of Tate, however, significantly departed from Tate's exclusive interest in the issue of religion. What the Humanists failed to understand, Ransom argued, was that the code of classical ethics they upheld was based on an older way of life, that of the gentleman, which modern society no longer fostered. Schoolmasters like himself, Ransom stated, must take heed of the economic realities of the world in which their students lived. "Now we know," Ransom declared, "we must reckon with the fact that the life of our scholars is unsound at its economic base, and we are not doing anything very important by pouring in soft materials from the top." Citing John Ruskin as an authority, Ransom argued that art, as well as religion, is only possible in a society in which people live in a right relation to nature. Where the tempo of life is leisurely, the time spent in industrial occupations does not preclude time spent in living, the idea of progress does not claim all of a person's thoughts, and humans are not told "to take up arms against nature, and never to drop them again."[71]

Davidson agreed with Ransom's inclinations on this issue. He echoed Ransom's ideas in a March 1930 review of the Humanist symposium. The Humanists, Davidson insisted, must reach the "Man in the Street" and not merely academics if they wanted to make a difference. This meant reaching factory owners, newspaper editors, movie magnates, grammar school teachers, preachers, and politicians. But the Humanists ignored the fact that Americans lived in an age of materialism and had, for the most part, been converted to "a system of utterly materialistic values." Rather than attempt to "super-impose fine ideas and noble schemes on a civilization which is dominated entirely by contradictory values," the Humanists must go to the base of society. "I do not see how the doctrines of Humanism, inspiring as they may be, can be introduced into our society from the top, by means of a movement which is purely literary and philosophical and which while condemning wholly the creative aspects of modernism, cannot show in its ranks a single creative writer of proved ability," Davidson wrote. "A movement of reform must begin at the base of our life—that is, with its economic base. And the Humanists have practically nothing to say on the subject of economics."[72]

Ransom had pushed to publish the introductory manifesto to the volume early in the year, as a prelude to the forthcoming book, but the plan proved unworkable. Tate favored the plan because he wanted to take advantage of the furor raised by the New Humanists, who published their own symposium early in 1930.[73] The need to refute Humanism was evident in Tate's proposed additions to the opening statement of principles. He specifically contrasted the "genuine" humanism produced by the old southern order with the Humanists' "system of abstractions." Culture arose from the concrete details of daily life, residing in tables, chairs, portraits, acres, laws, and marriage customs. "Humanism, properly speaking," he wrote, "is not a philosophical system, for the sure reason that a given man is not a systematized gentility, but a living example of it; it is not an abstract value, like Truth or Honor, but a descriptive term, and it applies to a certain kind of imaginatively balanced life lived out in a definite social tradition."[74]

I'll Take My Stand incorporated Ransom's critique of the New Humanists. Humanism was not an "abstract system" but a culture, declared *I'll Take My Stand*'s statement of principles, "the whole way in which we live, act, think, and feel." In this, Ransom, Tate, and the other contributors to *I'll Take My Stand* were reflecting a contemporary shift to a more anthropological view of culture in the 1920s and 1930s. A humanistic culture "is a kind of imaginatively balanced life lived out in a definite social tradition," the Agrarians declared. "And, in the concrete, we believe that this, the genuine humanism, was rooted in the agrarian life of the older South and of other parts of the country that shared in such a tradition." Humanism accurately conceived, they argued in a formulation borrowed from Tate, "was deeply founded in the way of life itself—in its tables, chairs, portraits, festivals, laws, marriage customs. We cannot recover our native humanism by adopting some standard of taste that is critical enough to question the contemporary arts but not critical enough to question the social and economic life which is their ground." As Davidson declared:

> Mr. Eugene O'Neill may have every wish to be Sophocles, but he cannot be Sophocles in a New York skyscraper, any more than Mr. Thornton Wilder can be God by sending his astral body to Peru. The Humanists commend us to Sophocles and God, *in vacuo*. Their thinking stops where it should begin, with social conditions that shape the artist's reaction. Like Arnold, they imagine that culture will conquer Philistinism and have faith that the "best" ideas will prevail over the false ideas or non-ideas of the great Anarch.

In Arnold's time it was reasonable to entertain such a hope. Today it is the academic equivalent of Y.M.C.A. "leadership."[75]

Tate and Ransom argued that attitudes toward religion, tradition, and nature, which themselves were inextricably intertwined, were intimately connected to the socioeconomic structure of society as well. "The social structure depends on the economic structure, and economic conviction is the secular image of religion," Tate declared in *I'll Take My Stand*. Religion and myth, by defining the relation between humans and nature and validating human values, demarcate the range of social and economic customs. The fact that a myth attains a popular audience and widespread repetition shows that the myth maker has effectively defined a value. As Ransom wrote of the "myth-maker" in *God without Thunder*, "The community in accepting his myth professes to a certain view of the human relation to the universe, and to an economic theory which is appropriate to that relation. *The religion of a people is that background of metaphysical doctrine which dictates its political economy.*"[76]

Tate had come around to the ideas expressed by Ransom in his essay and that were amplified in the statement of principles beginning *I'll Take My Stand* and in the text of the book itself. Tate praised the essay in a letter to Bernard Bandler of the *Hound and Horn*. Ransom, he stated, "points to a far profounder humanism than any of the current brands." Indeed, Tate confessed to C. Hartley Grattan, editor of an anti-Humanist collection of essays, that he retained an essential sympathy for the New Humanists. "I myself am not certain just what label I ought to apply to myself," he stated, quite revealingly, on 19 February 1930, as the Agrarian volume was being prepared. "If I had to identify myself with a school—which I don't intend to do—I should prefer the Humanists to any other, in spite of grave faults in the position of the two leaders." He was not, he wrote Bandler, "anti-Humanist at all." He merely differed with the Humanists on "questions of method." Babbitt "looks to education in the strict sense; I look to it in the larger sense and the more radical sense of the total background. If the homes of college boys are one thing, you can't make Humanists of them with another thing that will not be relevant to their practical needs after college."[77]

Agrarianism was a humanistic and economic attack on industrial culture, the effects of the market on society, and a capitalist economy no longer responsive to human wishes. It was also, even in the hands of so outwardly dispassionate a writer as Ransom, a defense of the South. Richmond Croom Beatty, a Vanderbilt graduate student in English at the time the book was published, later recalled the emotional impact of *I'll Take My Stand*, an impact that would be replicated many times in later generations of southern readers. The shared tradition of southernness, he believed, was what *I'll Take My Stand* was all about. "I will simply say: *the book waked me up!*" Beatty declared.[78] For Beatty, the book was defined by the legacies it impelled him, as a southerner, to confront. The power of these legacies, as well as the depth of the divisions beneath the surface of the book, ultimately swallowed Agrarianism, but it is important to remember that *I'll Take My Stand* was about more than just being southern and was shaped primarily by intellectual currents arising from outside the South. The authors were dissatisfied with merely rhetorical appeals to the superiority of southern living. Instead, they insisted, every culture is built upon a material establishment. Even a superior culture can be maintained only if the economic substructure of society is compatible with it. *I'll Take My Stand* was humanistic in its appeal and rhetoric, but it was a carefully tempered humanism, one that recognized that the preservation of the South's cultural legacy might first of all require a battle for its economic soul.

CHAPTER THREE

The Failure of a Political Faith
Agrarianism, 1930–1940

Since we lack that deep unity of mind which is brought about by centuries of participation in a mythical religion, the sole scheme of principles, the sole standard of truth that we can call upon is a conception of man in his political role. And a political faith is the most difficult of all, for it is essentially pragmatic and the act of faith must be individual, based on individual reason; the religious motive for action is, as Kant would say, apodeictic, beyond question, and common—not individual.

Allen Tate to John Gould Fletcher, 3 December 1930

The internal divisions and unstated assumptions that lay beneath the surface of *I'll Take My Stand* broke through in the 1930s, resulting in a rather brief and abortive career for Agrarianism as a social movement. The Agrarians attempted to elaborate their social theory, publicize their views, and forge alliances with like-minded thinkers. But the movement's energy and focus dissipated by the mid-1930s. John Crowe Ransom and Allen Tate shifted their attention away from social criticism to literary criticism. Their criticism grew out of the ideas on religion and myth that had been so important to their understanding of Agrarianism (if not terribly evident in *I'll Take My Stand*). Donald Davidson did not participate in the turn toward literary criticism but, instead, transmuted his southernism into what promised to be a more politically palatable regionalism.

Above all, however, it was the rigorous demands of loyalty to the southern past and southern identity that most sapped the will of the Agrarian intellectuals. This was certainly true of Tate, who moved steadily away from southern particularism and, in the process, promulgated his own vision of Agrarianism as a more general Christian humanism. Allen Tate wrote Andrew Nelson Lytle in July 1929 that there was no use in merely "brooding over the past." "We must *use* the past for daring and *positive* ends," he wrote. In the same month Tate wrote Ransom that what he admired most in Ransom's writing was its lack of sectionalism. His own "Southernism," he confided to Ransom, would lead, in all likelihood, to an order "superficially very dissimilar" to that of "our fathers." Tate did not elaborate on this dissimilarity, but in November 1929 he distinguished his position from that of Donald Davidson and Lytle. "We are not in the least divided, but we exhibit two sorts of minds," he wrote Davidson. "You and Andrew seem to constitute one sort—the belief in the eventual success, in the practical sense, of the movement." The other mind, he suggested, that of Ransom, Robert Penn Warren, and himself, saw "that the issue on the plane of action is uncertain." At root, Tate declared, he believed that "there is enough value to satisfy me in the affirmation, in all its consequences, including action, of value. If other goods proceed from that, all the better."[1] As the decade progressed, Tate sought to detach ever more clearly the conservative principles in which he believed from the southern context in which he articulated them.

Tate consistently argued that the true object of the southern movement should be the definition of certain humanistic principles at the heart of the Western tradition. His reservations about Agrarianism were evident in his objections to the title of the symposium, which he believed appealed to southerners, not Americans in general. In early 1930 John Donald Wade apparently suggested "I'll Take My Stand." Tate, Warren, Lytle, and Lyle Lanier all objected.[2] Tate, joined by Lytle, backed *Tracts against Communism* as an alternative, since the Agrarians argued that the evils of industrial capitalism were akin to those of communism. Tate lost the argument but was able to explain his opposition to the title in a footnote to his contribution: "It emphasizes the fact of exclusiveness rather than its benefits; it points to a particular house but omits to say that it was the home of a spirit that may also have lived elsewhere and that this mansion, in short, was incidentally made with hands."[3] He felt vindicated after reading a prepublication notice of the book by a newspaper columnist, probably T. H. Alexander of the *Nashville Tennessean*. "It is over now. Your title triumphs," he wrote Donald Davidson, revealing some ambivalence about the socioeconomic agenda of Agrarianism. "And I observe that Alexander today on the basis of the title defines our aims as an 'agrarian revival,' and reduces our real aims to nonsense. These are, of course, an agrarian revival in the full sense, but by not making our appeal through the title to ideas, we are at the mercy of all the Alexanders—for they need only to draw portraits of us plowing or cleaning a spring to make hash of us before we get a hearing."[4]

Tate's judgment was in part confirmed by the reviews. Although often respectful of the Agrarians and their motives, the reviews tended to be critical of the symposium. Indeed, the Agrarians faced an avalanche of scorn for being historically myopic and, in terms of practical reform, hopelessly romantic. Reviewers attacked the book in two general ways. They criticized the Agrarian view of progress, suggesting that the Agrarians ignored pervasive southern problems, such as rural poverty and disease, and absurdly rejected technology. But many also attacked the Agrarian understanding of southern history, feeling it was romantic and blind to key elements of the past.

Critics often portrayed the Agrarians as backward-looking, unrealistic, and romantic. "Twelve Canutes are these," editorialized the *New York Times*, in a figure that was used more than once. Critics took the Agrarians to task for ignoring both the material benefits that accrued owing to mass production and modern science and the social pathologies endemic to the South in their absence. Gerald W. Johnson, writing in the *Virginia Quarterly Review*, ridiculed the Agrarians' glorification of the rural South:

> Have they never been in the modern South, especially in the sections still completely ruled by agrarianism? Have they been completely oblivious to the Vardamans, the Bleeses [*sic*], the Heflins, the Tom Watsons, who are the delight of Southern agrarianism? Are they unaware of pellagra and hookworm, two flowers of Southern agrarianism? Have they never been told that the obscenities and depravities of the most degenerate hole of a cotton-mill town are but pale reflections of the lurid obscenities and depravities of Southern backwoods communities?

The *Macon Telegraph* lambasted the "Neo-Confederates" for desiring a return to a burdensome past:

> They desire horses and buggies and music boxes to replace automobiles and radios. They want huge Georgian plantation homes with well fitted slave quarters to take the place of suburbs and industrial villages. They want plows and hoes to take the place of looms and cards. Their housewives will wrap cheese cloth around the butter and lower it into the well instead of placing it in automatic refrigerators. They pine for a return of the agrarian civilization and its crinoline embellishments.

At least one reviewer pointed out that the cultural values advocated by the Agrarians were not exclusively agrarian. "Leisure and calm are no doubt necessary for reflective and artistic life," the reviewer for the *Buffalo News* observed. "But industrialism is not incompatible with leisure and repose. One may live in an industrial society without being of it."[5]

The most damning line of criticism, however, focused on the Agrarian assumptions about the southern past. Most frequently, critics accused the Agrarians of falling prey to a weakness William S. Knickerbocker identified as "reconstructing the truth that one needs." While not attacking leisure as such, a writer in the *Dallas News* observed that the Agrarian ideal of the leisurely life was inherently elitist:

> In the Old South which they recall through the softening mist of years, the surplus which meant leisure was only for the few. The slaves had to sing in the moonlight without much leisure, or get a hiding; and the small farmer worked incessantly, buoyed up by the hope that he might some day buy slaves and be received into the aristocratic caste. Only a few in the Old South had to have the economic surplus; only a few were expected to cherish the amenities, dispense hospitality, and cultivate the nobler virtues.

Historian William B. Hesseltine, writing in the *Sewanee Review*, disparaged the very idea of an agrarian culture. "At no time in its history, from Jamestown to Dayton, has the American South been other than a horrible example of the spiritual failure of agrarianism," Hesseltine wrote.[6]

When Andrew Lytle responded vituperatively, defending the folk culture of yeoman farmers but also accusing Hesseltine of being a "galvanized Yankee" who advocated communism, Hesseltine retorted that the "diabolical slave economy" characterized the Old South. Antebellum southerners would have industrialized if they could have, Hesseltine declared, and they had tried to do so unsuccessfully. He pointed out that former Confederate generals happily went north after the war to serve railroad corporations. The Tennessee war hero Nathan Bedford Forrest, of whom Lytle was writing a hagiographic biography, was himself a slave trader, which was "an antebellum form of mass production," Hesseltine insisted. "The reason why the south has failed to produce anything more than a false tradition is that it is an agrarian section," Hesseltine relentlessly continued. "It was, as I have pointed out, valiantly struggling to bring industrialism into its territory, and it would have succeeded if there had not been a conflict of interests with the slaveholders who diverted the energies of the southern people into a defense of slavery."[7]

Critics accused the Agrarians of substituting myth for history. Henry Nash Smith, in an early example of the myth-and-symbol interpretation of American culture for which he became famous, analyzed Agrarianism as a myth—"a selection from experience on the basis of desire." The Agrarian version of history was completely false,

he argued: slavery was not humane; work in the South was not leisurely; the South did not reject commercial agriculture; the South
did not have a particularly democratic or leisurely civilization; and the
code of aristocratic benevolence was a sham.[8]

W. T. Couch made perhaps the most insightful observation on the
Agrarian symposium in 1936. He focused not so much on the my-
thologizing of the past but on the narrowness of the Agrarian vision,
and he rightly perceived that much of the power of the Agrarian argument was based not on an appeal to the importance of traditional social customs but to a particular understanding of southern history.
There is more than one southern tradition, Couch argued. If one must
speak of a single southern tradition, then this tradition must be very
broadly conceived. "It must include the almost ideal life of some plantations and the indescribable brutality, filth, and ignorance of others,"
Couch observed. "It must include a large number of yeoman farmers
and their families. It must not forget the poor whites or the free as well
as the enslaved Negroes. It must remember the emancipation societies that flourished in the South at one time, and it should learn of
such settlements as Salem in North Carolina, where an admirable and
almost unknown way of living prevailed. It must remember the diversity of the regions, the tidewater, the river valleys, the sandhills, the
Piedmont, the mountains, each making possible its own characteristic types of life and its own traditions." Only at the price of "historical truth," Couch concluded, could one speak solely of the plantation
tradition in the South.[9]

These criticisms struck at the core of Tate's preferred myth of an
organic and European-style South. They also struck at his elitism. *I'll
Take My Stand* was soaked in this southernism; the mere addition of
a footnote did not enable Tate to be free of it. The southernness of
the symposium caused Tate to begin to lose faith in it even before it
was published. He had initially seen the projected book as a way to affirm a body of ideas that he identified with Western civilization. "We
must be the last Europeans—there being no Europeans in Europe at
present," he wrote to Davidson in August 1929. In Tate's view, the
most important values of the West—those having to do with religious
wholeness and the "unity of being"—were no longer evident in any
lived culture, whether in the South or anywhere else. Tate was too
close to T. S. Eliot to believe it possible simply to affirm the value
of a whole and healthy culture. Spiritual wholeness was dead, and the
ashes of Western civilization could not be kindled into flame so easily.
Inevitably, then, Tate was frustrated when the Agrarians seemed to
fall prey to the same fallacy that characterized the Humanists. The
simple affirmation of ideas would not make them emotionally compelling. This was "the fallacy of men like Gorham Munson," Tate had

written Ransom in 1929: "They expect a set of abstractions to create the equivalent emotion out of the air." [10]

Tate's New York friends were dismissive of his neo-Confederate tendencies while appreciating his opposition to capitalism. After Tate's 1928–29 Guggenheim fellowship in Europe, Allen's brother Ben purchased an old southern mansion for him and his wife, Caroline. The new home overlooked the Cumberland River near Clarksville, Tennessee. The Tates named it Benfolly in Ben's honor, and it became the site of frequent visits from their friends. After visiting Tate at Benfolly, Edmund Wilson wrote "Tennessee Agrarians" for the *New Republic*, which, while giving the Agrarians' social criticism its due, characterized their southernism as an affectation of the young and self-absorbed. Constructing a composite picture of the typical Agrarian, Wilson portrayed a young man who fled the obsessive provincialism of the South only to recoil, after the newness had faded, from the cosmopolitan worlds of New York, Oxford, and Paris. Ultimately, though, Wilson concluded, the young Agrarians were no different from the other free-floating, youthful intellectuals of the time: "As lacking in a common ideal or religion as their compatriots of Paris and New York, they try to make one of ancestor worship. They revive the old myths of the family, sustain themselves with the bravery of their fathers. And they find at last a common cause and purpose in agitation against capitalists, largely Northern, who are bringing the textile and other industries to the South." [11]

Tate was stung by Wilson's piece, which he believed an unfair satire. Wilson had evidently touched a sensitive chord within him. "Can you really with such unblushing glibness reduce our position to *ancestor worship*?" Tate challenged Wilson, accusing him of not having read *I'll Take My Stand*. Tate bristled at the image of himself "mooning over the past." The Agrarians, he argued, "don't care a damn for the past as such"; but, as southerners, they were forced to know the past in order to understand the present. [12]

Immediately after the publication of *I'll Take My Stand*, the Agrarians organized committees to purchase a county newspaper, plan a second symposium, coordinate public statements, and hold local meetings in the South. Indeed, eager for the group to acquire a county newspaper, Ransom even declared his willingness to leave academia to edit it, if he could bear it financially. When Lytle, who ran a farm, suggested that his current crop might supply a down payment, Ransom inquired into the purchase of several county papers in Tennessee. In the end, the Agrarians never acquired a paper, and Ransom remained a college professor. [13]

Ransom and Davidson participated in five debates in the six months after the book's publication. The locations included Richmond, New Orleans, Atlanta, and Chattanooga and Columbia, Tennessee.[14] The Richmond debate, organized by Lambert Davis, editor of the *Virginia Quarterly Review*, and sponsored by the *Richmond Times-Dispatch*, was held on 14 November 1930, two days after the publication of the volume. It pitted Ransom against the historian Stringfellow Barr, who argued that industrialism was a positive development and should be welcomed by the South. A capacity crowd of thirty-five hundred attended the debate, and the audience included such notable literary figures as Ellen Glasgow, James Branch Cabell, Henry Seidel Canby, H. L. Mencken, and Sherwood Anderson, who served as moderator. Barr had written in the *Virginia Quarterly Review* that the South should welcome industrialism but use government to regulate it. In the debate Ransom declared measures such as workers' compensation, unemployment insurance, old-age pensions, and collective-bargaining guarantees to be contrary to the spirit of individualism and tending inevitably to socialism and, eventually, communism. In a lively rejoinder, Barr declared progress to be inevitable and argued that Ransom's communism was better understood as "paternalism." "When problems are complex," Barr declared, "you ought never to cry 'I'll Take My Stand' but 'Sit Down and Think.' " Applause from the audience seems to have awarded the debate to Barr.[15]

In addition to pondering life as a county newspaper editor, Ransom attempted to write an Agrarian economics, delving into the subject while on leave in England in 1931–32. During his long sabbatical he wrote an economic primer promoting subsistence agriculture entitled "Land!," while also giving talks on economics now and then to Rotary clubs. Ransom never found a publisher for the manuscript, but he considered it an "economic sequel" to *I'll Take My Stand*. In it, he advocated the return of the unemployed to the land, which could be the source of a good, humane life, one lived outside the money economy. In a February 1931 debate in Atlanta with William D. Anderson, president of the Bibb Manufacturing Company of Macon, Georgia, Ransom warned of the evils of one-crop agriculture, overproduction, and the concomitant need for incessant advertising. "Industrialism has but one genius," he declared, "and that is the genius of production, in which it makes no provision for emergencies. As part of the genius of production, it developed advertising and salesmanship to overcome the natural good taste of the people and their natural thrift." The belief that underconsumption was the key weakness of industrial capitalism shaped Ransom's economic thought. "It is an inevitable consequence of progress that production greatly outruns the rate of natural consumption," the Agrarians declared in *I'll Take My Stand*. Demand does not always match supply, Ransom observed in "Land!," and, in fact, supply was running far ahead of demand. Having established that the economy is prone to misalignment, Ransom attributed the crisis of the 1930s to "overcapitalization"—too much money in the service of production. Too many farmers were producing goods for the market, and more land was still available, Ransom observed. For this reason, commercial farming, Ransom argued, had been in crisis even before the depression. "Money-making, so far as American farmers are concerned, is like the grace of God; it cannot be pursued successfully as an end in itself." [16]

Overcapitalization could not be solved, Ransom argued, by the expansion of markets or investment in new industries. Nor, he believed, would businessmen ever abide centralized planning. Although in his manuscript he was supportive of the labor movement and the graduated income tax, he dismissed socialism out of hand. Socialism simply went against the American grain, in particular the American commitment to private property. Most important, socialism would not solve what Ransom considered the defect of capitalism: the industrial machine would be preserved; only the distribution of ownership, responsibility, and income would change. Overproduction and underconsumption would continue to characterize the economy. Socialism, he argued, was not the opposite of capitalism; it was really the opposite of a principle he valued—individualism. Capitalism's true opposite was, instead, agrarianism. Ransom promoted a return to subsistence farming, for the farmer, he argued, is an "amphibian," capable of living both in the money economy and out of it. He advocated government policies that inhibited commercial expansion, shifted the burden of taxation from land to income, encouraged homesteading, and gave preferential treatment to small farmers. "Land!" was Ransom's reworking of the old Jeffersonian agrarian myth. He envisioned a society of healthy, virtuous, and individualist peasants. ("Happy Farmers" was the title of one of his economic articles that reached print.) [17]

During this same period, Tate grew disgusted with the progress of Agrarianism, which he considered to be languishing. Tate confessed his frustration at the lack of Agrarian action to Bernard Bandler of the *Hound and Horn* in late 1931. "We are all grinding our own axes," he wrote. "Last year I gave about six months to the Cause—with the result that I'm being sued for debt, and may have to cease living the agrarian life for a few years unless dollars can be persuaded to raise themselves by their own bootstraps." [18] He returned to France in the fall of 1932, this time on a Guggenheim fellowship awarded to Caroline. Perhaps recalling his plans for a disciplined academy modeled on Action Française, he began to criticize the original project of the Agrarians. He was disgusted with what he now considered the "Anglonostalgia" of their program and began to feel that the program was too impractical. They should have pursued the "immediately possible."[19]

Tate did, however, make several efforts to move the program forward. He attempted to spread Agrarianism through *Hound and Horn*, a small but respected journal of the arts founded by the young critic Lincoln Kirstein. Kirstein, Bandler, and the other editors of the magazine had contemplated a critical forum on *I'll Take My Stand*, but they discovered themselves to be in general sympathy with the Agrarians.[20] In January 1932, Kirstein and Bandler asked Tate to be the southern editor for the journal. Tate accepted and tried to make *Hound and Horn* into an organ for Agrarianism, sponsoring a series of articles on southern figures such as John C. Calhoun, Thomas Jefferson, and John Taylor. He advocated a sectionalist attitude committed to a limited role for the federal government and to the need to secure a "just balance of power." Bandler and Kirstein planned to convene a large meeting of Agrarians and *Hound and Horn* editors, as well as an assortment of independent, nonleft critics, in June 1932, but it never materialized. Nonetheless, articles, poems, and stories from Tate, Caroline Gordon, Andrew Nelson Lytle, and Frank L. Owsley appeared in the journal, as well as an important essay on regionalism by Donald Davidson. Tate's association ended in late 1933, however, when the editors' enthusiasm for Agrarianism waned, in part because of the hostility of Yvor Winters, *Hound and Horn*'s western editor.[21]

The Agrarians always longed for a magazine or newspaper to express their views, and, for a brief period, Tate believed the *Hound and Horn* would fit their needs. Beginning in 1933, the Agrarians finally found an effective outlet when Seward Collins converted his literary journal, the *Bookman*, into the *American Review*. Collins intended to make the *American Review* an organ for contemporary "Revolutionary Conservatives": the New Humanists (whom he had long supported), led by Paul Elmer More and Irving Babbitt; the English Distributists, led by G. K. Chesterton and Hilaire Belloc; the Agrarians; and neo-Scholastics (or neo-Thomists), including, according to Collins, T. S. Eliot, Ernest Sellière, Charles Maurras, Léon Daudet, Henri Massis, Wyndham Lewis, and Christopher Dawson. Collins visited the Agrarians in Nashville and at the Lytle family's Cornsilk in Guntersville, Alabama, in the spring of 1933. A memorandum prepared by the Agrarians in Nashville around the time of Collins's visit outlined their principles and aspirations regarding an alliance with the *American Review*. The authors took pains to emphasize that their current focus on economics was only a part of their larger opposition to specialization, which was intellectual, political, social, and aesthetic as well as economic in nature. Their "closest allies," the Humanists, lacked an economics; the classical values that once underwrote the arts would not be restored without attention to the "social background." The Communists understood life purely in terms of the social background. It was the Agrarians who provided a full view of the world. The memorandum's authors refused to advocate a particular religion, although some members of the group "might want to name Roman or Anglo-Roman Catholicism," but rather declared their faith in "regionalism, sectionalism, provincialism."[22]

The *American Review* was, according to historian John P. Diggins, "notable for the perversity of its brilliance." Collins made it a forum for the voices of the antimodern Right in the 1930s, many of whom admired the medieval and royalist past of Europe, but some of whom appreciated modern experiments in corporatism and fascism. Some of the Agrarians, in particular Tate, later came to regret their association with Collins, who won notoriety later in the decade because of his profascist sentiments.[23] Through Collins, however, the Agrarians came into contact with the Distributists, who shared the Agrarians' propensity for linking radical economic nostrums with social and religious conservatism.

Defined chiefly by the Catholic apologists Chesterton and Belloc, Distributism was an amalgam of Catholic Agrarianism and English libertarianism. Chesterton and Belloc railed against government bureaucracy and paternalism. In contrast to the suffocating restrictions imposed by industrial capitalism and government regulation, Belloc posed the just social order of medieval Christendom, which he claimed fostered free individuals — independent peasants and guildsmen. Chesterton and Belloc were an inspiration to the Catholic Land movement in England, which eventuated in the founding of the Distributist League in 1926. Popular among American Roman Catholic intellectuals for many years, Distributism was inspired by papal teachings on social justice and decentralization. Distributists advocated the widespread redistribution of property in order to create an agrarian mixed economy of farming and small industry. The Distributist impulse in England manifested itself in diverse ways, including efforts to form rural collectives. The Dominican priest Vincent McNabb became an itinerant preacher, rejecting modern conveniences, traveling by foot, and dressing in homespun. American Catholics responded to the English initiatives with their own rural life movement, establishing the National Catholic Rural Life Conference in 1922. Some American Catholics channeled this neomedievalist type of thought into the liturgical arts, but others, such as priests Virgil Michel, Gerald Ellerd, and Paul Hanley Furfey, developed a more radicalized fusion of Catholic neomedievalism with American republicanism, which challenged capitalism and proposed embedding property owing in religious obligation. Dorothy Day, who established co-operative farms as well as urban missions, represented a radical form of Catholic agrarianism.[24]

The Agrarians published more than sixty articles in the *American Review* in its four-and-one-half-year life span. In an article published in September 1933, Andrew Lytle defended the medieval feudal order. He traced the history of the English revolution against the feudal state, which began, he wrote, in the sixteenth century and provided the relevant historical context for understanding early American politics. In the Middle Ages, property was (rightly, Lytle felt) conceived of as a "thing-to-be-used" rather than a "thing-to-be-sold." The older notion of property preserved the family; the newer, rights in property. England's Glorious Revolution in 1688 confirmed this new idea of property and created a state designed specifically to protect private property rights. This revolution was transmitted to the American colonists. In the early national period, Thomas Jefferson's Republican faction had stood against the modern state, but Jefferson came to be too devoted to the abstractions of natural rights. Modern revolutionaries destroyed the best foundation for a state, which was the "dogma of one religion." "Jefferson wrote some mighty pretty words: life, liberty, and the pursuit of happiness; and in their name he destroyed the Church and primogeniture, the high tower and strong rock of traditional society," Lytle wrote in a study of the Virginia statesman John Taylor in the fall of 1934. Taylor and the Founding Fathers were early Distributists, in Lytle's reckoning. What was now needed was a means to again "bind" people to the land, for the small, independent, subsistence farmer was, Lytle believed, the bulwark of the agrarian state.[25]

Frank L. Owsley presented perhaps the most detailed political program ever produced by an Agrarian in "The Pillars of Agrarianism," published in the *American Review* in March 1935. Owsley proposed that the government purchase land owned by insurance companies, absentee landlords, and any struggling landowner wishing to sell it and then distribute it in eighty-acre allotments (along with a log home, barn, fenced pasture, two mules, two milk cows, and three hundred dollars) to landless tenants. He estimated this might "rehabilitate" up to five hundred thousand people. Unemployed city dwellers should likewise be resettled and rehabilitated on the land. The recipients of these government homesteads would not be able to sell or mortgage them, and the government would limit the mortgage of farmland through courts of equity and bar the sale of land to real estate and insurance companies and banks. In this way, Owsley hoped to reestablish a "modified form of feudal tenure." He blamed the new status of the United States as a creditor nation as well as rising

American tariffs for the slack export markets for agricultural goods. Nations that once purchased cotton from America were now switching to countries in debt to them; and southerners had always seen tariffs as evidence of the fundamental disparity of interests between the South and the industrial Northeast. Owsley proposed constitutional reforms that would essentially reverse the verdict of the Civil War: the nation should be broken into regional governments, each having much of the power of the current state governments and the federal government, including the right to set aside national tariffs and set their own, if need be; the central government would regulate interstate commerce and finance, establish a currency and military, and conduct foreign policy. In this way, Owsley reasoned, "leisure, good manners, and the good way of life might again become ours." [26]

In general, the Agrarians opposed the New Deal Agricultural Adjustment Act (1933), which tended to benefit large farmers at the expense of small farmers, tenants, and sharecroppers. Senator John Bankhead of Alabama expressed interest in Owsley's "Pillars of Agrarianism," and Owsley and Agrarian Herman C. Nixon supported the Bankhead-Jones Farm Tenant Bill, which Bankhead cosponsored in the spring of 1935. The bill would have provided low-interest, long-term loans to help tenants, sharecroppers, and agricultural laborers purchase farms. Davidson felt the bill was inadequate; Nixon, who had believed the AAA tended toward fascism, supported it enthusiastically. Perhaps the most liberal of the Agrarians, Nixon eventually came to support farm cooperatives, government ownership of natural resources and public utilities, and the socialization of medical care. When finally passed in modified form in 1937, the Bankhead-Jones Act established the Farm Security Administration, which was charged with making farm purchase loans but provided little aid to tenants and sharecroppers.[27]

Tate spearheaded the Agrarians' attempts to align themselves with the Distributists, whose chief spokesman in America was Herbert Agar, a well-connected newspaperman associated with the wealthy Bingham family of Kentucky and their *Louisville Courier-Journal*.[28] Tate's support for Distributist economic proposals was, in fact, the fulfillment of the strategy he had outlined at the end of his contribution to *I'll Take My Stand*. Realizing that the spiritual reality of a feudal society was gone, he had suggested that the only option was political radicalism. The fulcrum of Tate's renewed passion for Agrarianism was the wide distribution of property. "The big basic industries must be broken up and socialized, and the small businesses returned to the people," he wrote John Peale Bishop, explaining the Agrarians' new alliance with Collins and the Distributists in the spring of 1933. "The Distributists differ with us on this in no respect.

The end in view is the destruction of the middle class–capitalist hegemony, and the restoration with the material at hand, not a literal restoration, of traditional society." Planning a second symposium for the
spring of 1934, Tate placed much weight on an elusive distinction between the Agrarians' desire for a "planned society" and others' desire
for a "planned economy." He also took to referring to the project as
a projected "Conservative Revolution."[29]

Who Owns America?: A New Declaration of Independence, published
in 1936, was the culmination of Tate and Agar's collaboration. The
volume was composed of twenty-one essays, with contributions from
eight of the original Agrarians as well as Agar, English Distributists
Douglas Jerrold and Belloc, the Catholic Agrarian and Jesuit John C.
Rawe, and Cleanth Brooks, another alumnus of Vanderbilt who was
beginning his career as an English professor and literary critic. The
essayists criticized big business, monopoly capitalism, and mass production; called for political and economic decentralization; and advocated the Agrarian-Distributist program of widespread land ownership, subsistence farming, and regionalism. The high point of the
Agrarian-Distributist coalition occurred in June 1936, when a convention for the Committee for the Alliance of Agrarian and Distributist Groups met in Nashville. By this time the movement consisted of the Agrarians (with a large contingent of the Nashville circle
in attendance, including eight of the original Agrarians as well as
Brooks), Distributists, the Catholic Land movement, the Coopera-
tive movement, the National Committee on Small Farm Ownership,
and eccentric planners such as Ralph Borsodi, a writer from New York
who organized modern homesteading operations in order to rejuve-
nate the moral character of Americans. The convention's platform
had a pronounced libertarian cast. After declaring the imminent danger to freedom, the platform stated: "Philosophically, we would assert
that the end of man is the complete development of his own individual and social nature, and that institutions—political, economic,
social, educational, and religious[—]are but means to this end. These
institutions are good in the degree that they assist him in his free development, and evil in the degree that they hinder him." Human freedom, the platform read, depends on "the freedom of men as economic
agents." It identified finance capitalism, communism, and fascism as
the greatest dangers to economic freedom and called for the decentralization of population in the United States as well as of ownership
in agriculture, industry, and trade.[30]

The subtle ways in which the intense southernism of Agrarianism worked to undermine it can be seen in the rather unsuccessful
efforts to forge an effective political movement based on an Agrarian-

Distributist alliance. The further the Agrarians moved from the rhetorical power and emotional fervor of their "reconstructed but unregenerate" stance as southerners, the more their voices became indistinguishable in the raucous, crowded, and, more than ever, radical organs of American debate during the Great Depression. Agrarianism stripped of its intense particularism and the concrete example of the South's noncommercial cultural traditions became a rather abstract and colorless cry for economic decentralization. The southernism of *I'll Take My Stand*, however, although providing vivid rhetoric and powerful symbols, undercut the ability of the Agrarians to construct a cultural criticism of wide appeal. The greater depth of Distributism in both moral philosophy and political economy is evident. The Distributists tapped into a deep stream of antimodern social thought and literature; their appeal to the Catholic tradition presented them, at least in theory, with a rather large, international audience. Aside from a particularly striking rendition of the cultural losses due to modernization, the Agrarians had little to offer beyond a parochial appeal to their own backyard. Moreover, the tragic history of the South, marked as it is by multiple perversities of human bondage and repression, can tax even the sternest of loyalties. No Agrarian seems to have found loyalty to the southern past more emotionally draining than Tate. Indeed, he began to detach his social thought from the South as soon as *I'll Take My Stand* was published.

Tate sought to clarify his ideas concerning religion and the South in response to concerns of John Gould Fletcher about his essay in *I'll Take My Stand*. His point, Tate wrote Fletcher in December 1930, was that the *motive* for defending tradition was no longer religious, as with the Irish, but political. "Since we lack that deep unity of mind which is brought about by centuries of participation in a mythical religion, the sole scheme of principles, the sole standard of truth that we can call upon is a conception of man in his political role," Tate wrote. "And a political faith is the most difficult of all, for it is essentially pragmatic and the act of faith must be individual, based on individual reason; the religious motive for action is, as Kant would say, apodeictic, beyond question, and common—not individual." One month after the publication of the *I'll Take My Stand*, Tate was diagnosing what, for himself, was a devastating failure of Agrarianism. The Agrarians were left, as he told Fletcher, "trying to make a political creed do the work of religion—and by religion I mean a profound conviction about the way life should be lived." The validation of values was now left in the human realm of politics and individual reason. Tate found himself in 1930 a reluctant pragmatist.[31]

Tate was—ambivalently and with some anxiety—fleeing the southern past from 1930 onward. After *I'll Take My Stand*, he became troubled by his deep immersion in the southern past, confessing to his friend and fellow southerner John Peale Bishop that he feared he was identifying his own self with the social and political failure of the South—something he believed characteristic of southerners. "The older I get the more I realize that I set out about ten years ago to live a life of failure, to imitate, in my own life, the history of my people," Tate wrote in the summer of 1931. As an artist, he instinctively sought this complete identification with his people. "We all have an instinct—if we are artists particularly—to live at the center of some way of life and to be borne up by its innermost significance. The significance of the Southern way of life, in my time, is failure," he observed ruefully. Tate believed that, paradoxically, for a southern artist to succeed, it was necessary to become deeply entwined with and disconnected from one's southern heritage.[32]

Tate worked to break the link between Agrarianism and the South. This entailed a steady movement away from the stance of Davidson, who marked the outer limits of commitment to sectional loyalty among the Agrarians. Davidson had argued that the wellspring of art was an intense attachment to one's home region. Tate distanced himself from such a stance. The Agrarians did not intend *merely* to defend certain sectional prejudices and prerogatives, he wrote the critic R. P. Blackmur in December 1933: "Sectionalism is not sectionalism, any more than French culture is a sectionalism within Europe. We use the term because of the superficial domination of the political structure." Tate contrasted the "man of letters" with the politician. The politician is a sectionalist, but the man of letters is the spokesman for tradition, a less politicized notion in Tate's mind. Although politics was the defense of tradition, the two were necessarily at odds. Tradition, Tate held, is unselfconscious and private: "it should not be put up on a billboard or debauched in a conquest of the world."[33]

Throughout the fall of 1932 and spring of 1933, Tate and Davidson reconsidered Agrarianism with some asperity. Davidson was beginning work on the essays that would become *The Attack on Leviathan: Regionalism and Nationalism in the United States* (1938), his major statement of regionalism. In the general idea of sectionalism, one that could appeal to Americans in regions outside the South, Davidson believed he had found a way to revivify Agrarianism. Tate saw little advantage in Davidson's sectionalism. He criticized the first drafts of an article Davidson had prepared for *Hound and Horn*, which embodied many of Davidson's new ideas. Tate believed Davidson was forsaking a universalist position. Davidson suggested that each section may use its own language in speaking for itself; self-professed regionalists "are prone to write of Gopher Prairie in terms of itself, not of what New York may think of Gopher Prairie." Tate bridled at this sort of talk;

Gopher Prairie did not deserve the privilege of its own idiom because it would merely comprise everything against which contemporary critics of the American business civilization revolted. "We constantly hate the Gopher Prairies, and not merely from a Southern point of view," Tate wrote Davidson. "It is rather that our Southern point of view is largely made up of the traditional and civilized view of human culture that prevails in France at this moment, and to some extent in England—the common humanistic tradition." As Tate explained to Kirstein, "What Davidson is really fighting here is a small war against cosmopolitan aesthetic fashions; but, as I have told him, if he is erecting a Southern mind that cannot understand and assimilate, and use for its purposes, the technique of James Joyces, I will have to secede from it. This is literary Know-Nothingism, and I am agin it."[34]

Faithfulness to a sectional language was not a good in itself; Tate's southern agitation had been based not on his faith in the South but on his conviction that the South represented humanist values of universal application. Artists must not pay automatic obeisance to whatever beliefs are current in their section. Artists will inevitably find fault with their culture, Tate believed. The very argument for tradition is that it will occasionally produce artists and critics who will take the universal point of view. "I do not want to restore the Old South; I wouldn't if I could," Tate wrote Blackmur.[35]

At the same time that he valorized the independent cosmopolitan intellectual, Tate moved to a more open acknowledgment of his inner division over the southern heritage. He believed the history of the South was the source of his art but also, paradoxically, corrosive of it. He was unable to avoid internalizing the legacy of failure; by the 1940s Tate was routinely frustrated by writer's block, publishing little poetry thereafter. The Tates—Allen, Caroline, and their daughter Nancy—established themselves at Benfolly, only an hour from Nashville, in the spring of 1930. They lived there in genteel poverty but still entertained the Agrarian "brethren" and their families as well as guests from the New York literary world and beyond. "The Tates were stately yet bohemian, leisurely yet dedicated," recalled Robert Lowell, who as a young man camped out on the Tates' lawn in 1937 in order to meet Ford Madox Ford. "A schoolboy's loaded twenty-two rifle hung under the Confederate flag over the fireplace. A reproduced sketch of Leonardo's *Virgin of the Rocks* balanced an engraving of Stonewall Jackson."[36]

Benfolly was near the home of Caroline's large, extended family, the Meriwethers. In the spring of 1933, returning from their second Guggenheim expedition abroad, the Tates decided to stay the summer with the "Meriwether connection," as Caroline called her family,

Malcolm Cowley and Allen Tate shaking hands in front of a monument to
the Confederate dead, June 1933. (Courtesy Robert Cowley)

since Benfolly had been rented for the spring. Malcolm Cowley came
to spend part of the summer in the area while he worked on his book
Exile's Return, published in 1934. He lived at a nearby home of one
of Caroline's relatives and saw the Tates almost every day. Cowley
completely disagreed with the Agrarians' social and economic conservatism but admired their feeling for the folk culture of their region, which resonated with his own feelings for the western Pennsylvania country of his childhood. He visited Nashville and ate at the
home of the Ransoms, where, he later recalled, John Ransom carved

a country ham "with the air of performing a sacrament." Visiting Fort Donelson on the Cumberland, Cowley and Tate posed for a mock-serious photograph solemnly shaking hands before a Confederate monument.[37]

The ideas of Tate merged, to a degree, with those of Cowley. Indeed, Tate's only novel, *The Fathers*, published in 1938, a declaration of his own sense of disconnection from the South, was, in part, a development of the theme of generational disinheritance found in Cowley's *Exile's Return*. In that book, Cowley wrote that the "lost generation" of writers, which included F. Scott Fitzgerald, Hart Crane, John Dos Passos, E. E. Cummings, Ernest Hemingway, and himself, had come of age during a period of transition, caught between two eras and two sets of values, with none to claim as their own. Members of his generation "were seceding from the old, and yet could adhere to nothing new; they groped their way toward another scheme of life, as yet undefined." Cowley agreed with the Agrarians' claim that a better and more rooted culture was being destroyed by modernity. Industrial capitalism was making moderns into exiles, "homeless citizens, not so much of the world as of international capitalism."[38]

In the summer of 1933, as Cowley was visiting, Tate was experiencing a personal crisis. The submersion in Caroline's huge Meriwether clan proved difficult for him to bear. At the end of June, he disappeared; when he returned in July, he admitted to Caroline that he had had an affair with her twenty-seven-year-old cousin. When the affair ended, he had been distraught and so had fled. The affair deeply wounded Caroline and irreparably damaged the Tates' marriage. What drove Tate to the first (he claimed) of numerous extramarital liaisons is unclear, although the causes seem to have been deeply embedded in Tate's psyche. Later in life, Tate would often claim that Caroline's family on her mother's side was paranoid. He told Caroline that she was obsessed with her family. Recapitulating the affair twenty years later as he was undergoing Jungian psychoanalysis, Tate told Caroline that he associated her with his mother, who, he claimed, tried "to cut [him] off from the outside world." "In the summer of 1933 I heard you, for two months, speak to me in the collective tone and meaning of a Sho Nuff Maywether, as if you were possessed," he wrote Caroline. In the 1950s with the aid of dream analysis, Tate came to believe that he had for years "been trying to make the family shadow something it couldn't be: the past as a living centre." Caroline later believed that the roots of his infidelity lay in his own impermanent and somewhat vagabond youth. "I think that, louts as they are, as he is always saying they are, they still have something that his family has lost," she wrote Katherine Anne Porter of the Meriwethers in 1945.[39]

Even before his emotional reaction to the tradition-bound Meriwether family, Tate was intellectually blocked in his attempts to evaluate the southern past. He began a biography of Robert E. Lee in 1929 but was soon critical of Lee. As he wrote in *Jefferson Davis: His Rise and Fall* in 1929, Tate believed that southern leaders should have defended the true heart of the Confederacy, which was the lower South —Georgia, Mississippi, Florida, Alabama, and Louisiana—rather than squandering their resources on Virginia. Lee, the great Virginian, had allowed the interests of Virginia to come before those of the Confederacy as a whole. Further, Lee shrank from a merciless prosecution of the war, in a way Stonewall Jackson never would have. Lee placed honor above independence, Tate wrote Lytle in 1929. "If he had taken matters in his own hands, he might have saved the situation; he was not willing to do this," Tate argued. "It would have violated his Sunday School morality. Here we have an example of a man whose character was greater than his creed, but the creed won."[40]

Tate was unable to write the biography. As the years passed and the biography, the advance for which the penurious Tates had already spent, became the Tate family's "very own albatross" (in the phrase of Ann Waldron, Caroline Gordon's biographer), Tate's feelings toward Lee became entwined with his feelings about the South and his own past. Throughout the summer of 1931 Tate struggled to write the Lee biography, eventually writing about fifty pages before more or less abandoning it. He confided his difficulties to Andrew Lytle, asking him to intercede with their mutual publisher, Earle Balch. Tate's graphic explanation of his problem reveals the way in which southern history easily mingled with more deep-seated attitudes. "The longer I've contemplated the venerable features of Lee, the more I've hated him," Tate wrote. "It is as if I had married a beautiful girl, perfect in figure, pure in all those physical attributes that seem to clothe purity of character, and then had found when she had undressed that the hidden places were corrupt and diseased. Can any man alive write this way about Lee?" Tate identified Lee with a failing that he believed latent in a certain type of southernism: a self-righteous turning from effective action, a type of social impotence. "In the case of a man like Davis," Tate observed, "there is weakness but a certain purity, but in Lee, who was not weak, there is when we see under the surface an abyss, and it is to this that I do not want to give a name."[41]

During 1932, Tate began to experiment with fiction; ultimately he produced a novel, *The Fathers* (1938), which drew freely on stories and models from his own family history. And the Lee biography consistently took on autobiographical implications. The section Tate managed to finish included a detailed account of the failings of Lee's father, who fell from political and military glory to a debtor's prison.

The failings of Lee's father, which paralleled those of Tate's own, promised to be central to Tate's interpretation of Robert E. Lee. As his biography of Lee languished, Tate began a new project in 1932. He intended to render his own family history as a type of southern history and tentatively entitled the work "Ancestors of Exile." Drawing on his own divided heritage, the book, mixing genealogy with fictional elements, was to chronicle the coming together of a Virginia Tidewater family with a Scotch-Irish pioneer clan. Tate provided Bishop with a brief outline of the proposed work: "The fundamental contrast will be between the Va. tidewater idea—stability, land, the establishment—and the pioneer, who frequently of course took on the Va. idea, even in Tenn., but who usually had some energy left over, which has made modern America. My brother and I show these types fairly well."[42]

In Ransom's original Agrarianism, the pioneer versus the establishment constituted the essential social tension. Tate now saw both the pioneer and the establishment strains working in his own family. Tate's brother, Ben, a coal and power entrepreneur nine years older than Allen, had supported the family when Tate was a boy, while their failed father had lived reclusively, carrying on extramarital affairs. Ben, the wealthy entrepreneur on whom both the chronically impoverished Tate and his family depended, was the man of action, the pioneer. Tate himself represented the old Tidewater culture of establishment, which he viewed with ambivalence. The personal scrupulosity of the establishment culture encouraged inaction; further, Victorian pieties had led to his plain-born father's social ostracism and, in his own mind, to his own marital guilt. Tate saw both legacies as constitutive of the modern South. Writing to Ellen Glasgow in May 1933, he described a climactic chapter for "Ancestors of Exile," entitled "Anonymous Confessions," which would feature the "chaotic protest of a woman produced by the union of the Tidewater and Scotch-Irish strains—her protest against the aimless life to which she is committed without quite understanding why it is aimless." "Through her," Tate observed, "I am offering my judgment upon the modern mind."[43]

"Ancestors of Exile," like the Lee biography, remained unfinished. In the fall of 1933, in the aftermath of Allen's affair, the Tates struggled to put their ruptured marriage back together. They resolved that Tate would give up the Lee biography, which had hung over their heads for three years and which, Caroline observed, seemed to make Allen sick whenever he attempted to work at it. In October, Tate gave up the genealogical project. As he tried to explain to Robert Penn Warren, the work on his ancestry seemed at first an easy project but had now become impossible. "I discover in myself a great reluctance in trying to make my ancestry 'illustrate' anything, even if I could honestly find that it illustrated virtue in its rarest forms," Tate admitted. "The mistake consisted in assuming that it is easy to turn one's private resources into propaganda, even for a good cause." [44]

Tate had never believed that the South bequeathed a functioning, premodern culture to modern southerners. This was evident in his contribution to *I'll Take My Stand*, in which he ended by highlighting the rationalistic legacy of Jefferson. Yet, after the mental and emotional turmoil of his marriage and failed writing projects in the early 1930s, Tate gave up any faith he had ever possessed in somehow recovering an effective humanistic society from southern history. In this sense, *The Fathers* was a post-Agrarian work, for it was an acknowledgment of the complexity of southern history and the divided lessons it taught.

The novel's narrator, Lacy Buchan, was an aging southerner recalling the disintegration of his family on the eve of the Civil War. Lacy is a modern exile, a product of the Old South forced to live in the modern era. This sense of being drawn to a past culture yet forced to live in a new informed Tate's understanding of himself and his southern literary contemporaries (and was informed by Cowley's analysis of the spiritual exile of the lost generation). Indeed, his suggestion that the efflorescence of southern writing in this period—the "southern renascence" that Tate vigorously promoted—was a product of this tension between the southerner's knowledge of the premodern and disenchantment with the modern was influential for a generation of southern literary scholars. "With the war of 1914–1918," Tate wrote in 1945, "the South re-entered the world—but gave a backward glance as it skipped over the border: that backward glance gave us the Southern renascence, a literature conscious of the past in the present." [45]

The Fathers is a book of remembering in an almost Proustian vein. Lacy comments on the smells or items that cause his memory to jog and that momentarily jar his sense of time. The book's opening is an image of remembering: the smell of salt fish stirs Lacy's memories of the Buchan home at Pleasant Hill (the actual name of a home owned by Tate's ancestors) (3). [46] Although Lacy enacts the drama of the southerner's encounter with the past, the central figure in the book is George Posey, the strong and dashing interloper who desires Lacy's sister, Susan, in marriage and comes to be a competing "father" in the family. The novel is about the way in which Posey, representing the aggressive and capitalistic spirit of the new age, disrupts the tradition-bound Buchan family, which exemplified the culture of manners, courtesy, chivalry, and elaborate social conventions. In the process, Posey brings catastrophe.

The character of George Posey is oblivious to the rituals and conventions of southern civilization. He announces his marriage to Susan rather than asking for permission from her father, Major Lewis Buchan, much to the chagrin of Major Buchan. He engages, somewhat subversively, in a ridiculous jousting tournament set up by the young men of the county to win Susan's favor, only to erupt in laughter when presenting the hard-won laurel wreath to her. He refuses to follow the elaborate prescriptions of the *code duello*, unceremoniously knocking his drunken challenger to the ground rather than engaging in a potentially lethal contest of arms.

At root, Posey does not understand the elaborate cultural barriers erected by the South—its manners, rules, decorum— or the reason they exist. As Lacy explains in the novel, the conventions of southern culture protect men from unrestrained emotions and desires but also from the abyss of complete evil and the horror of man's finitude (46). George Posey, Lacy explained, was "unprotected." He was too sensitive and experienced events too personally, "a man who received the shock of the world at the end of his nerves." "Is not civilization the agreement, slowly arrived at, to let the abyss alone?" the aged Lacy asked (185–86).

But the Old South was dying and possessed only an ineffectual culture, as symbolized in the character of Major Buchan. Major Buchan attempted to run the plantation according to the paternalistic credo of the Old South, but he was failing. Posey, in contrast, is driven by material concerns. He knowingly sold his half brother, a mulatto slave who served as the Poseys' butler, to acquire a fine horse for the jousting tournament. Gradually obtaining control of Major Buchan's affairs, he defied the major's wishes and sold some family slaves in order that the Buchan plantation remain solvent (53–54, 131, 134). The elder Buchan was out of sync with his times. A steadfast Unionist, he refused to face the reality of southern secession. His opposition to the coming war led to the final breach of his authority. When Posey, whose family lived in Georgetown in the District of Columbia, chose to defend the Confederacy, Major Buchan's sons chose to follow this charismatic alternative father, and not their blood relation (149–50). In *The Fathers*, the Confederate rebellion becomes the vehicle for the ultimate triumph of the acquisitive capitalistic spirit and the sealing of the old culture's doom.

Lacy Buchan's family embodies the collapse of the Old South. By the end of the novel, the union of the Posey and Buchan clans has led to disaster and resulted in the death of both George Posey's black half brother and Lacy's brother Semmes, the burning of the Buchan family home, and the suicide of Major Buchan (the foremost representative of the culture of the Old South). His people, Lacy observed at the beginning of the novel, were "scattered into the new life of the modern age where they cannot even find themselves" (5).

It is, however, Posey—"a man without people or place," the unsentimental and business-oriented man who disrupts the traditional customs of the Buchan family—and not Lacy Buchan, who represents the plight of the modern southerner (179). Lacy compares Posey to a force of nature that lacks self-control (268). Disaster for the Buchan family followed on Posey's presence not because he was cruel or unfeeling. Quite the opposite, Posey was capable of great passion and even, in some fashion, longed for the heritage of the South; he desired, after all, marriage into the Buchan family. Rather, the character of George Posey is poignant because of his ultimate frustration. He could see what his people had lost and yet could not have it. In possessing it, he destroyed it. It was in this capacity that he was the true father of Lacy and spiritual analogue of Tate. "In a world in which all men were like him," Lacy observes, "George would not have suffered—and he did suffer—the shock of communion with a world that he could not recover; while that world existed, its piety, its order, its elaborate rigamarole—his own forfeited heritage—teased him like a nightmare in which the dreamer dreams a dream within a dream within another dream of something he cannot name" (180).

In a 1936 letter to Tate, Ransom confessed that he felt "patriotism" was harmful to the artistic sensibility of them both. "What is true in part for you (though a part that is ominously increasing) is true nearly in full for me: *patriotism* has nearly eaten me up, and I've got to get out of it," he wrote.[47] Indeed, from the mid-1930s onward, Ransom, Tate, Warren, and Cleanth Brooks were actively involved in defining what came to be labeled the New Criticism. Ransom self-consciously channeled his energies into his literary criticism. Lured by the offer of an increased salary and more time to devote to his writing, as well as his regret that Vanderbilt University was moving away from a traditional liberal arts curriculum, Ransom made the difficult decision to leave the university (and the South) in 1937 and assumed a faculty position at Kenyon College in Gambier, Ohio. His move coincided with the rise of the New Criticism, which dominated American academic English departments from 1938, when Ransom's first collection of critical essays, *The World's Body*, appeared, until the mid-1960s. Ransom's second major critical work, *The New Criticism* (1941), an analysis of the criticism of I. A. Richards, T. S. Eliot, and Yvor Winters, gave the movement its name. Shortly after his arrival in Gambier, Ransom established the *Kenyon Review*, which became an important outlet for the New Criticism.[48]

The study of literature in American colleges first arose as the study of the classical languages, rhetoric, and poetry declined in the nineteenth century. Since the end of the nineteenth century, historical and philological scholars had contended with genteel generalists in the tradition of Matthew Arnold for dominance in departments of English. The philologists and their allies won, in part because their emphasis matched the methodological rigor and scholarly assumptions that were shaping the modern research university. The model of English study in the 1890s, as exemplified by Harvard University, for example, was extensive training in linguistics and historical philology. The Vanderbilt group had cultivated an opposite approach to literature—one centered on the close study and discussion of the dynamics of particular texts—since their days as Fugitive poets. By the 1930s, Ransom and his former pupils were ready to champion their rigorous focus on the text as an aesthetic object to the profession as a whole, just as the conflict between scholars and critics in college English departments was reaching its climax.[49]

The New Criticism was a formalist approach to the study of texts, characterized, above all, by a system of close reading. The intention was to focus on the literary object itself as an organic and self-sufficient whole. The critic paid greater attention to the structure of the work, its symbolic patterns and metaphorical and rhetorical intricacies, than to the mind of the author, the work's effect on the readers, or historical context. For critics such as Ransom, Tate, and Brooks, a work of literature was ontologically superior to other writing, an avenue to a distinct and unique form of knowledge.[50] The Agrarians were by no means the only or original New Critics. Richards, Eliot, and William Empson were important inspirations; aside from Ransom, Tate, Warren, and Brooks, important New Critics in the 1940s included R. P. Blackmur, Robert Heilman, Arthur Mizener, William Van O'Connor, Mark Schorer, Robert Stallman, Austin Warren, René Wellek, William K. Wimsatt, and Yvor Winters. But the southerners were excellent literary politicians and crucial leaders of the movement. In addition to Ransom's *Kenyon Review*, Brooks and Warren edited the *Southern Review* at Louisiana State University from 1935 to 1942. Their 1938 undergraduate text, *Understanding Poetry*, was a landmark in transmitting the new critical approach into the college classroom. Brooks's *Modern Poetry and the Tradition* (1939) provided a succinct revisionist history of poetry along New Critical lines. In 1939, Tate established himself in Princeton University's creative writing program. He published a stream of critical essays and briefly edited the *Sewanee Review* in the 1940s. Wellek and Austin Warren's *The Theory of Literature* (1942) systematized the body of thought for graduate application; in 1948, Ransom established the Kenyon School of English (later moved to Indiana University), an annual summer program designed for graduate students. Brook's *The Well-Wrought Urn: Studies in the Structure of Poetry* (1949) was perhaps the supreme example of New Criticism in practice.[51]

For Ransom, his shift from Agrarian organizing to criticism was a means of defining and preserving the conditions of artistic production. He considered "Criticism, Inc.," an essay included in *The World's Body*, in which he called for a "precise," expert criticism to be practiced by professionals employed in the academy, a "postscript" to Agarianism. By associating philological and historical analysis with other disciplines and by promulgating a set of aesthetic characteristics and critical standards that define good poetry and require extensive methodological training in order to teach, Ransom was not only carving out a distinct discipline but also creating a program of research and study. Ransom was also, by stressing objective critical standards, promising a depoliticized criticism at a time when Marxist calls for social realism and judgments based on the political ramifications of a text were influential in American literary life.[52]

The New Critics, then, played a vital role in the professionalization of academic literary study after World War II. Their approach to literature, which originally was less disengaged and apolitical than it later became, met fierce resistance at the time from both critics on the left and old-fashioned Humanists. Leftists saw the New Critics as apolitical, draining literature of its historical and political significance in order to privilege the preferred values of high modernism: hierarchy, order, ambiguity, and irony. Genteel humanists of the older school saw them as soulless mechanics, blind to the moral purposes behind art and literature. Nevertheless, by the late 1950s, the New Criticism was so dominant, it had already calcified into a rigid orthodoxy. Although sapped of its critical potency, it remained a dominant pedagogical presence in American universities. It became the "normal criticism," an assumed set of techniques for literary analysis.[53]

Literary historians more interested in Ransom, Tate, Warren, and Brooks as literary critics than as social thinkers have argued that the New Criticism was a continuation, or transmutation, of their Agrarian conservatism. Mark Jancovich, for example, argues that the southern critics' move into the academy was "merely a change of tactics." "They hoped to establish an institutional basis for the distribution of their social and cultural criticism," he argues. Inspired by the Marxist Antonio Gramsci, Paul Bové has argued that the Agrarian movement into academic criticism represented the absorption of a radically conservative but nonetheless oppositional force into the hegemonic capitalist state.[54] The New Criticism, however, was not a simple transmutation of the radical conservatism of *I'll Take My Stand*, nor was it necessarily a co-optation of Agrarianism by the dominant system.

Rather, Ransom, Tate, and Warren's shift to a more exclusive concern with literary criticism was, in part, the function of the particular characters of each man as well as the dynamics of academic politics in America. Warren was a relatively minor figure in Agrarianism (and Brooks was even more peripheral). Ransom's increasing concentration on literature was a continuation of his deepest concerns, and Tate's reorientation was the culmination of his rejection of southern particularism and his new desire to articulate what had been an incipient Christian social criticism.

Ransom and Tate's Agrarianism had always been informed by a deeper concern with the problem of religious faith in the modern world. Religion, Ransom had argued in *God without Thunder*, gained its power from its mythic components; in his contribution to *I'll Take My Stand*, he had attempted to vindicate and defend the life of the leisured gentleman, which was the life that made art possible. In his literary criticism of the 1930s, Ransom conceived art, religion, and manners to be interrelated. (Religion and art became essentially interchangeable in his thought.)[55] Together, religion and art were cultural practices necessary for a complete and good life. Civilization, science, the hectic, workaday world of modern life—all conspired against art, religion, and manners. In poetry, Ransom argued in 1941, we can appreciate the rich density of the world—we can be "delicate and sensitive"—in a way that we cannot in everyday life.[56] Thus, the role of the artist is to present the "world's body" for the renewed appreciation of the audience. Furthermore, for Ransom, poetry presented an avenue of knowledge of the world distinct from that of science, with its incessant abstracting of nature: "It is as true today as yesterday that the actual world is not clearly made like its scientific transcripts; the material components in its structures are indeed concrete and insubordinate; and it is in this respect that poetry makes its representations of the world as an alternative to the docile and virtuous world which science pictures." Poetry as an art form, he argued as a New Critic, had a unique ontological status; it provided a way to understand the world through the union of meaning and structure, words and metrical form. "Poetry is the kind of knowledge by which we must know what we have arranged that we shall not know otherwise," he declared in *The World's Body*. "We have elected to know the world through our science, and we know a great deal, but science is only the cognitive department of our animal life, and by it we know the world only as a scheme of abstract conveniences. What we cannot know constitutionally as scientists is the world which is made of whole and indefeasible objects, and this is the world which poetry recovers for us."[57]

Our science-driven culture, then, deadens our ability both to love nature and truly to know the universe. It is in leisure that we develop art as the means of expressing this love of nature.[58] It is leisure, too, by extension, that allows us to develop religion and manners as well as art and thus introduces a fuller knowledge of the universe. After Agrarianism Ransom no longer defended the social economy of the South, which, he had argued in *I'll Take My Stand*, promoted the leisure necessary for the good life of aesthetic appreciation, love of nature, and religious practice. Now he would defend art, not through social theory, political agitation, or cultural criticism, but through aesthetic theory and by shoring up the project of criticism in the academy. If American industrial society no longer provided the conditions for a rich art, the academy might at least preserve the principles of that art.

Writing in the *Kenyon Review* in 1945, Ransom responded to two articles on art and religion by W. P. Southard and Theodor W. Adorno. The Agrarians, Southard argued, had failed to live out the convictions of their Agrarianism and had not made actual the ideals of organic community. Adorno's more philosophical article reflected on the impossibility of artistic and religious unity in a modern, nonhierarchical, and individualistic society. Ransom agreed with Adorno: the time when art and the economy were in harmonious relation was over. At one time humans worked in small settings, close to one another and often close to nature. Now labor was specialized, and individuals were part of a vast, interconnected web of impersonal relations. Southard, Ransom argued, was the victim of a "phantasy" if he truly desired to go back to an earlier economy. It was a "phantasy" he, too, had shared as a Southern Agrarian but now rejected. The new economy, Ransom argued, must be accepted, for "without consenting to division of labor, and hence modern society, we should have not only no effective science, invention, and scholarship, but nothing to speak of in art."[59]

While the Agrarians had previously seen the atrophy of a rich and communal art under industrial capitalism, now Ransom believed that it was the dream of an Agrarian nonindustrial economy that must be sacrificed for the possibility of art. Modern Americans could recapture the spirit of organic unity of the agrarian past, but only through its presence in art. The Agrarians had not gone back to the farm, Ransom acknowledged. Indeed, he as well as Tate and Robert Penn Warren had gone to northern universities to teach. They could not invite others to do what they themselves had not done, he concluded. Remarking that the fate of postwar Germany appeared to be a return to an agricultural economy, Ransom observed ironically, "Once I should have thought there could be no greater happiness for a people, but now I have no difficulty in seeing it for what it is meant to be: a heavy punishment."[60]

In a 1952 symposium for the literary journal *Shenandoah* entitled

"The Agrarians Today," Ransom declared that no part of the country, North or South, would ever possess an agrarian society again. An agrarian economy was a hopeless idyll, if not actually an undesirable retrogression, Ransom argued. He welcomed the South's embrace of the New Deal economy. The makers of the New Deal, he wrote, had realized "that you cannot have mass production unless you have mass consumption too; and that the cue for all future government in this country is by every possible indirect means to distribute purchase-money among the groups which have not had it."[61]

Tate's immersion in Agrarianism had always been marked by the jarring incongruity between the kind of culture he believed the Old South possessed and its lack of what he believed should necessarily accompany it. The South had an established, feudal way of life, one that provided for the "unity of life" treasured by Tate, but it lacked the feudal religion of medieval Christendom. It was, instead, Protestant and, moreover, strongly influenced by the rationalist tradition of the Enlightenment and Thomas Jefferson. Thus, Tate's decade-long research into southern history convinced him that the South, in a crucial respect, had not lived up to the ideal of a feudal society, and so the contemplated Agrarian return to the traditions of the southern past would necessarily fail. The political faith of the Agrarians would necessarily be inadequate. As Tate declared in the *Southern Review*, responding to Dudley Wynn, who had suggested that the Agrarians' and Distributists' defense of authoritarian religious faith tended toward fascism, one cannot just will a faith in religious authority.[62] Moreover, Tate's deep obsession with southern history had been personally draining, leaving him unhealthily fixated on failure, loss, and inadequacy. As was made plain in *The Fathers*, the legacy of the Old South was precisely the alienation that was the fate of all moderns.

At root, Tate longed for the simple faith of the premodern Christian. He was an admirer and advocate of Christian feudal society; yet, in the 1930s, he could neither believe in Christianity nor submit to religious authority. Nor did he believe that the South, despite its traditional social structure, inherited such a Christian tradition of "unity of being." Even if the vestiges of a traditional social order survived, to be practiced by modern southerners on weekends or in their free time, the spirit of these traditions was gone, Tate argued in an address delivered at the University of Virginia in 1936 entitled "What Is a Traditional Society?" For the old traditions to be truly operative, modern southerners' way of making a living would have to accord with their way of living; the economic base must accord with the social order. Traditional man "dominated the means of life; he was not dominated by it," Tate argued. "I think that the distinguishing feature of a traditional society is simply that. In order to make a livelihood men do not have to put aside their moral natures. Traditional men are never quite making their living, and they never quite cease to make it. Or put otherwise: they are making their living all the time, and affirming their humanity all the time." The 1936 address marked a shift in Tate's thinking, for he was using *traditional*, the adjectival form, to describe the optimal way for men to live with one another, rather than *tradition*, the noun, to refer to what is handed down from one generation to the next. It was clear that the South did *not* hand down the traditions (a feudal economic order or religion) that made for a traditional society. If a traditional society "could come into being now, and had no past whatever, it would be traditional because it could hand something on," Tate declared. "That something would be a moral conception of man in relation to the material of life." But if the South were to become a traditional society, it would not be due to southern ancestors.[63]

From the late 1930s onward, Tate would conceive of the good society—one that was traditional and allowed a unity of being—as something that would be attained not by returning to the past but by creating anew. History merely proved that such a society, in which "absolute beliefs" had reigned supreme, had existed at one time. Now, the task was to look forward toward reestablishing such a society. We waste our time, Tate exclaimed in 1936:

> if we suppose that St. Thomas, religious authority, the Catholic Church, the Old South, were ever more than expressions of certain degrees of achievement in traditional life by certain men at certain times under certain conditions. It is a special "psychosis" of modern man that impels him to "restore the past." Those ages of the past that he cries for had restored nothing whatever: they created something, and although they levied upon the past, they quickly transformed their borrowings, and amalgamated past and present into a whole.[64]

This was a stark repudiation of Agrarianism.

As it was, Tate did find the absolute he sought in the 1940s, as he gradually moved closer to the Roman Catholic Church, finally converting in 1950. As he did so, like Ransom, Tate focused his energies on criticism. He defended the role of the independent "man of letters" and fought to preserve the independence and integrity of the critic. He participated wholeheartedly in promoting the New Criticism. Over the course of the decade, he became an increasingly Catholic critic. Following the Thomist philosopher Jacques Maritain, Tate traced the dissociation of feeling and reason to René Descartes. Modern man has "set himself up in quasi-divine independence" since the sixteenth century, Tate wrote in 1951. He no longer restrained his intellect and will with feeling, the property that alone allows man to submit in humility to the natural world. Those who think that they may have full knowledge of nature using their reason alone are falling prey to what Tate termed the "angelic imagination." The only true path to knowledge is the "symbolic imagination"; humans may know the divine, thus the fullness of nature, only through symbols, or analogies, to the natural world. "The human intellect cannot reach God as essence; only God as analogy." The sensible world is but a mirror, reflecting God.[65]

Louis D. Rubin Jr. has suggested that Tate's progression in the 1930s, culminating in the writing of *The Fathers*, was unique among the major Agrarians. Tate did "what none of his fellow Agrarians really attempted to do," Rubin argued: "turn the Agrarian concerns inward, and undertake, in his more important writings, an intensive search into their meaning so far as his own personal identity was involved. Agrarianism became not only a program or even a defense of religious humanism, but also a complex problem in history, society, family ties, and personal allegiance. The question 'What should the South do?' became 'Who am I?'"[66] And yet Tate was not the only Agrarian to conceive of Agrarianism as a search into personal identity. To suggest this was so is to ignore the very different, yet equally intensive, search of Donald Davidson.

CHAPTER FOUR

Citizens of an Americanized Nowhere
Donald Davidson's Southern Regionalism

We are all Rebels, Yankees, Westerners, New Englanders or what you will, bound by ties more generous than abstract institutions can express, rather than citizens of an Americanized nowhere, without family, kin, or home.
Donald Davidson, "Sectionalism in the United States"

Donald Davidson conceived of social memory as a "folk-chain" that binds a people together. The folk-chain transmits tradition, Davidson declared, and tells southerners *"who we are, where we are, where we belong, what we live by, what we live for."* It is extended through history by one person teaching another: "What passes from memory to memory, without benefit of the historian's record, is as old in time as the memories that it expresses, and if it is accepted it endures as long as the land and people that accept it."[1]

Again and again, the Agrarians returned to one crucial question: How could southerners retain what they have? Yet Agrarianism was a flexible set of assumptions, criticisms, and principles, which meant fundamentally different things to different Agrarians. While Allen Tate resisted southern particularism both personally and intellectually, Davidson's Agrarian social criticism increasingly turned to the social memory of the South. He delimited the scope of community and the possibilities for social change according to his interpretation of the past. The cultivation of memory and tradition became the source of Davidson's southern regionalism. *The Tall Men* had prefigured this development. There the process of remembering was a means of personal sanctification and purification, the sacrifice of one's ancestors being the agency of redemption.[2]

Over the course of the 1930s, Davidson articulated a variant of Agrarianism that he closely linked to the particularities of region and community. In the process, he turned from the modernism that Tate and John Crowe Ransom espoused and, much to their distaste, embraced a romantic southern nationalism. Davidson replaced "tradition" and "traditionalism" with "region" and "regionalism," but the locus of his thought remained the same. "Don, I should say, is the least clear-headed person in Tennessee," Tate wrote to Bernard Bandler of *Hound and Horn* in February 1932. "Of all our people, Don is the great literalist in doctrine, and probably our finest character, but sheer, realistic intelligence—no," Tate wrote. Despite Tate's opprobrium, Davidson pressed ahead with his regionalist program. Unlike Tate or Ransom, who pursued their careers at universities in the North, Davidson did not leave the South, and he became openly critical of the literary modernism they upheld.[3]

The challenge Davidson's writings pose to modern readers lies in his particularist understanding of citizenship. Citizenship, Davidson believed, derives from a particular identity, and it must, therefore, imply membership, with all the limitations, responsibilities, but also privileges that membership entails. For Davidson, this sense of citizenship precluded social equality for African Americans in the South. The social memory Davidson shared upheld white supremacy. He expressed his feelings on segregation as early as *The Tall Men*. Addressing the southern blacks, the narrator says:

> There is a wall
> Between us, anciently erected. Once
> It might have been crossed, men say. But now I cannot
> Forget that I was master, and you can hardly
> Forget that you were a slave.

Social memory was the functional equivalent of race in Davidson's thinking, and racial segregation was a logical extension of his version of Agrarianism. It was a social institution developed by white southerners to preserve their culture and their identity.[4]

Unlike Ransom and Tate, Davidson never displayed an ironic or detached perspective on the South. He saw Agrarianism as a defense of localistic attachments in general and the South in particular. Over the course of the 1930s, Davidson argued that regional identifications were at the core of American society. The national government, he argued, had become an impersonal, inhuman juggernaut, a "leviathan." In arguing this, Davidson revealed a convergence of his thought with the American Right, which shared with Davidson a resistance to the cultural, social, and ethnic pluralism of the increasingly cosmopolitan and urban-based United States. The Right, too, singled out the state and a national financial elite as enemies of the vital, local communities of America. Throughout his career, Davidson assiduously resisted the modernization of social identity. His attention to social identity suggested that he did not see it as malleable or suited to individual retailoring; rather, it was an intractable attribute of race, region, and history. Davidson's characteristic response to modern America was intransigence—traditional folk were the "Immovable Bodies" that alone stood against the "Irresistible Forces" that threatened American culture. The careful cultivation of social memory was the source, Davidson believed, for a cultural politics of Agrarianism. The same currents of romantic nationalism that fed fascist myths of the folk in Europe pushed Davidson, too, into racism. By the 1950s, Davidson was a vocal defender of segregation in the South and the head of one of the primary organizations of massive resistance in Tennessee.

Indeed, Davidson admitted to Tate a preference for fascism over communism. The taint of fascism accounted, in part, for the declining appeal of Davidson's brand of romantic nationalism after World War II; in its place, liberal intellectuals expounded cosmopolitanism and cultural pluralism. Nevertheless, the weak hold of the modernized identity of suburb and bureaucratized social structure would become a staple of postwar American social commentary. The needs addressed by romantic nationalists did not diminish, even if the rhetoric of the prewar years did. Moreover, Davidson's antipluralism and antistatism did survive on the Right. Davidson scorned a national identity, which produced, he argued, "citizens of an Americanized nowhere." He was the most vocal of the Agrarians in insisting on the importance of an identity rooted in southern tradition, one that could only be maintained by an implacable resistance to modernity. The alternative, he argued, was to have no identity at all.[5]

Davidson's departure from the modernism of Ransom and Tate was already clear in the 1920s. *The Tall Men* was a work intended to appeal to the average Tennessean. It was to have been an alternative to the alienation, pessimism, and lack of answers in T. S. Eliot's poem "The Waste Land." Davidson repeatedly praised regional literature, whether of the South or Scandinavia, in his *Nashville Tennessean* book columns. An intense exploration of the particular, he argued, was the truest path to universal insight. Davidson's respect for regionalism was informed, moreover, by a southernism that he was not hesitant to express in print, as, for example, in a September 1929 review of Claude Bowers's history of Reconstruction, *The Tragic Era*. Like Bowers, Davidson considered Reconstruction a moral disaster. The former masters had been subjected to the rule of their former slaves, he charged. The greatest travesty of Reconstruction, in Davidson's mind, was black suffrage: "the slogan of black heels on white necks" and suffrage were the "*sine qua non* of the Radical plan," he believed.[6]

Davidson's southern regionalism derived from his own experience. Just as the southern past constituted a sacrament of purification and revitalization for the semiautobiographical protagonist of *The Tall Men*, Davidson's immersion in history—his "mystical secularism," as Tate termed it in 1942—provided balance in a life that, in his own view, was often disappointing and burdensome. Davidson's academic career was fraught with insecurity and hardship, which, as Michael O'Brien has suggested, fostered and compounded an ever present defensiveness. Davidson was wracked by intellectual self-doubt and become increasingly embittered at the emotional distance of his old Agrarian colleagues and his consequent intellectual isolation. As the planning for *I'll Take My Stand* proceeded, Ransom and Tate grew irritated with Davidson over what they interpreted as a lack of commitment to the practical organization of Agrarianism. Davidson failed in attempts to negotiate a contract for the anthology; refused to try obtaining a Guggenheim grant for an Agrarian newspaper because of scruples about northern funding; annoyed Tate by refusing to support the free speech rights of New York writers who had converged on the Harlan, Kentucky, strike; and, in general, was reluctant to make decisions.[7]

Davidson's Agrarian colleagues often found him morose and recalcitrant. Lytle blamed much of the controversy surrounding the symposium's title on Davidson's inscrutable personality. "Poor fellow, dark vapors gather in his mind to plague him," he wrote Tate. Tate believed that Davidson unconsciously framed his numerous projects in such a way as to prevent their completion, that he was "temperamentally incapable of action." In response to Tate's disappointment at lack of support for the jailed writers during the Harlan labor dispute, Davidson grew defensive. "Don't you dare put the blame of giving up a project on po' me," he wrote Tate. He continued in a self-pitying tone: "You know how I'm situated. You know how many times I have put my hand to the plough, when I could hardly afford to do so; and did so, in fact, often enough without respect to my personal interests." Ransom, expressing his regret at Davidson's refusal, sympathized with Tate. He often found Davidson's "fretfulness" useless, despite his affection for Davidson, and predicted that Davidson's inability to act would only worsen over time. "His trouble is pretty deep," Ransom wrote Tate. "He can't be jollied out of his melancholy, and as for intimidation, Don is like a large Tennessee knob of limestone." Agrarianism was good for all the brethren except, perhaps, Davidson, Ransom wrote Tate late in 1932. The "rebel doctrines" were "flames to his timber." He believed Davidson "one of the most intransigent spirits incarnated since Saul of Tarsus kicked against the pricks."[8]

Davidson did, indeed, suffer a series of personal disappointments and setbacks between 1928 and 1932. He had agreed to write a history of southern literature for Oxford University Press but was unable to complete the book, even after a summer at the writers' colony in Yaddo. Davidson complained to Tate in 1931 that his teaching load made it impossible for him to write the volume. He experienced new stresses with the collapse of his book page (and the loss of its salary, which had accounted for half of his annual salary) in 1930 and the death of his father in 1931. "Somewhere along the line I have had my fighting spirit knocked out of me," he confided to Tate. He was also plagued by a debilitating dental problem, which, Davidson later wrote Tate, had caused his "lassitude, grouchiness, rheumatism, and general no-countness" in the first years after *I'll Take My Stand* was published. Finally, Wesley Hall, the dormitory on the campus of Vanderbilt University where Davidson, his wife, and their daughter lived, burned to the ground in February 1932. His family saved only one-third of their possessions; Davidson lost books, correspondence, and back issues of the *Fugitive* magazine. In the wake of this shock, he requested a year's leave of absence from Vanderbilt. During this year, he was offered refuge in Marshallville, Georgia, at the home of his friend John Donald Wade.[9]

Davidson's sojourn in Georgia was an important time of healing for him. Yet he continued to grow away from his Agrarian friends. "Davidson has let the nation go to hell while he flirts with petunias in Georgia and escorts his wife to the local music society," a somewhat callow Robert Penn Warren observed of Davidson's stay in Marshallville. As early as 1929, Lyle Lanier had noted that Davidson tended to be, as Tate would have said, more literal than the other Agrarians. Lanier wrote to Tate that Davidson wanted a reconstruction of southern society "along lines indicated in the historical pattern." Although they all would like to see this occur, Lanier really thought it futile to expect such a turn of events. Davidson, he stated, "lives so within himself that he cannot read the handwriting on the wall."[10]

Further, Davidson's prickly personality separated him from his comrades' bonhomie. He disliked the bootleg whiskey common at their gatherings, and he and his wife rarely entertained his friends at their home. Davidson sent some poems for Tate's criticism in 1933 but betrayed a loss of self-assurance, afraid Tate would find them of poor quality, as well as the doubts of a forty-year-old man about the course his life had taken. "My prospects seem melancholy," he wrote Tate; "I think of my lost years of book page editing and literary chores and turn sick to my very gizzard. Perhaps, though, nature never intended me to be a poet or an essay writer. But what a refined sort of torture, to have the desire and the feelings, but not the power?" Davidson felt isolated, writing Warren in 1936, "I have become an outsider, and the state of my feelings is so confused and irritated that I cannot tell to my own satisfaction whether I have just stepped outside or been kicked outside." [11] The emotional distance can be seen in a 1936 letter from Tate. He accused Davidson of building a wall between himself and his friends and worried about the ill effect of Davidson's temperament on his well-being. Tate confessed to Davidson that he felt "some mild resentment for your withdrawing from us, for your difficulty of access, for your refusal to take part in the simple social pleasures that not only give us relaxation from the difficulties of a special kind of life, but actually strengthen the more serious ties that bind us together." [12]

The personal distances produced by Davidson's temperament and personality were, perhaps, a reflection of intellectual distances. As Ransom and Tate moved away from Agrarianism and, literally, out of the South, Davidson's romantic nationalism became more overt. Davidson's literary biographers, Thomas Daniel Young and M. Thomas Inge, observed that his poetry of the late 1930s became more Agrarian in choice of themes, with Davidson often adopting the pose of a prophet. "The emphasis is always on the necessity of preserving one's tradition," they observed, "but the poems are often so declamatory and argumentative that the poet emerges as an injured prophet—as one who has foreseen and suffered." Ransom tended to see Davidson's increasing southernism as in some way complementing his personal intransigence, feeding the demons that haunted him. After reading Davidson's 1938 volume of poetry, *Lee in the Mountains*, which was suffused in a brand of racial romanticism and social prophecy sure to rub against Ransom's modernist scruples, Ransom confided his opinion of the book to Tate: "Don just stopped growing before the rest of us did. . . . Don's case is partly private but partly, I'm afraid, the effect of ideology; his peculiar patriotism, consciously or unconsciously, is one that calls for no action, just speeches and poems; and I'm sure many Southerners are in the same way their own worst enemies." [13]

Whatever the ultimate source of Davidson's temperament, his southern regionalism was an intensely personal intellectual faith. Turning first to regionalism and then to the writing of history, Davidson articulated a politics of cultural identity. Louis D. Rubin Jr. later argued that Davidson's complete identification with the South came at a high artistic price; by rejecting the modernist idiom, Davidson became merely a sentimental poet. In Rubin's opinion, his early self-exploration, evidenced in *The Tall Men*, yielded to a fussy quarreling with nonsoutherners. He was incapable of intellectual detachment. Other scholars have concurred, characterizing Davidson as exceptionally rigid in his later work, motivated by a simple, less intellectual view of the world. Daniel Joseph Singal has argued that Davidson was incapable of living with tension or ambivalence; his intellectual life was "simple, visceral, and extremely limited." Davidson eventually came to appear, in Fred Hobson's view, "prudish, narrow, suspicious of modernism in any form, the defender of white supremacy above all else." Paul K. Conkin saw Davidson as emotionally beholden to his colleagues: "Simple, responsive, touchingly vulnerable, he needed the support of others and tended to flounder—in melancholy, self-pity, bitterness—when intellectually and emotionally alone. Then he would become cranky and defensive." Michael O'Brien agreed, suggesting that Davidson's insights consistently trailed behind the general trend of American thought. "His idea of the South had been rooted in an uncomplicated perception," O'Brien argued. "He had come to terms with the South by no elaborate route, from no critique of poetry or religion, but simply." Thus, in O'Brien's eyes, Davidson was motivated by the same "straightforward emotional need" as the average southerner. "The intellectual who defended the South was not uncommon," O'Brien observed, "but the intellectual who defended it on its own terms was rare." [14]

Much of this scholarly analysis is undoubtedly based on a distaste for Davidson's overt racism but also, most likely, on Davidson's preference for a romantic nationalism over the modernism favored by Ransom, Tate, and Warren. Yet it is too easy to envision a chagrined Davidson standing alone as his friends moved forward, past him. It must be remembered that Davidson was moving, too, and in a direction that he considered forward-looking as well. Nor was he really alone. If his southern patriotism called for no action, this was, in part, designedly so, for Davidson increasingly interpreted a defense of southern tradition as a defense of southern identity itself. His was a politics of culture. The socioeconomic argument at the heart of Ransom's conception of Agrarianism, which concerned Tate so much in the mid-1930s, increasingly diminished in Davidson's more romantic Agrarianism. For Davidson, Agrarianism embodied the special identity of the southerner. In 1935, John Gould Fletcher, prone to sharp displays of temper, threatened to disown Agrarianism over a relatively minor slight suffered by Davidson. Davidson wrote to reassure him, declaring that being an Agrarian was not a matter of membership in an organization but one of faith. We could not resign, Davidson wrote Fletcher, "because we couldn't stop being Southerners, ourselves, our father's sons." [15]

Davidson's ideas became clearer during the year he spent at Wade's home in Marshallville. Wade had deep roots in the small Georgia community and took an intense, paternalistic interest in it. Marshallville had originally been settled in the 1830s by a large group of emigrants from Orangeburg, South Carolina, and Davidson immensely enjoyed its persistent sense of cohesion and shared tradition. As O'Brien aptly stated, "Marshallville gave one precious commodity to a man deep in self-doubt—respect." Davidson was able to live peacefully and join in local affairs, including singing at the folk choral meetings in the countryside. On Confederate Memorial Day, Davidson read a poem about the Army of the Tennessee to the assembled villagers.[16]

An address, evidently composed to introduce Davidson's Confederate Day poem, communicates Davidson's faith, born in part of his experiences in Marshallville, in the ability of Americans to resist the encroaching culture of the industrial state. "People young and old, throughout the United States," he declared, "have become weary of the tedious and standardized existence which the ideal of a tightly unified, urban, industrial nation imposed upon them. They are not willing to become the robots of a Fordized and mechanized America." Instead, Davidson saw renewed regional loyalties emerging, as people discovered themselves to be not only southerners but westerners and New Englanders as well. "A kind of spiritual secession is taking place," Davidson exclaimed, more "far-reaching" and widespread than that which occurred in the 1860s. He applauded his Marshallville neighbors, and, by implication, all southerners, for remaining true to their roots, even while the rest of the country had been attracted by the false entreaties of an industrial culture. Southerners had always believed "the good life is not to be found at too great a distance from the land, or apart from the intimate fellowship of kinfolks and friends, the mutual graciousness of family life, the solace of a steadfast religious faith, and above all, the sense of belonging somewhere in a world which at best is changeable and insecure." By early 1933 Davidson was sure that a revival of sectional feeling was occurring across the nation. He wrote to Seward Collins, editor of the *American Review:* "The truth is, I believe, that the ideas of I'll Take My Stand are pretty definitely related to a groundswell that is going on in American life."[17]

Davidson's fullest statement of his new regionalism was *The Attack on Leviathan: Regionalism and Nationalism in the United States* (1938), a collection of his essays published between 1932 and 1937. The way for a southerner to take hold of his tradition, Davidson now argued—in opposition to Tate—was to reject modernism and the false individualism that modernity bred. Steadfast and dogged resistance to the "Irresistible Forces" of modernity was the prescription; southerners must become "Immovable Bodies." In *Attack on Leviathan*, the national government and the vaguely defined metropolitan network

from which it sprung emerged as the primary agent of these irresistible modern forces.

Davidson was heartened by the work of academics such as Howard
Odum, Rupert Vance, and their students at the University of North
Carolina, as well as historian Frederick Jackson Turner, whose posthumous publications on sectionalism had just appeared. For Davidson, regionalism was merely a polite way to phrase old sectional loyalties. "The New Regionalism," he wrote in Odum's journal, *Social
Forces*, "as it is now often called, is thus a powerful confirmation of
the justice of old southern claims, and perhaps also of the desirability
of maintaining the differentiations that once were damned and dismissed as sectional." Odum, busy consolidating an academic empire at
Chapel Hill, maintained a delicate balance between respect for southern sectional feeling and a desire to institute liberal programs of regional social reform. Davidson saw Odum's attempt to depoliticize
regional studies as futile. He viewed sectionalism as the necessary
political counterpart to the economic and cultural approach of regionalism. "I don't know whether I am a sectionalist or a regionalist;
but I know that I am a Southerner," he wrote John Donald Wade in
1934.[18]

Davidson's brand of regionalism was indistinguishable from a revivified sectionalism—his southern patriotism always lurking beneath
his scornful condemnations of America's "pseudo-culture." Davidson denied the existence of any national American heroes. The only
true heroes were sectional figures such as Andrew Jackson or Abraham Lincoln, whose great acclaim in one section was paralleled by a
proportional revulsion in others. When he was discussing Abraham
Lincoln, Davidson's rage became overt. "If Lincoln was a supporter,
as in a dim way he may have been, of the nation, then why did he fight
the South?" Davidson asked. "Lincoln made war upon his own idea,
and the fruit of his victory, represented in sprawling, confused, industrial America, is a more pitiful sight than the noble ruin." If fascism
or communism ever triumphed in the United States, Davidson sput-
tered, Lincoln would be in part to blame. The southerner merely tolerated the Lincoln Memorial in Washington, D.C., Davidson stated.

> To the sons of Confederates it is a reminder of tragedy, not an em-
> blem of exaltation. If the people of Illinois wish to erect a memorial
> to Lincoln in Springfield, that is entirely proper. But why should
> the Southerner be called on to respect as "national" symbol the
> great image of Lincoln in the attitude of a brooding god—Lin-
> coln, who did not receive a Southern vote in 1860; who was never
> president of the Southern states; who was, alas, though with some
> healing kindness toward the end, a destroying angel to them.[19]

In practical terms, Davidson advocated a new federalism—political and cultural autonomy for the country's different sections. In a summary statement of Agrarianism in 1935, Davidson articulated what he saw as its practical program: the conservation of land; its distribution as small, subsistence farms; limits on labor-saving machinery; the curbing of corporate powers; national support of small industry, noncommercial farming, and the arts; and, finally, regional governments in a new, revivified federalism. His program was similar to that outlined by Frank L. Owsley in "The Pillars of Agrarianism." In order to mitigate the South's status as a colony of the Northeast (the "greatest free trade area in the world"), Davidson argued in *Attack on Leviathan* for the establishment of trade barriers within the national boundaries to separate regions and enable them to stop the flow of "exploiting agents" across their borders. Like Owsley, Davidson wanted to reverse the result of the Civil War by empowering regions to impose taxes on "foreign" capital, exercise limited control of credit and money, establish their own educational standards and institutions, and preserve their distinctive systems of racial control (most important, the southern "bi-racial" system). "Whatever restores small property, fosters agrarianism, and curtails exaggerated industrialism is on the side of regional autonomy," Davidson believed.[20]

As he outlined a regionalist socioeconomic program, Davidson heaped scorn on the modernist intellect and on avant-garde and experimental art. New York City came to represent all that he disliked about America and bore the brunt of his accumulated resentments as a regional literary figure. For all of his assertions of independence, Davidson often betrayed a need to find acceptance in these cosmopolitan centers, even as he resented their supremacy. To his mind, nothing abrogated regionalist art so severely as the desire to seek patronage in the metropolis.

Davidson was unwilling to assign any credit for the increasing vogue of regionalist writing to the cosmopolitan centers that fostered regionalist authors; anything good that came out of New York, one suspects Davidson would have argued, only came as a result of demand from the hinterland. Metropolitan critics were, for the most part, castoffs from the provinces or descendants of new immigrant stock who "had no intimate share in the historical experience of any American place." They were all, from H. L. Mencken to Van Wyck Brooks, skeptics and cynics, misinformed about general American tastes. The essence of their doctrines—a witch's brew of antireligion, Freudianism, Marxism, and scientism—was "Decadence." Borrowing a page from Mencken, Davidson denounced cosmopolitan culture with florid rhetoric:

To a people the greater part of whom were schooled in Protestant religion and morality New York presented, with a knowing
leer, under the guise of literary classics, the works of voluptuaries
and perverts, the teeming pages of *Psychopathia Sexualis*, and all the
choicest remains of the literary bordellos of the ancient and modern
world. German Expressionism, French Dadaism, the erotic primitivism of D. H. Lawrence, the gigantic *fin de siècle* pedantries and
experimentalisms of James Joyce, the infantilism of Gertrude Stein
and various Parisian coteries—these furnished most of the catch-
words for all the clever people.

In contrast, Davidson apostrophized the plain folk of America as
"Immovable Bodies," stubbornly resisting the denatured cosmopoli-
tan culture. He placed his faith in the common folk of the various
American sections. These Americans knew the wisdom of trusting in
the particular. "The future is not yet; it is unknowable, intangible.
But the past was, the present is; of that much they can be sure."[21]

The growing regionalist movement caused Davidson's spirits to
rise. Many of the elements of his own regionalism were contained in
a 1933 article in *Hound and Horn*, which he later revised into an important section of *Attack on Leviathan*. Drawing on his own romantic nationalism, and on many of the currents of regional thought of
the day, Davidson outlined a regionalism with a nativist gloss. Regionalism, he argued, was a rejection of the false social identity impressed upon Americans by industrialism. In Davidson's regionalism, sectional identity tended to be rooted in racial homogeneity; the
national, synthetic identity that he decried resulted from an influx of
varied ethnic stocks. Davidson professed admiration, for example, of
the old New Englander, but this racial stock no longer represented
that section of the country. Instead, new ethnic stocks, "ignorant of
the American past," were becoming dominant. "Their rise to power
accelerates the detachment from the thought of other sections into
which the urban East is falling," Davidson argued. The America of
Waldo Frank's pluralist *Our America*, he added, was not that of Henry
Cabot Lodge or Will Rogers.[22]

Davidson's regionalism was not exclusively nativist, however. Although he attributed the loss of sturdy American identities to new
immigrants, he also spoke of "native immigrants," by which he meant
"careerists who have cut loose from their native soil." An upwardly
mobile middle class in which ethnic identity was erased was part of the
problem. Despite these tendencies, Davidson became convinced that
sectional loyalties were resurgent, even if this fact went unnoticed by
cosmopolitans. He pointed to popular interest in genealogy, histori-

cal societies, memorial associations, and historical landmarks. Sectionalism, he argued, fostered a loyalty that the nation-state, the great Leviathan, never could. The "Republic," he believed, had become too abstract, incapable of inspiring loyalty.[23]

Writers such as the Agrarians, Davidson argued, articulated this general American rejection of the artificiality of the metropolis in favor of a concrete allegiance to place and local tradition. The Agrarians "pointed out a road away from Leviathanism." Sectionalism, therefore, was a positive, not destructive, force; any excesses to which it might be prone would be checked by the national government and by the minority populations within each state. The truest American identity lay in its regional cultures. "Our most characteristic national songs are those that record sectional experience," Davidson observed. "Our literature, architecture, folk-lore, history, accent dissolve the national complex into sectional entities. Rivers, mountain ranges, deserts, degrees of latitude, differences of soil and climate divide us." To believe in an "American" identity was to believe in something that had no substantial existence—to subscribe to a "characterless and synthetic Americanism." Identity arose from America's regions. "Their national unity consists in the avowal which any section should rejoice for the others to make: that we are Rebels, Yankees, Westerners, New Englanders or what you will, bound by ties more generous than abstract institutions can express, rather than citizens of an Americanized nowhere, without family, kin, or home." [24]

Even as he celebrated the diversity of American regions, the sweeping generalizations Davidson was eager to make about Americans reveal an underlying faith that all true Americans were struck from an identical mold. He proclaimed the need to rediscover America, but the narrowness of his vision revealed little beyond a desire to enshrine the sturdy white pioneer as the ideal American type.[25] Davidson's best-known essay, "Still Rebels, Still Yankees," by its very title testified to Davidson's faith in the persistence of regional identities. First published in 1933, constituting a crucial chapter of *Attack on Leviathan*, it featured two lyrical character sketches.

Brother Jonathan of Vermont and Cousin Roderick of Georgia sprang from the earth, their values shaped by the very geography of their regions. The New England humanitarianism of Jonathan, for instance, could be explained by observing the neat ordering of fields and fences in the countryside. Thus humanitarianism "was the natural flower of good sense." New Englanders had been attracted to abolitionism before the Civil War because in their pretty and ordered region "it was hard to imagine a perverse land where so much could be so wrong without disturbing a people's composure or their happiness." Georgia, on the other hand, had a quite different impact on

human beings; people grew differently there. "The Georgia landscape had a serene repose that lulled a man out of all need of conscience," Davidson claimed. Nature for the Georgian was more ca-
pricious and exotic, "a fair but dreadful mistress, unpredictable and
uncontrollable as God." If a New Englander could impose symmetri-
cal order on his environment because he "knew exactly where to find
nature harsh and nature yielding," the Georgian had no such luxury.
"The Georgian never knew," Davidson claimed. "His safest policy
was to relax, and he readily developed a great degree of tolerance for
irregularity in nature and man." Thus, for Davidson, in the habit of
referring to Marshallville as Eden, southerners were initiated by circumstance to the ambiguities of human relations. "If New England
encouraged man to believe in an ordered universe, Georgia—and a
good deal of the South besides—compelled him to remember that
there were snakes in Eden." [26]

Davidson's defense of white supremacy was unabashed. He described the racial situation in the South in a 1937 review of John Dollard's *Caste and Class in a Southern Town:* "There are two races in
it, white and black, that live together and yet are separate in certain fundamental relationships. The white race keep themselves apart
in a superior position, and they see to it, if there is any question,
that the black race are kept apart in an inferior position. This bi-
racial arrangement is firmly established. It works under a code, for
the most part unwritten, which is rarely challenged or broken." The
white South would not tolerate any change in this system, Davidson
held. "No major change in Negro status can be achieved except at the
expense of the white race. The considerable elevation of the Negro
can only mean the degradation of the whites. The white South does
not wish to make this sacrifice, and that is all there is to it." [27]

At times Davidson descended into the crudest sort of racial stereo-
typing—all the while praising his face-to-face insights as superior to
the abstractions of liberal sociologists. At one point in the review, he
argued that a mutually distasteful difference in body odors between
whites and blacks was evidence for the need of racial segregation. At
another point, commenting on a case mentioned by Dollard of an
incidence of cannibalism involving a black man, Davidson adopted
the pose of decorous magnanimity. "Such atavism, however, is so uncommon as not to be worth noticing," he observed, highlighting his
own notice of it: "The South does not think of Negroes as cannibals,
even though it knows that large numbers of Negroes are a century or
less removed from savage life." Davidson made no claim that the system of segregation was a positive good; he only asserted, from a realist's perspective, that whites would not yield their control of southern

society. The Negro's status, he observed in the same review, "may or may not be an injustice."[28]

Davidson reduced the Negro to an element in the southern environment, "a grinning barnacle tucked away in all the tender spots of Southern life." At the core of Davidson's delimitation of identity was the irreducible element of race and skin color. There were southerners in Georgia, and they were white; there also existed Negroes, but they were an annoying parasitical growth on white society. They were certainly not southerners. Davidson never believed that whites and blacks were southerners in quite the same way. The Georgian, Davidson claimed, respected the Negro; he regretted lynching, "the work of hot-heads and roustabouts." Nevertheless, Davidson argued, speaking from within the mentality of the Georgian, "what did a few lynchings count in the balance against the continual forbearance and solicitude that the Georgian felt he exercised toward those amiable children of cannibals, whose skins by no conceivable act of Congress or educational program could be changed from black to white."[29]

Davidson's crude environmentalism and romantic racialism provided a rationale for his own bigotry and served to justify a closed society. Ironically, blacks appear in Davidson's essay as the ultimate "Immovable Bodies," providing a vivid model of Davidson's own counsel of stubborn resistance. To Davidson, blacks were an environmental "irregularity, taking a human and personal form, that had somehow to be lived with." From another perspective, their heroic preservation of identity might serve as a model of endurance for a marginalized culture. Such a doctrine, so effective in asserting cultural autonomy, however, could also, as Davidson illustrated, underwrite a program of social quietism for an entrenched majority. In Georgia, life was viewed "horizontally," Davidson claimed: "You never crossed a bridge unless you came to it—and maybe not then."[30]

Davidson was less interested in crossing bridges than in fortifying an insular notion of folk identity. Despite his gesture toward regional diversity, the social types characteristic of each region he analyzed tended to be variations on the yeoman agrarian. Brother Jonathan might live in Yankeetown and have beliefs different from those of Cousin Roderick, but they were spiritual kin all the same. Jonathan still ran a two-hundred-acre farm and rejected modern conveniences in favor of homemade crafts. As a type of independent New England farmer, Brother Jonathan was in the spirit of those citizens Jefferson saw as "the foundation of liberty in the United States." When Davidson contrasted the settlers of the Old Southwest with those of the Old Northwest, or the cowboys out west with the farmers of the Great Plains, any differences in outlook ultimately seemed of less account than a common independence of spirit. All were shaped by their native region, jealous of their liberties, and in harmony with nature. All, too, were white and native-born.[31]

Despite Davidson's regional and racial bravado, an underlying sense of frustration remained in *Attack on Leviathan*. He identified the perennial southern tension between progress and tradition. The dilemma of southern intellectuals persisted in many different forms and for all types of southern thinkers. Southern liberals were hamstrung, in Davidson's opinion, because the more they pushed for social reform, the more they undercut any support from traditional southerners who knew that such reforms originated in the alien North. Likewise, Odum and his colleagues hoped to organize southern support for regional planning, but to do so required arousing sectional feeling. Aroused sectionalism, in turn, led southerners to oppose social planning and was sure to alienate the needed northern support.[32] Finally, southern artists and writers were beholden to a cosmopolitan establishment for the resources necessary to pursue their art; yet, in Davidson's view, those cosmopolitan centers devalued the products of their native genius. Davidson wanted reform, but only on southern terms; he would support limited economic planning, but only directed by southerners; he desired national acclaim and a national audience, but not at the cost of betraying his southern identity.

Divided loyalties posed a personal dilemma, as well. In a letter to Wade, Davidson tried to distance himself from sectional extremists: "Underneath it all, I suspect Odum of suspecting us as guilty, or about to be guilty, of some heinous indiscretion, such as starting a new Ku Klux Klan, or failing to salute the colors, or preferring Dixie to 'America the Beautiful.' Or, more gravely, that we are a new school of secessionists or De Valeras, about to revive an old and bloody argument." Such actions were not forthcoming, Davidson promised. Nevertheless, Davidson based his politics of identity on a belief in white supremacy that would, ultimately, lead him to become chairman of Tennessee's version of a pro-segregation Citizens' Council in the 1950s.[33]

For Davidson, the critical test of southern integrity was the preservation of racial purity. His major defense of segregation, "Preface to Decision," was published by Allen Tate in the *Sewanee Review* in 1945. "Back of the total system is, of course, a racial decision of long standing," he wrote. "The white South denies the Negro equal participation in white society, not only because it does not consider him entitled to equality, but because it is certain that social mingling would lead gradually to biological mingling, which it is determined to prevent, both for any given contemporary generation and for its posterity."[34] Davidson attempted to prove that racial mixing had not occurred between whites and blacks to any great extent in the South, ignoring the population of mixed-blood individuals in America and concluding, rather illogically, that large numbers of white people proved his point.[35] At various times Davidson also used many classic defenses in discussing the southern "bi-racial" system: that no harm was intended blacks; that slavery would have been abolished eventually in the nineteenth century; that slavery had been an unwelcome inheritance from the British to begin with; that, in any case, southern (meaning white southern) customs could not be abrogated by mere laws; that the North, by the way, was marked by segregation and racial conflict as much as the South; and that, in the final analysis, personal bonds of respect and mutual regard existed between whites and blacks all over the South that mitigated the apparent harshness of the system.

Furthermore, the peculiar racial system of the South necessitated a delicate balance, Davidson argued. In a review of W. J. Cash's *The Mind of the South* (1941), Davidson proposed the antebellum South as a model of a society that balanced tradition, loyalty, and democratic principles. In the antebellum South, extreme individualism coexisted with a high degree of social unity; society was led by elites but elites who evidenced a widespread devotion to the public good; the masses acquiesced to an economic system that was generally disadvantageous to them; there existed a rigid class structure but one in which classes did not have a well-developed class consciousness.[36]

The key to this was not slavery, Davidson claimed, yet his own analysis of southern social equilibrium placed racial homogeneity front and center. He rejected as a myth Cash's theorized "proto-Dorian" bond that unified all classes of whites in their mutual subjugation of blacks. The presence of a large black population, he argued, threatened to disrupt the delicate social and political equilibrium of the southern republics, as happened when debate developed on the slavery question. There was simply no position for blacks as full citizens in the South, in Davidson's view. "The South knows that it could not maintain its society in the desired equilibrium unless the alien element, now vastly enlarged, could be strictly controlled," Davidson explained. "And if it could not maintain the equilibrium, it could not maintain democracy for white people."[37]

Democracy, Davidson was essentially arguing, was possible only in a homogeneous society. The inclusion of blacks on an equal social footing would tear white society apart, he declared; any political rights blacks gained without an accompanying higher social status, which the white South had no intention of recognizing, "would be only a cruel and dishonest fiction, worth nothing to him." The nation as a whole, Davidson believed, was neither an organic society nor a true democracy. "We keep the fiction of democracy, but behind the fiction, what do we see?" Davidson asked. "The strongest central government we have ever known; the most elaborately restrictive and regulative laws; a continually increasing tendency of the government to call for and indeed to exact unanimity of opinion, to brook no criticism, to demand almost servile obedience." By a neat rhetorical trick, Davidson turned Cash's savage ideal upon the North, indicting it for what he argued was the North's inability to tolerate the peculiar southern settlement on race — the biracial system.[38]

In Davidson's segregationist Agrarianism, history functioned as the equivalent of race in the definition of southern identity and community. In his 1945 defense of segregation, Davidson contrasted two John Smiths, whom a sociologist would classify as identical except that one was white and the other black. The sociologist, Davidson argued, would ignore the different histories of these two men. But for Davidson, the fact that the ancestors of the white John Smith had once owned the ancestors of the black John Smith, left out by the sociologists, was the "prime cultural fact." History, for Davidson, was everything. The black man lost his history in the same way that he had lost his true name (which, Davidson speculated, in Africa might have been "Crocodile-killer" or "Spear-maker" — "a valiant and honorable name"). "It is a tragic business that the Negro John Smith cannot enjoy contemplating his own name in quite the same way the white man does," Davidson wrote, "since there is hiatus or lurking humiliation where there ought to be history."[39] In other words, the fact that the black man was enslaved, brought to America, and denuded of his historical identity may be unjust and tragic, but the fact that he is now a historical nonentity cannot be changed. Davidson saw no possibility of contemporary blacks embodying their heritage, and he saw no black heritage in America.

The white man, on the other hand, is in a completely different situation, for he "can think back for many centuries without discomfort, or often with pride, if he cares to. His history is with him wherever he goes." The political philosopher Hannah Arendt once wrote that it is law and citizenship that alone guarantee human freedom; for Davidson it was history and connection to a past. History, he held, permeates the institutions of the white South. The white John Smith remembers it the moment the black John Smith in any way challenges the racial status quo. At this moment, Davidson wrote, "the historical element becomes the most powerful element in the whole environment of the two men, indeed in their very being. And white John Smith recalls that his grandfather before him, and his father and he afterwards, never at any time agreed to accept the Negro John Smith

as a member of white society, save under such limitations as are symbolized by the separate waiting rooms and other much more intricate
but carefully ordered customs."[40]

The unhappy consequences that resulted when southerners lost
their sense of identity were a primary theme of Davidson's major
attempt to provide a narrative of the southern past, *The Tennessee*,
his two-volume history of the Tennessee River valley, published in
1946 and 1948. Begun in 1940, *The Tennessee* was part of Farrar and
Rinehart's Rivers of America series, itself an example of the cultural
nationalism prevalent in the 1930s. Each volume in the series reaffirmed the American folk and their common democratic tradition.[41]
In the long history of the Tennessee River, from its original use by
Native Americans, through the encroaching arrival of white settlers,
to its use by Federal naval vessels to help defeat the South in the Civil
War, and, finally, to its taming at the hands of the Leviathan federal
government in the form of Franklin Delano Roosevelt's Tennessee
Valley Authority (TVA), with its dams and power plants, Davidson
produced a parable of the history of the South as a whole.

The most distinctive aspect of the Tennessee River—which doubles
back on itself and flows across the state of Tennessee twice, dividing
it into three sections—was its difficulty of navigation. It was a harsh
and inhospitable river boasting whirlpools and rocky shoals, which
were given such names as the Suck, the Narrows, Boiling Pot, Skillet,
and Pan. The river's utility as a thoroughfare for traffic in goods and
people was always limited, with the upper Tennessee effectively cut off
from the lower section of the river owing to the hazards of the Great
Bend, where the river doubled back on itself. This ungovernability
and wildness served as a metaphor for the free-spirited frontiersmen
and Native Americans—the hardy souls who made a culture for themselves in the unsettled Tennessee Valley. Their communities, organized into clans, embodied the virtues of a traditional society.

Davidson portrayed the American Indians positively (if stereotypically). They and the frontiersmen engaged each other in savage warfare, but theirs was a war on equal terms, marked by moments of
mutual respect. Davidson discussed the great burial mounds, surviving remnants of American Indian culture. This was not the first time
Davidson used the fate of Tennessee's Native American population in
his work. In *The Tall Men*, the Native Americans existed as memories.
They were dead, the victims of white pioneers. Their only remains
were the graves, the great burial mounds. With no descendants to remember them, the meaning of the dead Native Americans' sacrifice
was lost. *The Tall Men* ended with an image of a father and son on an
overgrown Indian burial mound:

> And there my father said,
> Pointing a low mound out to me: "My son,
> Stand on this Indian's grave and plainly ask,
> *Indian, what did you die for?*"

The answer is "Nothing!" The deaths of the Native Americans were meaningless, in Davidson's view, because they were not remembered.[42]

In *The Tennessee*, Davidson discussed the mounds again, this time giving an account of who left them and what function they served. But at least the mounds survived—as some sort of memorial. As a viable community in Tennessee, the Native Americans did not. They had lost the battle between themselves and the whites. It was not so much the battles with pioneers that destroyed their culture as the corrupting influence of trade and the world of commerce, which "brought the Indian tribes into the white man's power," he wrote. "Once they became dependent on guns, axes, and blankets which they must 'buy' and could not make, they lost their self-sufficiency and put themselves at the mercy of an economy and a politics which they could not understand." They agreed to treaties with the whites—and were persuaded to submit to a European crown, listening as a British agent admonished them not to break their solemn vow of loyalty lest they, in the stilted diction thought appropriate when addressing Native Americans, "would become no People." It was, of course, the whites who broke their solemn commitments; but it was not they who became "no People." It was the Native Americans who did, forced to follow a trail of tears to the West, leaving behind only the mounds beneath which lay their dead.[43]

The second volume of Davidson's history told of the decline of the sturdy Tennessee communities, as they came under incessant attack from outsiders, first in the form of Union soldiers, then under the authority of the Roosevelt-era federal government. The Civil War was, in Davidson's partisan account, a savage attack on southern society. In no way was it like the Indian fighting of the colonial era. William Tecumseh Sherman introduced total war into Tennessee: "Under Sherman's authority, ravage became an official Federal policy. During the later years of the war, therefore, the Federal invasion, especially in the Great Bend, could hardly be distinguished from the inroads of a Genghis Khan or an Attila." Davidson glorified such paramilitary agents of southern "redemption" as the Ku Klux Klan, whom he portrayed as a noble group organized to fight the agents of commerce, industrialism, and northern domination.[44] Industrial advance by New South boosters and spokesmen was the most insidious challenge to southern traditions of community. "History was repeating itself," Davidson observed of industrialization in the South, "with an irony that may or may not have been justifiable. They who had invaded the old Indian lands had now in their turn been invaded and worsted." The invasion had not ended but continued into the present. The TVA was its culmination.[45]

In his generally even-handed account of the TVA, Davidson did not question the agricultural reforms and navigational improvements resulting from the development of the river (although the reconstruction of the river was an irresistible metaphor for industrialization's defeat of the pioneering spirit), but rather the way in which these gains were made. Davidson was alarmed at the expansive power of the federal government. He referred to the TVA as "King Kilowatt" and suggested that the TVA directors held "powers that kings might have envied."[46]

Davidson recognized the value of much of what the TVA did, in particular the agricultural reform it fostered. But, in the end, he was deeply troubled by the scope of its activities and the authority with which it was invested — an authority he did not believe was sufficiently accountable to the people the TVA affected. By instituting a system of high dams and locks, the TVA completely changed the nature of the Tennessee River, in particular the upper river, making it, in effect, a series of lakes. The river, Davidson believed, was completely tamed, even lifeless.[47] In the process, thousands of individuals had been displaced and many old farms and small villages and towns had been permanently flooded. The TVA was the "Great Leviathan," pushing the natives off the land just as the Cherokees had been, this time not with soldiers but with marshals and eviction notices. Even old graves were exhumed, the bodies placed in new caskets and taken to new gravesites. Davidson commented elegaically on the displacement:

> Old landmarks would vanish; old graveyards would be obliterated; the ancient mounds of the Indians, which had resisted both the plow and the farmer and the pick of the curiosity seeker, would go under water. There would be tears, and gnashing of teeth, and lawsuits. There might even be feud and bloodshed. Yet these harms, inflicted upon a sizable and innocent minority, weighed less in the TVA scales than the benefits that would accrue, in terms of industrial and social engineering, to the nearby or the distant majority who sacrificed only tax money.

The natives of the river valley (and by implication all southerners) were in danger, Davidson warned, of becoming, like the Native Americans before them, "no People" whose ancestors had died for nothing. They were in danger of losing their history, and in losing this, their

identity and their citizenship. Davidson's career from the time of *The
Tall Men* had consisted of a series of attempts to present the urgent
imperative of cultural preservation to his fellow southerners. *The Tennessee* was his most extended attempt to explain his own interpretation
of the southern experience in straightforward historical narrative.[48]

In the 1930s, Davidson's romanticization of the folk allowed him,
like many other regionalists, to attack both a centralizing and homogeneous culture and the industrial economy that produced it. Although the rhetoric of prewar cultural nationalism faded, it fore-
shadowed the identity politics of postwar America. In one form,
cultural nationalism resurfaced in African American, Hispanic, and
Native American calls for the cultivation and assertion of their own
particular identities. But this impulse was also preserved among thinkers such as Davidson, who constructed a segregationist cultural politics of social exclusivity.

In the 1960s, Davidson looked back on the renaissance in southern
letters as a "moment of self-consciousness." Davidson had always seen
the preservation of social memory—of the "folk-chain" of meaning—
as his special vocation. The folk-chain that bound his white South
together, however, bound black southerners into a system of social
inequality and denied recognition of their heritage. As Allen Tate observed in 1962, Davidson's historical vision was defective. Davidson's
Old South was simple, patriarchal—and slaveless. "Mr. Davidson's
Old South has always seemed to me," Tate observed on the publication of a collection of Davidson's poetry, "to leave about half of the
Old South out of the account: the half, or third, or whatever the figures were, that included the Negro."[49]

As the decade of the 1940s drew to a close, Louise Davis, a reporter
for the *Nashville Tennessean*, profiled Davidson. She found an im-
pressive teacher, whose rigid and dignified presence made him seem
more than human, at times, to his students. Davidson railed against
"progress" and saw culture disintegrating in America. "Students today have great *facility*," he declared, "but they don't have anything to
apply it to. They have no experience at living." In Davidson's mind,
education had become a mere "processing." "The urban life of the
average student," Davidson observed, "takes him from the radio before breakfast to school, from there to the movie, to the radio and
to bed again. He never gets a chance to *live*." Davidson believed that
students were no longer being given the chance to be responsible as
individuals. As the folk-chains of memory became looser during the
civil rights era, however, many southerners, including students, did
in fact claim responsibility for their lives. It was the large part of the
South that Davidson would never recognize as being truly southern

that most seriously challenged his folk-chain of memory. Davidson's response to that challenge made evident the segregationist implications of his brand of Agrarianism.[50]

The postwar years would see the further splintering of the Agrarian tradition. The Agrarians had been torn from the outset between modernism and romantic nationalism. They wanted to speak to universal concerns but also to establish a provincial southern identity. They desired to use history but also to escape its burdens, to affirm community but also to retain a wide degree of individual freedom. And ultimately, the Agrarians were torn between faith in segregation and the impulse for social equality. As the years passed, the anti-industrial humanism of *I'll Take My Stand* faded. In its place, the Agrarian tradition increasingly became, for some, a politics of identity, and for others, a set of universal humanist ideals struggling to escape their earlier association with localist concerns and ill-considered economic nostrums. For still others, Agrarianism became the forerunner of an organic conservatism oriented around localism and traditional, family-based, patriarchal authority that was gradually rising to cultural prominence. In this, some argued, it was part of a longer tradition not of antimodern humanism but southern conservatism.

CHAPTER FIVE

The South as Synecdoche
Agrarianism and the Conservative Movement

The cause of the South was and is the cause of Western civilization itself.
  Donald Davidson, *Southern Writers in the Modern World*

The South changed dramatically in the years between the publication of *I'll Take My Stand* in 1930 and the end of World War II. President Franklin Delano Roosevelt's New Deal sparked a profound reorganization of the region's economic and social life. Although the South had industrialized rapidly after the Civil War, no industrial revolution had occurred. The region lagged behind the rest of the nation in industrial capacity and labor force employment into the twentieth century. Low-wage industries such as textiles thrived owing to the South's large pool of rural workers and its isolated labor market.[1] Beginning in the 1930s, however, federal policy sparked the economic transformation of the region. Roosevelt's short-lived National Recovery Administration, established in 1933, along with minimum wage legislation passed in 1938, narrowed the southern wage differential and spurred the modernization of southern industry. As companies raised their wages and updated their equipment, workers lost jobs, but the isolated, low-wage labor market of the South was put on the road to extinction.[2]

The effects of New Deal agricultural policy were even more far-reaching and resulted in the end of the sharecropping system. Southern sharecroppers had farmed a parcel of land for a share of the crop, usually one-half; they purchased supplies on credit, usually at exorbitant interest rates, from either their landlord or a local merchant. Tenants rented the land outright. In both cases, the landless farmer depended on the landowner. The Agricultural Adjustment Act (1933) fundamentally altered this system through its program of voluntary

acreage reduction. Landowners took fields out of cultivation in exchange for federal rental and parity payments. Although they were
supposed to share the federal benefits with their tenants and sharecroppers, landowners often kept the full payments for themselves or
applied the tenant's share toward his accumulated debt. In this way,
federal intervention in agriculture sundered the last vestiges of the
paternalist bond between landowner and tenant. Landowners now
had a financial incentive to decrease their reliance on tenants and
sharecroppers and shift to wage laborers, which eliminated any necessity to share their federal parity payments. As the number of tenants and sharecroppers decreased, the size of farms and the level of
mechanization increased. A variety of other federal programs, including marketing agreements and credit and conservation programs,
contributed to this mechanization of southern agriculture.[3] These
programs were skewed in favor of large and absentee landowners, historian Pete Daniel has argued. Rather than stabilizing and preserving the small-scale agriculture of the tenant, sharecropper, and small
farmer (a type of agriculture closer to the self-sufficient subsistence
farming advocated by the Agrarians), federal policy promoted a "vast
enclosure movement," mechanization, and a type of large-scale agribusiness identical to that of the nation's other major farming regions.[4]

World War II accelerated these trends, constituting, or so Morton Sosna has argued, a more important watershed in southern history than the Civil War because it promoted social migration, rural
depopulation, industrial growth, and, in a region previously marked
by poverty, prosperity.[5] In 1940, two-thirds of the South's population still lived in rural areas or small towns, but, during the war, military bases as well as assorted war industries, ranging from shipbuild-
ing yards and aircraft plants to munitions factories, fed the growth
of southern cities. Approximately nine billion dollars worth of war-
related investment poured into the South. The Oak Ridge, Tennessee,
nuclear plant, which produced uranium for the atomic bomb, employed 82,000 workers alone. By 1945, 4 million people, fully one-
fourth of the South's farm population, had migrated from the countryside. Mechanization of southern farms accelerated. Further, the
war spurred economic growth, which resulted in the doubling of
southerners' personal income and a 50 percent increase in the region's
industrial workforce. At the same time, 1.6 million southern civilians
left the region during the war.[6]

The agrarian South was slipping away, to survive primarily in memory and vestigial usages, habits, and customs. The legacy of Agrarianism, however, was just beginning to be seriously contested. Donald
Davidson did not agree with John Crowe Ransom's postwar assessment of the Vanderbilt group's previous endeavors as "agrarian nos-

Five contributors to *The Fugitive* at the Fugitives' reunion, Nashville, Tennessee, 1956. *L-r*: Allen Tate, Merrill Moore (a student at Vanderbilt University in the 1920s),

talgia." He was disgusted with Ransom's repudiation of Agrarianism in part because he did not recognize what Ransom repudiated as Agrarianism. To Davidson, Agrarianism was a politics of southern identity more than an economic program. It was a shame, he wrote Tate in 1945, "that, in recanting from his agrarian principles, John accepts as a valid interpretation of our principles the silliest and meanest version of our ideas that our critics gave." His disgust reveals the deep schism that had opened within Agrarianism. "If John intended to recant, why didn't he renounce the real thing and not the bogus thing?" a puzzled Davidson queried Robert Penn Warren. What must have been most exasperating of all to Davidson, however, was that conservative social views seemed finally to have a receptive audience in

Robert Penn Warren, John Crowe Ransom, and Donald Davidson.
(Courtesy Photographic Archives, Vanderbilt University)

America. Liberals, he wrote to Warren, were in "painful public distress," their chickens finally "coming home to roost."[7]

Other Agrarians, aside from Ransom, however, were rethinking and reinterpreting what they had done so many years before. In *Shenandoah*'s 1952 "Agrarians Today" symposium, Frank L. Owsley suggested that *I'll Take My Stand* was perhaps too strident and that the term "agrarian" had been a "strategic error." Andrew Nelson Lytle agreed, suggesting that the stridency of the term "agrarian" had played into their opponents' hands. At a reunion of the Fugitive poets in 1956, Owsley once again regretted that the group was "tagged" as Agrarian, as if everyone "ought to go out and plow." Agrarianism was a philosophy, not an economy, he maintained. This was an especially surprising statement, given that Owsley's essay from 1935, "The Pillars of Agrarianism," had been the most well developed statement of an Agrarian political program.[8]

Unsurprisingly, Tate, by this point a Catholic, was the most forthright in arguing that Agrarianism was an intellectual and spiritual affirmation and not a practical reform proposal. In the *Shenandoah* symposium, Tate wrote that Agrarianism had been an image of "unified Christendom"; it was this goal to which the Agrarians had been directed. Tate claimed never to have believed Agrarianism would be successful in any practical political sense. The Agrarians' attempt to revive the Old South, Tate argued in a misleading characterization of *I'll Take My Stand*, was a kind of "idolatry." The South possessed the virtues of the old spiritually unified order, but the attempt to remake it would be to "prefer the accident to the substance."[9]

Cleanth Brooks, responding to the *Shenandoah* symposium, agreed that "agrarian" was a limited term and that Agrarianism had, in fact, ultimately been about religion. The nation was now debating profound moral issues, he argued, noting the publication of T. S. Eliot's *Notes toward a Definition of Culture* (1948), the revived interest in Catholic and "neo-Protestant" orthodoxy, and the public feelings aroused by Whittaker Chambers's religious fatalism. The Agrarians did much to open this debate, Brooks claimed. The moves by Tate and others to explicitly religious standpoints were "inevitable clarifications and extensions of the central position," he believed. The South remained the best example of a traditional society.[10] Brooks's claim was significant, for other southern conservatives were increasingly making the same point. By the 1950s, many Americans, including intellectuals, were beginning to heed conservatives. As many Americans reconsidered the legacy of liberalism and progress, it was time, perhaps, to reconsider Agrarianism. As the reservations raised in the *Shenandoah* symposium suggest, the Agrarians themselves were fully engaged in this project.

An effective conservative movement emerged in the United States in the mid-1950s, in large part owing to the efforts of the young commentator William F. Buckley Jr. and the *National Review*, the conservative journal he established in 1955. In his standard history of the conservative intellectual movement in America since 1945, George H. Nash argued that the success of Buckley and the *National Review* lay in its ability to unite antistatist libertarians, who wanted to roll back the New Deal state; socially conservative traditionalists, who opposed the secularism and relativism of liberalism; and anti-Communists, who feared liberal weakness in the face of Communist aggression abroad and subversion within the United States. The explicit goal of the *National Review* was to "fuse" the various strands

of right-wing thought in American into a cogent and powerful ideology.[11] Nash's historical argument reflects the editorial content of
the *National Review*, in which diverse intellectuals vigorously debated
the definition of conservatism: Was it a faith in free-market capitalism? Or was it based on a belief in a quasi-aristocratic social order? A
divide between libertarians and traditionalists characterized the conservative movement through the 1960s. Yet the relatively quick dis-
sipation of the often cantankerous libertarian-traditionalist debates
in the 1960s, just as the conservative movement began to acquire real
power in American politics by tapping into a popular backlash against
racial and cultural liberalism, is testimony to the ideological achievement of the *National Review*.[12]

By asserting a new "conservative" identity, Buckley marginalized
both the older leadership of the Right and newer contenders for conservative leadership in the 1950s and thus transformed right-wing
politics. Buckley's movement was, as the libertarian economist Murray Rothbard shrewdly observed, a "Popular Front": he assembled
Catholic traditionalists, former Communist Cold Warriors, free-
market economists, southern states' rightists, midwestern isolationists, and other assorted right-wing thinkers in a common movement
despite the contradictions of their strongly held positions on the basis
of a common opposition to liberals and the liberal state.[13] His achievement was less in formulating a "fusionist" synthesis of traditionalist and libertarian positions than in formulating the neat ideological split itself. The split suggested that the primary form of political
identification for postwar Americans should be ideological, that the
choice of ideologies should in fact be between the *liberal* and *conservative* camps (the *National Review*, as Garry Wills observed, "for the
first time, made Liberalism (capitalized) the enemy"), and that these
contrasting ideological positions did not so much reflect real differences in class interest as rival sets of values and ideals.[14] The conservative movement was as much about power as ideas, but organizers
and activists such as Buckley defined it as a movement of ideas, not of
party or class. It was the purveyors of flawed and corrupted ideas who
were responsible for any ills in modern America, not the structure of
industrial capitalism itself or any other such large, impersonal force.

Buckley and other conservative publicists repeatedly targeted the
liberal establishment as their primary political enemy and relentlessly
attacked the power and programs of liberals. Liberals in control of the
federal government, conservative activists argued repeatedly, were
depriving Americans of the ability to define their own values and pursue their own vision of the good life. Liberals lacked religious faith;
their principled open-mindedness left them vulnerable to corrosive
values and godless communism. Liberal social engineering—a sur-

reptitious agenda geared toward reshaping human beings to conform to the liberals' own, vague "scientific utopias"—was the "profound crisis of our era," the editors of the *National Review* declared in the inaugural issue. Liberals were gradually making the United States a socialist nation.[15]

The strength of conservative ideology, sociologist Jerome L. Himmelstein observed, lay in its "capacity to picture a natural, spontaneous order (whether in American society or the world) and to blame the disruption of that order on liberal elites and their policies and ideas."[16] Buckley was able to contain rival claimants to leadership of the conservative movement. This was in part because he always paired a politics of liberty (and the pristine market) with a politics of order—an embrace of modernization with a rejection of cultural modernism. Buckley and the *National Review* sought to return to the conservatism of Victorian America, a cultural code that had held stern and repressive injunctions to curb the appetitive self in a tenuous balance with individualistic calls to maximize one's competitive drives and self-advancement. Buckley did not simply preach an unvarnished free-market liberalism; rather, he attempted to distill the essence of nineteenth-century Victorian culture into a new political philosophy, which he labeled "conservatism."

Radical conservative critiques of progress, such as that of the Southern Agrarians, were marginalized after World War II, not so much by liberals, who tended to be intrigued by conservative antimodernism, but by the postwar conservative movement, which aimed to co-opt the label "conservative." Ransom and Tate showed little interest in the conservative movement, but Davidson, among others in the Agrarian orbit, was attracted to Buckley's new coalition. Davidson and Richard M. Weaver, a younger Agrarian convert, were willing to adopt the rhetoric of traditionalism and conservatism. Moreover, they could argue that it was, in fact, the South that was the very model of a society that preserved both individualism and a firm sense of order. While conservative theoreticians split philosophical hairs and penned polemics attacking either libertarian or traditionalist excesses, southern conservatives quietly pointed to the South as a synecdoche of what they envisioned as an older America—one rooted in religiosity, localism, and a stable social order, one that united freedom and authority. Davidson refashioned his southern regionalism into a form palatable to a broader range of traditionalist thinkers. By the end of the 1950s, Davidson—as well as Tate, Weaver, and others in the Agrarian circle—had planted the seeds of a universalist reinterpretation of Agrarianism, one with only limited criticisms of industrial capitalism and fewer assertions of southern identity. "The cause of

the South was and is the cause of Western civilization itself," Davidson wrote in 1958.[17]

In a brief but suggestive analysis, Fred Siegel has suggested that
the laissez-faire conservatism so typical of the American business
class was the product of changes in the American social elite that
came to fruition after the Civil War. Previous American conservatives, whether they were Federalists, Whigs, or Tidewater aristocrats,
were skeptical of democracy. Gradually, however, a new entrepreneurial class gained standing among older social elites. This new bourgeois elite understood the acquisitiveness and self-reliance endemic to
American culture. Fearing that, in an era of mass-based reform movements and broad (if corrupt) democratic politics, the state would seek
to redistribute wealth, the new business elite promoted an ideology
of upward mobility defined in strictly pecuniary terms, expressed an
abhorrence of governmental regulation of the economy or interference with the rights of private property, and looked to the courts to
forestall "socialistic" reforms.[18]

Conservative alternatives to the laissez-faire faith of American
businessmen persisted, however. By the time Buckley and his associates scouted the possibilities of a new conservative movement,
right-wing critiques of modern American culture and both its
consumption-driven corporate capitalist order and its deep individualism existed. Not the least of these was the radical conservatism of
the Southern Agrarians. The Agrarians upheld a social order defined
not only by the norms of nineteenth-century proprietary capitalism
but also by a set of manners and customs rooted in an established culture and economy. They spurned notions of modernity and progress,
arguing that it was the leisurely rhythms of a stable and rooted organic
community that southerners should preserve. The modern industrial
economy promised ceaseless labor and moral exhaustion; the agrarian
life yielded play, art, and conversation, those qualities essential to a
life of spiritual and aesthetic fulfillment. The Agarians' New Humanist rivals garnered even more attention, as they condemned the hedonism and spiritual vacuity of a society built on a pecuniary definition of success and defended the classical principles of order over
and against the romantic individualism they believed characteristic of
Americans.

Aside from these strains of antimodernism emerging from the
academy and the world of American letters, a rather broad-based
American political Right also grew up during the 1920s. Several historians have recently emphasized the unique nature of the second Ku
Klux Klan, the popularity of which has long been a distinctive and

troubling feature of the 1920s. Millions of Protestant Americans expressed a distaste for the impersonality, pluralism, diversity, and disorder characteristic of modernity and newly evident in the increasingly pervasive national consumer culture. The kind of Americans attracted to the Klan in the 1920s were those who adhered to a Victorian moralism being challenged by bohemian enclaves of artists and socialites. Klansmen in the 1920s indulged in racist, nativist, and anti-Catholic rhetoric, but they also resented the authorities' failure to enforce Prohibition, were disturbed by the bohemian subculture of the cities, and feared the increasingly bureaucratized federal government.[19]

The 1920s Klan (or second Klan) attracted from three to six million Americans and was quite distinct from the paramilitary Klan that formed in the South during Reconstruction. The national leadership of the second Klan provided only loose direction to local chapters, the political focus of which often differed from locality to locality. Only 16 percent of its membership was in the South. The second Klan had chapters in the Midwest, West, and Northeast; there was even a chapter at Harvard University. As historian Stanley Coben noted, Connecticut boasted a larger Klan membership than Mississippi, New Jersey more than Alabama, Oregon more than Louisiana. There were more Klansmen in Indianapolis than in Mississippi and South Carolina combined, and Chicago was the largest Klan city in the country. Indiana, Illinois, and Ohio together contained 40 percent of the national membership. Indeed, Indiana was a Klan stronghold; the Klan enrolled a remarkable one-fourth to one-third of the state's native-born white men. The second Klan managed to gain control of state governments in Oregon, Colorado, and Indiana in the 1920s and achieved great mainstream success. Nor, after the early 1920s, was the second Klan especially violent or committed to vigilantism.[20]

Revisionist historians of the second Klan such as Leonard J. Moore, Robert Alan Goldberg, Christopher N. Cocoltchos, Shawn Lay, Larry R. Gerlach, David A. Horowitz, and William D. Jenkins have portrayed it as a mainstream social movement, tending to draw members from a broad social spectrum, reflecting dominant values, and committed to civic action. The Klan's animus was often directed less at blacks, Catholics, immigrants, or Jews than at local elites who would not or could not effectively address local corruption and disorder or who were affiliated with national corporations or liquor interests.[21] Moreover, the racist, anti-Catholic, nativist, and anti-Semitic rhetoric of the Klan in no way impaired its viability as a political movement in a nation where such sentiments were considered unexceptionable by the white majority. The Klan's brand of white Protestant nationalism focused on issues that reflected anxiety over the weakening of Victorian social norms: the failure to enforce Prohibition, public immorality and vice (including drug use and gambling), political corruption, public indifference to civic life, the erosion of traditional family values, waning church attendance, and the need for better public schools. This organization, the new Klan historians have argued, was a civic organization popular with the white-collar middle class and small businessmen of Protestant America and driven by an antimodern, racially exclusive, and anticosmopolitan mentality. As Coben wrote, "Klansmen in the mid-1920s decidedly were not a fringe group of vigilantes; they were solid middle-class citizens and individuals of high Victorian character." [22]

Leonard Moore pushed this argument further, seeing in the 1920s Klan the "social foundations" of the American Right. "The main forces that drove the Klan movement—the desire to uphold white Protestant cultural hegemony and an inflamed populist opposition to the growing power of political, economic, and cultural elites— have played a fundamental part in shaping conservative and right-wing movements from that time until the present," Moore argues. The second Ku Klux Klan was the leading edge of what has been a decades-long battle against secularizing trends in American culture on the part of a significant minority of Americans—initially Protestants but later Catholics, too. The Right in America, in Moore's view, has fought "racial, ethnic, and cultural pluralism; the loss of popular control over local affairs; the materialism of the new business and consumer culture; challenges to the cultural authority of religion; the 'new woman,' the youth culture, and other forces undermining traditional gender roles and family structures." [23]

The right-wing milieu of the 1930s reflected the values of small-town, Victorian America. Spokesmen for the Christian Right in the 1930s, such as William Dudley Pelley, Gerald B. Winrod, and Gerald L. K. Smith, reflected the bourgeois culture of the ministers and small businessmen who were their fathers. They preached the nineteenth-century gospel of work, extolling piety, propriety, upward mobility, hard work, and delayed gratification. They saw science, liberalism, and rationalism as undercutting these values. (As Leo Ribuffo observed in his history of the Christian Right in the 1930s, "Ethnic tensions and cultural conflicts that historians usually associate with the 1920s survived, somewhat recast, into the Depression.") Roosevelt's disdain for Prohibition and his gestures of inclusion toward blacks, ethnics, and Jews made evident his comfort with the cosmopolitanism characteristic of the cities and, thus, aroused the antipathies of increasingly marginalized small-town elites.[24] As president, he personified an expanded and interventionist government, the progres-

sive social science that guided government reformers, and a modernist, consumerist culture — all the things that threatened conservatives'
sense of order.

Other dissidents of the era reflected this intense localism. Louisiana's powerful Huey Long and the Roman Catholic radio priest
Charles Coughlin in the 1930s decried the power that large institutions held over individuals and communities. They favored augment-
ing governmental power, but only so the state could limit the power
of the national elite and powerful corporations. Both favored decentralization and small-scale, proprietary capitalism. "What had in the
1920s been a diffuse localism producing a wide range of disconnected
cultural protests became in the 1930s a powerful challenge to the
nature of the industrial state," argues historian Alan Brinkley.[25]

The "Old Right" that grew up in the 1930s in opposition to Roosevelt's New Deal was shaped by the tradition of laissez-faire conservatism (most evident in groups such as the pro-business Liberty
League) but drew also on some of the same values and anxieties per-
colating on the antimodern right, including the desire to retain the
social authority and defend the autonomy of the American provinces.
According to libertarian economist Murray Rothbard, the Old Right
flourished from 1933, the date of Roosevelt's inauguration, to 1954,
the eve of the founding of the *National Review*. Rothbard's experience provides a window into its milieu. He grew up in a middle-class
Jewish family in New York City in the 1930s but was not attracted
to the city's vibrant Left as were so many other young Jewish students. Rothbard's father, a Polish immigrant, was a steadfast individualist and a firm believer in the ability of the individual to advance in
America's free-market economy. While attending a private day school
(on scholarship) and, later, Columbia University, Rothbard was first
attracted to the right-wing press. After the war, he discovered the libertarian Foundation for Economic Education, founded by Leonard
Read in 1946 in Irvington-on-Hudson, New York. Rothbard began
to read older libertarian journalists and writers such as Frank Chodorov, Albert Jay Nock, H. L. Mencken, John T. Flynn, and Garet
Garett. The Old Right that he discovered was an open and expansive
coalition of cranky individualists, such as Nock and Mencken; southern states' rights Democrats; conservative Republicans, largely from
the Midwest (although Rothbard joined the Young Republican Club
of New York in 1946); and old progressives (among whom Rothbard
numbered Herbert Hoover).[26]

Rothbard discovered the Old Right, however, after its climactic
moment, which had been the fight against American involvement in
World War II. The anti-interventionist, or isolationist, movement
was rooted in a suspicion of the state, a proud provincialism, and a re-

jection of internationalism. Its primary embodiment was the America First Committee, which eventually sponsored 450 local chapters and enrolled at least 250,000 members. Liberals, pacifists, and socialists gravitated to the organization; the socialist leader Norman Thomas, for example, appeared at America First rallies, although he headed his own Keep America Out of the War Committee. For the most part, however, the Old Right dominated America First, which was as opposed to Roosevelt's domestic policies—and his very person—as his foreign policy. Midwestern business leaders—the Main Street segment of the Republican Party, which was traditionally opposed to the northeastern Wall Street elements—were the primary benefactors of the organization. The rank-and-file membership was mostly Republican. The movement's most prominent spokesman, Charles Lindbergh, expressed the vision of a "rural arcadia" that lay behind much of the movement (and sounded vaguely Agrarian): "How long can men thrive between walls of brick, walking on asphalt pavements, breathing the fumes of coal and oil, growing, working, dying, with hardly a thought of wind and sky, and fields of grain, seeing only machine-made beauty, the mineral-like quality of life?"[27]

Lindbergh's acceptance of a decoration from Nazi Germany and his refusal to condemn Nazi atrocities tainted the movement. In a radio broadcast in September 1941, he declared that the Jews, Great Britain, and the Roosevelt administration were the three major elements leading to war. "Instead of agitating for war, the Jewish groups in this country should be opposing it in every possible way, for they will be the first to feel its consequences," Lingbergh noted somewhat ominously. Tolerance was one of the first casualties of war, he observed. The "far-sighted" Jews realized this and opposed intervention. The "greatest danger" posed by Jews to the United States was "their large ownership and influence in our motion pictures, our press, our radio, and our Government." Lindbergh's statements irreparably damaged the America First Committee, discrediting it in the eyes of many. Although America First disbanded after the Japanese attack on Pearl Harbor and the German declaration of war on the United States, anti-interventionist critics persisted on the right and provided a little-heeded commentary on American Cold War policy that was, in some ways, peculiarly prescient, particularly in its warnings about American entanglements in the Third World. Many veterans of the Old Right deplored the diminution of Congress's role in making war, scorned what they considered war scares generated by President Harry S. Truman in support of his policies, and warned against the exaggeration of the Soviet threat. These rightist critics looked askance on foreign aid, which, they argued, resulted in only limited benefits, and suggested that the United States was becoming an imperial power. The nation would inevitably, they argued, be forced to support unsavory regimes around the world. Beginning in 1950, many isolationists warned against United States involvement in French Indochina. In Rothbard's recollection, most of the Old Right fiercely opposed the Marshall Plan, the Korean War, and much of the nation's Cold War policy in general, beginning with the Truman Doctrine, which articulated the policy of containment. Indeed, dissension over the Cold War and the rise of the national security state was a key element in the disintegration of the Old Right and the rise of Buckley's *National Review* circle.[28]

Many Americans were intrigued by conservative philosophy, if not the Right, after World War II. The rise of fascism and totalitarianism, world war, and the specter of nuclear annihilation were conducive to the questioning of modernity and progress. The "totalitarian" nation-state, if considered the epitome of modernity, was the negation of what, since the Enlightenment, had been the promised fruits of progress: science, rationalism, secularism, democracy, and liberalism. Conservatives had placed their faith in traditions built up over centuries and thus seemed to provide an alternative. "Those patterns of social organization which are essential either to progress or to stability come only with the maturing of time; the impatience of the radical can never recreate what he has been, by accident, able to destroy," wrote Francis G. Wilson, a conservative political scientist at the University of Illinois in 1941. "Stability is the keystone in the arch of social reality," he declared. "Stability is a value in itself." To many survivors of the war years, these words seemed self-evidently true.[29] The political passion and idealism of the depression years were exhausted. Now, the mood on college campuses, one observer remarked, was that of a discarded optimism. Another suggested that the 1950s would be remembered as the "Era of the New Conservatism." H. Malcolm MacDonald, a professor at the University of Texas, viewed this new conservatism as a major ideological shift in Western civilization. The history of the West for the previous fifteen years, he claimed in 1957, had been that of the new respectability of conservatism, which, he wrote, was the reassertion of the "Western view of man": skepticism of perfectionism and utopianism, respect for hierarchy, and faith in the transcendental reality of values and absolutes. Today's conservative, MacDonald declared, is the "twentieth-century humanist."[30]

Signs of the new conservatism were everywhere. Although rejecting the antistatism of the Old Right and abhorring the populist Right, which they associated with fascism, liberal and left-leaning intellectuals flirted with intellectual conservatism. Dwight Macdonald and the writers he published in *politics*, as well as the émigré political philosopher Hannah Arendt and cultural critic Lewis Mumford, were critical of radical visions of progress and examined the ways in which society might be reconstituted in order to foster a stronger individualism and sense of citizenship.[31] Many liberal intellectuals expressed doubt that the crass and superficial consumer culture of the West was capable of producing the character Americans needed to face down Soviet Communism. Few Americans were ready to assume the hard life of freedom, liberal historian Arthur M. Schlesinger Jr. suggested in his classic articulation of "existential liberalism," *The Vital Center* (1949). The blighting impersonality of the postindustrial state, he declared, was eroding society's "center," both the leadership class that mediated between the Left and the Right (the "group which holds society together") and the social nexus that bound individual and community.[32]

The Protestant theologian Reinhold Niebuhr, the leading liberal intellectual of the period, spoke powerfully of the sinfulness of all humans and the moral ambiguities of all political orders. In the process, he expressed a generation's disillusioned reassessment of radical ideologies that promised a new order of morality and social justice. Original sin ensured that "no matter how wide the perspectives which the human mind may reach, how broad the loyalties which the human imagination may conceive, how universal the community which human statecraft may organize, or how pure the aspirations of the saintliest idealists may be, there is no level of human moral or social achievement in which there is not some corruption of inordinate self-love," Niebuhr wrote.[33]

In addition, the New Critics were dominant after the war, and, led by Ransom, Tate, and Brooks, they played an important role in elevating to canonical status such conservative antimodernists as T. S. Eliot, W. B. Yeats, and Ezra Pound. They received much support from liberal and leftist critics based in New York City. The formerly radical "New York Intellectuals," including Philip Rahv, William Phillips, Lionel Trilling, Diana Trilling, Clement Greenberg, William Barrett, Irving Howe, Delmore Schwartz, Leslie Fiedler, and Alfred Kazin, promoted a complex, iconoclastic, and difficult modernist aesthetic in art and literature that was a reaction against both the politicized criticism of the Left in the 1930s and the Popular Front culture that persisted into the 1940s (and which many of the New York Intellectuals dismissed as mass-produced pap). America's liberal elite was engaged in a conservative rethinking of its intellectual heritage and its previous understanding of the role of intellectuals in politics. Modernist works and the modernist aesthetic became surrogates for a more explicitly conservative political criticism. The veneration of the individualistic avant-garde artist—with the disinterested and expert critic to serve as interpreter and critic—was one of the New York Intellectuals' contributions to America's Cold War consensus. The apolitical modernist genius was to prove the superiority of both the American character and the American system. The English writer Stephen Spender, noting the high estimation accorded such illiberal modernists as Marcel Proust, Joyce, Franz Kafka, Rainier Maria Rilke, Yeats, and even D. H. Lawrence by American intellectuals, was one of the critics to make the new conservatism explicit. It was time, Spender argued in August 1950, to move "beyond liberalism" and replace the liberal-conservative opposition with a "revolutionary traditionalism," which he defined as a "determination to improve conditions, inseparably fused with a determination that the most valuable characteristics of tradition should be reborn with the future." [34]

At the same time, the 1940s and 1950s were the peak years of the Catholic Revival, the predominantly lay movement of intellectuals led by Jacques Maritain and Etienne Gilson and shaped by the Thomistic philosophy that had so influenced Allen Tate as a young man. Revival thinkers believed that Western civilization was in a state of crisis, and they aimed to inspire Catholics to reestablish a Christian social order. [35] This Catholic intellectualism was gaining some measure of respect in the wider culture. Robert M. Hutchins and Mortimer Adler promoted Aristotelianism and Thomism at the University of Chicago. Maritain himself gained considerable respectful attention while living in the United States throughout much of the 1940s and 1950s and teaching at prominent American and Canadian schools, including Princeton University (where he established the friendship with Tate that led to Tate's request that Maritain be his godfather upon his conversion) and the University of Toronto, where Gilson headed the Medieval Institute. [36] Neo-Thomism spurred a revival in the discussion of natural law, as, for example, in Walter Lippmann's *Essays in the Public Philosophy* (1955). Waldemar Gurian's *Review of Politics*, published out of Notre Dame, provided a noteworthy forum for the critique of positivistic and behavioralistic approaches in the social sciences, publishing non-Catholic as well as Catholic intellectuals; Hannah Arendt, Hans J. Morganthau, and Herbert Butterfield appeared in its pages. [37] Other Catholic intellectuals, such as the historian Ross J. S. Hoffman, were instrumental in sponsoring a reconsideration of Edmund Burke, the Irish statesman credited with founding modern conservatism in response to the French Revolution. Hoffman helped establish a Burke Society at Fordham University in April 1945 and, with his colleague Paul Levack, published an anthology of Burke's writings in 1949. Francis Wilson, an early and visible proponent of conservatism and Burke, was a Catholic convert.[38]

Observers identified another school of intellectuals as the "New Conservatives," most notably Russell Kirk, author of *The Conservative Mind: From Burke to Santayana* (1953); Peter Viereck, a historian and poet at Mount Holyoke College who sparked the New Conservative revival with *Conservatism Revisited: The Revolt against Revolt, 1815–1949* (1949); John Hallowell, a political scientist at Duke University who propounded a political philosophy based on Christianity and, in *The Moral Foundation of Democracy* (1954), identified natural law as the basis of democracy; and Richard M. Weaver, a student of the Agrarians who published *Ideas Have Consequences* (1948), a plea for a renewed faith in moral absolutes. Other writers who reached a broad audience and were sometimes associated with the New Conservatism in the early 1950s were Clinton Rossiter, a historian of American political thought, and August Hecksher, the lead editorial writer for the *New York Herald Tribune*.

Viereck had coined the term "New Conservatism" in an article he wrote for *Atlantic* in 1940 at the age of twenty-three. He drew inspiration from the classicism of Irving Babbitt and the New Humanists and came to promote a kind of realistic, state-oriented conservatism in response to the irrationalist politics of the day. "My great dream," Viereck declared in 1940, "perhaps young and naïve, is for American youth to synthesize cultural, spiritual, and political conservatism with economic reform." What the world needed was a "New Conservatism," which would mediate between the evils created by laissez-faire capitalism and the irrational desires fed by revolutionary movements of the Right and Left.[39] Some, although not all, of the New Conservatives were comfortable with the liberal establishment. Clinton Rossiter shared the assumptions of the consensus liberals of the period, believing "change and progress" the American way of life. Conservatism was, for him, responsible liberalism. August Hecksher favored two-time Democratic presidential candidate Adlai Stevenson, declaring him the model American conservative of the twentieth century. Insofar as they believed New Conservatism to be compatible with liberal aims, many postwar liberals did not object to the label. In 1955, Reinhold Niebuhr's son Chris, head of the Liberal Union at Harvard, expressed approval for Peter Viereck. Conservatism in America, Chris Niebuhr argued, was the conservation of liberalism.[40]

"It used to be one of the fixed characteristics of an American conservative that he should deny he was one; now it appears to be expected of every liberal that he should insist that he is the *real* conservative," the New York critic Irving Kristol observed in 1958. Daniel

Aaron, writing in 1954, noted the "ever-widening influence" of the New Conservatives, among whom he numbered the New Critics and European existentialists, as well as Eliot and Protestant theologians Niebuhr and Paul Tillich. Such conservatism should be valued, Aaron argued, for it would serve as a counterweight to the weaknesses to which democratic societies were prone, "the sanctifying of majority will; an uncritical faith in manifest destiny; a delight in the new-fangled; an oversimplified conception of human nature; predilection for short-cuts and panaceas of all kinds; an intense absorption with the mechanics of life." Niebuhr expressed a similar skepticism of the Enlightenment faith in perfectibility and progress. Individual rights are worthless, he argued, unless recognized by a community, and communities are inevitably hierarchical and inegalitarian. "An academic liberalism with its abstract notions of liberty and equality has never been able to come to terms with these realities of the community," Niebuhr wrote. "There is, therefore, some truth in the aristocratic-conservative tradition which the most democratic society must reserve from the error of aristocratic pretensions and must incorporate into the wisdom by which the life of the community is regulated and integrated."[41]

This voguish conservatism was not without critics. In 1949 Robert Gorham Davis, an associate professor of English at Smith College, attacked the Southern Agrarians (in their guise as New Critics) and the New Humanists for leading, he claimed, an assault on the "assumptions of democratic liberalism." These two groups of conservative intellectuals may have failed to change American culture in the 1930s, Davis argued, but "during the forties, with the intense reaction against Stalinism, the socio-historical patterns of acceptance and rejection established by the humanist-agrarian movement quietly triumphed on the higher literary levels, and became the required postulates, curiously enough, for the proper evaluation of literature." To buttress his claim—that, in his formulation, conservatives had succeeded in substituting the values of hierarchy, catholicism, aristocracy, tradition, absolutes, dogma, and truth for those of liberalism, naturalism, scientism, individualism, equalitarianism, progress, protestantism, pragmatism, and personality in American literature— Davis pointed to the contemporary authority of Catholic and Anglo-Catholic writers such as Graham Greene, Evelyn Waugh, C. S. Lewis, and W. H. Auden as well as Niebuhr, Eliot, and the New York critic Lionel Trilling, who was publishing critical essays on the liberal imagination.[42]

The debate reached a peak between 1953 and 1955, in part owing to the publication of Kirk's *The Conservative Mind*, a widely noted attempt to establish an intellectual genealogy for the Anglo-American conservative tradition. Much attention centered on attempts to define a conservative philosophy, which, for most Americans, had long seemed identical to laissez-faire economics and social Darwinism. Many critics insisted that the constitutive elements of an authentic conservatism—an established aristocracy, a custom of deference to a social elite, an established church, an ingrained reverence for tradition—simply were not present in America. Liberals argued that the United States was, from its foundation, built on equality of opportunity and democratic government, an unalterably liberal nation. Louis Hartz's *The Liberal Tradition in America* (1955) was the definitive expression of this view.[43] There was no feudal period in the American past, no strong tradition of aristocracy, noblesse oblige, or social deference, Hartz argued. For many liberal intellectuals in the 1940s and 1950s, the United States was still the world free from its birth —one in which the Lockean social contract came nearest to being a true description of historical reality. "There are no institutions in the political, economic, and intellectual life of the nation which can claim the *Tradition* and *Authority* which are the essence of genuine conservatism," Harold W. Stoke observed in 1942. Stuart Gerry Brown declared emphatically in 1955: "*To be an American conservative it is necessary to reassert liberalism.*" In such a nation, no philosophical conservatism, defending hierarchy and prescription, could take root. Conservatives were "honorable, generous—and irrelevant," the historian Arthur M. Schlesinger Jr. wrote. They did not have ideas, ran Trilling's famous dismissal, but "irritable mental gestures which seek to resemble ideas."[44]

Both the Old Right and the New Conservatives posed particular problems for Buckley and the nascent conservative movement. Buckley sought to establish a conservative movement that retained a claim to the conservative philosophy so appealing to liberals but remained firmly on the Right. He was ideally suited for this task. As the son of a Catholic, Irish-American oilman who had stubbornly established himself in the world of Yankee Protestantism, he was able to bridge the divisions between social conservatives and right-wing liberals. Brilliant and precocious, he garnered national attention soon after graduating from Yale University in 1950. In *God and Man at Yale* (1951), the attack on academic freedom that made his reputation as a controversialist, Buckley declared the need for a social orthodoxy. Professors at Yale should be required to teach the religious and economic principles held by the Yale corporation and the majority of the alumni, Buckley argued. He provided an artful blend of tradition and libertarianism; he defended orthodoxy, but the orthodoxy was free-market capitalism as well as Christianity.[45]

The Old Right imploded, in part, as a result of the pressures of the Cold War. Many American conservatives, including Buckley, were galvanized by the threat of communism. They believed liberals to be either willing allies or hopeless dupes of Communist propaganda and judged Truman's containment policy to be feckless. The apocalyptic writings of Whittaker Chambers, a writer and former Communist who implicated Alger Hiss in a prewar spy ring, mesmerized many on the Right, including Buckley, who developed a close relationship with Chambers. In his powerful confessional autobiography, *Witness* (1952), Chambers portrayed himself as an existential witness to the evil of communism and the truth of Christian revelation. "The crisis of the Western world exists to the degree in which it is indifferent to God," Chambers declared. True freedom, he argued, is equivalent to religious faith; freedom is only found through religion. "Communism is what happens when, in the name of Mind, men free themselves from God," Chambers pronounced.[46]

Buckley ardently supported Senator Joseph McCarthy's attempts to uncover subversive Communist agents in the government. Before his fall in 1954, McCarthy was a potent force in American politics, and McCarthyism became a rallying point for the Right, a harbinger of a potent right-wing populism. For liberals, however, McCarthyism represented the power of demagoguery, the gullibility of the masses, and the abrogation of civil liberties. McCarthyism provoked a crisis for the Right. The question of countersubversive action by the government weakened anticommunism by alienating liberal from conservative anti-Communists and provided the Left with a convenient propaganda weapon against the Right. The Right, liberals charged, was "radical" and "extremist," indifferent to fundamental American liberties.[47] McCarthyism divided the Right itself. Many important (or soon-to-be important) conservatives were either critical of or intensely ambivalent toward McCarthy, including Will Herberg, Robert Nisbet, Viereck, Ralph de Toledano, Russell Kirk, and even Chambers. In the fall of 1952, divisions over McCarthyism ruptured the editorial staff of the most effective intellectual journal on the Right, the *Freeman*. The magazine's three principal editors left in early 1953; by 1954, the *Freeman* had become a more narrowly libertarian publication. The decline of the *Freeman* created an opening for the *National Review*, which, in fact, mimicked the older magazine's format and drew from its staff and contributors.[48]

Out of this crisis on the right, the *National Review* emerged to champion a new conservative movement. It was a firmly McCarthyite journal. Former leftist anti-Communists were vital to the *National Review*. In addition to Chambers, whom Buckley convinced to serve on the magazine's staff from 1957 to 1959, Buckley relied on James Burnham, a former Trotskyist who became the *National Review*'s expert on foreign policy; Willi Schlamm, an Austrian who had been a Communist in his youth; Frank Meyer, an active Communist from 1931 through 1945 who became a sort of in-house ideologue for Buckley; and Max Eastman, an accomplished and formerly Marxist critic who joined the staff when the magazine was founded, only to leave in 1958 because of the magazine's religious sensibility.[49] The magazine's editors promoted an aggressive foreign policy. Led by Burnham, they called for the liberation of Eastern Europe from Communist rule. Containment, Burnham argued, was a "policy of drift"; Western Europe, he declared, would not survive without a free Eastern Europe. Either war or surrender was inevitable. In 1959, Buckley's brother-in-law, L. Brent Bozell, speculated on a "preventive" war with the Soviet Union. If a war of attrition failed, he wrote in the *National Review*, the United States must destroy the enemy "in the middle of the night," in full knowledge that "it is God who ordains the cost."[50]

The editors of the *National Review* forged a new ideology, which they identified as conservative. Between 1954 and 1955, the Old Right succumbed amid a final flurry of polemics on anti-intervention, nationalism, and the Cold War. The aging isolationist activists were, quite literally, passing away. Further, the midwestern and Protestant base of the Right was expanding to include many strongly anti-Communist Catholics. Anticommunism was a great unifier, binding together the wings of the Right into a new conservative coalition. It represented, at one and the same time, a broad defense of capitalism and a passionate assertion of religious faith.[51] Buckley harnessed the energy of the Old Right and sought to expand its base. In place of the strains of anticosmopolitanism, isolationism, and antipluralism prevalent on the older right, Buckley promoted his own vision of the conservative movement — one that welcomed more Americans, including Jews and Catholics; was firmly behind corporate capitalism; and favored an interventionist foreign policy and vigorous prosecution of the Cold War. The *National Review* also functioned to proscribe anti-Semitism and other forms of extremism within the conservative movement.[52]

At the same time, Buckley moved to preserve the conservative label for the Right by emphasizing its integrity as a distinct ideology. He wanted no blurring of the lines between liberalism and conservatism; rather, the two must be clearly demarcated. Liberalism for Buckley meant the social engineering state and a soft moral relativism. An essential opposition to the New Deal state and an uncompromising commitment to anticommunism characterized the *National Review*. This implied, at root, an acceptance of the free-market economy. An early target was the type of aristocratic, or "traditionalist," conserva-

tism espoused by Viereck, Kirk, and other New Conservatives. Frank
Meyer observed in an attack on the New Conservatives that appeared
in the *Freeman* in 1955 that a sharp divide existed between individualists and traditionalists. "This is not a problem of tone nor attitude, not
a difference between the conservative and the radical temperament;
it is a difference of principle," he declared.[53] Buckley later scornfully observed that Viereck's New Conservatism was a label by which liberals
"designated people they thought respectable"; he briefly considered
an examination of the claims made by Viereck and other New Conservatives to represent "legitimate" conservatism as the topic of his
second book.[54]

Many politicians, including Herbert Hoover and Ohio senator
Robert A. Taft as well as Friedrich Hayek, insisted they were "liberal."[55] Buckley and the *National Review* never sought to recapture
the liberal label. Rather, Buckley attacked liberalism at every opportunity. From the first issue, the prime target of the *National Review*
was a misguided liberal elite, blinded by wispy delusions of perfect-
ing man and committed to the dream of an omnicompetent state.
Buckley set as his task the publication of a truly conservative magazine in a "country widely assumed to be a bastion of conservatism."
The editors of the *National Review* did not believe they lived in conservative times; rather, they perceived the nation as suffocatingly liberal and the conservative movement as beleaguered. The magazine,
Buckley declared in his "Publisher's Statement," "stands athwart history, yelling Stop, at a time when no one is inclined to do so, or to
have much patience with those who so urge it." It was this brand of
conservative ideology that pulled New Conservatives skeptical of the
progressive visions of liberals and social planners into the conservative movement. Buckley laid the onus for what he perceived as a
weakened American commitment to capitalism and republicanism on
liberal intellectuals. The causes of crisis in America lay in the corrupting influence of radical ideas, which liberals lacked the sense to resist.
"Our political economy and our high-energy industry run on large,
general principles, on ideas—not by day-to-day guess work, expe-
dients and improvisations." In the magazine's credenda, Buckley expressed opposition to an activist state, communism, superficial intellectual fashions, middle-of-the-road politicians, labor unions, world
government, and social engineering.[56]

Buckley's paradoxical goal was to mate a politics of order with a
politics of individual freedom. He oscillated between competing desires for both. Buckley was skeptical of democracy because skeptical of the political and intellectual capacity of the masses, particularly when he looked to emerging nations in Africa, for which he had
little but disdain.[57] "The democracy of universal suffrage is not a bad

form of government; it is simply not necessarily nor inevitably a good form of government," he wrote. "Democracy must be justified by its works, not by doctrinaire affirmations of an intrinsic goodness that no mere method can legitimately lay claim to." The danger of democracy, Buckley observed, is that the people will use power to *"diminish the area of human freedom."* The specter of a popularly supported liberal state haunted Buckley; conservatives consistently felt themselves to be pulling against the tide of public opinion in the 1950s. Although Buckley distrusted the masses as citizens, he did not distrust them as consumers. Buckley was attracted to libertarianism and urged the decentralization of power. "Societies are free according as people are free; the more free the individual, the more free the society," he argued.[58] He placed great faith in the market. For example, Yale University's willful indifference to the desires of its customers (or students) for a traditional education angered him. In a free economy, the consumer is sovereign, Buckley argued in *God and Man at Yale.* "It is of the essence of freedom that citizens not be made to pay for what the majority does not want, and there is no exception to this rule that does not entail a surrender of freedom and a substitution of minority for majority rule." [59]

With suspected Communists, however, Buckley was a forthright proponent of order over freedom. In this, he drew inspiration from Willmoore Kendall, an iconoclastic conservative political theorist who was his mentor at Yale University and later a colleague at the *National Review.* The concern to vindicate the legitimacy of the coercive power of the majority in a democratic society was a keynote of Kendall's thought from the 1940s through the 1950s. At the tail end of the depression, Kendall had claimed that the plutocratic elite ignored the will of the people. After World War II, as he gravitated to the right, he saw liberal intellectuals and policy makers as the primary opponents of the popular will. Kendall early argued that the internal cohesiveness of the community—its ability to unite around a set of common values and goals—was essential to a healthy democracy. He believed that the enemies that Americans faced in the Cold War included not only Communists but also the "more or less typical American liberal." The liberals' inability to recognize that society must possess a "minimum consensus of value" was their Achilles' heel.[60] Liberals opposed America "at its best" and were against the "American way of life," Kendall wrote in the *National Review* in 1957.[61]

Kendall was a vocal supporter of congressional efforts to ferret out Communists in the United States. He argued that a democratic government had the right to proscribe beliefs that challenged the essential orthodoxy undergirding American society. His views shaped the work of Buckley and Brent Bozell, who published *McCarthy and His*

Enemies, a defense of McCarthy, in 1954. "Not only is it *characteristic* of society to create institutions and to defend them with sanctions," Buckley and Bozell wrote. "Societies *must* do so — or else they cease to exist. The members of society must share certain values if that society is to cohere; and cohere it must if it is to survive." Kendall echoed this sentiment, which, in fact, was derived from his own views on majority rule, in a postmortem defense of McCarthyism, published in *The Conservative Affirmation* (1963). Every society has a consensus of values, Kendall argued, and it is perfectly just that a majority of that society insists that everyone accept that consensus as a condition of membership:

> Discussion there is and must be, freedom of thought and freedom of expression there are and must be, but within limits set by the basic consensus; freedom of thought and freedom of expression there are and must be, but not anarchy of thought or anarchy of expression. In such a society by no means are *all* questions open questions; some questions involve matters so basic to the consensus that the society would, in declaring them open, abolish itself, commit suicide, terminate its existence as the kind of society it has hitherto understood itself to be.[62]

Kendall simply believed that, in this democracy, all must, in the end, accept the authority of certain, basic American truths — an American orthodoxy that Kendall felt no scruples in rigidly defining. A 1960 attack on John Stuart Mill published in the *American Political Science Review* was, he confessed, "unabashedly egghead McCarthyism."[63] The American people are right, Kendall declared, to proscribe the Communist minority in their midst. The conservative, he argued "finds in the First Amendment no mention of a right to think and say whatever one pleases, or of a duty on the part of American citizens to tolerate and live with and interminably discuss any and every opinion that their neighbors may take into their heads."[64] The sentiment was echoed by James Burnham. "McCarthy was the symbol through which the basic strata of citizens expressed their conviction — felt more than reasoned — that Communism and Communists cannot be part of our national community, that they are beyond the boundaries," Burnham wrote.[65]

In this way, Buckley struggled to develop a coherent political theory. Yet his position was marked by inconsistencies. He feared a democratic government that would usurp individual rights in the market but was unconcerned with the political rights of Communists or their sympathizers. Federal enforcement of liberal social policies was unacceptable, even if supported by a majority, but federal enforcement of ideological orthodoxy was necessary. Buckley recognized the difficulty of his ideological balancing act: "Freedom and order and community and justice in an age of technology: that is the contemporary challenge of political conservatism."[66]

Frank Meyer made the most ambitious effort to promote the "fusion" of traditionalist conservatives and libertarians in the conservative movement. In part, he merely sought to stress the points of consensus that united all on the right, despite competing emphases.[67] But he also attempted to reconcile the conflict between freedom and order in his own thought. His most sustained attempt to do this was in his 1962 volume *In Defense of Freedom: A Conservative Credo*. For Meyer, the essential wisdom of nineteenth-century conservatism was the perception that the "objective existence of values based upon the unchanging constitution of being" should be the "criterion for moral thought and action." Meyer wanted to placate conservatives in the movement by recognizing this principle, with which he also fully agreed: Human beings must live within an order based on objective moral values. However, for Meyer as for Buckley, freedom remained the core of his philosophy. Seeking to reconcile the two claims, he stubbornly pursued the notion that true and authentic moral action must be voluntary and not coerced. In this, he articulated a libertarianism with existentialist overtones. "Acceptance of the moral authority derived from the transcendent criteria of truth and good must be voluntary if it is to have meaning; if it is coerced by human force, it is meaningless," Meyer argued.[68] He reiterated the point often in his book. "Men cannot be forced to be free, nor can they even be forced to be virtuous," he claimed. "To a certain extent, it is true, they can be formed to act as though they were virtuous. But virtue is the fruit of well-used freedom. And no act to the degree that it is coerced can partake of virtue — or of vice." The individual must voluntarily accept the moral authority of the transcendent. Human freedom is the ability to make an immoral choice, and only if fully free is a moral decision possible. The notion that freedom is the "essence" of a person's "being" was Meyer's "central axiom."[69] In the end, he rejected the imposition of values by the community or state.[70] His conception of the role of the state was unmistakably secular: "To achieve a good society requires men unremittingly devoted to the pursuit of good and truth, but it requires also that no one have the power to impose beliefs by force upon other men — and this whether those beliefs be false or true."[71]

Meyer was, as Brent Bozell pointed out, essentially libertarian. The fusionist effort, Bozell commented, "invariably consists in borrowing from the libertarians their principles and programs, and from the traditionalists the divine *imprimateur*."[72] Bozell favored a more traditionalist politics and a larger role for the state in enforcing moral standards. People are never in danger of losing the kind of freedom about which Meyer fretted, Bozell argued, because the "morally significant choice" is always an inner one, not subject, ultimately, to coercion. One may not be able to act on one's beliefs, but a good will is what defines moral virtue. Moreover, Bozell argued, by forbidding the state to take any means to inculcate virtue, Meyer was, in fact, simply seeking to make a virtuous choice as difficult as possible. If a state is empowered to imprison a thief, Bozell argued, why cannot it undertake a program to deter juvenile delinquency before a crime is committed?[73]

The disparate ideological impulses on the right were never "fused" by Buckley, the *National Review*, or anyone else. An ideology oriented to order is, in principle, at odds with an ideology based on freedom. But, in practice, postwar conservatives managed to achieve a balance, primarily by focusing attention on the liberal state, about which everyone on the right could find something to dislike. For a movement based on ideological presuppositions, it was vital that the leaders pursue even a chimerical fusion of philosophical opposites. Buckley and conservatives like him genuinely sought to bring philosophical order to their own competing impulses for both a conservative and Christian moral order and a robust capitalist free market. They sought to systematize a Victorian ethos that, in the nineteenth century, had existed in discrete cultural beliefs and practices situated in the church, the club, and, ultimately, the home. For the emerging conservative coalition, the "fusionist" project was successful even if not brought to a convincing intellectual resolution. It eased the tensions between political allies who disagreed in some rather fundamental ways, thus helping the conservatives on their path to power.

There was no necessary connection between conservative antimodernists, Catholic revivalists, Niebuhrian realists, Burkean defenders of tradition, "New Conservatives," or Agrarian critics of progress and the mainstream conservative coalition that developed in the 1950s. Allen Tate evinced little interest in the conservative movement. In a forum organized by Hiram Haydn, the editor of *American Scholar*, in response to Robert Gorham Davis's attack on the conservatism of the New Critics, Tate was careful to distinguish between artistic opinion and political convictions. Despite their conservative cultural views, he noted, practicing New Critics voted in all sorts of differing ways: Eliot voted Labor; Yvor Winters supported Robert La Follette and later the Democrats; an unnamed New Critic had voted for Norman Thomas. Tate himself claimed to have voted only once, and then for Franklin D. Roosevelt. He disclaimed any opposition to America's increasingly egalitarian society or its wide range of individual freedom. "I think, Mr. Davis," Tate declared at one point, "you are trying to equate us with what I heard called General Motors conservatives—or was it Western Electric reactionaries." Tate's primary commitment was to intellectual autonomy. Indeed, he later refused to write for Buckley's *National Review* because of its support of McCarthyism.[74]

There were some links between the world of antimodernist conservative intellectuals at midcentury and that of right-wing populism. Davidson's thought, as evidenced particularly in his attack on the federal "leviathan," had been converging with the Old Right. By the 1950s, he was eager to establish an alliance with Buckley's new conservative coalition. He recast Agrarianism as a form of traditionalist conservatism. Traditionalists were welcomed by Buckley as part of the movement, even as he contained any incipient challenge to the main course of corporate capitalism. The evolution of Russell Kirk's thought exemplifies the nature of this postwar traditionalist conservatism; Kirk, furthermore, was an important link between Davidson and the conservative movement.

Kirk's *Conservative Mind* played a vital role in sparking the debates over the New Conservatism, although Kirk himself professed to dislike the label. He considered ideologies to be the rationalistic and distorting aberrations of the liberal mind-set. Anyone, Kirk argued, could be a conservative. The true conservative could be a landowner or manufacturer, but just as easily a clergyman, farmer, or truck driver:

> The true conservative, in short, whether he knows Latin or not, has in him something of the temper of Cicero, and about him some touch of the high old Roman virtue. *Conservare*, to keep or preserve, is his principle of action. Preferring the old and tried to the novel and dubious, he endeavors to safeguard the institutions and wisdom which his own generation have inherited from dead ages. It is not wealth that makes him a conservative, nor power, nor timidity, nor class, nor even immediate interest, but rather this deep-seated prejudice in favor of prescriptive truth.

A conservative was someone who was shaped by religion, possessed a firm moral sense, was hostile to arbitrary power, opposed centralization, and favored prescriptive rights and the sanctity of private property. Such habits of mind were inborn; Kirk believed he had been conservative from the hour he began to reason. "Conservatism and liberalism and radicalism are states of mind, not of the pocketbook," he declared in *A Program for Conservatives* (1954).[75]

Born near Detroit in 1918, Kirk was the son of a railroad engineman who left school before the sixth grade. His mother read poetry and graduated from high school, but no one had attended college in his family except one grandfather. Some of his mother's family settled in Mecosta, a small town located in the stump country of central Michigan, an area cut over by lumbermen in the 1870s and 1880s and left desolate. Kirk spent much time there as a boy and loved the country. "Here I came to know the world of silence," he recalled.[76]

Kirk's preferred mode of self-presentation was picaresque. In an autobiographical essay, "Reflections of a Gothic Mind," published in 1963, he claimed to be a bohemian Tory. Even as a boy he recalled being suspicious of change and longing for continuity. Nevertheless, he loved traveling and was an avid hiker. He loved to explore, on his own, neglected sites and forgotten byways wherever he happened to be. "A connoisseur of slums and strange corners," he wrote, "I have dwelt in more garrets and cellars, forest cabins and island hovels, than I can recall." He pictured himself a wandering and impecunious man of letters, but one "attached to orthodoxy in church and state." Unmarried until his mid-forties, the congenial Kirk loved stories and anecdotes but was also something of an ascetic, never drinking to excess and with no prurient stories to relate in his memoir.[77]

As a young man, Kirk worked summers at Henry Ford's Greenfield Village, meeting and coming to respect the old industrialist. After graduating from Michigan State College in 1940, he took a master's at Duke University in Durham, North Carolina. There he completed a master's thesis on John Randolph, the flamboyant antebellum Virginia statesman and states' rights ideologue, and developed an attachment to the South. While at Duke, he traveled throughout the coastal South—visiting Charleston—and hiking in the North Carolina Piedmont. In the winter of 1941, he read *I'll Take My Stand*. He had previously read Davidson's *Attack on Leviathan* while in college, remarking to a friend that it was "Southern agrarianism at its almost-best."[78]

Despite the attention he has received as a New Conservative or "traditionalist," Kirk is a far better exemplar of the midwestern individualism that defined the mental world of the Old Right. He scorned unions, disliked bureaucracy, and opposed the expanding powers of the federal government. As a teenager, Kirk disapproved of Franklin D. Roosevelt and joined the anti–New Deal Liberty League. He expressed displeasure at big business, which he knew through his work in the payroll division of the massive River Rouge Ford plant, where he was transferred after Greenfield Village was closed early in World War II. During the war, he expressed disgust at the relocation of Japanese Americans in a letter to his friend William McCann. He opposed American entry into the war and had voted for socialist Norman Thomas in 1944 because of his anti-interventionist stance on the war. This midwestern conservative, however, had much sympathy for the South. When hearing of federal legislation designed to outlaw the poll tax in the South, Kirk expressed his opposition to McCann: "Virginia has preserved the highest level of political integrity in the South—and perhaps in the nation—largely by means of poll-tax restrictions; but senators and representatives will vote for any infamy, so long as [it] gives them a chance to roar."[79]

At Duke Kirk first became familiar with the social conservatism of the eighteenth-century Irishman Edmund Burke, and while stationed with the Chemical Warfare Service in Utah during the war, Kirk found himself experiencing a religious impulse. Burke's strictures against Enlightenment rationalism began to take a firmer hold on him. It was here, he later claimed, that he recognized the "Gothic" nature of his mind, its medieval "temper and structure." After the war, he taught off and on at Michigan State and completed a doctoral dissertation at St. Andrews University in Scotland.[80] In Scotland and England Kirk imbibed the sort of ordered and ancient (and fraying) traditions that were most congenial to his mind.[81] He chose as his dissertation topic the Anglo-American conservative tradition; the massive manuscript became *The Conservative Mind*.

The success of *The Conservative Mind* far exceeded its publisher's expectations. With the aid of a positive review in the *New York Times* by Gordon Keith Chalmers, the president of Kenyon College (and the man responsible for bringing Ransom to that institution), and a subsequent substantial treatment in *Time* magazine, for which Whittaker Chambers was partially responsible, the book attained wide notice and went through three printings before the year was out. William A. Rusher, longtime publisher of the *National Review*, remembered Kirk's book, as well as Friedrich A. Hayek's attack on government planning, *The Road to Serfdom* (1944), and Chambers's *Witness*, as influential in his conversion from a moderate, Republican Wall Street lawyer to a conservative activist. "Kirk introduced me to the traditionalist heritage of Burkean conservatism," Rusher recalled, "which dovetailed neatly with any instinctive hostility to the scientistic, programmatic bent of all forms of Marxist socialism, including communism." Kirk's book was published at just the right moment; conservatives subsequently installed it in their postwar canon. "With the advent of Russell Kirk," George H. Nash observed, "the new conservative or traditionalist segment of the renascent American Right reached full bloom."[82]

Kirk's conservatism is summed up in two sentences from his *Program for Conservatives*: "There is an order which holds all things in their places, Burke says; it is made for us, and we are made for it. The reflective conservative, far from denying the existence of this eternal order, endeavors to ascertain its nature, and to find his place in it."

This faith in a definable and eternal cosmic order, combined with a defense of the social elite, demarcates the heart of Kirk's conservatism.[83] *The Conservative Mind* was, in many ways, a defense of elitism. Reason was not an effective guide to political action, Kirk argued. Rather, one had to rely on established institutions and practices. It was the statesman's special office to know when prudent change was required. The "leader" loomed large in Kirk's book. Every thought and act of the people were influenced by some idea or leader. Indeed, without ideas and leaders, Kirk held, people would not rightly exist: "In the absence of such a leaven, the people subsist only as an amorphous mass of loosely cohering atoms, a tapioca-pudding state, which social planners contemplate with equanimity." To trust the people in the abstract was an "act of reckless faith far more credulous than medieval relic-veneration," Kirk declared. Kirk was unrelentingly elitist, larding his work with encomiums to the British upper class and calls for rule by a natural aristocracy.[84]

The Conservative Mind was intended as a history of the prescriptive philosophy of Edmund Burke. Kirk attributed great achievements to conservative ideas, especially those of Burke. "Burke's ideas did more than establish islands in the sea of radical thought: they provided the defences of conservatism, on a great scale, that still stand and are not liable to fall in our time," Kirk argued. Burke's heirs were a strikingly eclectic (and in many ways antithetical) set of political thinkers, novelists, and philosophers whom Kirk admired: all the leading Adamses; the Federalists; southern states'-rights theorists John Randolph and John C. Calhoun; the English romantics George Gissing, Walter Scott, and Samuel Coleridge; the American Tory James Fenimore Cooper; Alexis de Tocqueville, the sole Continental thinker Kirk treated; New Englanders John Quincy Adams, Orestes Brownson, and Nathaniel Hawthorne; Victorian legal theorists Henry Maine and James Stephen; the Tory statesman Benjamin Disraeli; and the New Humanists Irving Babbitt and Paul Elmer More, among others. As Bernard Crick observed, Kirk had gathered together under the label conservative "as weird a collection of unlikelies as ever went to sea in a sieve."[85]

The Conservative Mind, however, was less a history than a melodrama of ideas. There was little analysis in the work. Kirk proceeded from thinker to thinker, highlighting aspects of their thought, often giving extended extracts of their original writings, thereby assimilating them into the Burkean tradition. He gave no attention to the overall structures of a specific thinker's ideas, to contradictions within individual thinkers or between them, or to historical context. The entire book proceeded on a high level of generality, rarely descending from the plane of abstracted ideas.

Kirk attempted to outline a coherent prescriptive philosophy as an alternative to radicalism. Behind all political problems lay religious and moral issues, for Kirk believed that politics should be merely the application of divine will—the "Justice which is above nature." One had to rely on faith and prescription to know the divine pattern. At the heart of Kirk's sensibility, however, was a nostalgia for a lost past. Kirk warned of the potential "Americanization" of the world, expressing disgust at a cheap American culture founded on immediate gratification. Like Tate, Kirk lamented the decline of a premodern culture of unity, in which religion, art, and popular interests were part of a harmonious whole. In its place, he claimed, was "social boredom" or "social fatigue," exhibited in the pursuit of sensual or material gratifications, even to the exclusion of higher, spiritual ends and needs.[86]

Kirk wrote about Scotland and England the way Davidson wrote about the South. The Britain Kirk loved was the Britain of the eighteenth and nineteenth centuries, which he observed in quiet deliquescence as he hiked the highlands of Scotland while a student at St. Andrews. "Few places in Britain cling more affectionately to the old way," he observed of St. Andrews. It was fitting, he observed, that "cozy" was a Scottish word, for that is how Kirk felt in the tiny Gothic town and in the land to which he could trace his own ancestors. Kirk feared that the postwar British order, with its government planning and the destruction of ancient buildings in favor of new working-class housing, would destroy the "face of Britain" as it existed in his imagination and in such vestiges as Edmund Burke's decayed home. He found the new towns built for English workers in the coal-mining regions arid and monotonous, like suburbia transplanted in the countryside.[87]

The strong "chain of social continuity, linking generation with generation," was no stronger than in Britain, Kirk believed, and British planners would do well to conform their plans so as to renew it. To break the chain would have serious consequences. Perhaps bearing this in mind, in the 1960s Kirk married, converted to Roman Catholicism, and proceeded to limit his wanderings to the vicinity of Mecosta, planting an orchard and choosing to put down roots in his ancestral home. "To plant a tree, in our age when the expectation of change commonly seems greater than the expectation of continuity, is an act of faith," he declared. "No matter how far a man strays, it is well that his home should remain a place where his ancestors lie buried."[88]

Kirk also admired the Agrarians, styling himself at times a "northern Agrarian." *The Conservative Mind* contained a mention of Davidson and Tate. Kirk befriended neo-Agrarian Richard Weaver and in the mid-1950s was interested in having Tate as literary editor of the conservative intellectual journal he wished to establish (and which later became *Modern Age*). Kirk and Davidson became correspondents and friends; Kirk lectured at Vanderbilt in October 1955. Davidson, who actively opposed desegregation in the South, saw that issue "involved organically" with the problems he felt Kirk was addressing. After receiving two of Kirk's books in the mail, Davidson assured Kirk he would be "proselyting [*sic*] for [him]." "Your books are a great solace to me," he wrote. For his part, in 1956 Kirk declared Davidson's *Attack on Leviathan* the most neglected book of the past twenty-five years. "It is more than the chief accomplishment of the talented group called the Southern Agrarians: it is the most telling analysis in our time of the dread strength of Leviathan, that oppressive centralization which stifles liberty and art and all the proliferating variety of civilized existence."[89]

Although strikingly antimodern, Kirk upheld the importance of tradition and the need for renewed authority in philosophical terms. Kirk's instincts were those of a midwestern conservative, while his tastes and intellectual predilections were decidedly those of a British Victorian. He deprecated the desiccated landscape and mind-numbing bureaucracies of industrial capitalism, but, rather than attack the economic system itself, he lamented the growth of the centralized state and the decline of traditional values, customs, and moral authorities. He posed little challenge to Buckley's effort to assume control of the Right and, indeed, wrote for the *National Review*.

Kirk's sweeping defense of a Christian social order and of Western civilization in general was representative of a strong tendency on the right. A number of the Agrarians were, simultaneously, draining Agrarianism of its radicalism and interpreting it, along the same lines, as a conservative defense of the ideas and values of Western civilization. Davidson promoted this retrospective reinterpretation of Agrarianism. He was in general agreement with Tate and Brooks in their emphasis on the role of Christianity in their analysis of Agrarianism. "There can hardly be such a thing as a 'society,' in any true sense, without religion as the all-pervasive arbiter of value," he declared in the 1952 *Shenandoah* symposium. Davidson did not forsake the South, which remained for him more than an image of fading premodern social organization. He continued to hold that the South retained a superior way of life with strong bonds of family and religion, the wide ownership of property, and a hardy political conservatism. He also retained his southern prejudices. Ransom had pointed to the increasing role of blacks as consumers as a positive change in the South, a sign that the racial problem was easing. He urged southerners to move quickly toward giving the Negro equal rights. Davidson chose the rise of states' rights parties as a recent positive sign in the South.[90] But, in the 1950s, Davidson sought also to universalize the South and transform it into a symbol of traditionalism. In defending the South, Davidson now held, the Agrarians were upholding the endangered values of the West. Like Kirk, Davidson embraced the language and rhetoric of traditionalism as well as Buckley's conservative coalition. Kirk venerated old England; Davidson upheld the idea of the South.

Throughout the 1950s and after, Davidson cast his social and literary criticism in the rhetoric of tradition and reconceptualized Agrarianism as a form of organic traditionalism. "A traditional society is a society that is stable, religious, more rural than urban, and politically conservative," he argued in a 1950 essay. "Family, blood-kinship, clanship, folk-ways, custom, community, in such a society, supply the needs that in a non-traditional or progressive society are supplied at great cost by artificial devices like training schools and government agencies."[91] His second collection of essays, *Still Rebels, Still Yankees* (1957), contained section headings such as "Tradition and Experiment in Modern Poetry," "Tradition versus Antitradition in Prose Fiction," and "The Oral Tradition: Ballad, Folksong, and Myth." Indeed, Davidson resisted reprinting sectional pieces that had appeared in *The Attack on Leviathan* but that his publisher insisted on including in the later volume (one of which even supplied the title of the volume). "I got tired of arguing and let it go at that," he confided to Brooks. "But I think the title is a little misleading in certain respects. I really wanted this book to be wholly about the tradition v. anti-tradition theme in literature and the arts." Explaining the theme of the book to his editor on its publication, Davidson declared that tradition is "the living continuum that makes society and civilization possible" whereas "anti-tradition" is "the disintegrative principle that destroys society and civilization in the name of science and progress."[92]

Davidson presented his postwar revision of Agrarianism as the inaugural Eugenia Dorothy Blount Lamar Memorial lectures in the fall of 1957 at Mercer University in Macon, Georgia. He chose as his topic the history of the Fugitive and Agrarian movements and presented Agrarianism as an affirmation of absolute moral values and of the Western Christian tradition. Tracing the development of the group from the time he arrived on the campus of Vanderbilt University in 1909, Davidson stressed the shared assumptions of the group of eager and passionate young men who gathered periodically to discuss ideas and, later, poetry. They possessed a common understanding of people, nature, and God, an understanding derived from their culture. As poets, they soon came to realize that art requires a set of underlying religious beliefs. The form requires the myth. Thus,

Davidson argued, it was natural that he, Ransom, and Tate gradually saw the necessity of supporting the "traditional, believing society" of the South. In support of Tate's own retrospective reevaluation of Agrarianism as a form of Christian humanism, Davidson, too, suggested that Agrarianism was really concerned with the defense of the Christian faith.[93]

Davidson's thought had been converging with that of the broader American Right since his attacks on the federal leviathan in the 1930s. Deferring to the conservative ideology of the 1950s, Davidson portrayed Agrarianism as a response to *liberal* (not northern) attacks on the South. Davidson used the South as a synecdoche for Western civilization. It was not merely the South that was being assaulted, Davidson declared:

> It was the American political and governmental system in general. Not only religious bigotry in the South, but religion and religious institutions as such. Not only the meagreness of Southern educational provisions, but the ideal of liberal education itself. Not only the shallowness of Southern achievement in literature and the arts, but the validity of the entire Western tradition of literature and the arts, from Homer on down. Not only the disordered civilization of agriculture and industry, then admittedly unpromising in the South, but the basic American principle of free enterprise in labor, agriculture, and industry.

In Davidson's careful rewriting of the history of the movement, the Agrarians became defenders of the South and southern values, which meant they were defenders of imperiled Western cultural values at the same time. The primary villains were not northeastern industrialists but collectivists, materialists, and secularists.[94]

One of the more pronounced misconceptions that Davidson introduced into the history of the Agrarian movement had to do with the influence of the 1925 Scopes trial in Dayton, Tennessee, which tested that state's prohibition of the teaching of evolution in schools. Davidson linked the origins of *I'll Take My Stand* to the Agrarians' disgust with the trial in order to reinforce his argument that Agrarianism was, at bottom, a defense of a Christian perspective. As early as 1949, Davidson had planted the notion that the Scopes trial was one of the incidents that sparked the southern fervor of the Agrarians. In a long response to the draft of an essay by Richard Weaver on Agrarianism, Davidson commented, "The Dayton trial, by the way, was one of the events that turned the Fugitives into Agrarians." Weaver inserted a footnote into his typescript reflecting this information, albeit exaggerating its importance on his own: "It is most instructive to know that the Scopes 'anti-evolution' trial, which the press of two continents made into an unparalleled sensation, was the decisive factor in turning the Nashville group against scientific rationalism." The supposed connection was repeated by both Davidson and Andrew Lytle at the Fugitives' reunion in 1956. Previously, it had made its way into an article on the Fugitives by one of Davidson's students, Louise Cowan, in 1955. Davidson alluded to the Dayton trial again in his 1957 lectures, suggesting that there was "something more, perhaps, than a merely symbolical connection" between the Scopes trial and *I'll Take My Stand*. The trial, he argued, made it clear to both Ransom and himself "how difficult it was to be a Southerner in the twentieth century."[95] Since 1957, this connection has been repeated by a wide variety of historians and critics.[96]

Davidson's later memory that the Scopes trial was important to instigating Agrarianism was almost surely exaggerated.[97] Even granting that Scopes-inspired attacks on southern backwardness by writers such as H. L. Mencken fed Davidson's fierce southern pride and defensiveness, at the time of the trial Davidson held the rather conventional opinions about evolution of a moderate, liberal southern academic and was indifferent to organized religion.[98] A month before the trial, Davidson took the Carroll County Teachers' Association to task in his *Nashville Tennessean* book column for their hostility to Hendrik Van Loon's *Story of Mankind:* "If people are going to begin to rule out all books whatsoever that make use of the evolutionary hypothesis in presenting the history of man, not only biological studies, but literary studies, will have to be strenuously expurgated." Further, Davidson was aware of the perceptions of the South to which the trial would give rise. If Davidson was affronted, as he later claimed, by northern reaction to the trial, he most assuredly saw it coming:

> In the name of intelligence and common-sense, in the name of culture and progress, in the name of true religion which is broad enough to abide and absorb the truths of science without depending upon a militant, reckless, and narrow dictatorship for its subsistence, is it not time to resist with open speech and active endeavor this effort on the part of Tennesseans to plunge their own state back into the darkness of the Middle Ages? Is it not time for progressive minded people to put themselves on record, so that whether the victory be lost or won, the outside world may know that Tennessee is not a total fog of Bryanism?

There is no evidence that Davidson reacted to the Scopes trial at the time by vigorously defending religious absolutes. Later in 1925 Davidson commented on an article critical of antievolutionism by his department chair, Edwin Mims; it had shown, Davidson argued, that Tennessee had "more progressives than an uninformed person might think."[99]

Davidson's reinterpretation of Agrarianism laid the groundwork for an antiliberal neo-Agrarianism that some conservative thinkers would find attractive. For Davidson and those who followed his interpretation, the Old South became an image of a culture marked by spiritual wholeness and the union of art and life. Much of their rhetoric was indebted to Allen Tate, whose understanding of the southern spiritual heritage shaped his critical writings on the southern literary renascence. He argued that the efflorescence of brilliant southern writing between the 1920s and 1950s was the product of the transition from a premodern to a modern social world. This transition was delayed in the South because of the Civil War and the South's prolonged economic recovery, as well as the South's peculiar social heritage. The southern renascence, he declared, was a "backward glance" at a fading culture.[100]

The attraction of Tate's formulations in the postwar context, even for non-southerners, is illustrated by the engagement of the Canadian critic Marshall McLuhan with the Agrarians. Prior to his celebrated analysis of the mass media in the 1960s, McLuhan shared the Agrarians' antipathy to modern industrial society. Attracted to G. K. Chesterton as an undergraduate in the 1930s, McLuhan had joined the Distributists while on fellowship at Cambridge (where he studied under I. A. Richards and F. R. Leavis). While in England, McLuhan not only became a New Critic but also met Chesterton and began reading Jacques Maritain. He converted to Catholicism in 1936. Thus, McLuhan joined the Catholic Distributist milieu so important to Tate and sympathetic to Agrarianism. In "The Southern Quality," composed for an essay contest Tate instigated while editing the *Sewanee Review*, McLuhan argued that the South possessed a lesson for the rest of the world. The South, he claimed, exemplified a humanist culture, where the ideas of scholars and intellectuals actually attained social efficacy, filtering throughout the wider culture. Southern writers from William Byrd of Westover to the present had insisted on a "direct connection with the taproot of classical humanism and Ciceronian *humanitas* and eloquence." McLuhan was captivated by the South, having traveled to Nashville to meet with Davidson, Owsley, and a former pupil of the Agrarians then teaching at Vanderbilt, Richmond Beatty. "There does seem to exist some sort of pre-established harmony between me and your friends which can't be explained in terms of my own background," McLuhan wrote Tate. "It is a very strange thing to find oneself more at home among new acquaintances than one ever has been with the people one is accustomed to." [101]

In McLuhan's expansive vision, the South was a surviving remnant of Ciceronian humanism, opposed to the rationalist mainstream of Western civilization (the "autonomous dialectics and ontological nominalism"), best represented, he believed, in the New England mind. [102] The Canadian fell completely for the Agrarian myth; a revival of Agrarianism, conceived of as Christian humanism, was imperative. The South was a synecdoche for the most essential aspects of Western civilization. The United States' use of atomic weapons, McLuhan wrote Tate one day after the dropping of the second bomb on Nagasaki, was justification for rejecting the Allies' "exceedingly dubious 'cause.' " Civilization, he declared, had not survived the Second World War. The use of the bomb, he wrote in his essay, had shown for all to see "the abdication of all personal and individual character from the political and economic spheres." "The destructive energy postulated by the revolutionaries is here," McLuhan wrote, "and it is vastly in excess of any available human wisdom or political ingenuity to accommodate it." [103] It was in this context that McLuhan saw the "chivalric South" as the bastion of civilization in the English-speaking world. The South was a convenient and compelling symbol in a distressing time. [104]

The idea of a unique southern "quality" that would serve as a humanistic restraint in an age in which technology escaped human control took root among the Agrarians and their followers, including many southern literary scholars. Brainard Cheney, a political journalist, novelist, and playwright from Tennessee who was close to the Agrarians, argued in 1958 that Agrarianism was a defense of metaphysics against materialism. The ultimate solution to the moral crisis of the modern world lay beyond the South, however. Industrialism cannot be avoided, Cheney averred. "We have to go back further into our origins, our source of motivation, than the tradition of the gentleman, Southern or otherwise," Cheney wrote. "We have to conjure with greater Power. We have to go back to our Christian heritage. I am looking for Christians with the blood of martyrs in their veins, and ready to spill it." [105]

Russell Kirk and Davidson shared a common diagnosis of modern society's ills. Both emphasized the decline of rooted, traditional communities. Yet Kirk's evocation of the Scottish or English countryside was remote for most Americans. Kirk's proposed conservatism was an unencumbered and freestanding *pietas*, the "veneration of man's sacral associations and of the wisdom of man's ancestors." [106] His poli-

tics of rooted identity excluded no one; it was ultimately rooted in
the general history of the West less than that of any particular region
in the United States. While Kirk was decrying the homogenization
and sterility of modern America, his broad and inclusive traditionalism was suited to citizens of an Americanized nowhere. He shared a
quality of Irving Babbitt and Paul Elmer More that had so annoyed
Ransom and Tate in the 1920s — the schoolmaster's trait of disengage-
ment from the realities of contemporary culture. Kirk's highest attachment was to the generalized concepts of tradition, hierarchy, and
piety.

Peter Viereck criticized the Agrarians in the 1950s for possessing
something of this same quality of rootlessness. A conservative must be
rooted, he argued, and for Viereck, the liberal tradition was the only
true root in American society. The southern culture the Agrarians
venerated was dead, and thus their movement was purely nostalgic, he
declared. The more extreme contributors to *I'll Take My Stand*, whom
he refrained from naming, fell into the class of "doctrinaire counter-
revolutionaries," of whom he wrote: "Theirs becomes an unhistorical
appeal to history, a traditionless worship of tradition, a rootless appeal for roots." [107] But the distinctive culture and values of the South
were not nearly so dead as Viereck and others would have had it.

After World War II, however, the radical conservatism of Agrarianism faded; the conservative movement marginalized any right-wing
critique of industrial capitalism, whether intellectual or popular.
Neo-Agrarianism would be defined more by its intransigent defense
of the South, and traditionalist conservatives focused their attention
on ideas, not concrete social or economic institutions. The fusionist
conservatism of Buckley's *National Review* emerged triumphant. Attempting to make Agrarianism a conservative philosophy with wide
appeal, Davidson found at least some allies outside the South. Amid
anxieties over the nature of American individualism in the postwar
years, Davidson and his neo-Agrarian followers remade Agrarianism
as a form of traditionalist conservatism. The intellectual who most
decisively shaped this neo-Agrarianism was Richard Weaver. A student of Ransom's at Vanderbilt, Weaver shaped a political philosophy
based on a rooted individualism. In doing so, he was attempting to
bridge conflicting impulses to both particularism and universalism in
the Agrarian discourse, as well as a deeper, lingering gulf between the
romantic southernism of Davidson and the more astringent intellectualism of Ransom and Tate.

CHAPTER SIX

Agrarian in Exile
Richard M. Weaver and the Philosophy of Order

*Man is free in proportion as his surroundings have a determinate
nature, and he can plan his course with perfect reliance upon that
determinateness.*
    Richard M. Weaver, *Ethics of Rhetoric*

Sometimes the claim of exile rings hollow. In *Emigrants and Exiles*
(1985), his study of Irish emigration to America, Kerby Miller noticed
the unusual degree to which Irish emigrants thought of themselves as
political exiles, involuntarily fleeing the oppression of British tyranny
and relegated to a life of loneliness and misery. The fact is that most
Irish emigrants were voluntary, not involuntary. They left Ireland
for the United States in search of better opportunities, many drawn
to America more by their own dreams of a better life than by resistance to English oppression. Relative to other immigrant groups,
furthermore, few Irish returned to their native land. The sense of
exile can be as much a product of emotion as of reality, a rationalization that serves to make the carefully calculated decision to break
old connections seem beyond one's ability to control.[1] A widespread
and acute homesickness was ingrained in the minds of Irish emigrants
through such devices as the "American wakes"—night-long community gatherings that featured music, drink, food, and dance mixed
with lamentation and grief for the departing family member or vil-
lager. Through the motif of exile, Miller argued, the emigrant justified a break with his or her homeland, and, at the same time, those
left behind imprinted Irish memories and values on the emigrants. As
Miller speculated, there is something in the exile motif that appeals to
everyone's desire to belong. "It may be that we all—men and women
in modern societies—are in some sense exiles from the better, hap-
pier lands of our dreams," Miller wrote, "and that Ireland's past emi-

grants and present inhabitants only more starkly or poignantly reflect a universal dichotomy between aspiration and achievement."[2]

Richard M. Weaver was an exile in spirit, if not in fact. His thought and career reflect a balancing of the contending impulses within the Agrarian tradition. His primary Agrarian mentor was John Crowe Ransom, yet Weaver was eventually attracted to the southernism more characteristic of Donald Davidson. Like Davidson, he helped construct the idea of the South as a synecdoche for Western civilization. Agrarianism molded Weaver's mind, and he, in turn, decisively reshaped it. One student of southern letters labeled Weaver the "Saint Paul" of Agrarianism.[3] Weaver recalled his conversion to Agrarianism and the decision to pursue a Ph.D. in southern literature as a decisive moment of personal freedom. Yet he chose to make his career in a major northern urban center, and the major works he published during his lifetime were not about the South exclusively or the Agrarian tradition. His primary intellectual endeavor through the early years of his professional life was to leave the South behind and to fashion a conservative philosophy of order relevant to a national audience. In the process, Weaver established an identity as a conservative, not as an Agrarian.

Weaver is a difficult historical figure to understand; he was private by nature and a lifelong bachelor, and records that shed light on his emotions and inner life are only now being collected and archived. It does seem likely, however, that this reserved and austere man had some difficulty reconciling his intense feeling for the South with the freedom and convenience of life in the North.[4] As he aged and the times changed, Weaver eventually felt the need to reaffirm his southern heritage. Despite his endeavor to universalize Agrarian ideology, Weaver used his philosophy to defend racial segregation; and, at the end of his life, he intended to return to the South.

Richard Weaver's historical significance lies in his contribution to the conservative movement. The book on which his reputation primarily rests, *Ideas Have Consequences*, published in 1948, is a prime example of the post–World War II efflorescence of conservative thinking. He was instrumental, for example, in linking the postwar critique of a mass society to the conservative movement. George H. Nash, the preeminent historian of conservative thought in the United States, chose Weaver as a representative figure of the traditionalist segment of the movement. Sociologist Jerome L. Himmelstein, in *To the Right: The Transformation of American Conservatism* (1990), suggested that *Ideas Have Consequences* was "probably the most revered and influential" of traditionalist texts. Historian Forrest McDonald saw the book as an Agrarian form of traditionalism; many conservatives, he argued,

view *Ideas Have Consequences* as the "source and origin of the contemporary American conservative movement." In addition, Weaver's
appeal transcended the divisions of the conservative movement. Although usually thought of as a traditionalist, he was eulogized at his
death by the libertarian *New Individualist Review* as one of the most
important conservative intellectuals in America.[5]

Weaver was, by most accounts, a modest, gentle, shy, and quiet
man who lived much of his life alone. His sister Polly remembered
Weaver as a "strange guy" and "lonely fellow." He never married and
spent the bulk of his career as a professor at the University of Chicago. After moving to Chicago, he often returned to North Carolina in the summers, and in 1953 he purchased a home in Weaverville,
North Carolina, the Weaver family's ancestral hometown. Weaver
was born in Asheville, North Carolina, in 1910. His father, Richard
Malcolm Weaver Sr., a gregarious and outgoing man, was the junior
partner in a livery stable and automobile agency in Asheville. The
elder Weaver died of a stroke in 1915, when his oldest son, Richard,
was five. Weaver's mother, Carrye, widowed with two boys and two
girls, eventually moved the family to her hometown of Lexington,
Kentucky. She became manager of the millinery department at her
brother's clothing store, Embry and Company. (She had actually
founded Embry and Company as a millinery shop in 1902 at the age
of twenty-eight, about six years before her marriage to Weaver.) The
children were often left in the care of housekeepers and spent summers with their aunt back in Weaverville. Weaver remained devoted
to his mother all his life. He assumed primary responsibility for her
about 1944; after 1953, she as well as two siblings and a nephew lived
in his home in Weaverville.[6] As an adult, even while teaching in Chicago, Weaver fostered a connection to Weaverville. His great-aunt
wrote of Weaver in a family history, "He enjoys a bit of his heritage of
loving the land, makes a garden[,] knows every fruit tree and grape-
vine by name and manages to get home at the right time to prune,
spray and gather the fruits of his labors."[7] He often took automobile
trips with his mother when on break.[8]

At the University of Chicago, Weaver's life was ascetic and regi-
mented, although there is no reason to believe unhappy. The author
of an obituary for a University of Chicago publication recalled a quiet
man who kept people at a distance by his "reticence, his sense of decorum, his rather formal courtesy, and by a calm stability which seemed
to invite neither offers of aid nor the exchange of confidences." Weaver's life, the writer observed, tended to be "confined within a special
and self-imposed routine." He taught his classes early in the morning, left his office for lunch at the same time every day, usually to eat
at the same place (a school dining hall, the closing of which made

Weaver quite upset), returned in the midafternoon to do his work, and went home in the evening to his apartment in a local residential hotel. (He rented an apartment in his final two years in Chicago.) Weaver lived as a boarder in Chicago, but he was not a recluse; he enjoyed good conversation and was congenial. He also returned often to the warm relations of the small town of Weaverville. All the same, Weaver enjoyed his life in Chicago. One colleague recalled that he shared in the conviviality and drink of social gatherings, sometimes singing folksongs or telling stories. His fellow conservative and friend Willmoore Kendall was disgusted with accounts that tended to portray Weaver as solitary and dislocated. (In a remembrance, Russell Kirk, a friend of Weaver's, actually quoted an acquaintance who suggested that Weaver was becoming "more like a little gnome every day.") Weaver was happy, enjoyed his friends, and loved Chicago, Kendall declared, walking home by a different path every day in order to see the city. Indeed, a colleague later remembered that Weaver had declared that no institution could tempt him to leave the University of Chicago—except Vanderbilt University.[9]

Weaver was intensely "southern," a friend recalled, even while attending college. Weaver described himself as "gloomy, ardent, stupid" on entering the University of Kentucky at age seventeen in 1928. The argumentative Weaver, who majored in English, was skilled in debate and tended to make his fellow students furious. As a student, Weaver gravitated toward progressive causes, winning a debate sponsored by the Intercollegiate Peace Association in May 1929 with an address entitled "Our Big Business of War" and helping to organize the school's Liberal Club. As president of the club in 1932, Weaver led a protest against local officials in Bell County who barred representatives from eastern colleges who were attempting to examine conditions in the strike-torn coal fields of eastern Kentucky. The university's Men's Student Council condemned the Liberal Club for its stance, and thirty-four students and alumni petitioned the university's president in protest at the group's actions. Upon graduation, Weaver became secretary of the local chapter of the American Socialist Party. He spent two years in the party but did not particularly enjoy his new associates. Unable to find a job or obtain a fellowship to continue his studies elsewhere after graduation, Weaver enrolled in the University of Kentucky's graduate program in English. The next year, however, he won a scholarship to Vanderbilt University. Weaver had been aware of the Agrarians since at least August 1931, when, in a book column coauthored for the student newspaper with his friend Clifford Amyx, he remarked on *I'll Take My Stand*, calling it a "striking if ineffectual rally against the onward sweep of industrialism." He completed a master's thesis in 1934 under John Crowe Ransom and stayed on two years with a teaching fellowship. He intended to write a dissertation on John Milton, but, needing work, he left Nashville to teach, first at Alabama Polytechnic Institute (later Auburn University) and later at Texas A&M University in College Station. The dissertation languished.[10]

When Weaver first arrived at Vanderbilt, the Agrarian agitation was in full bloom. *I'll Take My Stand* had been published just three years before. Although enthusiasm had subsided immediately after the symposium's publication, some of the Agrarians were experiencing a second wind. In the fall of 1933, Ransom had begun to publish sections of his economic treatise. Tate, while patching together his marriage with Caroline, became more committed to Agrarianism as a practical program. And the Agrarians had found a national outlet for their writings in Seward Collins's *American Review*. Weaver chose as his master's thesis topic the Humanist controversies that had played such a significant role in the origins of Agrarianism.

The thesis was Weaver's first step in his reinterpretation of Agrarianism. The themes of the thesis were the position of humans in the world; the significance of "experience," a term rich in connotations for both modernist critics and their opponents at the time; and the problem of the origins of values. Weaver framed his discussion with Joseph Wood Krutch's *The Modern Temper* (1929), an account of the modern loss of values and the resulting cultural anxiety. The New Humanists had responded to this anxiety. Like Ransom and Tate, Weaver was very critical of them. Weaver shared Ransom's philosophical bent and was shaped by his teacher's preoccupations. The critique of Humanism in his thesis relied heavily on Ransom's own philosophical proclivities.[11]

The source of values, Weaver maintained, lay in the elemental flux of experience. The Humanists' repudiation of the world, then, led to an inadequate aesthetic theory. Weaver argued that the Humanists made an almost mystical affirmation of their values but that such a mystical stance was simply unpersuasive. In modern society, people were brought up to look for empirical proof of reality and values, which the New Humanists did not supply. Moreover, because they so discounted human experience, the Humanists belittled art, which, following Ransom and Tate, Weaver believed a distinctive form of knowledge. Humanist attempts to judge art by the moral lessons it embodied were misguided. Art did not teach simple moral lessons; it illuminated deep sources of value in human experience. The Humanists, with their shallow aesthetic theory, Weaver believed, failed to ap-

preciate that art contributed moral values only insofar as it reached
the deeper levels of human experience. "It is the world of reality which
is father to value," Weaver declared.[12]

In a 1953 autobiographical essay entitled "Up from Liberalism,"
Weaver recalled that he had come to Vanderbilt nominally socialist
but left feeling attracted to "the Agrarian ideal of the individual in
contact with the rhythms of nature, of the small-property holding,
and of the society of pluralistic organization." He was deeply influenced by Ransom's gentle tutelage and his philosophical musings on
religion and poetry, in particular his mythological treatment of religion in *God without Thunder*.[13] Weaver assimilated the basis of Ransom and Tate's scorn for what they considered an ineffectual New
Humanism and adopted some elements of their critical theory, but he
gradually moved away from the modernist sophistication of Ransom
and toward the deep identification with the South characteristic of
Donald Davidson. By 1940, unlike Ransom and Tate, he came to see
his southern heritage as somehow tied to the deeper sources of value.

In the autobiographical essay, Weaver highlighted two events in his
intellectual development. The first concerned Weaver's adoption of
the Agrarian outlook. The intellectual turning point in his life occurred, Weaver wrote, when he embraced Agrarianism while teaching
in Texas in 1939. He had completely repudiated the Left by this point.
("I am junking Marxism as not founded in experience," he wrote his
friend John Randolph.) Now, he woke up, converted to the "poetic
and ethical vision of life." Weaver's conversion experience, in his telling of it, occurred on the road: "I recall very sharply how, in the Autumn of 1939, as I was driving one afternoon across the monotonous
prairies of Texas to begin my third year in this post, it came to me
like a revelation that I did not *have* to go back to this job, which had
become distasteful, and that I did not *have* to go on professing the
clichés of liberalism, which were becoming meaningless to me." "It is
a great experience," Weaver observed, "to wake up at a critical junc-
ture to the fact that one does have a free will, and that giving up the
worship of false idols is a quite practicable proceeding." [14]

Weaver recounted his conversion to Agrarianism as a liberating
moment. It was a discovery that, at the age of twenty-nine, the pattern of his life had not yet been set, his life was not determined, and
he yet possessed a free will. ("I did not *have* to go back to this job. . . . I
did not *have* go on professing the clichés of liberalism.") His immediate impulse was to turn toward a deeper study of southern culture
and the southern past. He chose to pursue a Ph.D. in literature. "I
want to have a part in the re-evaluation of Southern culture which is
now under way," Weaver wrote the chair of the English Department
at Louisiana State University, preliminary to applying to its graduate

Richard M. Weaver.
(Courtesy Ted J. Smith III)

program. The "intoxicants of Progress and Development" had worn off in the country, and Weaver believed that the South held valuable lessons for the rest of the nation. On his application, he called himself a southern nationalist and declared his intention to "do an important piece of research in the history of [his] section." [15]

In December 1942, Weaver defended his dissertation, a study of postbellum southern writers titled "The Confederate South, 1865–1910: A Study in the Survival of a Mind and Culture." The thesis was directed by Cleanth Brooks, but only after Weaver's first adviser, the literary historian Arlin Turner, went into the military. Brooks later recalled giving only nominal direction to the work. Weaver, thirty years of age at the time he entered the program in the fall of 1940, came to the university with a clear idea of what he wanted to do. [16]

In his dissertation Weaver attempted to interweave the cultural criticism of Ransom and Tate with Davidson's politics of southern identity. Shaped by Ransom's and Tate's writings on religion and myth in *God without Thunder* and *I'll Take My Stand*, Weaver interpreted the South as a living embodiment of premodern values. In the modern world, he believed, the individual became a democratic mass man, economics usurped politics and morals, relativism eroded moral standards, and religious orthodoxy crumbled under rampant skepticism. Unlike the Agrarians in *I'll Take My Stand*, however, Weaver talked less of the South as a concrete way of life than as a set of values, or a "mind." For the Agrarians in 1930, the South had been both a culture and a social economy; in Weaver's telling, it was a set of cultural values. There were no loving descriptions of country life or meticulous sketches of recognizable southern types. Rather, Weaver's model was Ransom's philosophical *God without Thunder*. The South became, in his hands, a set of myths that functioned to maintain social order and provide an agreeable way of life. The mind of the antebellum South, Weaver declared, had been rooted in feudal tradition, the code of chivalry, the concept of the gentleman, and a deep religiousness. A particular set of cultural beliefs, not socioeconomic institutions, defined the Confederacy.[17]

Weaver outlined a rudimentary cultural theory in the dissertation. Modernity stripped away the veils of culture, he argued, only to find that these veils themselves constituted culture. In a text of the study revised for publication in 1944–45 (although not published until after Weaver's death), he wrote, "When the men of the new order did strip aside these veils and found that there was nothing behind them, but that the reality had existed somehow in the willed belief, or the myth, they marked the beginning of modern frustration." Much like Ransom but less clearly a skeptic, Weaver conceived of religion as a necessary myth that revealed ontological truths. If we say "man lives by his myth," Weaver wrote, "by a projection of ideals, sentiments, and loyalties, which constitute the world of truth—not the world of nature—then the conservation of the pattern becomes obligatory, and the underminers of the faith and the mockers of the vision deserve the obloquy which has traditionally been theirs." This was Weaver's own unorthodox defense of religious orthodoxy: religion was one of the vital cultural "veils" that humans strip away at their own risk.[18]

Weaver was as cavalier in treating religious dogma as Ransom. He did not explore the intricacies of doctrine as Ransom had in *God without Thunder*, in part because his treatment of religion was only a small section of his overall work but also because his approach to the South was on the whole rather detached and abstract. Therefore he eulogized the piety of the Old South but not any particular religious doctrine. "Whether he was a Virginia Episcopalian, dozing in comfortable dogmatic slumber, or a Celt, transplanted to the Appalachian wilderness and responding to the wild emotionalism of the religious rally, he [the southerner] wanted the older religiousness of dreams and drunkenness—something akin to the rituals of the Medieval Church, and to the Eleusinian mysteries of the ancients," Weaver wrote. What the South possessed, Weaver argued in a 1943 article that echoed Ransom's contribution to *I'll Take My Stand*, was a piety that took the form of a "submissiveness of the will," a general respect for nature and institutions. The South for Weaver was a symbol of a premodern faith in absolute values that was endangered by modernity.[19]

Weaver returned again and again over the years to the idea of the South as a model of the "spirit of feudalism" and of "a rooted culture which viewed with dismay the anonymity and the social indifference of urban man." He blurred the distinction between past and present, suggesting that traits such as the older religiousness still characterized southern culture. "The typical Southerner," Weaver wrote in 1952, "is an authentically religious being if one means by religion not a neat set of moralities but a deep and even frightening intuition of man's radical dependence in this world." But from the mid-1940s on, Weaver more often than not in his published writings made no reference to the "stubborn humanism" of the South to buttress his own humanistic prescriptions. The South represented a set of cultural values, the metaphysical veils that unbelieving and empirically minded moderns pulled aside at their own peril. But veils were not peculiar to the South; rather, the entire heritage of Western Christianity was such a veil, and Weaver came to believe it was being pulled aside entirely too easily.[20]

The Agrarians believed that the Civil War meant the destruction of a revered way of life. Weaver came to see World War II in much the same terms, only it was not a region's way of life that was falling prey to the expansive, bourgeois culture of a neighbor but an entire civilization's institutions and values that were victims of the rationalizations and technologies of world war. "This war is not going to improve anything," Weaver wrote John Randolph. "We are going to get out of it poorer, more disillusioned, more bankrupt in purpose than ever before. . . . The war is like some giant automaton set going by an evil spirit. Nobody thinks it is creating anything, nobody wants it to go on, but nobody can stop it." Weaver's disillusionment was bitter, particularly after the dropping of the atomic bomb by the United States. He felt the bomb was "a final blow to the code of humanity. I cannot help thinking that we will suffer retribution for this." "The official lies, the cunningly manipulated hysteria, the repudiation of moral standards by sources we had been taught to respect most— these have been nauseating," Weaver lamented. Many on the left— including Dwight Macdonald, C. Wright Mills, and Lewis Mumford—were making the same arguments at the time. "The emperor or dictator, of completely pervasive authority, backed by an oligarchy of scientists—that is the situation into which forces are hurrying us," Weaver wrote in an epilogue that appeared in the posthumous edition of his dissertation. "The state becomes a monolith, rigid with fear that it has lost control of its destiny. We all stand today at Appomattox, and we are surrendering to a world which this hypostatized science has made in our despite." [21]

After completing his dissertation, Weaver returned to North Carolina and taught at North Carolina State University in Raleigh while living with his mother. Although he enjoyed his students, most of whom were young soldiers, Weaver desired to move on. Cleanth Brooks interceded with his friend Ronald S. Crane, the leader of the school of neo-Aristotelian critics at the University of Chicago, to help Weaver gain a position there. [22] The University of Chicago was a place of great intellectual ferment in the 1930s and 1940s, much of it inspired by its president, Robert M. Hutchins. Hutchins and the philosopher Mortimer Adler, whom he brought to Chicago in 1929, were critical of the modern academy, with its increasingly specialized disciplines, rigid departmental divisions, and scientifically oriented research. They sought to place general education in the classical liberal arts at the center of undergraduate education and were particularly enamored of the "Great Books" approach to teaching pioneered by the literary scholar John Erskine at Columbia University in the 1920s. Hutchins was in search of a source of moral certainty in the modern world. Convinced that theology could no longer be used to order higher education, he looked to philosophy to meet this need. [23]

In 1942, the University of Chicago approved Hutchins's plan for a four-year program that would combine the last two years of the University High School and the first two years of undergraduate College in an experiment in general education. In Hutchins's College, discussion of generally assigned texts displaced lecturing, and graduation depended on passing fourteen comprehensive examinations. The university recruited a separate teaching faculty, many without the standard academic credential of the Ph.D., to staff the College. Weaver received an appointment in 1944. At least in its early years, teaching at the College was an intense experience. The staff held weekly meetings to review the content of courses; students ruthlessly judged poor teaching by migrating to those sections taught by more effective faculty. Although Weaver thrived in this atmosphere, winning an award for outstanding teaching in 1949, there is little evidence to conclude that he played a leading role at a university that, by the 1950s, was home not only to the neo-Aristotelian criticism associated with Crane (a minor but influential formalist rival to the New Critics) but also to the natural-law political philosophers grouped around Leo Strauss and the rising Chicago School of neoclassical economists that included Milton Friedman. [24]

Nevertheless, it was on a fall morning in 1945 in his Ingleside Hall office that, according to Weaver, the second significant event in his intellectual life occurred. That morning Weaver jotted down a series of chapter headings for a book inspired by the "holocaust" through which the world had just passed. "The persistence of the fact of evil was then being underlined for me by the dreadful events of the Second World War," he wrote in "Up from Liberalism." Those notes became the basis of Weaver's most significant work, *Ideas Have Consequences*, published in 1948. Weaver was most disgusted by the Allied refusal to protect Finland from the Soviet Union in 1940 and the accords reached at the Yalta Conference. American war policy led Weaver, on the very cusp of the Cold War, to shift from an Agrarian to a more self-consciously conservative stance.[25]

The conduct of the war, Weaver believed, revealed the failure of chivalry, and this idea first suggested the thesis of *Ideas Have Consequences*. Chivalry symbolized the vital capacity of culture to constrain human passions and to limit individual aggressiveness. It was a cultural embodiment of a rooted and constrained individualism. The loss of chivalry, which Weaver dated to the nineteenth century, came to represent for him, too, a general decline in Western cultural standards. Any final vestige of chivalry was almost completely shattered, Weaver believed, by the massive bombing campaigns of World War II and the creation of the atom bomb. The advanced technology of war made a mockery of rules of combat; Allied capitulation to Soviet pressure was the betrayal of an earlier commitment.[26]

Weaver opposed Franklin D. Roosevelt's policy of unconditional surrender. It "impiously puts man in the place of God by usurping unlimited right to dispose of the lives of others," he wrote in *Ideas Have Consequences*. His opposition to unconditional surrender and his skepticism toward the atom bomb reflected similar sentiments of many partisans of the Old Right during and after World War II. Although in abeyance for a period after Pearl Harbor, the noninterventionist Right continued to be active throughout the war and was highly critical of the aggressive American foreign policy of the early Cold War years as well as Roosevelt's concessions to the Soviets at Yalta. One of the Old Right's most powerful voices was Robert R. McCormick and his *Chicago Tribune*, and it is noteworthy that Weaver openly and stoutly defended McCormick's editorial policies, to the chagrin of some of his University of Chicago associates. Although Weaver is often classified as one of the New Conservatives of the postwar period, in many ways he, like Russell Kirk, shared much of the worldview of this deep-rooted midwestern, small-town Right. Indeed, he participated in the postwar convergence of the Davidsonian stream of Agrarianism with the Old Right.[27]

The actual idea of writing a book on these issues seems to have originated in a conversation between Weaver, Brooks, and W. T. Couch, the former editor of the University of North Carolina Press. Weaver began writing in the fall of 1945 and wrote most of the first draft of the manuscript—which was variously called "Steps toward the Restoration of Our World" and "The Adverse Descent"—over the summer of 1946. Couch, who had become director of the University of Chicago Press, enthusiastically picked up the manuscript. His bid to get the publication committee's approval for the book was aided by a positive reader's evaluation from Brooks.[28] Much to Weaver's consternation the book was published as *Ideas Have Consequences*, a title Couch found more "popular" than Weaver's suggestions. Couch also solicited positive appraisals from Ransom, Paul Tillich, and Reinhold Niebuhr, the latter of whom called the book a "profound diagnosis of the sickness of our culture."[29] *Ideas Have Consequences* evoked strong responses, one reviewer labeling it a "pompous fraud" and "essentially evil." Others praised it; Clare Booth Luce supposedly bought ten copies to distribute to friends.[30]

Ideas Have Consequences was, in effect, an attempt to universalize Southern Agrarianism and signaled the shift of Weaver's attention away from the rationalizing effects of industrial capitalism to what he considered the weaknesses of the post-Enlightenment liberal philosophical tradition. In his book Weaver attacked the relativism of modern times, arguing that the modern person was a "moral idiot" and that humankind had endured a long descent since the fourteenth century, when William of Occam first successfully propounded the doctrine of nominalism, by which it was denied that universals have a real existence.[31] Rationalism had usurped religion and religious understandings of life. In the modern world, materialist social theories, various forms of social and economic determinism, and theories of psychological behaviorism were common currency. This was the process of the "adverse descent." The specter of world war drove Weaver to his pessimistic evaluation of the modern, much as it had a host of other cultural critics in the postwar years. "At the height of modern progress," Weaver observed, "we behold unprecedented outbreaks of hatred and violence; we have seen whole nations desolated by war and turned into penal camps by their conquerors; we find half of mankind looking upon the other half as criminal." The war was only a logical product of a widespread decline that had produced a pitiable modern person: "Look at him today somewhere in the warren of a great city. If he is with a business organization, the odds are great that he has sacrificed every other kind of independence in return for that dubious one known as financial. . . . Not only is this man likely to be a slave at his place of daily toil, but he is cribbed, cabined, and confined in countless ways, many of which are merely devices to make possible physically the living together of masses." [32]

Weaver intended, however, not only to indict modern culture but to argue that an objective basis of value was needed in order to undergird a renewed humanism. As early as 1942, he had stated that the world "will not regain order and stability until it returns to the kind of poetic-religious vision of life which dominated the Middle Ages." He wrote John Randolph in August 1945 that he felt the "essence of civilization is ethical." His already well-developed predilection to conceive of ideas as the driving force of history may well have been strengthened during the writing of *Ideas Have Consequences* by his friendship with his officemate at the University of Chicago, Pierre Albert Duhamel. Duhamel was well versed in medieval Catholic philosophers as well as contemporary Catholic critics, such as the Distributist Eric Gill. He and Weaver became fast friends and intellectual companions, often sharing drinks together at Duhamel's home on Saturday nights (sometimes in the company of guests such as Cleanth Brooks and Marshall McLuhan). [33] In an essay written shortly after the war, Weaver talked of humanism's need to "seek transcendental help"; humanistic actions must be "measured, pointed up, directed by some superior validating ideal." [34] Yet *Ideas Have Consequences* added nothing new to the Agrarians' argument that humanism was no substitute for religion. And because he limited his discussion to the most general terms of reference, Weaver did not strongly link a humanistic culture to larger socioeconomic structures, as the Agrarians had.

Nevertheless, Weaver incorporated the understanding of culture derived from his Vanderbilt and LSU writings into *Ideas Have Consequences*, including the idea of chivalry. Chivalry embodied a conception of "something spiritual which stood above war itself and included the two sides in any conflict." Weaver considered the medieval code of chivalry the most concrete example of a code of civilization that bound humans and set limits to their self-destructive impulses. Chivalry stood against the whole idea of total war. "The Christian soldier," Weaver had written in his dissertation, "must seek the verdict of battle always remembering that there is a higher law by which both he and his opponent will be judged, and which enjoins against fighting as the barbarian." It was just this code, the ancient human ability to "contain" war "*within* civilization," Weaver later observed, that had broken down in World War II. Although Weaver disliked the title of his book, the degree to which he saw intellect or mind as the moving force in cultural decline is striking. [35]

The first third of the book contained Weaver's theory of culture. Culture, Weaver argued, in a departure from Agrarianism, was less a product of social practices or the customs of small-town or rural life than a philosophical system, or set of rationalized sentiments, such as the code of chivalry. At the center of every culture, he asserted, lies an "intuitive feeling about the immanent nature of reality," what he termed a "metaphysical dream." This "dream," the term itself suggesting an aesthetic representation, was the source of value, "the sanction to which both ideas and beliefs are ultimately referred for verification." Once again Weaver argued that reason alone did not instruct as to good or bad, for reason could never be a source of value. "Sentiment" was "anterior" to reason. Rather, human judgments of right and wrong were always based on cultural "yea-saying." That is, notions of what was good were always based on what a culture defined as good, what was given higher status in some sort of cultural hierarchy. "A developed culture is a way of looking at the world through an aggregation of symbols," Weaver argued, "so that empirical facts take on significance and man feels that he is acting in a drama, in which the cruxes of decision sustain interest and maintain the tone of his being."[36]

A weak and flabby culture, one that was marked by sentimentality and the inability to make distinctions, would not contain visions of the good strong enough to bind human beings' destructive tendencies. We must cultivate an "unsentimental sentiment," Weaver declared, much in the vein of Reinhold Niebuhr's *Children of Light and Children of Darkness.* Only then would human reason have the basis for strong codes of morality. In a striking passage, Weaver defended the medieval theologians who had debated how many angels could stand on the point of a needle. This was not a ridiculous enterprise, he argued, for the underlying point to such questions was to define a system of teaching "with which they bound up their world." It produced a "heuristic principle" that "made one's sentiment toward the world rational, with the result that it could be applied to situations without plunging man into sentimentality on the one hand or brutality on the other." Human beings relied on formalized cultural codes to define their values and guide their behavior.[37]

With this argument, Weaver returned to a line of reasoning that had been present in Tate's early writings. Tate had conceived of religion as a product of human reason, but one based on an elemental perception of the pure flux of nature. Weaver spoke in very similar terms in *Ideas Have Consequences.* Man "conceptualizes in order to avoid an immersion in nature," Weaver declared. Weaver still believed that "experience," that modernist notion of the flux of pure sensation, was the source of all value. Yet Weaver no more came up with a means to make religion operative in the world than did the original Humanists. The strength of Agrarianism lay in its appeal to a particularistic culture. The Agrarians knew what they sought to preserve: the culture of the South. Weaver spoke in the most abstract of terms. In the wake of World War II, however, his ideas found a more attentive audience than had those of either the New Humanists or the Agrarians.

The second third of Weaver's book constituted an indictment of modern decadence, clearly marking his turn from Agrarianism to a traditionalist conservatism. Weaver believed that the end of social distinctions and social hierarchy led to social fragmentation and the creation of mass men. Further, specialization exacerbated the moral failings of the age. As men and women no longer understood the far-reaching effects of their actions, their sense of moral responsibility declined. He pointed to the thousands who labored unknowingly for the atom bomb project at Oak Ridge, Tennessee. "It is just possible that a few, and I should be willing to say a very few, had they known that their efforts were being directed to the slaughter of noncombatants on a scale never before contemplated, or to a perfection of brutality as we have defined the term, might have refused complicity," he argued. Chivalry is meaningless in such a context, in which the individual becomes something of an "ethical eunuch." "The chance that the world will not use atomic bombs if it goes on making them is infinitesimal," Weaver observed elsewhere in the book.[38]

Weaver argued that the mass media of print, radio, and film, what he called the "Great Stereopticon," purveyed diverting but ultimately bland and deadening fare to the public. There was no greater force that undercut the kind of culture that he deemed vital to the support of a metaphysical dream. Advertisements or variety shows jarringly followed announcements of the devastation of great cities, reducing the moral import of American actions. Human suffering and social crisis become, Weaver charged, perverse sources of entertainment: "The extremes of passion and suffering are served up to enliven the breakfast table or to lighten the boredom of an evening at home."[39] Finally, Weaver condemned the "spoiled-child psychology" promulgated by a consumption-oriented middle class. Although admiring of producers and competitive capitalists, Weaver decried what he considered the materialistic and acquisitive mind-set of the middle class. He disdained popular demands for economic reform or economic democracy, dismissing them as self-aggrandizing demands of those who had been told they deserved rewards for no labor.[40]

In the final third of the book, Weaver articulated the remaining resources for a humanist society. In at least one aspect a metaphysical dream was active, for men and women still respected the "last metaphysical right" of private property. Weaver retained enough of the original Agrarianism, however, to distinguish concrete forms of property from abstract forms, such as ownership of stocks. He saw corporate capitalism, the rationalization of industry, and much that transpired in the name of private enterprise as anathema. Instead, he articulated the Distributist position, hailing the moral value of independent farms, local businesses, and family homes. To counter the descent into barbarism, Weaver called for the restoration of philosophical realism and the cultivation of piety, the "discipline of the will through respect." This entailed a respect for nature as something greater than the individual ego, perhaps meaning the curtailing of technology but definitely a revival of chivalry.[41]

By arriving at the logic of Donald Davidson's politics of rooted identity without Davidson's immersion in regionalism, Weaver decisively shifted the terms of the Agrarian discourse. His thought represents a neo-Agrarian position, one more oriented to philosophy than to economics, and one that attributed the problems of modern rationalization and social atomization not to socioeconomic change but to the post-Enlightenment liberal tradition, particularly secularism, social equality, and an unrooted individualism.

For many, Weaver was a major figure in the postwar conservative movement. The conservative sociologist Robert Nisbet, for example, labeled him "the morning star of the contemporary renascence of conservative thought in the United States." Weaver had never simply rejected individualism; rather, he believed that the individual must be firmly embedded in the limiting myths, symbols, and traditions of a cultural hierarchy. "Man is free in proportion as his surroundings have a determinate nature," Weaver declared in *The Ethics of Rhetoric* in 1953, "and he can plan his course with perfect reliance upon that determinateness." Few statements captured the mind and personality of Weaver so well. His suspicion of the state, most evidenced in his strictures on modern warfare, as well as the cultural elitism implicit in his social criticism, further suited him to a movement that, before the infusion of conservative populism in the late 1960s, was marked by a skepticism toward democracy and distrust of an open society.[42]

As the importance of industrial capitalism faded in Weaver's philosophy, so too did any residual hostility to big business. By the 1960s, Weaver had moved far from the economics of Agrarianism, celebrating instead the virtues of free enterprise. The American contribution to Western civilization, he eulogized in the manner of the Chamber of Commerce, was the idea of merit and individual advancement. "This respect for freedom, initiative, and enterprise has given us the most wonderful, productive system in the history of the world." In the 1930s, the Agrarians had decried the onslaught of a northern industrializing economy, which they believed would destroy local cultures and folk arts and centralize power in the hands of a plutocratic elite.

In 1962, Weaver praised the "genius" of the businessman. Americans must not be blind to the fact, he declared,

> that we have the highest popular standard of living in the world by far; that we have so much food stuffs that we are looking for ways to give them away; that we produce so much cotton fiber, tobacco, etc., that we have to contrive schemes to hold down the annual crop; that we have so many automobiles that the streets of every city, large and small, are clogged with them; that we are so prolific in appliances and gadgets that the makers are looking for new ways to get them into the hands of customers. It is hard for me to believe that in the midst of all this plenty, some people could feel called upon to apologize for our failure.

Agrarianism had come a long way. "Capitalism has delivered the goods and it is absurd to go on the defensive about that," Weaver declared.[43]

The ideas Weaver expressed in *Ideas Have Consequences*—the chastened view of humanity, the suspicion of a soulless technological and materialist culture, the desire for the classical virtues of humility, restraint, and moderation—echoed the ideals of Niebuhr and the New Conservatives of the immediate postwar era. His hostility to strategies of total war and the use of atomic weapons echoed the postwar Left. Yet Weaver cast his lot with the conservative movement that developed around William F. Buckley Jr. and the *National Review*. "I believe it will appear increasingly," he wrote Randolph in December 1942, "that the real war is between Anglo-American rightism and the various forms of European leftism." "Liberalism today is bankrupt," Weaver wrote Brooks in 1944. "It has nothing to offer, nothing even to say." As early as 1946, Weaver was asked to be the academic adviser of a student conservative league at the University of Chicago. He gave the students a talk on "creative conservatism." In his autobiographical essay, which Weaver labeled "Up from Liberalism," he expressed his scorn for liberal ideology. "The chief result of what I now think of as my re-education has been a complete disenchantment with the liberalism that was the first stage of my reflective life," he wrote. "Liberalism is the refuge favored by intellectual cowardice, because the essence of the liberal's position is that he has no position. . . . It is the state of mind before we have made up our mind."[44]

Weaver was an early and devoted worker in the conservative movement. He was on the list of contributors to the *National Review* from its inception until his death, writing many reviews for it in its fledgling first two years. He was an editorial adviser, and, later, associate editor, of the major conservative journal of ideas, *Modern Age*, which

Russell Kirk founded in 1957. With Milton Friedman and Friedrich
Hayek, Weaver was one of the three editorial advisers to the *New Individualist Review*, a journal of libertarian economics that Hayek's students at the University of Chicago began in 1961. Weaver became a
trustee of Frank Chodorov's Intercollegiate Society of Individualists.
The extent to which Weaver assimilated the free-market orientation
of the conservative movement is attested by his receiving a grant from
the Volker Fund, an anti–New Deal philanthropy generally used to
subsidize laissez-faire economists. The fund provided Weaver with a
sabbatical for the 1955–56 academic year, which he devoted to work
on *Visions of Order: The Cultural Crisis of Our Time*, a more rigid reworking of his ideas on the prescriptive role of culture that remained
unpublished until after his death. Indeed, shortly before his death,
Harold Luhnow, president of the Volker Fund, offered Weaver a job
at his full Chicago salary.[45]

Weaver reinterpreted Agrarianism as a nonparticularist conservatism fundamentally concerned with issues of value. The Agrarians,
Weaver argued in "Agrarianism in Exile," published in the *Sewanee
Review* in 1950, had traveled to Europe, discovered that the South
embodied key organic elements of European culture, and organized
in order to preserve what was essentially European in southern culture. The essay displays the influence of Ransom and Tate in both
their Agrarian and post-Agrarian, New Critical phases. Weaver cited
their ideas on metaphor in order to claim an Agrarian belief in absolutes and adopted, in general, Tate's understanding of Agrarianism as
merely a form of Christian humanism. Ransom's *God without Thunder*, Weaver declared, was the most profound of the Agrarian books
because it showed that myth can be an expression of ultimate truth,
thereby presenting the ambiguous Ransom as far more of a believer
than he actually was. The superiority of Agrarians over the New
Humanists, Weaver claimed, lay in their understanding from the beginning that "man requires some conception of the absolute to maintain his humanity."[46]

"Agrarianism in Exile" deemphasized Agrarianism's anticapitalist
bias, defined Agrarianism in terms of philosophical positions and the
defense of absolutes, and, most strikingly, minimized its southernness. The South, Weaver argued, in an elitist and somewhat rueful
tone, lacked sufficient intellectual depth to appreciate and support the
Agrarian message. Many of the Agrarians, he suggested, had found
the South unreceptive to their doctrines. "What has been represented
as the flight of the Agrarians may appear on closer examination to be
a strategic withdrawal to positions where the contest can be better
carried on," Weaver argued.[47]

Davidson's response to Weaver's article places the implications of Weaver's project into stark relief. Davidson was sympathetic to Weaver, for he was reinterpreting Agrarianism along the same lines. Yet there were limits to Davidson's revisionism. Weaver forwarded the manuscript to Davidson, and Davidson responded with a three-page letter and a nine-page single-spaced, typed "Notes on 'Agrarianism is Exile.'" Weaver's singling out of *God without Thunder* for special praise was sure to rankle Davidson, who was disgusted with what he considered Ransom's betrayal of the movement. In his response to Weaver, Davidson took pains to argue the essential unity of Agrarianism. "All the books of the agrarians are but one book," he declared, "in the sense that nothing they have done has been unaffected by their central purposes; and their differences are, in a sense, not so much departures as variations in the grand design." The movement as a whole deserves attention, not just the "exiles," Davidson further argued.[48] Davidson did not see the "general exodus" of Agrarians that Weaver claimed existed and suggested that Weaver pay more heed to the Agrarians who left Vanderbilt to teach at other southern universities. The Agrarians had received notable attention in New York-based literary quarterlies (several of them, including Ransom, Tate, Davidson, John Gould Fletcher, and Stark Young, were relatively well known literary figures at the time), but Weaver's suggestion that they were received more widely and positively in the North is exaggerated. Nor did Davidson agree with Weaver's condescension toward southern intellectualism. "Until he had been corrupted by New Deal subsidies, war, and socialist intimidation," Davidson wrote, "the average Southern farmer, wherever he could be physically approached, was naturally, in the early 1930's, a more sympathetic and understanding person than another crowd, who were our real enemies — the 'liberals,' the educated jackasses."[49]

Although Weaver heeded many of Davidson's suggestions, he did not change the theme of his essay, which was that Agrarianism had less to do with the South than previously thought. The passions of the Civil War have receded, Weaver wrote, and one need no longer play the role of the sectionalist. "The sections fade out, and one looks for comrades wherever there are men of good will and understanding," Weaver argued. "I think the issue has broadened in this way for all who saw it first under narrower horizons." Agrarianism was not about the South; it was about modern civilization. The Agrarian "upheaval" was a "particular instance of a movement which is taking place all over the world," Weaver held. "It is, to repeat, a phase of the general retreat of humanism before universal materialism and technification. And this is the real reason that geographical residence has ceased to be an important fact about the Agrarians." The secret to the lasting power of the Agrarians, he argued, was their "admission of a theism."[50]

Weaver was prone to criticizing modernity in the most abstract, universalized terms. This tendency, which led Weaver away from the vivid particularism of *I'll Take My Stand*, particularly annoyed James Burnham, Buckley's most reliable editorial adviser on the *National Review*. Burnham argued against printing Weaver's full-length articles (as opposed to Weaver's book reviews, of which he approved) for the magazine. Weaver had "to learn how to communicate on a less abstract plane," Burnham advised Buckley in a memo. He grouped Weaver with a set of *National Review* contributors who tended to start with an empirical issue and then moved straight into dialectical abstractions. (He was particularly annoyed at a piece by Weaver that was ostensibly about advertising but gave no concrete examples of what he criticized.) "This kind of philosophizing is the lazy academician's way of ending problems; it smells of the lamp most smokily," Burnham observed, adding that it was boring to read as well. Nevertheless, much conservative writing in the 1950s and 1960s was devoted to defining conservative first principles.[51]

One of the most influential writers in this vein was Frank Meyer, William F. Buckley Jr.'s in-house ideologue at the *National Review* and the architect of "fusionism." Meyer was at the center of conservative debates about the individual and society, and his thought sheds light on Weaver's own ability to navigate a middle course between libertarians and traditionalists. Meyer had been an active Communist Party member from the 1930s through the end of World War II. After the war, he shifted to the Right, cooperated with the FBI to identify midwestern Communists, and maintained a dogmatically individualist outlook. The aristocratic culture of Britain and certain aspects of Christian traditionalist thinking attracted him, and he loved the classics. A Jew, he converted to Catholicism on his deathbed. Meyer first met Weaver personally at a 1959 conference in Brown County, Indiana. There he recalled being surprised that Weaver, who was supposed to speak as a representative of traditionalist conservatism, agreed to a great extent with himself. In fact, Meyer insisted in 1970, *Ideas Have Consequences* played a formative role in his own personal development. It "adumbrated" the "informing principle" that united the conservative movement—"the unity of tradition and liberty." The book, he declared, was the "*fons et origo*" of the conservative movement.[52]

Meyer identified a basic conservative consensus on several key issues: opposition to the growth of centralized power in the state and any utopian schemes for social change originating with the state; faith in the existence of an objective moral order; a rejection of communism; and a conviction that the individual was primary. Some conservatives might stress the importance of tradition, he suggested, others might stress freedom, but all shared certain fundamental convictions.[53] Meyer believed that freedom was the essence of being human. The fundamental element of his "fusionist" synthesis of traditionalism and libertarianism was that moral authority could never be imposed by the state but must always be accepted voluntarily. For Meyer, the only authentic approach to life was one founded on free choice. Although affirming Christian orthodoxy (God's grace alone heals the "lonely horror" of the soul, he declared), he insisted that virtuous action must be freely willed to be meaningful. "Only the independence and autonomy of the person makes love or any other valid relationship between persons possible; were human beings but parts of a larger whole, their love, all their reachings out one to another, would be but the cellular interactions dictated by the tropisms of the larger organism."[54]

The degree to which Weaver did, at times, echo Meyer's position—despite very significant differences on the nature of individualism and the role of traditional social authority—is striking. In "Education and the Individual," an essay first published as a pamphlet by the Intercollegiate Society of Individualists in 1959, Weaver sounded very much like Meyer. "One cannot *be* a being unless he feels within himself the grounds of his action," he declared portentously. He decried the "other-directed" and "hollow" men of the time.

> The real person is, in contrast, the individual who senses in himself an internal principle of control, to which his thoughts and actions are related. Ever aware of this, he makes his choices, and this choosing is the most real thing he ever does because it asserts his character in the midst of circumstances. Then the feeling of freedom comes with a great upsurging sense of triumph: to be free is to be victorious; it is to count, whereas the nonentity by his very nature does not count.

In this essay, Weaver articulated a standpoint parallel to the central dictum of Meyer's fusionism: "*The unfree man cannot be good because virtue is a state of character concerned with choice, and if this latter is taken away, there is simply no way for goodness to assert itself.*"[55] Fusionism was a means by which conservative activists could cement traditionalist intellectuals to the emerging conservative movement. Meyer and Weaver's stress on ideas and faith—on the individual moral decision—helped shift traditionalists' attention away from the individualistic social philosophy and capitalist economics so prominent among other segments of this movement.

In *Ideas Have Consequences*, Weaver had engaged in a delicate intellectual balancing act that persisted throughout his career—attempting to preserve a conception of rooted individualism that was analytically distinct from the bourgeois individualism he condemned as, in part, the root of modern decadence. In 1948 he argued that piety entailed a respect for the individual within community, what he chose to denominate "personality" as distinguished from individualism. Personality, he argued, is the "little private area of selfhood" in which a person integrates a relationship both to something transcendental and to the community. Individualism was potentially destructive. "Individualism, with its connotation of irresponsibility, is a direct invitation to selfishness, and all that this treatise has censured can be traced in some way to individualist mentality," Weaver declared.[56]

Weaver never developed this argument from *Ideas Have Consequences* any further. Yet a consistent feature of his thought was a faith in the ability of cultural constructs like chivalry to contain individual appetites. Above all else, Weaver was a philosopher of order, believing that a good and moral life can only be lived ensconced within the firm embrace of culture and tradition—chivalry, religion, law, myth. He had harsh words for human egotism and selfish individualism. In "Up from Liberalism," Weaver viewed his own conversion to Agrarianism as liberating, but it was a liberation achieved through a commitment to the southern past. Social traditions, a shared past, chivalric customs—all buttressed his own sense of individual capacity. To Weaver's way of thinking, a true individualism, one built on rootedness and connection, came only when a person was embedded in a social order. Weaver labeled this " 'social bond' individualism" in a late essay. Such an individualism "battles unremittingly for individual rights, while recognizing that these have to be secured within the social context."[57]

The tension between individual freedom and an ordered society was a central theme of Weaver's last book, *Visions of Order*, which was written for the most part between 1955 and 1958 and published only posthumously. This tension was very real in 1950s America, particularly in the wake of Cold War spy scandals, loyalty review boards, and McCarthyism. In *Ideas Have Consequences*, Weaver had spoken of the "yea-saying" function of culture, the way in which a culture organized values in a hierarchy. But where he had previously spoken of a "metaphysical dream," in *Visions of Order* Weaver described the center of culture as a "tyrannizing image," a "focus of value" that discriminated, selected, and preferred the material of daily life. Culture was by definition exclusive. "Such differentiation is possible only if there is a center toward which the parts look for their meaning and validation," he wrote. Only insofar as a culture was able to discriminate, to separate what threatens the integrity of the culture, was it able to integrate itself.[58]

Weaver had assimilated some of the criticisms of an open society made by Willmoore Kendall, Buckley's mentor at Yale. Weaver had become acquainted with Kendall in the 1950s, and the two men had tinkered with the idea of a joint project. (Many of the reviews Weaver wrote for the *National Review* in its early stages were written when Kendall was book editor.) Kendall, who insisted that Weaver was neither a traditionalist nor a Southern Agrarian, considered *Visions of Order* to rank with *The Federalist* in terms of political wisdom.[59] In the book, Weaver argued, just as had Kendall, Buckley, and Bozell in defense of McCarthyism, that every society was defined by a consensus of values that must remain unchallenged in order for the society to survive. Every culture must exclude certain ideas and values, Weaver declared; the binding images of a culture should exercise a tyranny that bars challenge.

Weaver used the term "status" to connote those prescribed social attributes, such as name or title, that defined identity. It was these social elements, Weaver believed, that gave human beings continuity and permanence, despite physical changes in size or appearance, or even an alteration in personality. They constituted the "thread" of a person's selfhood.[60] The central element of Weaver's delicately balanced social bond individualism was based on this idea that effective personal identity is, in some sense, a social quality. Status and memory were connected, Weaver argued, for status was transmitted by memory. "No man really exists except through that mysterious storehouse of his remembered acts and his formed personality," Weaver argued. A man's "very reality," his identity, "depends upon his carrying the past into the present through the power of memory." Weaver, as had Davidson, came to see memory, both social and personal, as constitutive of self. The rejection of memory seemed to him something like suicide. If a man "does not want identity, if he has actually come to hate himself, it is natural for him to try to get rid of memory's baggage."[61]

Frank Meyer's embrace of Weaver's work and his claim for its importance to fusionist conservatism are testimonies to Weaver's ability to finesse the full implications of his "social bond" individualism. Weaver envisioned social authority lodged in internalized cultural codes and not the state, which made his thought more palatable to libertarians. Weaver's "social bond" individualism converged with a celebration of the virtues of free enterprise—"the best productive and distributive system." And even as Weaver warned against the "anarchic individualism" of Henry David Thoreau and his heirs, his instincts, he confessed in 1960, were libertarian.[62] Most important, his tendency to write in generalized and abstract terms, while it may have limited the appeal of his work, allowed him to leave the details and implications of his social theory to more polemical essays or reviews.

The burgeoning civil rights movement in the South had begun to attract public attention with the *Brown v. Board of Education* decisions in 1954 and 1955 mandating the gradual desegregation of schools. The *National Review* opposed federal efforts to promote integration. The Supreme Court's desegregation cases, it declared in January 1956, were "patently counter to the intent of the Constitution, shoddy and illegal in analysis, and invalid as sociology." Issues of school desegregation should be decided on the local level. A February 1956 *National Review* editorial carefully based the magazine's opposition to federally enforced integration on constitutional, and not racial, grounds. Meyer opposed the *Brown* decision because it "rode roughshod over precedent and reason and constitutional obligation." James Jackson Kilpatrick, the editor of the *Richmond News-Leader*, was the most respected intellectual opponent of federal desegregation efforts. After the publication of *The Sovereign States* (1957), which presented a constitutional defense of segregation, Kilpatrick became a frequent contributor to the *National Review* and, in historian George H. Nash's words, became the "more or less 'official' " conservative spokesman on constitutional issues and civil rights.[63]

In an August 1957 editorial, William F. Buckley Jr. opposed guarantees of black rights to vote on racial grounds. In disenfranchising blacks, Buckley argued, white southerners were simply asserting that the "claims of civilization" should "supersede" demands for universal suffrage. Buckley asked whether the white South is "entitled to take such measures as are necessary to prevail, politically and culturally, in areas in which it does not predominate numerically." "The sobering answer is *Yes*—the white community is so entitled because, for the time being, it is the advanced race." The editorial was laced with condescension and some naïveté. "The great majority of the Negroes of the South who do not vote do not care to vote, and would not know for what to vote if they could," Buckley wrote. He called on white southerners to aid in the advancement of blacks and warned them not to exploit "Negro backwardness." Buckley was an elitist and a skeptic concerning democracy. After Brent Bozell sharply dissented from Buckley's position on black voting rights, Buckley retreated and suggested that the vote be denied to the uneducated, whether white or black. "The South should, if it determines to disenfranchise the marginal Negro, do so by enacting laws that apply equally to blacks and whites, thus living up to the spirit of the Constitution, and the letter of the Fifteenth Amendment," he wrote.[64]

Buckley's position on racial issues and civil rights evolved over the years, revealing the central, if often unspoken, position race has held in conservative politics since the 1950s. In *Up from Liberalism* (1959), he argued that an effective response to African nationalists was to declare that their people were not ready to rule themselves. Turning to the United States, Buckley argued that whites in the South might legitimately claim political authority on the basis of whites' leading role in American civilization. "The white South perceives," he wrote, "for the time being at least, qualitative differences between the level of its culture and the Negroes', and intends to live by its own."[65]

Yet Buckley became disenchanted with the crude populism of southern segregationist leadership. He deprecated racism while upholding the principle of states' rights. In 1962, he attacked Mississippi governor Ross Barnett's motives in denying the admission of James Meredith to the University of Mississippi even as he defended the right of Ole Miss to bar blacks. Buckley had a particular animus against Governor George Wallace of Alabama, considering him a lower-class demagogue.[66] At the same time, Buckley anticipated the conservative critique of liberal policies on crime and welfare in his campaign for mayor of New York City in 1965.[67] Mainstream conservatives in the late 1950s and early 1960s were well aware of the potential appeal of their principled opposition to federal civil rights policies for southern whites and northern working-class and lower-middle-class ethnics. Senator Barry Goldwater's *Conscience of a Conservative*, ghostwritten by Bozell, declared that the federal government did not have the right to integrate public schools. Goldwater had strongly supported black voting rights (although he backed away from this during his 1964 presidential campaign), but he opposed federal action to bring about desegregation. "We are being asked to destroy the rights of some under the false banner of promoting the civil rights of others," Goldwater declared in an address televised across the South in the last days of the 1964 presidential contest.[68]

Shortly after the violence surrounding Meredith's admission to the University of Mississippi in the fall of 1962, Weaver wrote Buckley in praise of the *National Review*. "As far as I can see, you are the only journal north of the Mason-Dixon line which keeps putting the right argument forward in the Mississippi affair, *i.e.*, this is a matter that involves the fundamental structure of our government."[69] Weaver displayed a patronizing and chauvinist racism in his writings. In his dissertation, he presented an amiable view of slavery—"only under the rule of gentlemen was the peculiar institution tolerable." At least slaves, unlike northern workers, he observed, knew they were cherished by their masters. Blacks were stereotypically childlike, loyal, and aware of their incapacity in Weaver's eyes. "The Negro is one of the most sensitive creatures on earth," he observed, "but he resents not so much his implied inferiority as the sharp word and the unsympathetic look which tell him that he is not wanted."[70] He opposed racial integration, arguing that, as imposed on the South by the North, it amounted to "racial collectivism" and "communization."[71] In *The Lasting South: Fourteen Southerners Look at Their Home* (1957), a symposium organized by Louis D. Rubin Jr. and Kilpatrick that self-consciously echoed *I'll Take My Stand*, Weaver accused the North of hypocrisy, pointing to northern white flight as blacks entered previously all-white neighborhoods and the de facto segregation characteristic of many parts of the North. He urged the advice of Booker T. Washington on blacks: "When they create something that the world desires the world will come and ask to have it, and will have to accept it on the Negroes' terms. That is the way other races have raised themselves, and it is the only permanent way." The South has and must continue to maintain the "standards of white civilization," he argued. Writing to Russell Kirk, Weaver explained that his opposition to integration was based not on prudence but on principle — "the principle that racial and cultural groups have the right and even the duty to protect their integrity."[72]

Visions of Order was, at least in part, a defense of segregation. "A culture integrates by segregating its forms of activity and its members from those not belonging," Weaver wrote. "The right to self-segregate then is an indispensable right." Court-ordered integration, he concluded, is a challenge to the cohesion of southern society. Democracy, a "valuable but limited political concept," should not be extended beyond the political realm. "The most pressing duty of the believer in culture today," Weaver wrote, "is to define democracy and keep it within its place, in doing which he not only will preserve it as a viable form but also will protect those other areas of activity which are essential to supply a different kind of need."[73]

Weaver's conception of citizenship was akin to Donald Davidson's. He likened culture to a "brotherhood." "If you belong to it, you live in and by it; if you are outside it, you find the gulf impassable, except to certain superficial contacts," he wrote in *Visions of Order*.[74] The issue became, then, how to determine membership in a culture. Weaver argued that culture, by definition, excluded, but he did not clearly examine *how* a culture excluded, which was the crux of the issue. "Southernness," for example, could be defined on the basis of any number of factors — locality or shared history, not necessarily race alone.

As Weaver surveyed the changes wrought in the South by the civil rights movement from his academic past in Chicago and summer residence in Weaverville, he was faced with another question: Had he forfeited his southern identity, his membership in the culture, by his self-imposed "exile"? There is more than one way to be outside a culture, Weaver suggested in *Visions of Order.* Some are born outside it. But another type of outsider is one who voluntarily leaves. Such members of a culture have "estranged" themselves from it "through study and reflection," he argued. Yet such a person "has not lost the intuitive understanding which belongs to him as a member." In fact, Weaver claimed, this outsider may have the special ability to serve as a "doctor" or healer of the culture, owing to his special vantage point. "For diagnostic and remedial work we may have to turn to those who have in a way mutilated themselves by withdrawal, by a special kind of mental discipline, and by a kind of fixation upon a task which even impedes free cultural participation," Weaver declared, in exculpation, one suspects, of his own freely chosen life in Chicago, which was an exile only by the most tenuous of standards.[75] He had, in fact, been faithful to the South all the time—more so because of the sacrifices he endured, Weaver pleaded in the familiar rhetoric of the voluntary exile.

Before his sudden and unexpected death at age fifty-three, Weaver was planning to return to the South full-time. He had accepted a one-year appointment to replace Davidson in the English Department at Vanderbilt University. Davidson was retiring, and the English faculty had every expectation of asking Weaver to assume the chair permanently. But Weaver was found dead in his apartment, the victim of a heart attack, in April 1963, before he had a chance to occupy it.

Thirteen years before, in a speech at a family gathering, Weaver suggested that the city dwellers' condition is one of anonymity. "They are people without names. They come to be like mass-produced parts polished, machined, and what is worst of all to say—interchangeable."[76] It is unfortunate that Weaver, an outsider, perhaps, in both Chicago and the South, was not more attuned to the irony of his remarks. Throughout the time Weaver lived in Chicago, during the 1940s and 1950s, his adopted city was the endpoint of a massive exodus of blacks from the South. These men and women were, in a way, spiritual exiles just like Weaver; they, however, sought to escape the oppression, social and economic, visited upon them by southern whites. For them, Chicago was, indeed, a "promised land," one of potential freedom, dignity, and prosperity. That the plight of these black folk was so completely invisible to Weaver is not surprising, for the exile motif has everything to do with identity, and it was a racially exclusive identity that Weaver's carefully tended sense of exile nurtured.

And it was the politics of identity, of an assumed bond between white southerners, that lay indelibly at the heart of Southern Agrarianism and the evolving organic conservatism of Davidson, Weaver, and later neo-Agrarians. No amount of universalizing, not even self-imposed exile, altered that fact.

CHAPTER SEVEN

The Awful Responsibility of Time
Identity, History, and Pragmatic Agrarianism

> *For nothing we had,*   *All is redeemed,*
> *Nothing we were,*   *In knowledge.*
> *Is lost.*
>
> Robert Penn Warren, *Brother to Dragons*

In the late 1970s, long after he had been a precocious student at Vanderbilt University and more than two decades since he had tried to explain the sometimes agonizing inner conflict of white southerners over segregation, Robert Penn Warren recalled his old teacher Donald Davidson. Davidson was a man "somewhat divided against himself," he believed. Although Davidson was a "superlative" teacher and gifted writer of prose and poetry, Warren felt that his lyrical voice had been soured by his sectional passions. Davidson's stubborn stance in support of white supremacy and segregation in the South was in marked contrast to Warren's opposition to both. Nevertheless, relations between the two men were always cordial, although Warren was the object of occasional lectures about his racial beliefs. Warren remembered their friendship fondly: "Davidson and I remained dear friends to the end, and I'd go see him every time I could, and he would always forgive me. Call me a damn fool, and then start the friendship over again." [1]

Perhaps this long friendship survived the fierce contest of political convictions because Warren and Davidson were so alike in the importance they attached to the southern past and the disappointment with which they viewed the southern present. The problem with the modern South was that it increasingly resembled the rest of modern America. Of all the original Agrarians, Warren and Davidson were the two most concerned with the issue of identity. Warren believed that the nature of modern life effectively thwarted the achievement

of what he termed "identity and community." "In our world of rest-
less mobility," he wrote, "where every Main Street looks like the one
before and the throughway is always the same, of communication
without communion, of the ad-man's nauseating surrogate for family
sense and community in the word *togetherness*, we look back nostal-
gically on the romantic image of some right and natural relation of
man to place and man to man, fulfilled in worthy action."[2]

For both men, the contemporary specter of an Americanized nowhere was offset by the memory of a more rooted, organic, and humane past. True to the Agrarian program, they looked to the past
when addressing the distressing conditions of modernity. Both relied on the past for identity and the validation of values, and both
attached intense importance to efforts to engage past actors, even to
commune in some sense with forebears. Yet how they understood the
past and what it told them about modern life were radically different. Davidson saw the past as a mirror; into it he looked for recognition and understanding of himself. He understood the South through
the civil religion of the Lost Cause. His highest loyalty was to the
South, which, by the 1950s, had come to be, for him, a symbol for the
most cherished values of Western civilization. For Warren, the past
was altogether more ambiguous, containing both good and bad. He
could neither identify with the past as unquestioningly as Davidson
nor turn from it as completely as Allen Tate, for the southern heritage meant too much to him. He believed history to be a rebuke. Not
only did the nobility of past sacrifices contrast favorably with current
failings, but the record of human travesties and injustice punctured
national myths of superiority. Warren was a philosophical pragmatist, inspired by William James; he believed that human beings necessarily constructed their own identity and, in this way, defined moral
value. Moral values are not given; they must be discovered and realized anew by each human being in a process of relentless testing, an
"agony of will."[3] A confrontation with one's own past and cultural
history is integral to this process.

If Agrarianism was divided between modernism and romanticism,
Warren and Davidson's relationship revealed a second and deeper set
of divisions over individual responsibility, the role of history, and
racial justice. Davidson was, Warren recalled, "an absolutely unreconstructed Rebel," "just fanatical" on the race question.[4] The controversies over segregation and the status of blacks in the South revealed, more than anything, the moral ambiguity of Agrarianism. The
question of race loyalty tested southern definitions of community and
freedom. To Davidson, segregation was an extension of the logic of
Agrarianism. It was a means of preserving the southern tradition.
From Warren's viewpoint, the racial question was the ultimate test of

the modern southerner's ability to come to terms with the past and renounce an unjust and immoral social system. The southern past, in and of itself, was unable to clarify values; it was southerners, Warren believed, acting in light of the past but not determined by it, who were required to assume this task.

Warren's upbringing was not unlike that of Davidson. Both were from small towns and from families that placed an emphasis on reading and study. Warren was born in 1905 in the town of Guthrie, Kentucky, just over the northern border of Tennessee. Built on a railroad line, Guthrie was in decline before World War I and had the rough and violent character of a frontier town. Warren's father had set aside his youthful literary ambitions and hopes of being a lawyer in order to support his widowed stepmother and her family. He became a small-town banker and merchant, only to go bankrupt in the Great Depression. Warren's mother was protective and a bit meddling; she died in 1931, when Warren was twenty-six years old.[5]

All his life Warren loved the outdoors. He was an athletic boy and loved to swim and run. He hunted, collected butterflies, and studied birds. A town boy who chose to associate with the country children, Warren was lonely at times, sometimes teased and harassed by his classmates for being studious. The abundant forests and fields around Guthrie were a means of escape, but so were the summers he spent at his maternal grandfather Penn's antebellum home in Cerulean Springs, Kentucky. There he felt welcome in the eccentric presence of his white-haired grandfather, whom Warren most vividly recalled sitting in a split-bottom chair, leaning against a cedar tree. Like Davidson, Warren imbibed a love for the southern past at the feet of a grandparent. Gabriel Penn had fought under Nathan Bedford Forrest at Shiloh (as had Warren's paternal grandfather and a great-uncle). The young Warren would listen to his grandfather recite poetry, or the old man and his avid grandson would plot military strategy in the dust, although they were as likely to re-create Napoleon's campaigns as those of Robert E. Lee. In such a world, Warren recalled, where the past was ever present in the tales of the older folks, life took on the quality of a double-exposed photograph. "The real world was there and the old world was there, one photograph superimposed on the other," he recalled. "Their relationship was of constant curiosity and interest."[6]

After finishing high school in Guthrie at the age of fifteen (not an especially difficult feat, according to Warren) and completing one year of school in Clarksville, Tennessee, Warren enrolled at Vanderbilt in 1921. As a boy, Warren had dreams of a navy career. His father even obtained an appointment for him at Annapolis through a friendly congressman. But a stone thrown by his brother Thomas blinded Warren in one eye; the accident ruined Warren's prospects of a navy career and left him physically and emotionally wounded. He felt a sense of shame and apartness because of his injury.[7] While he was in college, the vision in his left eye deteriorated, and Warren worried that his good eye would be affected. In his junior year, this nagging fear combined with overwork, stress, and the disappointment of an unrequited love for Chink Nichol, a cousin of Andrew Nelson Lytle, drove Warren to the point of nervous exhaustion and depression. In May 1924, at age nineteen, he made a halfhearted attempt at suicide.[8]

Warren later recalled the importance of his circle of friends at Vanderbilt, especially Allen Tate, at this difficult time. Concern for his welfare was not limited to his fellow students. Warren had come under the influence of John Crowe Ransom and Donald Davidson, the two people most important to him at Vanderbilt; Ransom, indeed, became something of a second father.[9] Aside from their friendship, however, the two older men also stimulated Warren's interest in poetry. Warren later recalled a day at his home in Guthrie that changed his life. Ransom was reading some poetry of Thomas Hardy when Warren became convinced, he remembered, that "this is the real thing." In Ransom's own poetry Warren saw "a world [he] could feel some recognition of." "You see," he remarked, "I could feel *his* experience, not mine; I could feel experience, human experience, through his work. Ransom made me see poetry in the common light I saw around me every day, in the country." Poetry helped him come out of his depression. "It was the one thing, it seemed, that could take me out of my fear," Warren later wrote.[10]

Warren joined the circle of Fugitive poets in 1923, publishing several poems in the magazine. And he contributed to the Agrarian symposium. But he was always a junior member, never really at the center of Agrarian organizing. His career, too, had a longer, more sharply ascending arc. He became the most widely recognized of the Agrarian circle. Before he died in 1989, Warren had published ten novels and sixteen volumes of verse. He won the Pulitzer Prize for *All the King's Men*, published in 1946. He won Pulitzer Prizes, as well, for two volumes of poetry, *Promises* (1957) and *Now and Then* (1979). In 1986, he became the nation's first official poet laureate; uniquely among the Agrarians, his birthplace home is preserved and open to the public. Unlike Tate, Warren's creativity never stopped; he continued to produce prose and poetry through most phases of his career, while achieving some popular success as a novelist. Also unlike Tate, Warren pursued his academic education. After graduating from Vanderbilt in 1925, he obtained a master's degree in English at the University of California at Berkeley and studied further at Yale University

Allen Tate and Robert Penn Warren near Guthrie, Kentucky,
1933. (Courtesy Robert Cowley)

and, on a Rhodes scholarship from 1928 to 1930, at Oxford, where he
earned a B.Litt.

After his graduate work, Warren wanted to return to the South.
In 1930 he turned down a better job in California to teach at South-
western College in Memphis, Tennessee. From 1931 to 1934, he was
assistant professor of English at Vanderbilt, but he could not obtain
a regular position there. He considered middle Tennessee "heaven"
and did not want to leave, but he accepted an offer to teach with his
friend and fellow Vanderbilt alumnus Cleanth Brooks at Louisiana
State University in 1934. There he achieved his greatest academic success, helping to edit the well-regarded and influential *Southern Review*
for seven years, and with Brooks published *Understanding Poetry* in

1937. But Warren felt unwanted at LSU and claimed years later that he was "somehow squeezed out of the South." From 1942 on, Warren made his career in the North, principally at the University of Minnesota and Yale, and eventually made his home in Connecticut.[11]

By the 1950s, Warren was speaking in an existentialist idiom distinct among the Agrarians. His first book, a biography of John Brown, was a case study of idealism grown indistinguishable from fanaticism. A sainted radical to some, Brown was, in Warren's southern eyes, motivated by equal parts delusion and self-interest.[12] Warren was skeptical of democracy and of the moral capacities of the average person. He believed that the impulse that lay behind the ideological conflicts of the 1930s and 1940s was the "*passionate emptiness and tidal lust* of the modern man who, because he cannot find long-range meaning, seeks meaning in mere violence, the violence being what he wants and needs without reference ultimately to the political or other justification he may appeal to."[13]

The central dynamic of Warren's work was what he considered the modern person's compulsive search for knowledge in a disenchanted world.[14] The old systems of belief and meaning had fallen, and the individual was thrown back upon his own resources to achieve "identity" or "definition." These words, according to literary biographer Charles Bohner, had an almost "cabalistic" implication for Warren.[15] Warren held that people must create their own meaning, a meaning purchased at a high price in the flux of human discord and conflict. It is an illusion to see in a person any ultimate innocence or natural goodness; any such illusions were unalterably shattered by the knowledge gained in world war and genocide. Rather, humans must accept ultimate responsibility for and complicity in the evils of their nature and the fact that good ends often are the product of less than noble means. Only by first experiencing the "pain of isolation" and realizing the "tragic pathos of life" would human beings come to a chastened and nonsentimental understanding of the nature of love and justice.[16]

The influence of Reinhold Niebuhr can be seen in Warren's work in the 1940s, as well as an acknowledged debt to the pragmatism of William James. Warren also developed a more serious interest in exploiting historical materials in his work. This was in part due to his friendship with the historian C. Vann Woodward. Woodward received his Ph.D. from the University of North Carolina, the Vanderbilt Agrarians' institutional rival. Toward the end of World War II Woodward and Warren were both in Washington, D.C. Woodward was a historian with the navy; Warren, the chair of poetry at the Library of Congress. They renewed a previous acquaintance then, but it was not until the following decade that they developed a strong friendship and fruitful exchange of ideas. Warren's existentialist viewpoint shaped Woodward, and Woodward's historical imagination interested Warren. It is not surprising that Warren would have found Woodward's vision appealing, for Woodward's sense of history as noncontinuous and open to reinterpretation, as well as his belief that the appropriate use of historical knowledge was to affect the present, best evidenced by his role as an expert adviser to the team that successfully argued *Brown v. Board of Education*, paralleled Warren's own sense that southerners must struggle with their past and not be bound by it. In an interview with the scholar Marshall Walker, Warren expressed his agreement with Woodward's controversial thesis that legal segregation was not a deep-rooted southern tradition but a comparatively recent product of the late nineteenth-century New South.[17]

Warren's mature philosophy informed his masterpiece, *All the King's Men*, published in 1946. The book, inspired by the career of Huey Long, Louisiana's powerful and flamboyant governor and, then, senator in the late 1920s and early 1930s, chronicled the career of a demagogic southern politician. It began as a verse play, the bulk of which Warren wrote in Rome in the summer of 1939, while observing the maneuverings of Benito Mussolini. In the novel, Warren revealed deep affinities with the major tenets of Niebuhr's worldview: the realization that the noble is always mixed with the base; that good actions may come from bad motives and vice versa; and the insistence that human beings must accept responsibility for all results of their actions, even when unintended, and yet continue to act boldly to shape their world. The central characters were Willie Stark, the populist demagogue, and Jack Burden, an ineffectual journalist who narrates the book. Willie was all action, at one time an idealist but, in his maturity, corrupt and unscrupulous; every political accomplishment was tainted by his egocentrism as well as by his methods. Willie extorted, intimidated, manipulated, and used brute force. But he also possessed a cynical variant of the realist, unillusioned perspective of Niebuhr. Men come from dirt, he declared, "conceived in sin and born in corruption and he passeth from the stink of the didie to the stench of the shroud" (49).[18]

Willie was also a pragmatist of sorts. William James, Warren later declared, was as much an inspiration for the character of Willie Stark as Huey Long.[19] The law was something manipulated and altered to fit circumstances, Willie declared. He compared it to a too small bedspread or the outgrown pants of a young boy: it is in constant need of additions and alterations (136–37). Moreover, it was necessary to engage in the sometimes dirty details of politics to effect change. It was people themselves who created values, Willie argued. Society defined the good on the basis of its needs. Asked how he recognizes the good, Stark replied: "You just make it up as you go along." "When your great-great-grandpappy climbed down out of the tree he didn't have any more notion of good or bad, or right and wrong, than the hoot owl that stayed up in the tree," Willie lectured Adam Stanton, a character who embodied an other-worldly idealism and an unbending standard of moral purity that were also features of Jack's character. "Well, he climbed down and he began to make Good up as he went along. He made up what he needed to do business, Doc. . . . That's why things change, Doc. Because what folks claim is right is always just a couple of jumps short of what they need to do business" (258–59). Ironically, it was Adam Stanton, in the name of honor, who murdered Willie.

If Willie was a model, albeit a morally dubious one, of action, Jack was the epitome of inaction. He lacked direction and consistently fled or withdrew at critical moments of his life, falling into fits of depression (which he glibly referred to as the "Great Sleep") when walking out on his wife, quitting the doctoral dissertation he had almost completed, or, crucially, when learning that his ideal of southern femininity, his childhood love, Anne Stanton, was sleeping with Willie Stark. Jack was an idealist, holding himself aloof from the corruptions and the compromises to which a full engagement in life might potentially lead. His life as a graduate student was, he admitted, a way of "hiding from the present" (160). Jack's inability to consummate his teenage affair with Anne (he was unable to separate Anne his lover from his adolescent vision of her innocence—sex with her would not be "right," he declared) was only the most poignant and crucial incidence of a general character defect (295).

The moral progression of the book was the movement of Jack Burden through three succeeding life philosophies, from his youthful idealism, through a false naturalism (a belief that all is biology and that society and human beings are governed by the "great twitch"), to a mature and chastened pragmatism and moral realism. By the end of the novel, Jack was a redeemed character, having united with Anne and accepted moral responsibility for the unintended consequences of his actions, which included the death of his biological father. But Warren presented this redemption as a function of Burden's personal reconception of the nature of the past and his own personal history. Burden's ultimate realization was that, although the past limits human action, it is not fate.

Warren created a compelling portrait of depression in the character of Jack Burden, who, when falling into the "Great Sleep," was unable to get out of bed and face the world. Jack was unhappy and alone, trapped by past decisions, by the circumstances of his upbringing, by failure and missed opportunity. From the time Warren originally conceived *All the King's Men* as a play, the character of the newspaperman (which evolved into Jack Burden) was redolent of lost youth. In the play, Warren later remembered, Adam Stanton, preparing to assassinate the southern politician, turned to the journalist, his boyhood friend, "with a sense of elegiac nostalgia for the innocence and simplicity of the shared experiences of boyhood."[20]

Jack's depression paralleled Warren's own emotional life. The 1940s were a difficult period for him. Warren's 1930 marriage to Cinina Brescia was an unhappy one, and Warren lacked the comforts of serene home life. Cinina was a jealous and sometimes abusive alcoholic, eventually requiring clinical treatment; she fought with his friends, including the Agrarian "brethren." As a consequence, Warren withdrew emotionally, minimizing the contact between his wife and his friends. She and Warren divorced in 1951.[21] It was not until the 1950s, after a second marriage to writer Eleanor Clark and the birth of two children, that Warren was able to construct the kind of loving home that he desired. From the mid-1940s until about 1954, he experienced a drought in his ability to write lyric poetry.[22]

Throughout *All the King's Men*, Jack's search for knowledge was almost always historical. The book is laced with Jack's historical research, whether the history of Willie Stark, Jack's own past, his incomplete dissertation on Cass Mastern, or his final research project into the personal history of Judge Irwin. Ineffectual in many areas of his life, Jack was a dogged seeker of truth. Life is motion toward knowledge, ran one of his early philosophies (150–51). One defines oneself through knowledge of the past, but it was this that Jack could not face. He was tortured by history. After his discovery of Anne's affair with Willie Stark, Jack fled to the West, one more example of his inability to deal with the world. His intentional retreat, though, unintentionally became an extended reliving of his own past. "To the hum and lull of the car the past unrolled in my head like a film," he recalled (273, 309).

Jack's redemption and healing occurred only when he became able to face the past, which was the result of a changed understanding of one's relation to the past. The paradox of mutability is a recurring motif in the novel. Indeed, it is always clear that Jack the narrator is writing about earlier versions of himself. "I (who am what Jack Burden became)," he said at one point; a little later Jack recalled Willie saying something "to me (to Me who was what Jack Burden, the student of history, had grown up to be)" (188, 191). When looking back over the past, Jack was fascinated by the idea that a human being can sometimes seem so different (so much younger, more naive, perhaps innocent) at different times in life as to be almost a different person. Yet, he asserted, they are always, "metaphysically," the same (13). The younger, immature Jack could not see how people can change. This was the defect of his idealism. Human beings tended to be reified values for the young Jack. They were most importantly defined, he believed, by some metaphysical essence. His "Anne problem," for example, lay in the way she represented virginal and innocent southern womanhood. When Jack looked around him, he did not see people; he saw walking, talking ideas. His love for Anne was tempered by the fact that he saw her less as a human and more as an icon of purity.

The problem of what in people could change and what was the metaphysical essence that cannot is at the heart of *All the King's Men*. The young Jack Burden's entire view of history was static and imprisoning. Actions once taken could not be changed or replotted; an object once shattered (or once defiled) could not be made whole, not with all the king's men, nor all the king's horses. Once we understand "the pattern we are in, the definition we are making for ourselves," the immature Jack believed, we are unable to break free of it. "We can only live in terms of the definition, like the prisoner in the cage in which he cannot lie or stand or sit, hung up in justice to be viewed by the populace." The only way to break out of this definition was, of course, to make a "new self." The immature Jack saw this as an impossibility: "But how can the self make a new self when the selfness which is it, is the only substance from which the new self can be made?" (351). He was unable to answer the paradox. Yet it is the very mutability of self that contained the answer. Warren intended the character of Jack to represent a superior, pragmatic understanding of self, one in which identity was not a Platonic essence but the product of human interaction and historical evolution. Identity was an ever changing relationship to a people and a past. Reality is not a function of an event, Jack argued, but of the "relationship of the event to past, and future, events" (384).

"The truth," Jack said self-mockingly, "shall make you free" (260). Yet the truth of the past never set Jack free. It only entailed responsibility, gave lessons in his own failings, or emphasized the spiritual weaknesses of his mother and presumed father. The immature Jack conceived of the past as merely a reflection of his own character. If it did not show him perfection, he shrank from it, collapsing into one of his "Great Sleeps." He was afraid of the past, Jack wrote, because it was a "reproach" to him (189). It did not reflect the moral purity or unassailable character that Jack craved, and, absent the pragmatic belief that identity was an ever changing product of human action, Jack found this historical reality morally incapacitating.

Such a static conception of the past—a sense of the past as a mirror that faithfully reflects oneself—drains one's life of moral responsibility, for it promotes a sense of the past as fate, a view that negated a belief in free will. In *Pragmatism* (1907), William James argued that free will is a wonderful "doctrine of *relief*," a "general cosmological theory of *promise*." "Free-will pragmatically means *novelties in the world*, the right to expect that in its deepest elements as well as in its surface phenomena, the future may not identically repeat and imitate the past," he wrote.[23] Warren clung to this notion, and it informs his account of Jack Burden. Jack's new approach to his past was shaped by empathy and acceptance, an approach he attempted to explain to Anne Stanton: "I tried to tell her how if you could not accept the past and its burden there was no future, for without one there cannot be the other, and how if you accept the past you might hope for the future, for only out of the past can you make the future" (435). At the end of the novel, Jack was poised to leave his childhood home of Burden's Landing, able, at last, to break free of the demand for moral innocence that characterized his youth. He and Anne may return some day: "But that will be a long time from now, and soon now we shall go out of the house and go into the convulsion of the world, out of history into history and the awful responsibility of Time" (438). He and Anne literally left Burden's Landing, but they were not leaving their pasts, only an unhealthy and nostalgic vision of the past, one that inhibited social change, excused moral injustice, and instilled enervating and self-deluding visions of innocence.

Although the trajectory of Warren's career lay away from the South and he had played only a minor role in the original Agrarian agitation, his concerns and outlook remained recognizably shaped by Agrarianism. Indeed, after the 1940s, Warren retreated from the stark and lonely vision of *All the King's Men* and reconsidered the way in which the past might function as a source of spiritual revitalization. In this task, his inspiration lay partly in Native American mysticism, but he also continued to blend Agrarian insights with the pragmatic and ironic philosophy that shaped *All the King's Men*.

Very much like Richard Weaver, Warren was influenced by John Crowe Ransom's *God without Thunder*. In a 1935 essay on Ransom's poetry, Warren observed that Ransom believed the modern "dissociation of sensibility" could be remedied by myth. Myth healed the dissociation, for it entailed the exercise of both the intellect and the imagination; thought and feeling became one. Some myths were harmful. Ransom condemned the "myth of rationality," a poor and inadequate myth, which substituted the satiation of the artificial desires generated by an industrial society for the free play of sensibility, feeling, and emotion. In 1931, Ransom, pouring Warren a bourbon, expressed his own puzzlement at *God without Thunder*: "I found it very odd that I who am not a religious man, should write such a book; but

Robert Penn Warren. (Courtesy Yale Collection of American
Literature, Beinecke Rare Book and Manuscript Library)

I had to write it for the truth that's in it." Recalling the remark sixty
years later, Warren was still struck by the way in which it clarified his
own thinking, for he was not a religious man, either. Yet he was not
antireligious. He was, rather, a "yearner"—"I mean I wish I were religious," he told an interviewer—and Ransom had given him a way of
accepting religion as a "necessary myth."[24]

Warren saw the same logic in Joseph Conrad's novel *Nostromo*. The
attempt to escape the "sea" of human illusions and dreams, which
buoy up the struggling human, would result in death. Man is not fit
to live outside the sea; he is not designed to walk on the dry land of
"naturalism." This insight lay behind Conrad's idea of a "true lie."
"The last wisdom," Warren wrote, "is for man to realize that though
his values are illusions, the illusion is necessary, is infinitely precious,
is the work of his human achievement, and is, in the end, his only
truth."[25]

In 1953, Warren published a book-length poem in blank verse,
Brother to Dragons, which revisited many of the themes of *All the King's
Men* but was at once more personal and more broadly concerned with
the role of history in a people's life. In many ways, this poem was
a counterpart to Allen Tate's "Ode to the Confederate Dead" and

Donald Davidson's *The Tall Men*. It was Warren's definitive treatment of the southern past and the role of history in the life of the modern southerner. In *Brother to Dragons*, which was based on true incidents in the lives of two of Thomas Jefferson's nephews, Warren attempted to reconcile the imperative for historical accuracy with the imperative for "true lies," or in Ransom's term, "myth." "Historical sense and poetic sense should not, in the end, be contradictory," he wrote, "for if poetry is the little myth we make, history is the big myth we live, and in our living, constantly remake."[26]

On 15 December 1811, the night, coincidentally, of the great New Madrid earthquake in the Mississippi Valley, Lilburn Lewis, the nephew of Thomas Jefferson, murdered with an ax a teenaged slave named George; either Lilburn himself or a slave under his order butchered George and burned his body. The murder was performed in front of Lilburn's slaves and was only discovered when part of the remains were found. The breaking of a pitcher that belonged to his deceased mother was the ostensible reason for George's brutal murder. Lilburn and his brother Isham were indicted for the act by the local authorities of the frontier western Kentucky community near which their parents, Charles Lewis and Lucy Jefferson Lewis, had bought some land and settled. Lilburn died in an apparent suicide pact with his brother, but Isham escaped and, according to legend, was one of the few Americans to die with Andrew Jackson at the Battle of New Orleans. Jefferson is not known to have ever mentioned the shocking incident.[27]

Brother to Dragons was an imagined dialogue in verse between Jefferson, his sister Lucy, her sons Isham and Lilburn, and Jefferson's cousin Meriwether Lewis, who had been charged with exploring the great Louisiana Purchase. "R.P.W.," the narrator, served to draw out the story of what happened and, with Jefferson, develop a stronger understanding of human nature and history as a result. The personalization of the work, with the inclusion of R.P.W. and the relation of details from the actual process by which Warren wrote the poem (including visits to the ruins of the old Lewis home that Warren had made with his father), rekindled Warren's lyrical voice. He had not composed a short lyric for almost a decade before the publication of *Brother to Dragons*, but its writing led to experiments with a more personal style of writing, which eventually characterized the poems collected in Warren's well-received *Promises* in 1957. The fully developed R.P.W., James H. Justus observed, marks *Brother to Dragons* as a "watershed" for Warren, "an enabling work that allowed the poetry to develop in a more open and confessional manner."[28]

In the poem, Jefferson symbolized Ransom's "myth of rationality." He represented what Warren considered to be a fatally misleading optimism about the nature and abilities of human beings and the possibilities of democracy. Jefferson preferred the rectilinear grace of classic architecture, representative, for Warren, of his dream that order and symmetry could be imposed on the teeming variety of nature. Reason would conquer all, and traditional religion and conceptions of evil were the antiquated myths of the Dark Ages. Warren's Jefferson was repulsed by the leering gargoyles and vicious serpents he saw in the gothic architecture of France, the "Flotsam and the frozen foam / Of an ebbed disturbance in Time's tide, / The nightmare of a sick child who screamed in the dark" (39). He preferred the classic lines of the Maison Quarrée in Nîmes, an example of Roman architecture he had recorded in his journal (and that Jefferson used as the model for the Virginia state capitol, which he designed). "I stood in the place, and saw it," Jefferson stated in the poem:

> I stood there, and I saw the law of Rome and the eternal
> Light of just proportion and the heart's harmony,
> And I said: "Here is a shape that shines" (39–40)

Warren denied any essential innocence or purity in nature. It was not a source of light; rather, borrowing from Joseph Conrad, Warren pictured the raw American wilderness of the early nineteenth century as the heart of darkness, untracked and wild, revealing the depravity inherent in human nature to all those who entered it. The West was not virgin land; it was a teasing harlot, taunting the American to "come git it . . . git it deep" (16).[29] The savage butchering of the slave George by Jefferson's own kinsmen—indeed, implicitly, the fact of slavery itself—was testimony to the flawed nature of Jefferson's conception. There was much darkness even in the blood kin of one of America's most enlightened of men. Warren used Meriwether Lewis to condemn Jefferson. Lewis was like a son to Jefferson and, with William Clark, had led the expedition to map and explore Jefferson's Louisiana Purchase, which was to be his empire of liberty. Yet on returning east, Lewis had fallen into debt and scandal. He eventually committed suicide. In the poem, Lewis bitterly blamed Jefferson for his fate. It was the miserable disillusionment of his return to civilization that drove him to suicide, he claimed. When he returned, he discovered that "in the populous place of the civil contract / The civil breath breathes out the life" (181). Like Jack Burden, Lewis's peculiar malady seems to have been the inability to come to terms with a world that fell short of his moral ideal. The inculcation of false hopes, the "great lie" that a nation could be formed based on the "brotherhood of justice," was worse even than the realization of the evil in people. Lewis was the very personification of bitter disillusionment:

Listen, had I but known the truth of the heart.
Had I not dreamed that good comes, even if not easy.
Had I not dreamed that man at last is man's friend
And will long travel together and rejoice in steadfastness.
Had I not loved, and lived, your lie, then I
Had not been sent unbuckled and unbraced
To find the end—oh, the wilderness was easy!—
But to find, in the end, the tracklessness of the human
    heart. (184)

Jefferson's myth of rationality was pernicious and inadequate, Warren believed, leading only to disillusion and misfortune.

Jefferson's "lie" was not a "true lie" but rather a wrong and self-serving myth of history. It was bred of Jefferson's own vanity. Jefferson did not see the persistent potential for evil in human nature. Further, he evaded responsibility. In the poem, he refused to acknowledge Lilburn as his kin, merely disparaging him and his deeds, unable to face the crime of his own blood. ("I'll have no part, no matter / What responsibility you yourself wish," he told his sister Lucy, who insisted on tracing her son Lilburn's actions, in part, to her own deficit of love [188].) Responsibility was of primary importance to Warren and entailed the recognition that all actions produce results, whether intended or unintended. In a famous image from *All the King's Men*, Warren compared human actions to the touching of a web, each movement reverberating to the outermost corner and potentially instigating action on the part of the deadly spider at the center.[30] Meriwether Lewis claimed more respect for the ax-wielding Lilburn, whose derangement was more honest than Jefferson's "special lie," concocted for the aggrandizement of Jefferson's own ego and the maintenance of his noble self-image (186). In refusing to recognize Lilburn or his act, Jefferson was merely repeating the essential crime of moral irresponsibility (what the institution of slavery represented for the South as a whole). If anything, as Lucy told her brother, Jefferson's crime was "more monstrous still, / For what poor Lilburn did in exaltation of madness / You do in vanity" (189).

The absence of a serious consideration of slavery and racism was a crucial lacuna in Agrarianism. African Americans were not substantially present in the Agrarians' South. Warren's vision of blacks was doubled. They played a dual role in *Brothers to Dragons*. In one sense they represented the evil or blackness in human nature and served, in several of Warren's writings from the 1950s and early 1960s, as complementary figures to white southerners. They were the other half, the secret sharers of white consciousness. Neither the light of rationality nor the light of love (represented by Lucy in the poem) penetrated

the dark that enveloped Lilburn, who was driven by a paranoid suspicion of his slaves, in particular of George, the slave he eventually
murdered. The darkness of the wilderness only magnified the "dark
fear hiding" in Lilburn's breast. And this darkness was personified in
the dark people whom he held in bondage. "He saw poor George as
but his darkest self," Lucy explained to R.P.W., "And all the possibility of the dark he feared, / And so he struck down that darkest self"
(189). Warren also had Jefferson comment on the omnipresence of
the slaves, whose "picklock gaze" revealed the guilty secrets of the
heart (108). The gaze was present even in the most private of moments, "when / You turn inward, at the heart's darkest angle" (109).
There was no escape from conscience, and Lilburn's attempt to murder George was, in its nature, a futile gesture. No more effective was
Jefferson's attempt to deny Lilburn or to affirm the Enlightenment
myth of the noble savage.

At times, however, blacks become more than merely the embodiments of projected white guilt. They were also the existential heroes
of the poem, for they lived with the knowledge of darkness and evil
and engaged every day in the elemental struggle for meaning in a
hostile universe. They lived in the blackness of the world, without illusions, free of the delusive dreams of human perfection and brotherhood. When Jefferson was brought to a recognition of his shared
responsibility with Lilburn in the poem, he arrived at a new understanding of the past. He recalled that once he had told John Adams
that the dream of the future outshines any dream of the past. But
now he saw that the "fact of the past" was prerequisite to any accomplishment in the future, the same lesson learned by Jack Burden in
All the King's Men. In his culminating speech, Jefferson pronounced,
in existentialist fashion, that the future must be "forged beneath the
hammer of truth / On the anvil of our anguish." At this point, at the
end of Jefferson's revelatory speech, Warren placed the lines that had
first come to him four years before he began continuous work on the
poem, and he had them spoken as an existential cry of anguish by the
victim George, constituting George's only lines in the book:

> I was lost in the world, and the trees were tall.
> I was lost in the world, and the dark swale heaved.
> I was lost in my anguish, and I did not know the reason. (194)[31]

Redemption comes in the poem both through love, which links all to
one another, and knowledge, which teaches the shared responsibility
of all in evil and injustice. His vanity punctured and his dream of a
universal "brotherhood of justice" revealed to be a sham in a nation
that countenanced human bondage, Jefferson realized that he was not
only "brother to dragons and companion to owls" (Job 30:29) but

also a brother to the black man and a sharer in his condition. He, George, and everyone else was lost in a moral world that was terrifyingly empty. Values were not given; they had to be created.

Warren proposed history as the source of direction for modern human beings, yet not in the sense that some southerners conceived it. History was and should not be used as a justification for the moral failings of a society or culture. Warren's persona chastized Isham for seeking to evade his responsibility for George's brutal murder by pleading ignorance and incapacity. Isham was calling upon "the great Machine of History," whose gears were oiled, R.P.W. observed scornfully, with the "sweet lubrication / Of human regret" (127). Everyone deserves pity and grace, R.P.W. declared, "but, by God, that's still no reason / To regard all history as a private alibi-factory / And all God's gleaming world as a ward for occupational therapy" (112).

Like Tate's "Ode" and Davidson's *Tall Men*, *Brother to Dragons* was structured around the perambulations of a narrative persona in the present. As the narrator walked the earth and observed the world, he walked, too, through history, either to reject it or to weave and reweave it into the substance of his being. Both at the beginning and the end of the poem, R.P.W. recounted a journey with his father to see the ruins of the Lewis household in western Kentucky. To get to the old house, R.P.W. climbed a steep hill, the path overgrown with tangled vegetation. After ascending the hill a second time, R.P.W. experienced an epiphany that recalled but crucially differed from the narrator's in Davidson's *Tall Men*. Thinking of the dead under his feet, R.P.W. looked out over the flowing Ohio River, the ever changing but historically permanent marker of the division between North and South, which, he imagined, represented the passage of time and human lives over the course of history (209–11). At that point, Warren evoked the image by which so much history became real for southerners of his generation and upbringing: the grizzled old man, sitting around telling tales. Such were the men who told Davidson tales of war outside stores as a boy; and such were the old folks who had made Warren's childhood seem double-exposed in some sense, the dead always co-present with the living. Yes, yes, R.P.W. thought, "We believe you, Pap. / Yes, you were there and saw it." But the patronizing tone fades, for R.P.W. realized that by the passing down of stories and traditions, such old men took not only themselves but also Warren back "there." As R.P.W. continued, he began to recount the narrative of Lilburn and Isham and Meriwether Lewis's journey in the first-person plural. "We" fought our way across the continent, "we" were thrilled and terrified by what was found. But also, "we" wielded the meat ax that murdered poor George, and "we" were the slaves who watched in terror as the deed was committed (213).

History became not only a way to partake of the past glories of the human experience and to assume the values of a past age but also a call to moral responsibility that emphasizes the commonality of all human experience. As R.P.W. declared:

> The recognition of complicity is the beginning of innocence.
> The recognition of necessity is the beginning of freedom.
> The recognition of the direction of fulfillment is the death of
>   the self,
> And the death of the self is the beginning of selfhood.
> All else is surrogate of hope and destitution of spirit. (214–15)

If history had served for Davidson as a sacrament of identity, in which the Confederate war veterans played the Christ-like role of savior, it served for Warren as a less sacramental and more mystical ritual of spiritual regeneration.

The agnostic Warren looked to American Indian traditions and myths for inspiration. He had chosen a saying from the Paiute prophet Wovoka ("when it shake the earth dont be afraid no harm anybody") as one of his epigraphs for the book, and the Ghost Dance religion Wovoka founded became a metaphor for Warren's own faith in history. Warren derived this epigraph from an 1896 report of the federal Bureau of American Ethnology on the Ghost Dance religion. The report had been written by a pioneering anthropologist named James Mooney. Mooney began the first of six trips he would make to the West over the course of three and a half years in December 1890, the same month as the armed confrontation between United States soldiers and a band of Miniconjou Lakota Sioux outside the Pine Ridge reservation by Wounded Knee Creek.[32] The immediate cause of the fight at Wounded Knee was a new federal allotment policy, which divided the Great Sioux Reservation and entailed the forcible relocation of some Native Americans. Wounded Knee was a symbolic last stand for the Sioux in their long-running series of western wars with the United States. Thirty-nine soldiers and 153 Sioux, including women and children, died. A contributing factor to the tensions between the federal government and the Sioux was a new religious ceremony sweeping through Native American nations in the West — what the Sioux called the "spirit dance" and whites translated as the Ghost Dance. For agents of the Bureau of Indian Affairs, the new Ghost Dance religion was a sign of incipient rebellion.[33]

James Mooney became interested in this Ghost Dance religion. Born to Irish immigrant parents in Indiana, he sympathized with the Native Americans, who were displaced by the more powerful force of white Americans, perhaps because of his own intense identification with the cause of home rule for the Catholic majority in Ireland. In 1896, Mooney published *The Ghost-Dance Religion and the Sioux Outbreak of 1890*, in which he analyzed the Native American Ghost Dance within the context of other ecstatic religious movements in world history.[34] Religious movements driven by a nostalgia for a lost paradise were, he argued, a function of oppression. People naturally yearn for a redeemer who, he wrote, "shall return from exile or awake from some long sleep to drive out the usurper and win back for his people what they have lost." "The hope becomes a faith," Mooney declared, "and the faith becomes the creed of priests and prophets, until the hero is a god and the dream a religion, looking to some great miracle of nature for its culmination and accomplishment."[35]

The quotation from the prophet Wovoka used by Warren was originally from a letter written by Casper Edson, a young Arapaho man who knew some English, which detailed an encounter between a group of Cheyenne and Arapaho visitors and Wovoka in 1891.[36] Also known by the Euro-American name Jack Wilson, Wovoka lived in Mason Valley in western Nevada. On 1 January 1889, during a total solar eclipse and while ill and feverish, he lost consciousness and claimed to have been transported to heaven. It was then, Mooney wrote, based on his own interview with Wovoka early in 1892, that

> he saw God, with all the people who had died long ago engaged in their oldtime sports and occupations, all happy and forever young. It was a pleasant land and full of game. After showing him all, God told him he must go back and tell his people they must be good and love one another, have no quarreling, and live in peace with the whites; that they must work, and not lie or steal; that they must put away all the old practices that savored of war; that if they faithfully obeyed his instructions they would at last be reunited with their friends in this other world, where there would be no more death or sickness or old age.

God also gave Wovoka a dance, which, if performed according to instructions, would hasten the eventual reunion of living and dead.[37]

After his vision, Wovoka established himself as a prophet, proselytizing and promoting what the Paiute called the "dance in a circle." At times, when the dance was being performed, Wovoka would, using a familiar Native American technique, wave an eagle feather in front of a dancer to induce a trance.[38] Wovoka's religion spread throughout western Nevada, California, the Northwest, and the Great Plains. It became the Ghost Dance religion of the Sioux that so worried federal Indian agents and led to the massacre at Wounded Knee.[39] It was, in fact, a movement of cultural transformation—a revitalizing movement by which Native American peoples experiencing profound distress as a result of epidemics, aggression, and poverty sought to preserve their culture and adapt to changing circumstances. Other American Indian prophets had previously developed ecstatic religious devotions in the nineteenth century similar to Wovoka's, including the politicized messianism of the Shawnee prophet Tenskwatawa, which was the basis of a pan–American Indian rebellion organized in the Old Northwest by Tenskwatawa's brother Tecumseh but which ended in the Native American military defeat at the Battle of Tippecanoe in Indiana in 1811, and the religion of Handsome Lake, a Seneca prophet who preached against drunkenness, witchcraft, and promiscuity in the early nineteenth century and was the subject of a pioneering study of revitalization movements by anthropologist Anthony F. C. Wallace. Religions similar to the Ghost Dance preceded Wovoka's prophecy, and other Native American peoples readily adapted Wovoka's teachings. The Pawnee, for example, believed that, through their Ghost Dance, they were able to commune with the spirits of deceased ancestors and were thus able to pass along the rituals and healing arts of their people, which would otherwise have been lost.[40]

In *Brother to Dragons*, Jefferson's new vision of the possibility of spiritual rebirth was embodied in a call for a Ghost Dance. The poem itself was, in fact, a Ghost Dance, a colloquy of the living and the dead, with R.P.W. as the interlocutor. It was a means by which Americans today can commune and learn from their ancestors. Davidson's *Tall Men* was, too, in this sense, an artistic transmutation of the Ghost Dance ritual. Both Warren and Davidson's works were efforts to promote cultural transformation by communion with wise ancestors. Warren, however, rejected the earlier Ghost Dance of the Lost Cause and Davidson's *Tall Men*. The climax of *Brother to Dragons* is a call by a redeemed and chastened Jefferson for a new and different Ghost Dance, one built on the recognition of human frailty, sin, and moral complicity in the evils of humankind. Just prior to this moment, he had recalled what he once wrote John Adams, "my old enemy and friend" — that "the dream of the future is better than the dream of the past" (193). Although Jefferson had learned that this was true only if one reconciled oneself to the terrible facts of the past, Warren held the sentiment to be true. Jefferson, in fact, calls for a new, "grander" Ghost Dance, one oriented toward the future, the "awful responsibility of Time," not any idealized vision of the past:

> Dance back the buffalo, the shining land!
> Our grander Ghost Dance dance now, and shake the feather.
> Dance back the morning and the eagle's cry.
> Dance back the Shining Mountains, let them shine!

Dance into morning and the lifted eye.
Dance into morning past the morning star,
And dance the heart by which we have lived and died.

"For nothing we had, / Nothing we were, / Is lost," Jefferson declared. "All is redeemed, / In knowledge" (195).

Warren's hope for a type of spiritual revitalization built on historical remembrance was informed by Reinhold Niebuhr and C. Vann Woodward. Man's nature is to sin, Niebuhr stated in *The Irony of American History* (1952), but he is responsible for the consequences of his actions all the same. In Niebuhr's view, power was never wielded by a nation or a people without some guilt; no actions were unambiguously virtuous. A recognition of the way even the most noble of aspirations may become distorted in practice counseled humility. "The ironic elements in American history can be overcome, in short, only if American idealism comes to terms with the limits of all human striving, the fragmentariness of all human wisdom, the precariousness of all historic configurations of power, and the mixture of good and evil in all human virtue."[41] Woodward expressed this Niebuhrian viewpoint in *The Burden of Southern History*, a collection of essays published in 1960 and dedicated to Robert Penn Warren. The South, Woodward held, is changing, no longer defined by one-crop agriculture, Jim Crow, lynching bees, white primaries, sharecropping, or one-party politics. All the same, the South retained its identity, which was based not on these fading sociopolitical institutions but instead on a shared and distinctive history of poverty and defeat. The South, more than any other region, Woodward argued, allows Americans to see the irony of their past. The South, he observed in 1997, "has experiences of failure, defeat, and military occupation in its history that should, but rarely have, restrained the North's faith in success, victory, and invincibility." Similarly, *Brother to Dragons* was a rebuke to modern Americans, whose faith in technology, science, rationality, in short, progress, caused them to miss the commonalities that they share with all those generations that have preceded them.[42]

Not every southerner viewed the past in the same way as Warren; nor did all draw from it the imperative to rearticulate their values in a time of moral confusion. Nowhere was this more evident than in the struggle over segregation in the South and the subsequent black crusade for civil rights in the 1950s and 1960s.

In general, the Agrarians had portrayed blacks in racist stereotypes when not ignoring them altogether. Owsley had pictured black slaves as scarcely removed from cannibalism, a people no society in its right mind would accommodate on any level of equality. Davidson

tended to portray blacks as happy simpletons, contented and stolid
in their submissive acceptance of white leadership. At other times
Davidson evidenced a certain sensitivity to the deprivation experienced by blacks in America, feeling that black culture was hopelessly
weakened, a view perhaps influenced by his own sense of the fragility
of white folk culture. Elsewhere, there was the faintest suggestion in
Davidson that blacks, in their rock-ribbed religiosity and stubborn
preference for the good ways of country life, were closer models of his
own most favored social type, the yeoman farmer, than many whites.
"The Negro, so far as he had not been corrupted into heresy by modern education," Davidson wrote in 1949, "was the most traditional
of Southerners, the mirror which faithfully and lovingly reflected the
traits that Southerners once all but unanimously professed."[43]

Yet, on the whole, the Agrarians paid little attention to black southerners. Nor were there especially cordial social relations between the
Nashville Agrarians and blacks. An incident involving Tom Mabry,
a cousin of Caroline Gordon's, illustrates the point. Progressive on
race, Mabry attended Vanderbilt in 1931–32, seeking a master's degree in English. He became acquainted with James Weldon Johnson, a leading black author who was on the faculty of Fisk University, an all-black college also located in Nashville. The Agrarians
rebuffed Mabry's attempt to bring them together with Johnson and
the poet Langston Hughes (who was a visiting faculty member at
Fisk). Allen Tate wrote Mabry that "there should be no social inter-
course between the races unless we are willing for that to lead to
marriage."[44] Although Warren later remembered his racial attitudes
becoming liberalized in the years after he returned to the South in
1930, his own outlook at the time was marked by racism. Remarking on Mabry's acceptance of a position at Fisk, Warren observed
that he "has definitely decided to commercialize his talent for nigger-
loving." L. D. Reddick, a student at Fisk in the early 1930s and later
a professor of history at Alabama State College, noted in a review of
Warren's study of segregation that there were few mutual contacts
between Fisk and Vanderbilt. "There may have been two or three
furtive friendships and an occasional individual visit or a group tour,
but there was no general fraternizing, no intellectual communion,"
he wrote in the review. "Fisk had Negro students and a mixed—
Negro and white—faculty; Vanderbilt had white students and a white
faculty."[45]

The original Agrarians accepted the racial status quo. In 1929,
Davidson wrote Will Alexander, head of the Commission on Interracial Cooperation in Atlanta, that the "Southern View of the Negro
question" was one of the elements of southern culture he wished to

preserve. He carefully identified himself with the "*better* Southern view": blacks should be free of "political injustice" and "vindictive oppression." But the southern view, he stated, "means segregation, no social equality, probably economic subjection for a long time to come," and, he added, as complete disfranchisement as possible.[46]

A 10 May 1933 letter from Allen Tate to Lincoln Kirstein, the editor of *Hound and Horn*, reveals the stark terms in which he viewed the racial problem. Tate frankly stated that he considered blacks racially inferior and that, of the two races, only one could rule. The southern racial problem was simply insoluble, he argued, resorting to the argument from fate that Warren would later so detest. Social order, Tate declared, must come before justice, and equality for blacks would only result in social disorder. Blacks in the South might hope for legal justice but not social justice. Aside from arguments cast in the mold of this sort of conservative realism, Tate also railed against miscegenation. He distinguished between sexual unions involving white men and black women and those involving white women and black men. The latter were the direst threat to the southern order, in Tate's mind. "If a white woman has a negro child, then negro blood has passed into the white race," declared Tate, in crude racial terms. The southerner's purpose, he claimed, is to prevent this. White women bore the weight of the "dogma of racial integrity." It was not so much the presence of mixed-race children that endangered society, for these children, whether of white or black mothers, would be considered black and hence inferior. Rather, it was the "sexual consent" of white women that threatened to be explosive. Here, Tate appealed to the "psychology of sex," by which women are altered by sexual relations in a way men are not. The question was one of "moral symbolism," he argued. "A white woman pregnant with a negro child becomes a counter symbol, one of evil and pollution," Tate wrote.[47] Ultimately, blacks were a mystery to the Agrarians. They simply did not understand black culture, nor did they make an effort to try and understand it.

In Warren's writings into the 1950s black characters usually represented the darkness in which whites confront their innermost selves. Blacks were the whites' secret sharers in *Brother to Dragons*. In *Band of Angels*, a novel published in 1955, the central character, a young mixed-race woman raised as a white plantation mistress, was tortured by her racial identity, in turns fascinated and repulsed by blackness. Another character, rescued by a slave-trading master from what Warren extravagantly depicts as a morass of African cannibalism and primitiveness, becomes his master's *k'la*, or second self. A *k'la*, the master explained, is a slave who is "almost like a brother or son or something. It's the one you tell your secrets to. It's the one when you die that dies with you." Blacks were symbols of white guilt. Warren defined them by their relation to whites; they existed as complements to white identity.[48]

Nonetheless, Warren's attitudes were models of liberalism compared with those of southerners who persisted in defending segregation into the 1950s and raised the call of "massive resistance." Among those was counted Donald Davidson. Davidson was swept up in the emotion of the segregation controversies in Tennessee and in the South as a whole. He enthusiastically supported Strom Thurmond's 1948 Dixiecrat bid for the presidency, itself the result of President Harry S. Truman's modest civil rights proposals. Davidson helped to get Thurmond on the Tennessee ballot and canvassed his associates on and off the Vanderbilt campus before the election in his eagerness to predict the election results. "I shall take the greatest pleasure in voting for Thurmond," he wrote W. T. Couch. "This is the first time in my life that I have had a chance to vote for a real Southerner, a decent and intelligent Southerner, who is brave enough to express views that I can accept, or at least vote for without qualm — views that, ten or even five years ago it was worth a man's political or academic or literary life to express. Don't think I'd lose such a chance!" In 1950 Davidson joined the Tennessee States' Rights Committee. With the *Brown v. Board of Education* decisions handed down in 1954 and 1955, Citizens' Councils were formed throughout the South, and tempers flared. (Warren contemptuously referred to the Citizens' Councils, the primary organizations of white massive resistance, as the "uptown Klan" and "reading-and-writing Klan.")[49]

The Tennessee Federation for Constitutional Government (TFCG), Tennessee's version of a Citizens' Council, was formed in June 1955 to fight desegregation, with Davidson as its chairman. While many other Citizens' Councils appealed to working-class and poor southern whites, the TFCG drew its support from the middle class and was the only statewide organization fighting desegregation in Tennessee. Its goal was to coordinate peaceful opposition through public education and the filing of court challenges to school desegregation. Headquartered in Nashville and relatively well financed, the TFCG included, aside from Davidson, local business executives, attorneys, an artist, and other members of the Vanderbilt faculty. It was loosely affiliated with the national Federation for Constitutional Government, an organization of which Davidson was also a member. Senator James O. Eastland of Mississippi was the guiding voice behind the larger federation, which aspired to direct massive resistance across the South, but the organization never lived up to his ambition.[50]

Davidson saw the situation as perilous. "Please remember me in your prayers," he wrote his good friend John Donald Wade in August 1955. "It's going to be tough going from now on." Davidson was both optimistic and ambitious to widen the scope of the TFCG. Writing to Louis D. Rubin, then a young scholar and writer who was briefly pro-segregation, Davidson expressed his view of the battle ahead. "All this large conflict—which is speedily going to widen beyond the mere segregation issue—has many serious aspects that I can't go into here. But of course it has been on the way for a long time. On the whole, despite the rather bleak outlook at present, I rather incline to believe that we are entering a new 'climate of opinion' under which the views that you—and I—cherish will have a far better chance than they have had in the twenty or thirty years past."[51]

Like Eastland and other conservative white southerners, Davidson traced the root of the opposition to segregation to communism. "The trouble is that the pressure from the NAACP and the radicals of the North never lets up, and is always extreme, always has the official or semi-official backing of government, and influences both political parties," Davidson wrote in a June 1956 letter. "Behind it all, in the last analysis, is Communist and Socialist pressure and their long-distance planning." Davidson had earlier warned fellow Agrarian Stark Young of the same menace. "The liberal-leftist-Communist-socialist crowd around here of course waged continuous and systematic war upon what you (and I, and others) stand for," he wrote in 1952. "I don't know whether you realize, or not, how far-reaching and how unscrupulous their long campaign has been, and how many forms it can take."[52] Davidson's belief that civil rights activism played into the hands of the Soviet Union is also seen in *Tyranny at Oak Ridge*, a TFCG pamphlet on desegregation in the town adjacent to a federal nuclear laboratory in east Tennessee that may be the work of Davidson himself. "Khrushchev, Bulganin, Molotov, and their Politburo no doubt are well acquainted with what is going on at Oak Ridge," the pamphlet charged. "It is a victory for Moscow. Anything that weakens state governments and swells the power of blind bureaucracy makes it that much easier for Russian Communism to take over the United States from the inside."[53]

Although the TFCG sponsored speeches by such leading pro-segregation politicians as Thurmond and Eastland and surveyed candidates for elected office about their views on segregation, the organization was essentially ineffectual (one historian labeling it "politically impotent"). It was one of the least effective of the major massive resistance organizations in the South. The TFCG sought to prevent the integration of the Nashville public schools but without much success. Nashville had a long and proud tradition of black independence and autonomy, and the black community brought pressure on the city's white leadership to desegregate, which it succeeded in doing in a series of step-by-step plans. Overall, Tennessee was relatively moderate on the issue of segregation. The bulk of the support for the TFCG outside Nashville came from west Tennessee, where most of the state's blacks lived. Statewide it never enlisted a broad following. Although its efforts drew editorial support from some newspapers, the *Nashville Tennessean* and other more moderate papers ridiculed the organization. In an editorial, the *Tennessean* labeled TFCG's members "homegrown bigots." Even the pro-segregation *Nashville Banner*, its editor recalled years later, "never subscribed to some of the extreme positions of Mr. Davidson." Nor did the *Banner* agree with TFCG vice chairman Jack Kershaw's suggestion that Nashville abandon its public parks and Tennessee abandon its schools rather than desegregate.[54]

The nadir of TFCG's activism was an attempt to prevent desegregation in Clinton, a small town fifteen miles northwest of Knoxville in the eastern section of the state, where support for segregation was weak. The TFCG filed a lawsuit, subsequently dismissed, to prevent Clinton school officials' plans for an orderly process of integration. The organization's appeal to the state's supreme court eventually resulted, quite unintentionally, in the court striking down the state constitution's provisions for segregation. In the meantime, integration began in Clinton on a limited scale. Although the TFCG renounced violence (it condemned the Ku Klux Klan, for instance) and disapproved of the smaller pro-segregation organizations active in the state, it agreed to cosponsor, with such groups as the Tennessee Society to Maintain Segregation, the States' Rights Council of Tennessee, Pro-Southerners, and White Citizens' Councils, a protest rally on 1 September 1956. Representatives of the TFCG (but not Davidson, who was at Bread Loaf in Vermont) were at the rally, which almost ended in violence. One thousand National Guardsmen were ordered to the small town by Governor Frank Clement to restore order. Arriving at the last minute, they dispersed an angry crowd on the brink of violence. In an editorial aptly entitled "Stay the Hell Out," the *Tennessean* criticized the federation's intervention in Clinton, denouncing its members as "white-collar race baiters."[55]

The fight for segregation was Davidson's chance to reenact the historical struggle of the frontiersman, which he had chronicled in his poetry and his two-volume history of the Tennessee River. In "The New South and the Conservative Tradition," an abbreviated version of an address delivered in April 1958 at Bowdoin College that was published in the *National Review* in 1960, Davidson lay claim to the southern tradition of the "actual South." The "actual South," Davidson wrote, is "a truly American society, organic with its past and inescapably alive in its present." The "New South" was not part of the southern tradition but rather "*the expectation that the North has of the South*" and "*the South's response to that expectation.*" New South support of business development, industrialization, progressive government, interracial unity, and the moonlight-and-magnolias sentimentalization of the antebellum past were northern habits. New South spokesmen, Davidson claimed, were bankrolled by the North.[56]

In effect, Davidson arrogated to himself the right to define who was southern and who was not, who belonged and who did not. As far as Davidson was concerned, proponents of the New South were defectors, their identity in some sense counterfeit. "The New South man is sabotaging Southern principles, and must be regarded as an alien," Davidson declared. Actual southerners would never accept the romantic, high-sounding, but deceptive myths retailed by Henry Grady and others like him. "Nothing Henry Grady said could ever fool my grandmother," Davidson wrote, "who, in the sixties, had seen her childhood friends captured by marauding Federal soldiers and shot in cold blood on the main street of her home town." This incident, told to him by his grandmother when he was a child, was also included in *The Tall Men*. His grandmother's memory had become Davidson's own, and it produced in him not redemption but anger and defensiveness.[57]

Davidson's opposition to federal efforts to desegregate the South was shared by many in the nascent conservative movement. The *National Review* opposed federally enforced integration from the start. Buckley's magazine printed not only Davidson's commentary on southern values and the dangers of the federal leviathan but also Richard Weaver's defense of segregation.[58]

Davidson wrote to Warren in 1958 that he believed the nation was approaching "some sort of 'Civil War.' " "Things *are* falling apart and the center is *not* holding!" he exclaimed pessimistically. After reading Davidson's *National Review* article, Tate wrote Warren complaining of its "tortured and disingenuous" nature. "I fear his Southernism, for all its cunning and learning, is now at the level of mere White Supremacy," observed Tate, whose views had become more moderate since 1933. "The Nigger is literally in his woodpile; he refers only twice to him, though we know he is motivating the entire argument." Warren himself had long since dismissed Davidson's views on race. He counseled Davidson's publisher not to reprint one of Davidson's old pieces on the race issue. "The tone is frenetic, the irony not very effective, and the reasoning sometimes, to me at least, fallacious." But for Warren the issue went deeper than Davidson's white supremacy. It touched on Davidson's view of history, and the role it plays in human affairs. "The argument from history is a very important one, but it isn't an absolute one," Warren observed. "And it ignores the argu-

ments from political justice or Christian charity." Davidson, in Warren's view, had adopted history as an alibi. "Don really argues that
history is fate, unalterable fate," Warren wrote.[59]

As the 1950s progressed and the federal desegregation decisions
were handed down, Warren felt the need to repudiate the nationalistic
use of southern history exemplified by Davidson and those like him.
But Davidson's sacramentalism of the past revealed certain contradictions in Warren's own ideas. The southern history that Warren
found redemptive also served as the bulwark for the most retrograde
of southern emotions. Many southerners were using their region's
myths and traditions to support race hatred, violence, and lynching.
Warren's 1956 book, *Segregation: The Inner Conflict of the South*, an expanded version of an essay commissioned for *Life* magazine, was his
personal attempt to come to terms with the tensions within his own
understanding of the Agrarian use of the past. As James W. Prothro
observed of the little volume, "Mr. Warren does not subject the inner
conflicts of the South to systematic analysis, he mirrors them."[60]

Warren the author is very much a presence in *Segregation*, for it
is a record of his return to the areas of the South with which he
was most familiar—Kentucky, Tennessee, Arkansas, Mississippi, and
Louisiana—and the interviews and discussions he had there. Warren
attempted to report the reasons why white southerners clung to segregation, as well as to define what it was that blacks wanted. He was
noticeably more successful at the first task than the second, for the
inner division of the South to which the subtitle referred appeared in
Warren's book more as the inner division of the white South. As Prothro observed, the division existed in Warren himself. Warren quoted
a girl from Mississippi who felt that "it's all happening inside of me,
every bit of it," adding, "I know what she meant." Warren saw the past
as a source of value but also realized, as a fellow passenger stated on
the plane trip back to the North, that southerners needed to "claw
out" of their troubles. "It is hard to claw out from under the past and
the past way," the man reflected.[61]

Despite all the reasons Warren saw for the widespread support of
segregation—including pride, money, racial differences, backwardness, power, hatred, constitutional scruples—he emphasized one in
particular, "piety." Many in the South were disoriented, he concluded,
"uprooted, driven from the land, drawn from the land, befuddled
by raw opportunities, new ambitions, new obligations. They have
entered the great anonymity of the new world." Segregation was for
them, after all, a means by which to retain what they valued from an
earlier way of living. In this sense, as a defense of traditional values
against modernity, segregation fit the Agrarian program. And al-

though Warren explicitly opposed segregation, he indicated that he believed desegregation would come only gradually. As L. D. Reddick noted, there were "loud echoes" of *I'll Take My Stand* in the book, for in "The Briar Patch," too, Warren had suggested that segregation would end only after a very long period of time. Reddick believed the real ordeal of the South was that experienced by blacks and not self-absorbed whites. He wrote cuttingly of Warren's book, "The picture that emerges is the old familiar one that may be noticed any day in cruder colors in the extremist press of the Deep South: The mistakes of the North are emphasized; the weaknesses of the Negro under-scored; and, above all, there is the determination of Southern white folk, they say, that 'nobody's a gonna *make* us. If we let the nigger in . . . we'll do so when we're good and ready!' "[62]

Warren was entangled in his own emotional attachment to the southern past. He saw that some who resisted court-ordered deseg-regation were motivated by high ideals:

> They dream of preserving the traditional American values of indi-vidualism and localism against the anonymity, irresponsibility, and materialism of the power state, against the philosophy of the ad-man, the morality of the Kinsey report, and the gospel of the bitch-goddess. *To be Southern again:* to re-create a habitation for the values they would preserve, to achieve in unity some clarity of spirit, to envisage some healed image of their own identity.

Yet, for southerners like Warren, who took very seriously the ambi-tion *to be a southerner again,* the moral obloquy of segregation stared them in the face, and the scurrilous and pathetic nature of the most ardent segregationists (for instance, the man Warren talked to who was a specialist in "ethnolology" and cited books showing blacks to be parasites) was distasteful. Southerners such as himself felt "the intellectual rub, the moral rub." The simple appeal to the southern past—the "argument of *mere* social continuity and the justification by *mere* mores"—was never adequate. For those who viewed the past in this way, Warren believed, "circumstances and values [were] frozen." They were fatalists. "The essence of individuality is the willingness to accept the rub which the flux of things provokes, to accept one's fate in time," Warren wrote. "What heroes would these idealists en-shrine to take the place of Jefferson and Lee, those heroes who took the risk of their own fate?"[63]

Warren was unwilling, however, to make sharp moral condemna-tions or ethical judgments in his reading of history. From his perspec-tive, all values were the products of individual negotiations with fate and circumstance. Such was the nature of moral decision making in our world of "action and liability." Warren's Agrarianism was a form

of pragmatism, the philosophy that Warren believed to be a "tenta-
tive, experimental, 'open' approach to the life process." He was suspicious of anyone given to moral absolutism, such as the abolitionists
and transcendentalists, whom he portrayed in *The Legacy of the Civil
War* (1961) as irresponsible idealists, scorning social action for fear
of moral contamination. Borrowing a page from historian Richard
Hofstadter, he suggested they were motivated to denounce slavery less
from moral principle than status anxiety in the face of a rising par-
venu industrial bourgeoisie.[64]

Gradually, however, blacks came to be for Warren something more
than the secret sharers of white people's guilt and fear. In part, this
was the result of his talking with more and more blacks. Aware, perhaps, of his inability to empathize fully with blacks, Warren produced
in 1965 a book of interviews with black leaders, old and young, from
varying political perspectives and with differing connections to the
civil rights movement. Blacks typified the challenges of modern life.
"I seize the word *identity*," Warren wrote, somewhat disingenuously,
as if it were a new word to him and not a concept central to his thought
since the 1940s. "It is a key word. You hear it over and over again. On
this word will focus, around this word will coagulate, a dozen issues,
shifting, shading into each other."[65]

The book was an extended investigation of the dynamics of black
identity. Armed with the concepts of Erik Erikson and other social
scientists and with the historical theories of Stanley Elkins, Warren
was more ready than ever to make sweeping generalizations about the
black loss of identity, the infantilization resulting from slavery, and
the dysfunctional nature of the female-centered black family. Warren found in Malcolm X the very model of the black existentialist
hero, as well as the ultimate "secret sharer," a man whose every word
seemed a reminder of white guilt.[66] Nonetheless, Warren remained
a gradualist, as wary of integration as he had ever been. A change
like integration, he explained, required that an old self "*die* into the
new life," a difficult process. Warren professed a great respect for
black leadership and considered the black leaders he met responsible
and dedicated, but he did not endorse civil disobedience. Indeed, in
a 1961 exchange of open letters with his friend Nicola Chiaromonte,
a European intellectual urging civil disobedience to protest French
conduct of the Algerian War, Warren argued that civil disobedience
was revolutionary and, in a democratic state, undercut democracy.
In April 1965, he spoke to a segregated audience at the University
of Mississippi's Southern Literary Festival despite a walkout staged
by a biracial delegation from nearby all-black Tougaloo College. The
delegation members had been harassed during their stay in Oxford,
Mississippi. Warren considered their treatment shameful but decided

to proceed with his lecture, in which he argued that Faulkner saw the rejection of blacks, brothers and kinsmen to southerners, as the "final crime against both nature and the human community." Warren bridled when *Newsweek* depicted him as a paternalistic and somewhat irrelevant moderate. Whites delude themselves, he declared in a response to the magazine, if they believe they can merely hand down a solution to the current problems. The Negro is in the right, he affirmed, and the matter is urgent.[67]

The figure in *Who Speaks for the Negro?* whom Warren most admired was Ralph Ellison, the moderate and respected novelist. Ellison sympathized with the plight of white southerners, agreeing with Warren that they were "imprisoned" by the emotions surrounding segregation. Ellison's pluralistic stance celebrated the distinctiveness of every culture but also the freedom to cross over racial and cultural boundaries as one's taste dictated. One of the privileges of being an American, he told Warren, is "to be able to project myself into various backgrounds, into various cultural patterns, *not* because I want to cease being a Negro or because I think that these are automatically better ways of realizing oneself, but because it is one of the great glories of being an American." Such pluralism allayed Warren's anxiety over integration. More important, Ellison rejected what Warren called the "gambit of the alibi," the impulse of blacks to adopt the self-justifying stance of the victim. This was a close analogue to the segregationists' use of history, which Warren condemned. Warren agreed with Ellison that the authenticity of black writing should not be determined by ideological measures. Ellison, Warren wrote, was "willing, pridefully, to head into responsibility," perhaps the highest compliment to be paid a person in Warren's way of thinking.[68]

Warren was disgusted with the resistance he saw in the South during the civil rights era, the same resistance that so warmed and reassured Davidson. Warren felt in some ways betrayed by the South. When he saw a picture of a young white man sympathetic to the civil rights movement being beaten during the 1960 Nashville sit-ins, the reality hit home, for this young man was ostracized and beaten in the city where Warren had spent so many happy and formative years when he himself was young. He was moved to write an essay on the incident, although he never published it. The event pictured, Warren wrote, "robs me of something: my identity." He himself would have been beaten, he observed, if he had sat at that stool at a dime store counter because he found that he agreed with the protest and admired its participants for their courage. The men who beat such protesters controlled public discussion in the South; they endangered Warren's own identity as a southerner, for they were redefining the South. "A man has his identity only in a right relation to his society," Warren declared. Without identity Warren felt condemned to the "spook-haven of exurbia," what he later termed the "no-society" and "anti-community" that too much of American was becoming.[69]

By the 1960s, it was not only the bureaucratized imperatives of modern society that threatened Warren's values. The new threat was not black southerners, despite the trepidation with which Warren viewed integration. Rather, the new enemy was the white southerners who had beaten the young student protester and all those other south-erners who would not effectively squelch such violence. It was pro-segregationists such as Davidson who had become the greatest im-pediments to Warren's vision of a revitalizing southern Ghost Dance. In the crucible of the 1960s, Agrarianism had come to be newly di-vided against itself. And so, too, was Warren divided against himself. It was Donald Davidson, Warren's old teacher and lifelong friend, and not the black man, who had come to be Warren's other self, the south-erner who could not break free of the chains of history.

CHAPTER EIGHT

The Survival of the South
The Agrarian Tradition, Southern Identity, and the Modern South

The only freedom which can last is a freedom embodied somewhere, rooted in a history, located in space, sanctioned by genealogy, and blessed by a religious establishment. The only equality which abstract rights, insisted upon outside the context of politics, are likely to provide is the equality of universal slavery. It is a lesson which Western man is only now beginning to learn.

M. E. Bradford, *A Better Guide Than Reason*

In 1981, the University of Georgia Press published *Why the South Will Survive*, a collection of essays written by Fifteen Southerners. The book was the product of a conference held in Columbia, South Carolina, in August 1979 in anticipation of the fiftieth anniversary of the publication of *I'll Take My Stand* and organized by Clyde N. Wilson, a historian at the University of South Carolina and editor of the John C. Calhoun Papers. Both volumes were concerned with what was perceived as an endangered southern way of life, but the latter volume differed from its predecessor not only in its assessment of what that way of life was and how to preserve it but also in the question that shaped the entire enterprise: Did the South still exist as a distinct and viable region? Wilson intended the book to be a reply to contemporary commentators who were proclaiming the disappearance of the South.[1]

The boom economy of World War II that had so changed the South continued to soar into peacetime, in no small part owing to the advent of the widespread use of air-conditioning throughout the region, a technological breakthrough that helped make the South attractive to industry, corporations, and retirees. The war had fostered the diversification of southern manufacturing, but, after the war, southern states established offices to lure industry and business to their region, which boasted a large, lower-wage, and predominantly nonunionized workforce. The number of factories in the South grew by 200 percent between 1939 and 1972. Such conditions provided the basis for the South's postwar "sunbelt" renaissance.[2] Further, by 1960, the South had moved to a substantially diversified agriculture. Highly mechanized plantations in Texas, Oklahoma, New Mexico, Arizona, and California accounted for more than half the nation's cotton production as early as 1949. Ten years later, only eleven counties in the South's old cotton belt still grew cotton as their principal crop. Between 1940 and 1960, the distribution of southern population had shifted from 65 percent rural to 58 percent urban. By the 1960s, then, the South had modernized. It was no longer an agrarian region in any meaningful sense. All told, more than 14 million southerners left the farm between 1940 and 1980; nonagricultural jobs tripled, industrial jobs almost doubled. By 1980, only 3 to 4 percent of southerners (about 1.6 million) farmed.[3]

African American migration to the North, occurring in great waves from around 1910 onward, accounted for much of the South's loss of rural population. The black southerners who stayed in the South, however, produced perhaps the most revolutionary changes in that region, shaking southern society to its foundations as thousands of local activists increasingly challenged the institutions of white supremacy and segregation. The civil rights movement may have fallen short of altering the fundamental economic inequalities of southern society, but it changed the face of southern social life and politics. Legal segregation collapsed by the 1960s; the Civil Rights Act of 1964 and the Voting Rights Act of 1965 introduced a mass of black voters into southern politics. Only one-fifth of the voting-age black population was registered to vote in 1952, constituting just 6 percent of the southern electorate. By 1972, more than 3.5 million southern blacks successfully registered to vote; in 1984, the number of registered black voters in the former Confederacy rose to 5.6 million. By the early 1970s, Mississippi—a state in which the percentage of blacks registered to vote had risen from 6.7 to 67 in the space of seven years—had the most elected black officials of any state in the Union, and African Americans had served as mayors of such towns as Tuskegee, Alabama; Fayette, Mississippi; and Madison, Arkansas. Former Georgia governor Jimmy Carter rode into the presidency in 1976, in part, on the strength of 90 percent of the black vote. (Fifty-five percent of white southerners voted for this southern Democrat's opponent.)[4]

Black political success shattered the solid South, which had voted as a bloc for Democratic presidential candidates from 1880 to 1944. Conservative Republican politicians such as Barry Goldwater, Richard M. Nixon, and Ronald Reagan successfully tapped southern white political support on the national level. In the 1950s, Democrats outnumbered Republicans eight to one in the South, but over the next thirty years the Democratic Party suffered a net loss of 25 percent of its membership, compared with a net gain of 20 percent for the Republicans. By 1988, one study reported that 35 percent of white southerners identified themselves as Democrats, 26 percent as Republican, and 39 percent as independents. The South increasingly became solidly Republican in presidential politics. As early as 1952, Dwight D. Eisenhower had broken the Democratic stranglehold on the South in presidential contests, winning Virginia, Tennessee, Florida, Oklahoma, and Texas. (In 1956 he added Louisiana as well.) In 1964, Senator Strom Thurmond of South Carolina switched to the Republican Party and supported the insurgent conservative presidential campaign of Senator Barry Goldwater, who, apart from his home state of Arizona, won only the southern states of South Carolina, Georgia, Alabama, Mississippi, and Louisiana. Richard M. Nixon swept the South in 1972.[5] Republican presidential candidates won the South in five of the six elections between 1972 and 1988 (prior to the candidacy of Democrat Bill Clinton in the 1990s). Segregationist Governor George C. Wallace of Alabama pioneered a politics of white racial backlash, creating a potent electoral mix of anticommunism, social conservatism, economic populism, and covert racial resentment, which he used to pummel the national liberal establishment. Wallace displayed electoral strength in the North as well as the South. In 1964 he entered Democratic presidential primaries in Indiana, Wisconsin, and Maryland and stunned political observers by winning 30 percent of the vote or better in each one. He won 33 percent of the southern vote in his independent presidential bid in 1968, coming in just below Nixon and carrying five states, and 13.5 percent of the vote nationally. Before the ill-fated Maryland rally on 15 May 1972, at which a disturbed gunman shot and crippled him, Wallace had won Democratic primaries in Florida, Tennessee, and North Carolina and had finished a strong second in Wisconsin, Pennsylvania, and Indiana.[6]

George Wallace's politics of rage and resentment, which grew out of the southern white strategy of "massive resistance" to desegregation and civil rights activism, was not the era's primary legacy for the white South, however. In fact, the end of segregation and black disfranchisement seemed to exorcise some of the South's racial demons, at least in northern eyes. The success of the civil rights movement combined with the burgeoning prosperity of the South and the election of a southerner to the presidency in 1976 inaugurated a vogue of southern chic in the late 1970s. Across the country, Americans exhibited a selective fascination with elements of southern culture —

including country music, redneck swagger, down-home cooking, and the tradition of gracious hospitality. While many southerners fretted that their newly urbanized and industrialized region was becoming homogenized, many northerners were charmed by the stubborn root-edness and family sense of the South.

It was in this context that Clyde Wilson, drawing from an ex-tended circle of his friends and acquaintances, organized the Colum-bia, South Carolina, conference that resulted in *Why the South Will Survive*. The volume's final contributors included four men who had either attended the University of North Carolina in the late 1960s and early 1970s (Wilson himself; Samuel T. Francis, a historian and aide to Senator John P. East; and Thomas Fleming, a classicist and headmaster of a small academy in South Carolina) or served on its faculty in those years (the sociologist John Shelton Reed). In fact, aca-demics dominated the book's roster of authors: William C. Havard, a political scientist at Vanderbilt University; M. E. Bradford, Fred Hobson, Thomas H. Landess, and Marion Montgomery, professors of English at the University of Alabama (Hobson), the University of Dallas (Bradford and Landess), and the University of Georgia (Montgomery); and George C. Rogers Jr., a historian, like Wilson, at the University of South Carolina. In addition, Wilson recruited two North Carolina attorneys, Hamilton C. Horton Jr. and David B. Sentelle; Don Anderson, an African American and the director of the National Association for the Southern Poor in Norfolk, Virginia; and the poet and novelist George Garrett. Finally, he secured contribu-tions from Andrew Nelson Lytle and Cleanth Brooks, who provided an essay on southern religion.[7]

When John Crowe Ransom, Donald Davidson, and Allen Tate plotted their symposium in 1929, they struggled to define an issue around which they might organize. They arrived at the notion of "agrarianism" relatively late, but it was admirably suited to their pur-pose, which was to articulate a self-consciously defiant response to modernity. The Agrarians took their antimodern stance in the name of what most of their Jazz Age contemporaries must have seen as a hopelessly antiquated and backward social order. In other words, not only did the Agrarians defy conventional opinion, but they did it in a flagrant and seemingly perverse way. It was this stubborn orien-tation to the past that gained them attention but also handicapped their efforts to be taken seriously. *Why the South Will Survive* was not an antimodern tract at all and was, in fact, much more explicitly about being southern than *I'll Take My Stand*. The Agrarians were concerned with the South's economy as much as its mores and cul-ture. The Fifteen Southerners assembled by Wilson were much more interested in the concept of southern identity. The Agrarians were pointing toward an alternative to industrial capitalism; the Fifteen Southerners produced a "manifesto of southern pride."[8]

Despite their differences, however, both volumes did attempt to assess the state of southern society; each contained essays on education, economics, literature, and religion. But the contributors to the later volume paid scant attention to the actual agrarian heritage of the South. Hamilton Horton's essay on the southern attachment to the land was Agrarian heresy. Horton identified a humanized "agrarian industrialization" taking root in the South, evident in new factories built in rural areas, which allowed the southern industrialist "the pick of the country youth at his machines." Reducing the Agrarian criticism of industrial labor to the fact that factories were located in cities, Horton argued that a rural-based factory labor force, able to retain its connection to the land through such devices as garden plots, would escape proletarianization. "The factory came to them, not they to it," he declared. "They have not left their homes, their churches, their ancestral cemeteries. Their roots in the Southern soil are intact."[9] Although Horton envisioned this decentralized industrialism as a means of preserving small farms by allowing farmers to supplement their income with part-time industrial jobs and although he advocated crop diversification and farmer-owned cooperatives as needed agricultural reforms, he was essentially boosting recent southern industrialization, in part by creating an image of a pastoralized industrialism, which featured factory managers fishing with their assembly-line workers on weekends and workers supplementing their incomes in difficult times by recourse to their vegetable gardens. The original Agrarians would have seen this as an absurd alternative to the culture they defended.[10]

A far stronger theme of the book was the attempt to define southernness. Sociologist John Shelton Reed wrote of southernness as the "substrate beneath the overlay of functional and utilitarian relationships imposed by a modern industrial economy," but this rigorous formulation was the exception. Most of the book's contributors preferred much broader conceptions. "Those elusive elements that have grown out of a common experience," William C. Havard wrote in elucidating the concept of the South, "cannot be expressed with total clarity through the use of any set of language or other symbols of which I am aware, and they cannot be readily confided to a list of codified propositions that we may apply in the conduct of our moral and political lives." Clyde Wilson declared that "the South has always been primarily a matter of values, a peculiar repository of intangible qualities in a society peculiarly preoccupied with the quantifiable."[11]

The authors shared a common anxiety that the intangible essence of southernness was, in fact, threatened by the cruder, quantifiable characteristics of modern American commercial culture. Taking as his inspiration Atlanta's 1960s-vintage slogan, "The City Too Busy to Hate," Fred Hobson investigated the dynamics of an economically booming, postracist South. With the growth of suburbs and the prevalence of air-conditioning, the South, Hobson observed, was part sunbelt skyscraper and industrial park, part historical museum. In addition, from Kentucky Fried Chicken to Opryland to "Hee-Haw," southern themes had become a popular subcurrent of American pop culture.[12] The South's public image recovered from the violent scenes of the civil rights protests, but Hobson worried that, in the process, the South had sold its soul:

> For all its cruelty and inhumanity, racism possessed a certain integrity, a commitment, however distorted and twisted. It would never sell out, never compromise simply to please. By contrast, public relations, to which Atlanta was committed, possessed no soul at all; it held only to the integrity of the dollar. Business required that Atlanta give up racism, so it did. But might not the City Too Busy to Hate also become, in other times and other circumstances, the city too busy to care, to help, to hold to anything in its tradition that did not benefit it in a purely economic or utilitarian way?

The commercialization and the homogenization of the public sphere, Hobson was arguing, had replaced those customs and institutions that, for good or bad, were the seedbed of a distinctive and impassioned southern culture.[13]

Hobson believed that a positive southern identity persisted, and in a deeper sense than conveyed by these superficial ephemera of pop culture. It was an identity rooted in a sense of time and place, in manners, religious temper, and a suspicion of material progress. Above all, he argued, southern culture possessed a healthy appreciation of the uses of leisure. The southerner was absorbed in life, Hobson wrote. "He was not too *busy*, that is—to hate, to help, to enjoy or to produce those elements of a vital folk culture: art, crafts, music, food." But Hobson's essay was marked by a note of wistfulness that betrayed the self-confident assertiveness of the book's title. "The American, a progressive creature, lives in his subdivision, drives on his interstate highway, shops at his mall, a captive of the moment, the present. He gives little thought to what occupied any particular spot fifty years before, to what happened there," Hobson commented. "The Southerner may not, either—but, with his tradition, he should."[14]

For a core group of contributors, *Why the South Will Survive* did, indeed, reflect an anxiety over the survival of tradition—not only the southern tradition but that of Western civilization and Christianity. For some, the South loomed as a synecdoche of Western Christian humanism, much as it had for Donald Davidson and Richard Weaver. The southern "way of life" transcended the geographical and historical existence of the South, Wilson argued, and had "an independent existence." For George C. Rogers, the South represented the Old Whig republican political tradition that culminated in the states' rights theorists of the antebellum period. To Samuel Francis, the South stood for a system of order rooted in church, family, and neighborhood.[15] Thomas Landess held that southern fellow feeling was rooted in a sense of Christian brotherhood. Ultimately, southerners share an orthodox, "Christocentric" view of the world. "In politics, in social arrangements, even in their literature there is always the implicit presence of God the Son, both as the crucified Jesus and as Christ the King," he wrote.[16] Marion Montgomery argued that the South represented a particular frame of mind, one poised against modernity in the name of family, hierarchy, and community. Thus, in his essay, "Solzhenitsyn as Southerner," he enlisted the Russian dissident Alexander Solzhenitsyn as a spiritual "cousin" of the southerner, even identifying him as a "Fugitive-Agrarian." Agrarianism was, Montgomery claimed, an attack on the "*secularist* aspect of industrialism."[17] In the book's conclusion, M. E. Bradford emphasized the common cultural identity of southerners, which, he asserted, is deep-rooted and organic: "Community is grown, not made. To repeat, community is something anterior, first submitted to and only then examined by those whose sense of personal worth and joy in life depend upon its survival." Andrew Lytle presented southernness as a kind of tribalism, referring to the clannishness and the role of kinship among the early Scotch-Irish pioneers of the Tennessee and Kentucky backcountry. It is this family sense, he argued, that makes a good society. "The chief or captain, as he was earlier called, was kin to everybody under his authority; this is the rule of blood," he wrote. "It had and has its blood feuds and other sins of pride, but I propose it to be more durable than the rule of purse or sword."[18]

Not all contributors to *Why the South Will Survive* identified with Lytle's atavistic clannishness and call for the "rule of blood," a worldview that the critic Richard H. King characterized as an unappealing "southern organicism." Yet the 1979 meeting of southern conservatives that resulted in the fiftieth-anniversary symposium was a key moment in the definition and self-awareness of a contemporary group of intellectuals who have, collectively, attempted to translate their version of southern conservatism into an effective national ideology and done so with an acute sense of kinship to the Southern Agrarians and Richard Weaver.[19] Ironically, key members of the group first met one another at the University of North Carolina, the old institutional archrival of the Vanderbilt Agrarians, in the late 1960s and early

1970s. The most explicitly neo-Agrarian member of the group, however, was M. E. Bradford, a product of Vanderbilt University and the
tutelage of Donald Davidson. Key members of the circle, first in the
Southern Partisan Quarterly Review and, later and more significantly,
in *Chronicles*, a conservative magazine published in Rockford, Illinois,
advocate a southern organicism rooted in insecurity and defensiveness.[20]

In *Why the South Will Survive*, the core of this circle's southern conservatism was an embattled defense of southern identity. The contributors to *Chronicles* betrayed a similar sense of being beleaguered
defenders of the Christian order who continue to fight despite being
under heavy siege by cultural liberals, black and Hispanic minorities, and the federal government. Most members of the circle identify
southernness with a Christian and organic social order built on traditional and patriarchal authority, but the circle is, in fact, politically,
socially, and intellectually diverse and loose-knit. Wilson, Fleming,
and the late Bradford have emphasized the southernness of their outlook. In doing so, they have developed a particularistic politics of
states' rights and localism, which they combine with a cultural and social criticism defined by Christian and patriarchal organicism. Samuel
Francis, by contrast, has more narrowly focused on politics and long
looked to the possibility of mobilizing "Middle American radicals" —
working- and middle-class Americans disaffected by the cultural and
racial liberalism of the post-1960s Democratic Party and economically distressed by the deindustrialization, retooling, and downsizing
of late-twentieth-century capitalism. Francis insistently pulled the
Chronicles circle toward a more populist right-wing politics and wider
political alliances, whether with the New Right conservative activists of the 1970s or the insurgent conservative candidacy of Patrick J.
Buchanan in the 1990s. In both cases, the cultural politics of the
Chronicles circle reflect a broader conservative antipathy to the cultural radicalism associated with the 1960s, and the aim of some members of the group seems to be a return to the perceived security, peace,
and order of the segregated, pre–civil rights American South, one in
which the prerogatives of white southerners were unquestioned.

M. E. Bradford and the *Chronicles* circle were not the only southerners who exhibited a possessive interest in the legacy of the Agrarians. In many ways, the generation of southern literary scholars who
came of age after World War II and were often trained by the Agrarians themselves constitute the most convincing claimants to the
Agrarian legacy. The members of this generation included Louis D.
Rubin Jr., who spent the majority of his career teaching at Hollins
College in Virginia and the University of North Carolina and men-

toring southern writers such as John Barth, Annie Dillard, Clyde Edgerton, Kaye Gibbons, and Lee Smith; Lewis P. Simpson, a Texan who began teaching at Louisiana State University in 1948; Thomas Daniel Young of Mississippi, who earned his doctorate under Donald Davidson and Richmond Beatty at Vanderbilt University and taught there after 1961; Walter Sullivan, a novelist and native of Nashville, who also taught at Vanderbilt beginning in 1949; Marion Montgomery, the Georgian novelist and poet who began teaching at the University of Georgia in 1954 and was also a contributor to *Why the South Will Survive*; Louise Cowan, a student of Davidson who headed the English Department at the University of Dallas; and C. Hugh Holman of South Carolina, who was both an administrator and professor at the University of North Carolina from 1946 to 1978. In addition, William C. Havard, the Vanderbilt political scientist who wrote on southern distinctiveness in *Why the South Will Survive*, was an active exponent of Agrarian ideas. A succeeding generation included Bradford as well as George Core, a literary scholar originally from Kansas City, Missouri, who began teaching at Sewanee in 1973. Between them, these scholars have held a powerful place in southern letters. Simpson became coeditor of the second series of the *Southern Review*, when that journal was revived in 1965; he also edited the Library of Southern Civilization series for Louisiana State University Press. Core became editor of the *Sewanee Review* in 1973. Rubin edited a number of southern literary journals over his career and, since 1969 has edited the *Southern Literary Journal*. In addition he edited Louisiana State University Press's Southern Literary Studies series.[21] As a group, they were indeed, quite powerful. The radical critic Paul Bové, in his study of the politics of American literary criticism, mordantly analyzed a type of academic critic he referred to as "Professional Southernist" (or "PS") with these men in mind. "The PS is both a monumental historian and an antiquarian," Bové observed. "Too often, the PS is a biographer. The PS's reproduce, in the form of explanation and apology, the tragic image of the Agrarians and their allies as failed prophets, bearers of refused alternatives, preservers of a better way, and guides to spiritual, imaginative renewal."[22]

The relationship between this group of southern literary scholars and the older Agrarians was deep. Lewis Simpson recalled visiting Allen Tate's grave in 1980, one year after Tate's death. He, Louis Rubin, and George Core went to the chapel at Sewanee where Tate was buried. After standing in silence a few moments, Rubin, hearkening back to an old custom of honorary address and the southern tradition of martial rhetoric, suddenly declared, "Colonel Tate!" The declaration, Simpson observed, was at once social and literary, "a gesture made in the name of those of us who in one way or another belong

to the second and third generations of the twentieth-century southern literary scene, and for whom, more than any other figure, Tate
had worn the aspect of a field commander of the literary troops."[23]

The most influential and comprehensive interpreter of the Agrarians of this generation of southern literary scholars was undoubtedly
Louis Rubin—the "primary architect and developer of southern literary study in this century" in the judgment of Michael Kreyling, a
younger student of southern literature.[24] Rubin's paternal ancestors
were German and Lithuanian Jewish immigrants from East Prus-
sia; his grandfather operated a small men's clothing store. Born in
Charleston, South Carolina, in 1923, Rubin grew up in a Reform Jewish family, but his Jewish identity did not have a strong hold on him.[25]
Instead, he absorbed the southern culture of the old city.[26] As a youth
he learned the mythology of the Lost Cause. While living in Richmond in 1932, he attended a Confederate veterans' reunion parade
and, on walks with his father, spoke with aged veterans as they sat on
benches outside the Confederate Home. He became an avid reader
of Confederate military history. He began college at the College of
Charleston, served in the army during World War II, and completed
his undergraduate degree at the University of Richmond. Aspiring to
a career in journalism after college, he worked as a reporter in Hack-
ensack, New Jersey; as city editor of a small daily in Staunton, Virginia; and, briefly, for the Associated Press out of Richmond. In 1948,
however, he entered the Creative Writing Program at the Johns Hopkins University, where he earned a doctorate in 1954 and developed an
abiding interest in the history of southern literature and, in particular, the relation between southern writers and their native culture. At
Johns Hopkins, Rubin studied with, among others, C. Vann Woodward; indeed, he considered writing a dissertation on Confederate
general James Longstreet under Woodward's direction.[27]

In accounts written from the 1950s through the 1970s, Rubin interpreted Agrarianism as, above all, a metaphor for the good life and an
example of a broader southern preoccupation with a distinctive cultural heritage. Rubin became acquainted with the Agrarians personally in the 1950s. As executive secretary of the American Studies Association from 1954 to 1956, he was instrumental in helping to organize
the Fugitives' reunion at Vanderbilt in 1956. Shaped by the Agrarians' own reinterpretations of what *I'll Take My Stand* had been about,
Rubin early dismissed the practical elements of their program, tending to view Agrarianism as a statement of southern cultural values.
Rubin chose sides early on. He argued that some of the early Agrarians had, at the time, misinterpreted the purposes of *I'll Take My Stand*.
They had, he wrote in a letter to Tate, "tended to mistake the acci-
dence for the substance, and to think that they were putting forward a

program of realistic action, particularly in the agricultural economics sphere, for the South, when actually the agrarianism was really a symbol, a metaphor even, for a much larger cultural position."[28]

This interpretation of *I'll Take My Stand* strengthened Rubin's own view of its worth. Rubin valued the image of the South proposed by many twentieth-century southern writers even if he believed it to be composed of more myth than reality. Attempting to define what he believed the Old South represented to the Agrarians, Rubin wrote:

> It was the image of a society that very likely never existed, but one that should have existed, in which men could live as individuals and not as automatons, aware of their finiteness and their dependence on God and nature, imbued with a sense of the deep inscrutability of nature, dedicated to the enhancement of the moral life in its aesthetic and spiritual dimensions. In contrast to the hurried, nervous pace of life in modern cities, the agrarian South was the image of a society in which human beings could live serenely and harmoniously. Not dominated by lust for money and power, they could be free of the tension and harassment of the modern industrial community.

Rubin shared this attachment to the ideal of southern community and of the rooted identity it provided—"in which all was fixed and ordered, and everyone knew everyone else, and who he was, and who and what his family was."[29]

Rubin's fullest treatment of the Agrarians was in a 1977 study of Ransom, Tate, Davidson, and Robert Penn Warren entitled *The Wary Fugitives*. Rubin paid special attention to the connection between the writers' social views and their poetry. The choice of the term "agrarianism," he argued, was a "strategic error of considerable magnitude." They resorted to it because "religious humanism" was an insufficient symbol and, moreover, the Agrarians themselves had forsaken religious orthodoxy. Their religion was, in fact, the South, Rubin claimed. "They thought and felt about the South in terms appropriate to religious belief." Rubin's perspective, greatly indebted to Tate's later interpretation of Agrarianism, discounted the Agrarians' socioeconomic argument; in his view, they should have simply championed the idea of the South. "This, I feel, is more or less what Tate wanted— a rigorous defense of the life and values of the traditional southern community, in the face of the forces of change that were bent upon transforming it—positive reaction, as he termed it," Rubin wrote.[30]

Much like the contributors to *Why the South Will Survive*, Rubin was preoccupied with southern identity. He tended to see the entire range of southern renascence writing as deriving from the attempt to define the "South." Practical Agrarianism—that which Tate and

John Crowe Ransom, in 1930, believed distinguished their social criticism—was inadequate and even, in some forms, "absurd" from a postwar perspective (as, to be fair, it had seemed to many critics at the time). Yet Rubin valued their moral and cultural criticism:

> There was and is no "practical" alternative to indoor plumbing and rural electrification; nor, I am convinced, were most of the Agrarians really interested in discovering one if it existed. What they wanted was to make people aware that plumbing and electrical appliances were not the be-all and end-all of existence, that there were qualities about community experience that were every bit as important as the securing of plumbing and rural electrification, and that if they did not recognize and look to the preservation of these qualities, a single-minded pursuit of septic tanks and rural electrification at any cost might result in their destruction. That, and not the economic virtues of subsistence farming, is what *I'll Take My Stand* was and still is all about.[31]

By equating Agrarianism with a set of cultural values, Rubin fit the Agrarians into a broader understanding of the southern literary renascence as, in Rubin's view, an evocation of an older southern way of life.[32] In many ways, Rubin argued, the renascence was the product of the West's "spiritual and moral dislocation" resulting from modernization and secularization. This was a view shared by other southern literary scholars. Walter Sullivan, for example, believed the literary renascence to be a reaction to the loss of the transcendent in society. Sullivan pinpointed the date at which the moral culture of the South could no longer support an understanding of the religious myth to the publication of Warren's *All the King's Men*, a position hotly disputed by other scholars.[33] Lewis Simpson, unlike Sullivan, was more skeptical of special moral claims made on behalf of southern culture. He argued that a false and nostalgic southern "culture of memory" lay beneath much of southern literature and took pains to point out that the Agrarians had resorted to a demonstrably false version of southern history to support their art. Drawing on the work of historian Eugene D. Genovese, Simpson dismissed the notion of a lost world of kinship, custom, and tradition as "feudal artifice," which "rang as hollow as an empty suit of armor."[34]

Rubin's relation to the southern "culture of memory" was more ambiguous. He based his own literary and cultural criticism on the southern decline of faith in transcendence but was less overtly religious than Sullivan, who eventually converted to Roman Catholicism.[35] As historian Michael O'Brien observed in the late 1970s, Rubin, Simpson, Sullivan, and Holman believed that a cohesive and coherent Old South culture had declined by the postwar era. These scholars were, in O'Brien's formulation, the "last theologians" of southern studies. Yet they subscribed, he argued, to a view of southern religion so vaporous as to lack any discernible theological principles. Indeed, Rubin's conception of the South was ultimately rooted less in spiritual considerations than in his own memories of a warm, hospitable, and leisured southern community.[36]

For a brief period in the mid-1950s, Rubin supported segregation in the South. While executive secretary of the American Studies Association, he was an assistant professor at the University of Pennsylvania, where he found no colleagues interested in southern literature or history. By his own account, Rubin's relative isolation as a southerner led him to a deeper emotional commitment to the South at the moment—in the wake of *Brown v. Board of Education* (1954)—when southern resistance to desegregation was beginning to swell. Despite his own previous convictions that segregation was wrong, Rubin accepted an editorial position on the *Richmond News-Leader*, which he held in 1956 and 1957, under James J. Kilpatrick, the foremost intellectual defender of segregation and quixotic exponent of John C. Calhoun's theory of interposition.[37] "As the chorus of criticism grew in the southern press," Rubin recalled, "for a brief period I was even able to rationalize myself into an intellectual concurrence in the traditional Southern position on race. It was totally an abstraction: I had no contacts with black people whatever." Rubin's work at the *News-Leader* and observations of the politics of massive resistance in Virginia, however, quickly led him to change his mind. Writing to Warren in the fall of 1956, Rubin confided that he felt the *News-Leader*, with its calls for massive resistance, was "on the wrong side of the segregation business." He credited Warren's writings on segregation with helping to change his thinking. "When my hometown paper, the Charleston News and Courier, referred to you as a turncoat and a traitor to the South, then I was more than ever convinced that I did not belong on the other side," he wrote Warren. He was chagrined, as well, when the *News-Leader* attacked Woodward. He remarked to Tate many years later, "I made a much better Diehard Confederate when away from the scene of the crime."[38]

Rubin coedited a 1957 symposium with Kilpatrick that was in some ways akin to *I'll Take My Stand* and *Why the South Will Survive*. The editors asserted in the preface of the symposium, which was entitled *The Lasting South: Fourteen Southerners Look at Their Home*, that the South's "identity" was "worth preserving." In his contribution, Rubin affirmed a distinctive southern way of life, marked by graciousness, historical awareness, attachment to family, and a strong sense of identity. Rubin wrote respectfully of what he considered an "inbred" southern conservatism of character, which placed family and region above material considerations. He agreed profoundly with the Agrarians' vision of an older South and their criticisms of modern culture. He asked in *The Lasting South* a variation of the classic southern question that was at the heart of Agrarianism: "How can a region retain the values of a traditional social order, based upon the individual and the community and ordered by a strong historical sense of life, in a modern, increasingly industrial and urban world?"[39]

Yet Rubin was not willing to take seriously the Agrarian hope that the social and economic structures of industrial capitalism could be resisted. It was the "values" of the South that must be preserved, not its socioeconomic structures. The "lasting South" was an identity, not an economy. Rubin's unwillingness to countenance Agrarianism as the preservation of particular southern social structures undoubtedly resulted, in part, from his realization that the system of segregation must end. Rubin hoped social values could remain firm while much else changed. The Negro, Rubin and his coeditor Robert D. Jacobs observed in *South*, a collection of essays on southern literature published in 1961, confronted the South with the issue of change. "In attempting to hold on to the traditional modes of thought and behavior so far as the Negro is concerned, the South seeks to retain a social structure doomed in and by time." The civil rights movement, Rubin believed, signaled the end of the Old South. The issue facing southerners in the 1960s was to control change so as to preserve those values most important to southern life. In Rubin's vision, Agrarianism was a reminder of what was worthy in the South. The southern identity would survive, but change must be accepted. In a symposium on southern fiction, Rubin claimed that southern life exhibited a continuity, despite urbanization. The Old South may have passed, but this only meant that southern culture was becoming more inclusive. Southern identity was broadened. What was changing, he argued, was that "the Negro is being brought *into* the community."[40]

With the exception of M. E. Bradford, the connection between the *Chronicles* circle and the Agrarians was not as direct as that of the southern literary scholars. Clyde Wilson grew up in a cotton-mill village in North Carolina. He was already a conservative when he enrolled in graduate school at the University of North Carolina in 1966 after having spent two years working as a journalist for the *Richmond News-Leader*. He eventually studied under Joel Williamson. Wilson's choice of the University of North Carolina as an undergraduate had been dictated by economic necessity and made despite his distaste for the liberal ambience of Chapel Hill. As an active conservative, he must have been relieved to find a circle of like-minded students in Chapel Hill, including Samuel Francis, who had taken the lead in organizing a student conservative group called the Carolina Conservative Society, which Wilson joined.[41]

Wilson had read the Agrarians by the time he was in high school and recalls reading Davidson's poetry in his junior year. Another young southerner who stumbled upon the Agrarians was John Shelton Reed, who first read *I'll Take My Stand* not in Tennessee, where he grew up, but in Cambridge, Massachusetts, where he was attending the Massachusetts Institute of Technology (MIT). He found a paperback edition of the book in the college bookstore in 1963 and read it straight through. "It was a revelation," he later wrote. Living in the North convinced Reed that the South possessed something worth defending, even in the midst of the South's vitriolic opposition to the civil rights movement, which decidedly was not worth defending, in Reed's view. The Agrarians identified something positive in the southern cultural inheritance—"manners, religion, tradition, community feeling."[42]

After graduation from MIT in 1964, Reed enrolled in the graduate program in sociology at Columbia University, where he studied southern cultural persistence under Herbert Hyman and Paul Lazarsfeld. He arrived at Columbia when it was reaching its peak as a center of student radicalism and protest during the 1960s. Reed ambivalently defended the war in Vietnam, believing the United States should either "win it or get out"; as a graduate teaching assistant, he insisted on meeting his class during the 1968 student strike. He and four students—a Roman Catholic priest from Australia, a former Marine, a South Carolina man, and a Jewish woman from New Jersey (whom Reed later remembered as a "premature neoconservative")— crossed the student picket lines as an act of defiance.[43] Reed arrived at the University of North Carolina in 1969 and became faculty adviser to the Carolina Conservative Society, a group of students that, Reed recalls, included Francis, Nancy Gustafson, Jeffrey Gaynor (later director of foreign policy studies at the conservative Heritage Foundation), Ben Steelman, and Lawrence Uzzell. The Carolina Conservative Society was essentially a reading group, which met to discuss conservative writings, sometimes retiring to a local bar, Clarence's. Both Reed and Wilson recall it as being important to them; Reed considers the group to have been a "band of brothers" (with, of course, one sister). In 1970 the group changed its name to the Orange County Anti-Jacobin League.[44]

Thomas Fleming was a graduate student in classics at North Carolina at about the same time, but he did not join the Carolina Conservative Society, although his friend and fellow classicist E. Christian Kopff was a member. At the time, Fleming considered himself a "countercultural leftist." Born in Wisconsin, Fleming grew up in Superior in the northwest corner of the state. When he was a teenager, his family moved South, and he lived in Florida and South Carolina. His father, although an organizer for the National Maritime Union and (Fleming believes) a Communist as a young man, was, by the time of Fleming's youth, a somewhat conservative businessman with whom Fleming found himself occasionally at odds. Fleming earned an undergraduate degree at the College of Charleston in 1967. While in college he did some work organizing blacks voters in South Carolina. Upon graduation he enrolled at the University of North Carolina; he loved Greek poetry and aspired to be a poet himself. Drafted in 1969 to fight in Vietnam, a war he opposed, Fleming was rejected because of flat feet and eye problems; he knocked around San Francisco for eight or nine months, listening to the Velvet Underground at local clubs and writing poetry, before returning to Chapel Hill to finish his dissertation on the lyric meter of Aeschylus under Douglas Young, a leftist émigré scholar from Scotland.[45]

Despite their common associations, not all members of this group knew one another while in Chapel Hill. Neither Wilson, Reed, or Fleming knew one another at the time. Nor was Agrarianism a unifying bond between them. Fleming does not seem to have read *I'll Take My Stand;* he knew Ransom and Tate chiefly as poets of whom he was not especially fond. Nevertheless, after a brief stint teaching in the Midwest, Fleming returned to the South. In 1975, he and his wife moved to McClellanville, South Carolina, a small town about forty miles north of Charleston. They looked after an old plantation on the Santee River, and for three years Fleming ran the Archibald Rutledge Academy, a classical southern academy for students ranging in age from five to eighteen. Eventually, through the good offices of Christian Kopff, Fleming and Wilson met and became friends. Fleming broached the idea of publishing a southern magazine, which would be written from, as he later recalled, "our point of view"; Wilson agreed. Together, they published two issues of the *Southern Partisan Quarterly Review* (a title later shortened to *Southern Partisan* by subsequent ownership). Fleming did much of the production work out of his home in McClellanville. Contributors included Russell Kirk, Bradford, Francis, and Reed (who published under the pseudonym J. R. Vanover).[46]

Money, however, was soon a problem, and in 1981 the two agreed to sell the magazine for a nominal fee to the Foundation for American Education, backed financially by Charles Scott Hamel, with the provision that they would retain editorial control. Prior to purchasing the *Southern Partisan,* Hamel had dreamed of bankrolling a Richard Weaver College to be established in South Carolina. The college never materialized, and one of the foundation's trustees, Richard

Hines, convinced Hamel to invest in a southern magazine. Fleming and Wilson were soon in conflict with Hamel's representative, Richard M. Quinn, a conservative Republican political consultant who vied for editorial control of the quarterly. Fleming felt betrayed, and he and Wilson soon left the magazine they had founded.[47]

Fleming and Wilson attempted to start a successor to the *Southern Partisan Quarterly Review* with no success. In the meantime, many of the contributors to the magazine had begun writing for *Chronicles of Culture* (a title later shortened to *Chronicles*), edited by Leopold Tyrmand and published by the Rockford Institute. Fleming knew James J. Thompson, a historian who had left the College of William and Mary to become an associate editor at the magazine. Thompson, however, had become disenchanted with Tyrmand and left the magazine. In 1984, Tyrmand offered Fleming the position of managing editor, which he accepted. The following year Fleming became the magazine's editor and, from Illinois, was able to again publish many of the southern conservative writers in his circle.[48]

Thomas Fleming first met M. E. Bradford at Clyde Wilson's 1979 meeting to plan *Why the South Will Survive*. Over time, the two became good friends. Because of his position as editor of *Chronicles*, Fleming was, in some ways, at the center of this circle of conservative intellectuals, but the heart of the group seems to have been Bradford. Bradford, too, is the most direct connection between the *Chronicles* circle and Agrarianism; he came to his neo-Agrarianism through the ideas and example of Donald Davidson. In Bradford's work, Agrarianism came to be a species of southern conservatism. He provided a genealogy of southern conservatism reaching back to the Old Whig "country" opposition to the Crown in seventeenth-century England and continuing through the Antifederalist opponents of the United States Constitution and antebellum states' rights theorists such as John Taylor, John Randolph of Roanoke, and John C. Calhoun. In the process, he delineated the principles of the organic and patriarchal conservatism characteristic of *Chronicles*. Richard Weaver, Bradford argued, "completed" Agrarianism. Unlike Weaver, however, Bradford never hesitated to defend the particularism inherent in his position. As with Davidson, southern history was central to his worldview, and strong opposition to the federal government defined his politics.

Born in Forth Worth, Texas, in 1934, Bradford was the son of a cattleman. His family's sense of its Confederate heritage was strong. Three of Bradford's great-grandfathers fought in the Civil War. "Reconstructing the past helped my family define who we were," Bradford once told an interviewer. He attended the University of Oklahoma and went on to serve in the navy from 1956 to 1959 and, after that, as an instructor at the United States Naval Academy. While he was there, some colleagues urged him to pursue his studies at Vanderbilt University after he finished his stint at the academy. Bradford took their advice and attended Vanderbilt, which he later remembered as a "veritable nursery of intellectual conservatism." (Thomas Landess, a friend of Bradford's at Vanderbilt, recalled the English Department of the late 1950s and early 1960s as being "utterly homogeneous, a department filled with Southern conservatives.") There Bradford met Davidson, who became his mentor and friend, and studied with Walter Sullivan and Thomas Daniel Young.[49] He was also introduced to the thought of two philosophical conservatives: Eric Voegelin, a German refugee scholar and author of *The New Science of Politics* (1952) and the massive, five-volume *Order and History* (1956–87); and Michael Oakeshott, the British political philosopher and author of *Rationalism in Politics and Other Essays* (1962). He cited both often in his political and social writings. From Oakeshott, Bradford borrowed a distinction between the "nomocratic" society, in which law and custom were supreme, and the "teleological" society, which was shaped by human purposes and rationalist theories. In Bradford's eyes, a nomocratic society, drawing on habits inherited through the generations, was obviously superior to its modern successor.[50]

Voegelin's influence was more pronounced. Indeed, Voegelin was a great influence on many conservative intellectuals, including southern thinkers, in the postwar period.[51] Trained in Vienna, Voegelin had traveled in the United States in the 1920s, even studying briefly with the philosopher John Dewey and labor economist John R. Commons. During the 1930s, he published refutations of Nazi racial doctrines, fleeing to Vienna in 1938 after the Nazi occupation. Eventually settling in the United States, he taught at Louisiana State University from 1942 to 1958, making the acquaintance of, among others, Cleanth Brooks.[52] Voegelin's most noticeable legacy for American conservatism was his claim that the intellectual underpinnings of modernity—humanism, rationalism, scientism, progressivism, the Enlightenment, and, ultimately, liberalism and Marxism—were rooted in a spirit identical to the Christian heresy of gnosticism. A wide variety of sects and intellectual currents have historically been classified under the label "gnostic," but, by the end of the second century, a specific sect was identified with gnostic beliefs by the emerging Christian Church and declared heretical. Rooted in pre-Christian beliefs, gnostics focused on *gnosis*, what they considered secret, even esoteric, knowledge, which, if obtained, explained God and the origins and destiny of humankind. Gnosis promised spiritual redemption. Gnostics were dualistic, distinguishing between an abased material world and its low "Creator" god (the vengeful God of the Old Testament) and a higher, spiritual realm governed by the "Unknown God," a truly spiritual being. They believed the material world to be a corruption of the spiritual realm. The hope for redemption lay in their belief that some humans contained seeds, or sparks, of divinity. These individuals might, by means of gnosis, apprehend this inner divinity and, by coming to know their God-like selves in this profound way, escape the limits of this corrupted material world.[53]

In Voegelin's view, a key achievement of the early Christian Church was to temper early Christians' millennialism and fascination with eschatology and the anticipated Parousia in which the Kingdom of God would be established on earth. The Book of Revelation, Augustine argued, should be seen as a collection of fables. He and others managed to "de-divinize" human history. Christians, Voegelin argued, were subsequently distinguished by their willingness to accept a world in which gods do not actively and regularly intervene in human affairs. In fact, for Christians, the divine impinges on the world only insofar as Christ remains spiritually present in the Church. "The life of the soul in openness toward God, the waiting, the periods of aridity and dulness, guilt and despondency, contrition and repentance, forsakenness and hope against hope, the silent stirrings of love and grace, trembling on the verge of a certainty which if gained is loss — the very lightness of this fabric may prove too heavy a burden for men who lust for massively possessive experience," Voegelin wrote.[54] This difficult life of faith, Voegelin believed, was indeed too demanding for the weak, and, from the twelfth century onward, the West experienced a widespread revival of gnosticism (somewhat broadly defined) — assorted attempts to "re-divinize" the world, to develop an understanding of history in which the world is progressing through stages, all tending toward a moment of historical fulfillment. This new, mundane philosophy inevitably entails the search for new prophets, messianic leaders, and chosen peoples, and it has mutated over time into theories of progress, trends toward secularization, and revolutionary movements aimed at achieving an earthly utopia. Thus, for Voegelin, a wide spectrum of modern movements (from humanism to socialism) and modern thinkers (from Hegel to Hitler) were in actuality pursuing the "immanentization of meaning" — seeking to find the ultimate meaning of history in human actions and human affairs. The growth of such gnostic impulses is the "essence of modernity." "The immanentization of the Christian eschaton," Voegelin wrote in *The New Science of Politics*, "made it possible to endow society in its natural existence with a meaning which Christianity denied to it. And the totalitarianism of our time must be understood as journey's end of the Gnostic search for a civil theology."[55]

Bradford first taught at Abilene Christian College in Texas. In 1967

Louise Cowan brought Bradford to the University of Dallas, the small, Catholic, conservative school where she was chair of the English Department. There he taught until his untimely death in 1993, specializing in the study of William Faulkner. Like Weaver, Bradford was active in conservative politics. A conservative Democrat who eventually switched to the Republican party, Bradford was once elected to the Texas State Executive Committee of the Democratic Party from Dallas. He opposed the Civil Rights Act of 1964. Much like Barry Goldwater, Bradford supported blacks' right to vote, he later explained, but opposed the act's provisions forbidding discrimination in hotels, restaurants, and public accommodations. In 1968 and 1972, Bradford supported the populist presidential campaigns of Alabama governor George Wallace. He also worked for the campaigns of Goldwater, Ronald Reagan, and Pat Buchanan.[56]

Bradford's political and social beliefs were remarkably consistent over the years, and his essays, particularly those collected in *A Better Guide Than Reason* (1979), *Generations of the Faithful Heart* (1983), *Remembering Who We Are* (1985), *The Reactionary Imperative* (1990), and *Against the Barbarians and Other Reflections on Familiar Themes* (1992), contain a consistent political and social philosophy. Crucial to this philosophy was the role of the "vatic spirit," or bardic poet. The vatic poet was entrusted with the community's memory, which defined identity. One's identity was not created; it existed independent of the individual will, possessing, Bradford argued, a historical and ontological reality. In the process of remembering, one literally discovered who one was.[57] Because this rooted and immutable social identity is at the heart of the social system, the poet's role as "memory keeper" was essential. In preserving the cultural heritage of a people, its oral traditions and stories of "blood and land," the poet revealed to them the definition of their society. In Bradford's view, Faulkner functioned as such a *"vates"* — an "artist who has submitted his imagination to the inherited corporate spirit of his people."[58]

In practical terms, Bradford envisioned a decentralized, patriarchal society. His politics were lifted whole from the antebellum South, which he saw as the fulfillment of the American political genius. Indeed, Bradford relished playing the role of the Confederate statesman redivivus. He venerated the Old Whig tradition of English opposition, which was grounded in a hardy republican skepticism of abstract theory and centralized power. This tradition of thought, based on ancient Roman principles, survived in America through the antebellum period, he argued. In this emphasis on the Old Whig tradition, Bradford fortified Davidson's politics of identity and Weaver's neo-Agrarian philosophy of order with insights gained from historians Bernard Bailyn, Gordon Wood, and J. G. A. Pocock, who had traced American colonial and revolutionary political thought to Old World and classical republican sources. The revolution was not very revolutionary at all, Bradford believed. It was merely an attempt to preserve the continuity of the English political tradition and to defend the prescribed rights of the English people.[59]

Bradford also drew on the revival of interest in Edmund Burke fostered by postwar traditionalists. Bradford believed Burke was the best guide to the Old Whig tradition, which retained an older, Roman conception of the self, one defined by social connections, as opposed to the Lockean concept of a punctual self imagined to exist somewhere in the mind. "A true Roman," Bradford observed, "was not an individual as we understand the term." The Roman, Bradford argued, was governed by personal pride and honor. "His was a shame culture, dominated by intense and personally felt loyalties to family, clan, and individual." This spirit of true republicanism animated the Antifederalists, who opposed, in Bradford's terms, the statist and gnostic implications of the proposed Constitution, which would favor the relatively weak, human faculty of reason over the better guide of experience. In his 1979 study of the political thought of the framers, Bradford provided a sort of Old Whig credo for himself: "The only freedom which can last is a freedom embodied somewhere, rooted in a history, located in space, sanctioned by genealogy, and blessed by a religious establishment. The only equality which abstract rights, insisted upon outside the context of politics, are likely to provide is the equality of universal slavery. It is a lesson which Western man is only now beginning to learn."[60]

Bradford assembled an eclectic array of sources to buttress his construction of an American political tradition of prescriptive rights, limited government, and patriarchal authority. He married this conservative political philosophy to a Davidsonian sense of exclusive social identity rooted in memory. Political liberty, in Bradford's view, had meaning only within the context of a society. As Hannah Arendt observed, commenting on the experiences of displaced Jews during and after World War II, without citizenship and without law, human rights mean precious little. A similar insight led Bradford to a radically restricted sense of individual freedom. He disparaged the attention Americans paid to the phrase "all men are created equal." Such a guarantee of equality applied only to those who were full members of the society that promulgated it. And it was only a declaration of equality before the law, in the "limited sphere of its operation." The wide social sphere not covered by law was open for the free play of inequality.[61]

The final exemplars of these republican and Old Whig ideals in America were the antebellum southern theorists of states' rights and organic community. Their thought elucidated what Bradford considered a southern idea of "corporate liberty."[62] This distinctive tradition of southern conservatism was defeated by the forces of gnostic northern imperialism in the Civil War, but it remained the taproot of Bradford's imagination. The antebellum South embodied the wisdom of a politics of identity and enshrined the prescriptive and patriarchal ethic of right social thinking.

Bradford believed the Old South approximated a premodern, clannish polity. A mutualism like that of a Highland clan characterized the Confederate army, he argued; the yeomanry looked to their betters, whom they respected because of their superior education and intellect, for leadership. Further, the average southerner was untainted by the liberal and overreaching deficiencies of the northern mind. The southerner, he argued in 1969, had a natural "piety toward Being" and was not burning with millennial fervor or haunted by eschatological visions. Rather, the southerner was safely and deeply (and conventionally) Christian. Southerners did not question their place in the social order, for all was ordained by God. "The effects of history, nature, and the fruits of personal choice enjoy in his eyes a prescriptive status; they are either the imposed will of an inscrutable Providence or the operations of a natural law set up by that Providence to accommodate human free agency to Its purposes," Bradford wrote.[63]

Nowhere were Bradford's neo-Confederate predilections more apparent than in his special animus against Abraham Lincoln, whose primary sin was to enshrine the ideal of equality in the American political discourse through the Gettysburg Address. Bradford saw Lincoln as an important target. He sent an early essay on Lincoln to Lewis Simpson, declaring his intentions in martial terms. "Nothing like this invasion of the millennialist sanctuary has occurred since W. G. Simms spoke in 1860 at the Cooper Union. I am going to do more of these rhetorical critiques from a Voegelinian viewpoint and then invade the American studies meetings."[64] Lincoln was a prime example of modern gnosticism, in Bradford's eyes, for, Bradford declared, Lincoln saw himself as a "rational, progressivist superman." Indeed, the whole antebellum Whig vision looked toward a "secular utopia," Bradford argued. Bradford cast all of Lincoln's life in the most sinister of terms. He gave Lincoln no credit for any intellectual or moral progression from his pronouncements in the 1840s to the years of the Civil War. Rather, Bradford freely juxtaposed the young Lincoln's comments on race and slavery, whether on the political hustings or otherwise, with his later statements and actions in order to convict him of hypocrisy. Neither did Bradford afford any consideration to the expediencies of politics; no sin by Lincoln could ever be justified by an appeal to political necessity. Bradford's Lincoln was a paragon of venality: hypocritical, corrupt, racist, unscrupulous, and duplicitous in his rhetoric. He was motivated by his own ambitions and thirst for power, provoking sectional conflict in order to attain his goals. Lincoln was guilty of war crimes for denying medicine to the South, complicit in the underrationing of his own troops, given to locking up political opponents in a "Northern 'Gulag,'" and, in general, an apt model for the twentieth-century dictator. Noting the dyspeptic Edmund Wilson's comparison of Lincoln to Bismarck and Lenin in *Patriotic Gore* (1962), Bradford added Hitler for good measure.[65]

Lewis Simpson observed after Bradford's death that, in the 1960s, many viewed Bradford as a successor to Richard Weaver. Bradford never made such a claim for himself, but he did argue that Weaver completed the Agrarian tradition by providing philosophical system and depth. Weaver, Bradford suggested, sought to root Agrarianism in a larger Western intellectual tradition. Yet Bradford asserted that Weaver's systematic philosophizing was foreign to the South, for the southern mind was, by definition, undogmatic and untheoretical. The guide for southerners was always experience, precedent, memory. Hearkening to Weaver's own writings about the classical rhetorical tradition, Bradford maintained that the statesman relied on rhetoric above dialectic. Elsewhere, citing Russell Kirk, Bradford declared that all valid principles must be identified from historical experience, as was the practice of the framers of the Constitution. Bradford declared that he himself listened only to "the broader authorities of reason and revelation, *once I am certain where I stand*."[66]

Southern conservatism, Bradford argued, was a unique ideology, and it was based on rhetoric rather than principles, being more an intellectual expression of dedication to faith, family, and tradition than social analysis. Political principles derived in a fundamental and sufficient sense from where one stood, Bradford argued in "Where We Were Born and Raised: The Southern Conservative Tradition," an essay published in the *Southern Review* in 1989. "Certain questions are settled before any serious deliberation concerning a preferred course of conduct may begin." The "prototypical" southern conservative, Bradford wrote, "cherished a clear sense of what Southern grandmothers have always meant in admonishing children, 'we don't do that': a prescription able to survive numerous violations, grounded in the memory of 'where [and how] we were born and raised.'"[67] Such a conservative ethic produced a "culture of families, linked by friendship, common enemies, and common projects" that, Bradford felt, was "something like a tribe."[68]

Southern conservatism was a philosophy universally applicable but also inextricably linked up with what Bradford considered to be "southern." In Bradford's mind, the South had come to be a mythic embodiment of a tribalistic culture. He assumed a shared body of values for all southerners. Bradford, and, indeed, Weaver and Kirk, both of whom he cited approvingly, spent little time considering the relation between culture and economics. They seemed to believe that without the deforming presence of the activist federal state and liberal social planners, traditional culture would assume the shape it always had. This was an assumption that John Crowe Ransom and Allen Tate had not made in 1930. Indeed, the Agrarians of 1930 had criticized the New Humanists for precisely this sort of thinking. Bradford cited the Agrarians' image of soft cultural material vainly being poured into society from the top. He believed it aptly described the ineffectual efforts of ideologues and liberals to impose social solutions on problems.[69] Rather, Bradford argued, culture grew from within a society, out of past experience and traditions. The Agrarians had meant that traditional culture depended on a premodern economy and its particular material establishment. They refused to believe that social change could be resisted merely by didacticism—by the pouring in of soft cultural argument. This was the logic behind their choice of agrarianism as a metaphor, for in it they appealed not only to the southern way of living but also symbolized the need to reform the economic structure of industrial society. The New Humanists were ineffective because they lacked such an understanding, the Agrarians argued.

Bradford's organic conservatism and defense of patriarchy was rooted in his understanding of the "country" tradition of republican thought and in an ethic of submission to tradition and heritage. Fleming rooted his defense of patriarchy in anthropology, genetics, and sociobiology, which he began to read in the 1970s, including the work of E. E. Evans-Pritchard, Edward O. Wilson, Robert Trivers, W. D. Hamilton, and Richard Dawkins.[70] Fleming believed that both patriarchy and the maternal nature of women were ordained by nature—an insight proven, he believed, by sociobiologists. Surveying what he considered the cultural decadence and social division of contemporary America (family breakdown, rampant pornography, lax sexual mores, increased incidence of rape, confused moral standards, and a balkanized people), Fleming wanted to provide a political theory grounded in the truths of human nature. His major attempt to do this was *The Politics of Human Nature*, published in 1988.[71] "The laws and decrees enacted by human government are mutable and sometimes tyrannical," he concluded, "but the laws of human nature, worked tight within the spirals of the genetic code, are unchanging and just."[72]

Fleming assailed radical feminism, which he considered "at best a fake and unnatural atavism, and at its worst, an assault upon the foundations of all human social life." He allowed that the decline of the home as a productive unit resulted in deadening domestic labor, but his prescription was not to liberate women from the bonds of the domestic sphere but rather to revive the home as a center of production. He advocated home crafts, home schooling, and women's control of childbirth—all efforts to bring meaning back into women's lives. Ultimately, the premodern family itself—at one time the primary productive unit in society, the maker of war, enforcer of social order, and primary agent of education and socialization—must be reconstructed in what would inevitably be a more patriarchal and clannish social order, with power devolved from the federal government to the local level. Contract law and the state had usurped the roles and functions of the family, through the creation of a maternalistic welfare state and through such individualistic legal reforms as no-fault divorces. The companionate ideal of marriage, women's liberation, and the professionalization of education had all contributed to the triumph of the state over the family.[73] The modern world has presided over an unprecedented weakening of the principles of social life, Fleming believed. These principles had conformed to the law of nature: they included the incest taboo; maternal nurturing and paternal authority within the family; the division of labor between the sexes; and the responsibility of the household to raise children, care for the elderly, and look after the infirm. "Destroy this foundation," Fleming declared, "and you wreck the entire social and political edifice erected upon these natural principles."[74]

Although ostensibly based on a rigorous review of modern anthropological, sociobiological, and sociological literature on the family, Fleming's impressionistic analysis was essentially an exercise in pure theory and an affirmation of Victorian notions about the nature of the family. He cited Henry Maine's *Ancient Law*, Aristotle's *Politics*, and Robert Filmer's *Patriarcha*, along with the work of E. O. Wilson and E. E. Evans-Pritchard, as his inspiration. Fleming's original aim in conceiving the book had been to discredit two bedrock notions of modern liberalism—the idea of "natural equality" and the theory of the social contract.[75] The social contract was a spurious conceit, he believed. Fleming rejected the Enlightenment claim of natural rights in favor of what he argued was the supreme authority of nature's law. He wrote favorably of communal forms of authority and punishment, such as enforced exile, shaming, peer pressure, taboo, even lynching and vigilantism. All these forms were potentially just and reliable. "A proper vigilante movement has all the elements of law and order: community support, concern for the solemnities of due process, even adherence to traditional forms," Fleming wrote. The presence of vigilante justice, he argued, usually signals a break between the community and the forces of law and order.[76]

Clan-based and communal authority—the true ingredient of a stable social order—is absent from modern America. For Fleming, the social order should be modeled on the family and so inextricably bound with traditional gender roles and gender relations. No-fault divorce laws, compulsory school attendance, social security, federal welfare, sex education, equal-rights legislation—all undercut the authority of the father and the mother. "The natural differences between the sexes, that issue into institutions of family, community, and state, delineate the contours of a healthy organic political system," Fleming declared. Or as he phrased it ten years after the publication of *The Politics of Human Nature*, "Only a community can close ranks against the federal judges, experts, and legislators who are taking away our children." Whereas liberals see judicial and welfare state officers as legitimate agents of the community, Fleming conceives them to be outsiders and enemies.[77]

Fleming focused the blame for the decline of a patriarchal social order not on capitalism (although he has been critical of it) but on the increasing power of the state and liberal individualism. In general, Fleming has equivocated on the role of the market in the social order. Although capitalism can damage natural institutions, the free market, Fleming argued in *The Politics of Human Nature*, is compatible with a competitive, organic social order. The free market, Fleming believes, is a "fact of nature," and he has called himself "more of an anarcho-capitalist than most of the free-marketers I have met." Yet he has expressed skepticism about forms of capitalist organization current in the United States, writing in 1982 that the free-enterprise system in the United States is often "a government encouraged monopoly or oligopoly of business interests." All the same, he hesitated to broach any interference by the community in the rights of private property. "The free market—that amoral competition for economic success—is the preeminent modern institution of society, although it is continually being hampered and restricted by communalists who hate the ideas of competition and excellence," he wrote in 1990. In a 2000 essay, Fleming argued that multinational corporations, the World Trade Organization, and an emerging "global economic bureaucracy" were threats to democracy and the integrity of nation-states, but he was wary of regulatory responses, feeling that governments imposed their own limits on freedom and that Western governments served corporate interests. Nevertheless, in 1994 he warned against mingling the values of the market with those of art, family, religion, and spirituality.[78]

The *Chronicles* circle gradually translated its patriarchalism and moral traditionalism into a program of cultural and political nationalism, self-consciously hearkening back to the pre–World War II, non-interventionist Old Right. Fleming, Wilson, and Samuel Francis consistently attempted to exert influence in national conservative circles and to affect practical politics through the pages of the *Southern Partisan Quarterly Review* and *Chronicles;* by contributing to conservative activist Robert W. Whitaker's 1982 collection of essays, *The New Right Papers*, an attempt to provide intellectual direction to the New Right in the wake of Ronald Reagan's 1980 presidential triumph; in intramural sparring with other elements of the conservative movement, particularly the more moderate neoconservative intellectuals, who came to prominence in the 1970s and were led by New York Jewish intellectuals such as Irving Kristol and Norman Podhoretz; by boosting the candidacy of Buchanan in the 1990s; by seeking alliances with socially conservative libertarians in the 1990s; and, in the case of Fleming and Wilson, by helping to establish the forthrightly secessionist Southern League (later League of the South) in 1994.

Samuel Francis specialized in formulating political strategies to tap the disaffection of dealigned middle-class American voters. Like Donald Davidson, Francis was born in Tennessee and heard Confederate war stories from his grandmother.[79] After earning his doctorate in history from the University of North Carolina, he worked as an aide to North Carolina senator John P. East before becoming an editorial writer for the conservative *Washington Times* in 1986. As early as 1982, in *The New Right Papers*, Francis championed the possible political strength of "Middle American Radicals," by which term he meant skilled and semiskilled middle-class and working-class Americans who were disaffected with liberalism.[80] He borrowed the term from Donald I. Warren's *The Radical Center: Middle Americans and the Politics of Alienation* (1976), and it became a leitmotif of his political writings.

Francis drew inspiration from the early work of James Burnham, the onetime Trotskyist and later adviser to William F. Buckley Jr. at the *National Review*, particularly his realist analyses of power: *The Managerial Revolution: What Is Happening in the World* (1941) and *The Machiavellians: Defenders of Freedom* (1943).[81] Francis argued that a new managerial elite arose as society modernized in the late nineteenth century and early twentieth. This elite installed itself in the emerging bureaucracies of the new corporations, the media, universities, foundations, and government. The elite's aim was to eliminate the power of its rival class—the older American middle class, which had come to power after the Civil War and had established a stable bourgeois order. Thus, the task of the new managerial elite was twofold: eliminate the economic power of the small and independent farmers and businesspeople who constituted the core of the older middle class and launch a cultural revolution that would discredit bourgeois culture. This new elite triumphed, Francis believed, with the passage of the state-oriented reform legislation of the Progressive Era and the New Deal. The post–World War II conservative movement represented the resistance of the old bourgeois elite in the face of these new managerial technocrats.[82]

Like others in the *Chronicles* circle, Francis had, by the 1980s, lost faith in the mainstream conservative movement, believing it to be dominated by statist and globalist neoconservative intellectuals. Francis's hope for a true, right-wing alternative to the accommodationist conservative movement lay in a program of Middle American nationalism. "What Middle Americans need is a political formula and a public myth that synthesizes the attention to material-economic interests offered by the left and the defense of concrete and national identity offered by the right," he argued in June 1992. This Middle American nationalism would shrink the federal government by, for example, eliminating the departments of Commerce, Education, Health and Human Services, Housing and Urban Development, and Labor as well as the National Endowment for the Humanities, National Endowment for the Arts, and federal civil rights enforcement divisions. Francis also advocated limiting American entanglements overseas. In a December 1991 issue of *Chronicles* celebrating the fiftieth anniversary of the isolationist organization America First, Francis outlined a Middle American nationalist foreign policy agenda, which included the termination of most foreign aid, an abrogation of national defense treaties into which the United States entered in the 1950s, the withdrawal of most American troops stationed in Europe and Asia, the implementation of the Reagan administration's antiballistic missile Strategic Defense Initiative, the establishment of a universal male draft, the proclamation of a defensive perimeter defined by the Western Hemisphere, and the elimination of any lobbying on behalf of a foreign government. This was a prescription for Fortress America with a vengeance.[83]

Much of Francis's Middle American nationalism was embodied in the political agenda that Pat Buchanan extolled in his bids for the Republican presidential nomination in 1992 and 1996 and in his Reform Party candidacy in 2000. Both Fleming and Francis provided political advice to Buchanan and helped on his campaigns. Both spoke at a 1993 meeting of Buchanan's American Cause organization. Francis attended a meeting at Buchanan's home in late 1991, at which the upcoming political campaign was discussed. He unsuccessfully urged Buchanan to break with the conservative establishment at that time.[84]

Although Buchanan failed to win the nomination, Francis argued that his campaigns focused the incipient Middle American rebellion and revealed the mainstream conservative movement's failure to capitalize on this enormous bloc of voters. Buchanan, Francis claimed in 1998, defined a "new paradigm in American politics" centered around trade issues, the erosion of national sovereignty, immigration, affirmative action, the right to bear arms, and cultural issues such as the abolition of the National Endowment for the Arts and the right to fly the Confederate battle flag. Buchanan's break with the Republican Party in 1999, Francis argued, betokened the emergence of a new brand of radical conservatism. During the 2000 presidential campaign, Francis argued that the culture war of the 1990s was, in fact, a class war. Buchanan, he suggested, must affirm and defend "such social particularisms—tribalisms, if you will—as class, cult, kinship, community, race, ethnicity, and nationality, each of which are legitimate and important parts of the politico-cultural complex." "The way to win Middle Americans," Francis argued, "is to communicate to them that you, as a candidate and a public leader, understand that they and their way of life are under siege, that the ruling class of the country in alliance with its underclass is besieging them, and that you are willing to ally with them against their enemies."[85]

Chronicles increasingly focused on immigration over the course of the 1980s. The issue reveals some of the contradictions of their politics. Francis's Middle American nationalism and the group's dalliance with Buchanan were, despite Buchanan's panegyrics to his Confederate ancestors, subtly at odds with the southern particularism that was a key element of the group's political viewpoint, particularly that of Fleming, Wilson, and Bradford. While celebrating all things southern and defending the Confederate flag, the *Chronicles* circle was, at the same time, postulating a unified and coherent Euro-American culture under dire threat from masses of nonwhite immigrants and from assorted racial minorities in America. The magazine's position betrayed a certain schizophrenia: while entertaining calls for secession and the radical devolution of power to regions, states, even neighborhoods and celebrating culturally driven secessionist movements, whether in the American South, Quebec, or northern Italy, *Chronicles* also featured articles bemoaning the disintegrative effects of multicultural liberalism on the national culture. At the same time, the magazine's writers outlined a highly exclusive sense of American identity, one reserved for non-Hispanic whites only.

Large numbers of recent immigrants to the United States were, Fleming claims, a concern of his from the time he assumed the editorship of *Chronicles*. Immigration, he believed, is a problem of national defense. In 1985, Clyde Wilson noted the rising proportion of racial minorities in the United States. He believed the figures posed a moral issue: What kind of nation were current Americans leaving to their posterity? Wilson proposed limiting grants of citizenship and restricting influxes of illegal refugees. In a March 1989 issue of *Chronicles* focused on immigration and ethnic identity, Fleming defined the immigration problem as specifically one of Third World immigration. Immigration policy is, he argued, the most "significant means of determining the future of our nation, and we owe it our children not to squander their birthright in spasms of imprudent charity." He proposed a tightening of immigration requirements for spouses and relatives, an end to mass immigration, the renewal of national quotas, and an end to welfare payments to immigrants.[86]

A primary concern for these writers was the integrity of American culture. "Immigration from countries and cultures that are incompatible with and indigestible to the Euro-American cultural core of the United States should be generally prohibited," Francis argued in December 1991. In June 1993, noting census statistics suggesting that whites will be near minority status by 2050, Francis proposed a complete end to immigration. "What sort of community can be created without the ties of blood, history, and faith to bind it together?" Fleming asked in July 1991.[87] Francis's and Fleming's concern for the cultural integrity of America, however, often shaded into anxiety over the racial composition of the nation. They tended to conflate race and culture. For example, Fleming argued in 1990 that European ethnic groups could more easily assimilate into American culture than non-European groups owing to common European and American ancestral ties. "So long as this was, fundamentally, an Anglo-American country with Anglo-American culture, language, and heroes, we knew who we were as a nation, whatever our individual backgrounds were," he opined. Insofar as he is an American, he is thereby English, Fleming declared. "If we really are the last generation of Anglo-Americans, than we are also the last generation of Americans, period."[88] The nation, Fleming argued, is a fictional extended family, although at times he seemed unclear whether the "ties of blood" need be merely fictional. At other times, he expressed alarm at any attempt to dictate a national cultural identity. In July 1995, for example, Fleming deplored attempts to impose a national identity, whether through enforced Americanization, identity cards, citizenship classes, laws mandating English as the nation's official language, or national education standards. Cultural nationalism, he declared, is an "unmitigated evil," and he lauded surviving local, provincial, and ethnic cultures. Moreover, in January 2000, Fleming, although identifying nationalism as a rational response to the "march of globalization," warned that it sowed discord and can pit ethnic and religious groups against one another. "Right-wing nationalists invite us to invent a white or Euro identity as artificial as the euro monetary unit, to establish it in schools and in the media at the expense of regional and foreign cultural identities," he wrote. "To heighten the national sense, other groups will have to be denigrated, their languages and cultures outlawed, and the reinvented nation—to prove its mettle—will embark on a series of imperial crusades to Americanize the world." Yet in 1995 Fleming asked, "Do people who call themselves African-Americans really regard themselves as Americans at all?" Black nationalism, he seemed to believe, is racist in nature and thus should be deprecated; Anglo-American particularism, however, is, apparently, rooted in culture and a shared history and thus legitimate.[89]

In fact, Fleming did not believe that blacks possessed a shared history. In 1997, he attempted to distinguish between racial and national identity. He took issue with biologists and geneticists who challenged the scientific validity of the idea of race as a distinct subdivision of human beings. "Anyone over the age of three used to know that race is a basic fact of life; today there are Ph.D.'s in the social sciences who do not know this, which is particularly strange in a place and time where race matters more, perhaps, than it ever has in human history." Race is a biological category, he insisted; the nation, by contrast, is defined by language, culture, and shared history. For Fleming, African Americans cannot aspire to a national identity (or, evidently, a legitimately particularist identity) because they do not possess a history or a culture. They lack, he argued, "even the minimum essentials of a common identity." Blacks' only "shared experience is bondage, which ended over 130 years ago," he declared. While arguing that identity politics should be rooted in national and not racial identity and claiming that racial nationalism is rooted in hatred (Fleming deprecated racialism and argued that its political applications led into a dead end), Fleming still affirmed the importance of race as a means of social classification and seemed to define American cultural identity in explicitly racial terms, equating it with Anglo-Americans. At the same time, he exhibited an unwillingness to interpret American racial history from an African American perspective or to believe that Confederate national aspirations could be inextricably tied up with race hatred. He wrote:

Liberals like to lump together Nazis, the KKK, and racial theorists, as if they were all part of a continuous movement aimed at maintaining white supremacy. But the original Klan was a national liberation army made up of ex-Confederates and their younger brothers who refused to accept their status as a subjugated people.

Black Americans have a perfect right to hate the original Klan, but they should understand that those postwar conflicts were part of a conquered people's struggle to defend itself. It was only accidentally a struggle between races.[90]

When making invidious distinctions between racial groups, Fleming and Francis tend to phrase the matter in terms of cultural difference. Any attempt by whites to preserve their cultural preeminence is, similarly, a reflection of cultural competition. But any black hostility toward white dominance is racist in motivation. Fleming is aggrieved when traditionalist conservatives sharing his views are accused of racism, arguing that it is, in fact, the National Association for the Advancement of Colored People (NAACP) that is a "race-baiting organization." The current American "regime," he declares, is built on "racism": "Those who dissent from the racist myths of white devils, patriarchal males, bigoted Southerners, antisemitic Christians — to say nothing of Uncle Toms, Oreos, and self-hating Jews—will find themselves the focus of a regime-sponsored hate campaign that will cost them their reputations and careers."[91] And both men display a remarkable lack of historical empathy for the experience of blacks in America. Francis displays little respect for the contributions of nonwhites to American success. "It is all very well to point to black cotton-pickers and Chinese railroad workers, but the cotton fields and the railroads were there because white people wanted them and knew how to put them there," he declared. "Almost all non-European contributors to American history either have been made by individuals and groups that have assimilated Euro-American ideas, values, and goals, or have been conceived, organized, and directed by white leaders." In an article on the fiftieth anniversary of the Supreme Court's 1954 decision mandating school desegregation, *Brown v. Board of Education*, Francis argued that blacks and whites voluntarily accepted racial segregation, as if it were a social custom equally shaped by both races rather than the law written by southern whites and enforced by all the formal and informal power of white society. His analysis of southern race relations stubbornly reflected the mentality of a massive resistance. The civil rights movement, Francis declared, "achieved the opposite of increasing freedom" because it "succeeded only in replacing what often was free and non-coercive (segregated) association with unfree and forced (integrated) association." In an article entitled "Prospects for Racial and Cultural Survival," which appeared in the March 1995 issue of *American Renaissance*, a newsletter edited by Jared Taylor, Francis's historical astigmatism on raced reached a remarkable peak, as he claimed that the causes of the Atlantic slave economy lay not only in whites' desire for inexpensive labor but also in the nonwhites' desire to gain access to the economically superior white society. The slave trade, in other words, was merely a clever means by which earlier hordes of nonwhite immigrants smuggled their way into white America.[92]

Francis wrote "Prospects for Racial and Cultural Survival" in response to proposals to divide the United States into separate racial zones. His essay was predicated on his belief that whites should not surrender "large parts of their own country to nonwhites." A larger theme of the essay was that conquered peoples inevitably, throughout history, dominate the conquerors. In the essay, Francis conflated racial and cultural identity, arguing that the biological category of race acquires concrete meaning in "community, kinship, nationality, territory, language, literature, art, religion, moral codes and manners, social class, and political aspirations." Whites in America have fallen to a "pitiable condition," he believed, because they surrendered their "will and identity" to such a degree that the "biological survival of the race is threatened." If the race dies, Francis declared, so does white civilization "because race is necessary, because no other race or people seems able to replicate or adopt the concepts on which white civilization is based."[93] Francis disclaimed any intention to restore white supremacy as it existed under slavery or segregation, but, in fact, his solution to the perceived crisis of white civilization was a forthright program of white supremacy or, in his own terms, "reconquest." Nonwhites would be guaranteed legal rights, but their ability to participate in the political system would be the decision of individual state and local governments. Further, there would be no bar on discrimination by private institutions, on laws outlawing interracial marriage, or on segregated schools, housing, public facilities, or transportation. The limited legal guarantees of the Civil Rights Act of 1866 constituted what Francis believed should be the full extent of rights guaranteed to blacks by the federal government. He proposed a three-part program: first, Francis sought to foster racial consciousness in whites. They must be aware of the "racial-biological endowments" that allow them to excel in self-government, economics, science, and scholarship. The deep racial insecurities lying behind some members of the *Chronicles* circle were betrayed in Francis's attitudes on this issue: "Whites would simply no longer countenance nonwhite aggression and insults or the idolization of nonwhite heroes, icons, and culture; white children would be raised in accordance with what is proper to being white, and norms openly recognized as appropriate to whites would be the legitimizing and dominant norms of American society as they were prior to the 1960s. Racial guilt and truckling would end." Second, Francis would end all immigration to the United States, seal the border, and expel illegal aliens (and, "perhaps," some recent legal immigrants). Further, he proposed a program of eugenics, calling for the end of welfare but also (presumably short of this goal) the enforced use of contraceptives for all welfare recipients. In general, contraception should be encouraged for all nonwhites and fertility promoted for whites. Third and finally, the political power of nonwhites and their "white anti-white allies" should be ended, as should affirmative action. Francis called for the dismantling of civil rights legislation.[94]

Fleming now disavows his youthful sympathies for the civil rights movement, disapproving of federal interference in state matters and feeling that the movement's legacy has been a race-based society.[95] Francis clearly would prefer a return to the white-dominated status quo that held before the 1960s. M. E. Bradford consistently opposed the civil rights movement. In 1966, he labeled an excess of concern for the rights of minorities "cupidity." In an article later that year, Bradford considered some intemperate remarks in which William Faulkner threatened forceful southern resistance to federal intervention on racial issues. Despite Faulkner's later disavowal of the comments, Bradford rose to the defense of the original remarks and argued, further, that they represented Faulkner's true outlook. Bradford defended segregation along the lines of his broader social philosophy. The values of a community arise from experience and are tested over time, he argued. Thus, they take on the character of what Burke thought of as "prejudices"—time-tested virtues and wisdom.[96] Desegregation imposed from without would irreparably rend the fabric of southern community. Truly "restorative reform" must come from within, evolving out of the past. "Its object is to preserve the integrity of the community," Bradford declared. "It is *never* imposed from without, *never* comes quickly, and is *never* the product of a few men, or even of a single generation."[97]

Bradford believed that Faulkner shared this view. "Faulkner's insistence that the responsibility for the stewardship of the Southern community must ultimately fall upon the white Southerner is nothing more or less than a recognition of fact," Bradford wrote. "It is not a defense of the status quo, not a reflection upon the Southern Negro. On the contrary, it is an acknowledgement of the irrevocability of history, of the necessity to work from what is and not from what one imagines ought to be." Although Faulkner would have wanted the communal family to include the African American, Bradford believed, he would not approve the "flight from patriarchal responsibility."[98]

Bradford further displayed a racial paternalism in a 1975 review of Robert Fogel and Stanley Engerman's *Time on the Cross* (1974) in *National Review*. *Time on the Cross* was a controversial assessment of slavery that suggested it was more stable and economically productive than previously thought. Bradford felt the book justified the traditional southern view of slavery; things had been, he declared, "just as we were told." He called slavery a "tenuous multiracial experiment," the wisdom of which had still to be decided. At the same time, he praised the "reluctant bondsmen" for their contributions to the building of a "prosperous and stable" South.[99] Bradford's position on race changed little over the years. Although he recognized the legitimacy of black grievances, he disapproved of federal civil rights regulation and of affirmative action. As late as 1986, he argued that tolerance for minorities and freedom from prejudice should not be placed ahead of the limited constitutionalism he preferred. Bradford's rigid politics of identity excluded blacks. In general, he did not believe that the demands of minority groups justified the expansive role the federal government assumed in responding to them, but he evaded the larger issue of whether minority demands were prima facie justified.[100]

As the promise of the New Right faded in the 1980s and the Reagan administration failed to roll back the welfare state (or even the level of federal spending), Wilson, Fleming, and Francis became disenchanted with mainstream conservatism. Francis's attempt to define a Middle American nationalism hearkening back to the isolationist Right of the 1930s and 1940s and his and Fleming's support for the quixotic presidential bids of Pat Buchanan reflected this alienation. The rift between what observers labeled the "paleoconservatives"—the *Chronicles* circle and those in its orbit, such as Russell Kirk—and the neoconservative intellectuals who held great influence in Washington and in many of the crucial foundations supporting the Right was bitter and acrimonious. The paleoconservatives felt the neoconservatives—many of whom had arisen out of the New York–based left Jewish intelligentsia of the 1930s and 1940s and had been Cold War liberals in the 1950s and 1960s—were latecomers to conservatism and had usurped and betrayed the true conservatives in the Right's moment of triumph. The neoconservatives pointed to attacks from Buchanan on American pro-Israel foreign policy and to the *Chronicles* circle's cultural nationalism as evidence of covert anti-Semitism and charged them with reviving anti-Semitic sentiments thought long dead on the respectable right.[101]

M. E. Bradford's failed bid to become head of the National Endowment for the Humanities (NEH) in the fall of 1981 initiated the rift. The Reagan administration's nomination of Sandra Day O'Connor to the Supreme Court had angered many on the right, and the administration briefly considered Bradford's appointment to the NEH as a gesture to mollify this constituency. Bradford pursued the post with alacrity, lobbying the White House and lining up support from conservative senators. In response, neoconservatives unleashed a quiet but effective assault. They found ready ammunition in Bradford's record of neo-Confederate rhetoric, particularly his vilification of the first Republican president, Abraham Lincoln. Although Bradford gained support from leading senators and a pledge from historian Eugene D. Genovese to testify in his behalf, he was never nominated. William Bennett, a protégé of Irving Kristol, was named in his stead. Conservative columnist George F. Will dismissed Bradford after the controversy as a representative of the "nostalgic Confederate remnant in the conservative movement," but the impetus for neoconservative hostility to Bradford may have had as much to do with dismay at the prospect of Bradford channeling NEH money away from the Northeast and to the Southwest as with conservative principles.[102]

The split between the paleoconservatives and the neoconservatives flared again in the spring of 1986 at the annual meeting of the conservative Philadelphia Society. At the time, Bradford was president of the association, and he fostered a debate on neoconservatism. University of Michigan historian Stephen Tonsor attacked the secularism and modernism of neoconservatives, identifying conservatism with Christianity and expressing the bitterness of traditionalist conservatives toward the neoconservatives. "It is splendid when the town whore gets religion and joins the church," Tonsor declared. "Now and then she makes a good choir director, but when she begins to tell the minister what he ought to say in his Sunday sermons, matters have been carried too far."[103] Fleming dates the conflict to the Rockford Institute's decision in 1989 to fire Richard John Neuhaus, a former Lutheran pastor (and later Roman Catholic priest) and neoconservative, as head of its Center on Religion and Society. In the late 1980s, this center served as a symbol of unity on the right: it received funding from foundations aligned with the neoconservatives but was associated with the paleoconservative Rockford Institute. Along with other neoconservatives such as Midge Decter, Neuhaus had been openly critical of the increasing cultural nationalism and opposition to immigration at *Chronicles*. A March 1989 issue focusing on immigration and national identity had particularly angered Norman Podhoretz, who considered it bigoted. As Neuhaus became increasingly disenchanted with what he perceived as the racism, nationalism, and nativism of *Chronicles*, he sought to ensure continued funding for the Center on Religion and Society should a break occur. In response, the Rockford Institute locked him out of the Center's New York office in May 1989, confiscating Neuhaus's files and depositing his personal belongings outside the office in garbage bags. Neuhaus promptly reestablished the religious center under a new name, taking with him approximately $750,000 in neoconservative funding. Beyond paleoconservative rhetoric, Neuhaus declared in his new journal, *First Things*, "one notes renewed attempts to invite back into the conservative movement a list of uglies that had long been consigned to the fever swamps. The list includes nativisim, racism, anti-Semitism, xenophobia, a penchant for authoritarian politics, and related diseases of the *ressentiment* that flourishes on the marginalia of American life." [104] Neoconservatives also had a hand in the decision of the *Washington Times* to fire Samuel Francis as an editorial writer. A young neoconservative publicist, Dinesh D'Souza, published an exposé of right-wing racism in the *Washington Post* that, among other items, detailed Francis's racist views as evidenced in a May 1994 speech that later became the basis for Francis's 1995 article in *American Renaissance* calling for white racial "reconquest." The editorial page editor of the *Times* demanded Francis's resignation soon thereafter. Francis claimed that the neoconservative Center for Equal Opportunity, headed by Linda Chavez, was behind his ouster; Chavez countered that Francis's own words were his undoing.[105]

Members of the *Chronicles* circle directed their energies in several directions, seeking allies within the broader Right. The libertarian economist Murray Rothbard struck up a correspondence with Fleming after the open break between *Chronicles* and the neoconservatives. Rothbard shared Fleming's respect for the Old Right and his antipathy toward the perceived globalism of neoconservatism. The two men plotted a coalition of socially conservative libertarians and paleoconservatives, formulating a "new fusionism" and establishing the John Randolph Club in 1990.[106]

During the same period, Fleming became increasingly interested in right-wing nationalist movements in Europe. This impulse led him to visit the Balkans and report on the ethnic conflict in that region from a pro-Serbian perspective. He was much more enthusiastic, however, for the Lega Lombarda (which later grew to be part of a larger Lega Nord), a localist movement in northern Italy, which fought for decentralization, cultural and linguistic revival, and, ultimately, political autonomy.[107] The model of the Lega Nord was on Fleming's mind when he and Clyde Wilson attended a 1994 meeting in Tuscaloosa, Alabama, organized by Michael Hill with the purpose of establishing an organization to defend the South's culture and autonomy. The Southern League (later League of the South), which grew out of the meeting, was loosely modeled on the Lega Nord. Hill became president and Fleming and Wilson board members. Hill was from northwestern Alabama, where his father ran a small building supply business. He earned a degree in history from the University of Alabama, studying with the southern historians Forrest McDonald and

Grady McWhiney. He went on to teach at all-black Stillman College and, on an adjunct basis, at the University of Alabama. (The University of Alabama did not renew Hill's contract in 1995, after he had become active in the Southern League and had begun voicing neo-Confederate opinions. Hill received tenure at Stillman College but resigned in 1999 to administer the League of the South full-time.) Hill advocates "cultural secession." "He refuses to eat at franchise restaurants or shop at Wal-Mart," observed journalist Gary Cartwright. "He does not watch television. He won't accept federal grants. And he grows much of his own food in his vegetable garden." Like the French Quebeçois, Scots nationalists, and the northern Italian separatists, the Southern League agitated for regional independence, declaring its support for southern secession. "All we ask," declared Hill and Fleming in explaining the Southern League's stance in "The New Dixie Manifesto," "are the rights the Constitution gave us and all Americans over 200 years ago: the right to be let alone to mind our own business, to rear our own children and to say our own prayers in the buildings built with our own money." By 1999, the organization claimed a membership of approximately nine thousand in forty-seven states. In March 2000, it promulgated a "Declaration of Southern Cultural Independence," declaring southerners to be a "separate and distinct people, with an honourable heritage and culture worthy of protection and preservation" and pledging to "cooperate economically to build and sustain our separate educational and cultural institutions." [108]

The quixotic call for secession was an extreme expression of the *Chronicles* circle's more general antipathy to the postmodern and multicultural nature of contemporary America. Some in the circle do not so much want to secede from the United States, it seems, as to return it to what they envisioned the historical reality of America to have been before the 1960s. The South that they hoped would survive was not one that included visible and vocal black and Hispanic populations. The southern identity that they valued was circumscribed by race. Not all members of the circle evidenced a strong faith in southern nationalism. Francis insistently looked to Middle Americans as the basis of a postconservative political movement. He thought southern secession a fantasy and sign of weakness and resignation and labeled the secessionist impulse of the League of the South an "infantile disorder." The South, he noted, has fed mightily at the federal trough, receiving farm subsidies, military bases, defense contracts, federal highways—and, from the perspective of blacks, federal civil rights protections, affirmative action mandates, and welfare—that it would be loathe to relinquish.[109]

One need not equate southern identity or southernness with a Christian, patriarchal social order or with whiteness. Not all members of the *Chronicles* circle did. John Shelton Reed is an instructive example. Reed is most noted for studying southerners, black and white, as a "quasi-ethnic" group. The South, he argued in *Whistling Dixie: Dispatches from the South* (1990), a collection of occasional essays, "has always been more a cultural entity than an economic or physiographic one." Reed has studied the cultural habits of southerners—from barbecue cooking to the rock-inflected music of Charlie Daniels, Waylon Jennings, and Hank Williams Jr., to NASCAR racing—and found a "down-home, funky, country" South for which he has much affection.[110]

He favors a nonexclusive southern identity, one that incorporates blacks as well as whites. Racism, he wrote, is an "insidious, soul-destroying poison." "If southern cultural revival means this, or even a larger voice for this, then to hell with it," he declared. He views the Martin Luther King Jr. national holiday—a sore point for many southern conservatives—to be a positive development as it welcomes "black citizens into full citizenship." On the Confederate flag—the defiant defense of which is a litmus-test issue among some southern conservatives—Reed staked out a moderate position, arguing that "trying to make all true Southerners salute the Confederate flag excludes altogether too many people who have a right to the label and who could be valuable recruits to the cause." "Maybe we've been brainwashed by 130 years of Yankee history, but Southern identity now has more to do with food, accents, manners, music than the Confederate past," he told *New York Times* reporter Peter Applebome in 1998. "It's something that's open to both races, a variety of ethnic groups and people who move here. It does not mean what it did at the turn of the century, when being Southern meant standing up for Dixie and saluting the flag."[111]

Indeed, Reed's essential libertarianism ("free men and women shouldn't be forced to do *anything* without a damn good reason") seems out of place in the *Chronicles* circle and hard to reconcile with the patriarchalism and organic conservatism so essential to much of the rest of the group.[112] This is evident in "The Same Old Stand?," Reed's contribution to *Why the South Will Survive*. In the essay, Reed argued, in direct contradiction of Bradford, that the South is primarily individualistic. Indeed, Reed declared, southerners are increasingly laissez-faire, even libertarian, in their approach to economics and culture. He alluded to the collapse of rigid racial barriers and illustrated the point with the example of a successful black college athlete who returned home and married a white woman to no ill effect. Southerners feel, Reed explained, that "an individual is entitled—indeed, obliged—to work out his own well-being, he is free to compete, without prescriptive restraints; and he is free to enjoy the fruits of success." Even southern evangelicalism is marked by an emphasis on individual conversion and salvation, Reed observed.[113]

Yet Reed sought to take account of the less tolerant aspects of southern culture and to reconcile the reputed strength of southern community feeling with his own libertarian reading of the South. The South is marked by "localism," he argued. Most southerners expect one to remain loyal to one's own community, one's own group. This loyalty, however, is freely chosen. It is easy to leave a group; in fact, the preferred southern method of handling dissent is to exclude the "deviant" from the group rather than to suppress him or her. "Theoretical hostility toward other groups, other communities, and other regions is often combined with a sort of workaday pluralism that lets folks get along pretty well most of the time, although it wouldn't satisfy the sponsors of National Brotherhood Week," Reed remarked. Outsiders are simply left alone.[114]

However, Reed's attempt to reconcile communitarianism and libertarianism leaves unanswered many of the questions that have bedeviled Davidsonian Agrarianism from the start. Who defines membership in the group? Who determines the circle of southern identity? It goes without saying that the social and economic goods of southern society will go only to members of the group in good standing, not to "deviants." Southerners just desire to be let alone, Reed argued, and tend, in fact, to tolerate the intolerable. Yet this assertion carries a note of obfuscation. Something truly intolerable will, by definition, not be tolerated. The white South's reputation for harsh defensiveness and close-mindedness reflects its long-standing intolerance of challenges to the racial consensus, as, for example, during the civil rights years. (To be fair, Reed did acknowledge the distinctive southern predilection for violence and retributive justice.) And blacks were excluded from southern identity entirely.[115]

Further, Reed argued that the South is a "nested set of communities," stretching from the region down through the neighborhood, then to the family—and all those in between. One is free to leave any of these communities. "The result is communities and groups which enlist the loyalty of their members, so long as they remain members, precisely *because* they are free to leave," Reed reasoned. "[W. J.] Cash's 'savage ideal' of conformity may well characterize relations *within* many Southern communities, while *between* communities a certain rough-and-ready tolerance (indifference, really) prevails."[116] Yet, as Reed's own metaphor implies, in a system of nested communities, one is never in between communities. To leave one is to still remain in a dozen others, all comfortably nested one in another. To be completely free of the coercion of community would necessitate leaving the South. Taken as a vision of society as a whole, to be completely free is to be completely outside community—to be nowhere. In other words, southern libertarianism and individualism are everywhere circumscribed by southern community.

Reed's attempt to describe a southern communal identity that would not be exclusive or coercive was almost a contradiction in terms. As Fred Hobson had suggested in his own contribution to *Why the South Will Survive*, southern hatreds and southern compassion and hospitality often derived from the same root. The strong virtues of a deeply rooted sense of identity often breed equally strong defects. In one sense, this was the lesson of Donald Davidson's career and thought. Davidson feared the loss of membership in a community and treasured his southern identity. He never did leave the South. Americans, Davidson believed, were sliding into nowhere. What Davidson saw, more than any of the other Agrarians in the 1930s, was the passing of a premodern sense of identity. In premodern or traditional societies, Alasdair MacIntyre argued in *After Virtue: A Study in Moral Theory* (1981), "it is through his or her membership in a variety of social groups that the individual identifies himself or herself and is identified by others. I am brother, cousin, and grandson, member of this household, that village, this tribe." Such attributes, MacIntyre argued, formed part of the core of a person's substance and defined his or her social obligations. Deprived of his or her "particular space within an interlocking set of social relationships," a person is "nobody, or at best a stranger or an outcast." [117] Lacking the bond of shared membership in a polis, one was a "citizen of nowhere, an internal exile wherever he lives." From an Aristotelian viewpoint, MacIntyre observed, "a modern liberal political society can appear only as a collection of citizens of nowhere who have banded together for their common protection." [118]

Davidson had a firm grasp on this insight, and he responded with defensiveness and insecurity, as did many in the *Chronicles* circle after him. Racism set narrow limits to his concept of friendship. Black men and women might be objects of his affection; they could not be full-fledged fellow citizens. Davidson's fear of modern anonymity and his hostility to a centralized government intent on forcing racial liberalism on the South led him to strong and active support of racial injustice and away from a critique of the socioeconomic factors that caused the atomization he condemned.

Bradford placed the Agrarians within a painstakingly reconstructed tradition of southern conservatism. Agrarianism was a politics, not a literary exercise, he argued. It was a mistake to lift the book from its context and make it into a "pseudopoetic tract or exercise in pastoral mythmaking." [119] This is a sound observation, yet Bradford's interpretation of *I'll Take My Stand* as an embodiment of patriarchal traditionalism was as great a distortion. Bradford argued that the Agrarians were "natural heirs" of Randolph, Taylor, and the "good," antistatist Jefferson:

> Community was their a priori ideal—an informally hierarchical social organism in which all Southerners (including the Negro, insofar as the survival of the community permitted) had a sense of investment and participation. In brief, a patriarchal world of families, pre- or noncapitalist *because* familial, located, pious, and "brotherly"; agrarian in order not to produce the alienated, atomistic individual to whom abstractly familial totalitarianism can appeal; classically republican because that system of government best allowed for the multiplicity that was the nation while at the same time permitting the agrarian culture of families to flourish unperturbed. [120]

Bradford remade Agrarianism, along Davidsonian lines, into a patriarchal version of republican political philosophy. Bradford had long planned a biography of Davidson, tentatively entitled "Down This Long Street: The Life and Times of Donald Davidson" but never completed. For Bradford, Davidson was an example of a "memory keeper," a "vatic poet" who played the elite role of validating and defining society. [121] "The idea that an elaborate and officially sanctioned memory is the best means of sustaining and perpetuating a particular culture is everywhere apparent in the work of Donald Davidson," he wrote in a posthumously published essay. [122]

Bradford made of memory a peculiarly truncated politics that upheld a rigidly defined identity and authority. And he justified this politics by an appeal to a conservative tradition stretching back to ancient Rome. Davidson's conclusions about southern life and segregation, in practical terms little different from Bradford's, derived not from a patriarchal political philosophy but from folkish romanticism. He did not appeal to prescriptive order to defend segregation but to white supremacy and baldly stated self-interest. Although Davidson became obsessed with the federal "leviathan" as he aged, his Agrarianism had begun as a celebration of pioneer frontiersmen and southern folk culture and a reaction against the homogenizing effects of a national business civilization. But doubts about industrial capitalism were rarely voiced in Bradford's writings, which were concerned, above all, with justifying a prescriptive and patriarchal social system and the power of a caste of memory keepers.

The original Agrarians had been forward-looking in their challenge of industrial capitalism, even if they advocated a return to an earlier scale of life. Too often, the work of Bradford and the *Chronicles* circle has been nostalgic and backward-looking, searching for solutions from the past to solve problems produced by pluralism and heterogeneity in American society. They remain immured in history, unable to see the past as anything other than fate. Their outlook is aptly described as nostalgic. "Nostalgia appeals to the feeling that the past offered delights no longer obtainable," the historian Christopher Lasch observed. "Nostalgic representations of the past evoke a time irretrievably lost and for that reason timeless and unchanging. Strictly speaking, nostalgia does not entail the exercise of memory at all since the past it idealizes stands outside time, frozen in unchanging perfection." [123]

If a consciousness of the legacy of their forebears lent crucial power to the original Agrarian manifesto, the Agrarians' interpretation of history could also have an enervating effect on the entire Agrarian tradition. In *Why the South Will Survive*, Andrew Nelson Lytle declared that Agrarianism had failed.

> Family and neighborhood made the world we inhabited. Travel through the countryside and you will find it empty. People dwell there, but as individuals, except in certain stubborn and traditional pockets. They do not compose a community. Travel to the towns and small cities and they all look stamped out of plastic. They differ mainly in size. The outskirts hold flat buildings of assembly plants owned from afar; more sinisterly, factories dealing in chemical poisons pollute our countryside. People as well as the towns are beginning to have an anonymous look.

Modern life, Lytle felt, was like a "wake for the living." At a wake one has the "illusory sense of life prevailing in the presence of death." Thus, we moderns live in the physical but not in the spiritual sense. Many of the late Agrarian accounts and interpretations of Agrarianism share this sense of loss, of something missing—the sense of being in a fallen order, and under the damning rebuke of history. Insofar as it partook of this sensibility, the neo-Agrarian tradition of cultural criticism risked becoming sterile and nostalgic. [124]

Of Southern Conservatism
and Agrarianism

*To renounce the principle of democratic property, which is the only
basis of democratic liberty, in exchange for specious notions of efficiency or the economics of the so-called free market is tragic folly.*
    Wendell Berry, *Home Economics*

By the 1980s, many literary professors and conservative thinkers propounded Agrarianisms quite different from what the Twelve Southerners advocated in 1930. For many of the leaders of the southern academic literary establishment, such as Louis D. Rubin Jr., Agrarianism
was a penetrating criticism of the spiritual and social costs of modernity. It was not an effective political or economic program; rather,
I'll Take My Stand surveyed the themes of hollowness and loss that
constituted the spiritual background of the southern renascence in
literature. Neo-Agrarian conservatives, such as Richard Weaver and
M. E. Bradford, and the broader "paleoconservative" *Chronicles* circle
considered the Agrarians to be prophets of cultural degeneration and
the loss of Christian authority in modern society. They saw in the
Agrarians an image of proper organic social order and the memory of
limited and republican forms of government. Southern Agrarianism
contained within itself the seeds of both interpretations. Nevertheless, later commentators tended to minimize what was arguably at its
core—a radical call to reject, at least in part, industrial capitalism and
the social values it promoted. The Agrarians confronted the modern
cult of progress with a call to slow down, to return to a more leisurely
but more limited way of life, one that they felt was vindicated by history and tradition. They sought to preserve what was best in their
tradition while accepting the changes that were necessary.
    The burden of this study has been to document the deradicalization
of the Agrarian tradition and to identify the ways in which a cultural

criticism originally insistent on the interconnection between culture and the economy came to be replaced by a traditionalist conservatism oriented around the image of the South as a synecdoche for Christian orthodoxy and a patriarchal social order. Contemporary traditionalist conservatives, if heeding much of the neo-Agrarian commentary on Agrarianism, stand to lose sight of the radical conservatism of *I'll Take My Stand*. They might also miss the vexing role that race has played in the Agrarian tradition. The legacy of slavery and the history of white supremacy and racism are deeply intertwined with the Agrarian tradition, which many of the principals understood, including even Donald Davidson and Richard Weaver, who felt that segregation was a vital bulwark of southern society. Through the writings of Robert Penn Warren, Agrarianism spawned a pragmatic, "liberal," variant, in which the guiding role of history was exceedingly more complex than for either Davidson or Weaver. Two contemporary writers, the historian Eugene D. Genovese and the essayist, poet, and novelist Wendell Berry, elucidate both the legacy of the original Twelve Southerners and the intellectual and political project of the neo-Agrarians. Although Genovese and Berry come to the Agrarian tradition from very different paths and with quite different agendas, they illuminate these important but sometimes hidden legacies of Agrarianism.

Eugene D. Genovese is the Brooklyn-born son of a working-class Sicilian American family and one of the most influential contemporary historians of American slavery and the slaveholding class. As a leading radical scholar in the 1960s and a longtime Marxist, he is an unlikely heir to the conservative southern tradition championed by Bradford. Genovese's radicalism, however, was informed by the same hostility toward bourgeois culture and radical individualism that shapes his current conservatism. And it is this hostility to bourgeois individualism that has enriched his historical work. Genovese's career has been defined by his effort to understand the slave South and, indeed, to rehabilitate the historical reputation of the southern master class, whom he believes articulated the most powerful native-born critique of the social relations of bourgeois individualism.

Genovese attended Brooklyn College and, after graduation in 1953, worked for a time as a newspaper copyboy before pursuing graduate studies in history at Columbia University. He earned his Ph.D. in 1959. Genovese was a member of the Communist Party at age fifteen and intended to work as a party labor organizer after college, but the party expelled him before graduation. Only then did he start reading the works of Karl Marx seriously. Genovese's expulsion from the party did not lead, as it did many intellectuals before him, into the anti-Communist Right or Left. Rather, Genovese became a confirmed Stalinist, forcefully attacking the anti-Communist New Left throughout the 1960s. Social revolution requires indiscriminate terror, he argued. Cultural radicals who envisioned middle-class students as a revolutionary vanguard and targeted the university were the object of his scorn.[1]

Genovese did not denounce Joseph Stalin's atrocities, but, even while consistently defending Soviet-bloc nations, he defended the Western liberal tradition of free speech and free thought, which was, for many radical intellectuals in the 1960s, the object of much abuse for its perceived racism, patriarchy, and elitism. This stance placed Genovese between radical and conservative factions. His embrace of a Vietcong victory in Southeast Asia at a 1965 Rutgers University teach-in caused Genovese to be a symbol of antiwar radicalism in the New Jersey gubernatorial election that fall. In 1969, however, he sided with conservatives and strongly opposed radical historian Staughton Lynd's campaign to become president of the American Historical Association and place that organization on record against America's conduct in the Vietnam War. Genovese defended the standards and autonomy of the academy and labeled the forces led by Lynd "totalitarians," declaring, somewhat extravagantly, that the historical association must "put them down, put them down hard, and put them down once and for all."[2]

Genovese's interest in the South began while a student at Brooklyn College when the economic historian Arthur C. Cole persuaded him to examine antebellum efforts at agricultural reform. This research led Genovese into a study of the southern master class. In his first major work, *The Political Economy of Slavery: Studies in the Economy and Society of the Slave South* (1965), Genovese argued that slaveholders composed a precapitalist and prebourgeois social elite struggling to maintain their noncapitalist system of social relations in the modern world. He questioned historians such as Kenneth Stampp who stressed the profitability of slave labor. At the same time, he patiently and controversially attempted to revise the tarnished reputation of the racist southern historian Ulrich B. Phillips, who had also viewed the slaveholders as a social elite struggling to preserve a stable and organic society. Phillips was, Genovese argued, perhaps as close to greatness as "any historian this country has yet produced."[3]

Genovese retreated from the claim that slavery was precapitalist and unprofitable, in part because of the arguments of Robert Fogel and Stanley Engerman. Engerman was his colleague on the faculty of the University of Rochester, which Genovese joined in 1969. Under the influence of historians such as George Rawick and Herbert Gutman, Genovese also moved from a more narrowly economic focus on southern slaveholding to a broader sociocultural approach to plantation relations in general. His new attention to slave culture, including African American folk tales, spirituals, and religion, and the role this culture played in shaping the African American community was reflected in his most famous work, *Roll, Jordan, Roll: The World the Slaves Made* (1974), his masterful exposition of the peculiarly intimate paternalism that characterized slavery in the American South. He stubbornly maintained his interpretation, however, of the southern master class as essentially anticapitalist and antibourgeois.[4]

The master class may have been deeply involved in the international market economy and, indeed, even internalized many of the values of the modern order, Genovese argued, but this slave-owning class remained, at the same time, opposed to the bourgeois mentality in crucial ways. The slaveholders clung to a premodern set of social relations and an understanding of the master-laborer relationship as defined by authority and benevolence rather than the cash nexus. When contrasted with the pattern of modernization in the North and elsewhere in the West, the slave South pointed in a "different direction." The South, he argued, "was *in* but not *of* the modern capitalist world." The contradictions of the master class's divided mind are the subject of a long-promised study by Genovese and his wife, Elizabeth Fox-Genovese, "The Mind of the Master Class: The Life and Thought of the Southern Slaveholders."[5]

Over the years, Genovese has become a cultural conservative. He is known and respected by many of the conservative intellectuals associated with *Chronicles*. Genovese was a friend of M. E. Bradford's and offered to testify in support of his potential nomination to head the National Endowment of the Humanities in 1981. He dedicated *The Slaveholders' Dilemma: Freedom and Progress in Southern Conservative Thought, 1820–1860* (1992), the inaugural lectures in Georgia Southern University's Jack N. and Addie D. Averitt Lecture Series, to Bradford, John Shelton Reed, and Clyde N. Wilson, "scholars, gentlemen, worthy heirs of a great Southern Tradition."[6] In his 1993 William E. Massey lectures at Harvard University, published as *The Southern Tradition: The Achievement and Limitations of an American Conservatism* (1994), and in a collection of essays published as *The Southern Front: History and Politics in the Cultural War* (1995), Genovese has attempted to defend elements of southern culture that he argues are valuable even if tainted by racism. The southern conservative tradition, he holds, is a healthy antidote to the decadence and radical individualism of contemporary liberalism and the cultural Left.

Socialism, Genovese now argues, was an utter failure; capitalism, in contrast, is a success and has expanded the possibilities of individual freedom and political democracy throughout the world. He harshly criticizes his erstwhile colleagues on the left. "Having substituted what may fairly be called a gnostic vision for Christianity and scoffed at the moral baseline of the Ten Commandments and the Sermon on the Mount," Genovese wrote, alluding to the thought of Eric Voegelin, "we ended a seventy-year experiment with socialism with little more to our credit than tens of millions of corpses." The Left, he declared, was guilty of a "blood-drenched romance with the Utopia of a man-made heaven on earth." In "The Question," published in *Dissent* in 1994, Genovese condemned the anti-Communist Left for complicity in Soviet atrocities because of its anti-Western tilt in national and international policy—atrocities, it should be noted, that the anti-Communist Left had, in fact, condemned for years while he had not.[7]

Genovese is much more sympathetic to the foibles of slaveholders. Indeed, he admires the anticapitalist ideology of the antebellum slave elite. He is struck by what Reinhold Niebuhr would have labeled an irony of history: How could such a great people have presided over a system of human bondage, such an "enormity"? The "tragic dimension of southern history," he suggested in *The Southern Tradition*, is "the extent to which courageous, God-fearing, honorable people rendered themselves complicit in slavery, segregation, and racism and ended up in defeat and degradation."[8]

In Genovese's interpretation, the southern conservative tradition is founded on a rejection of finance capitalism and what he considers the radical individualism of its bourgeois social relations. While Bradford traced the tradition to the "Old Whig" country opponents of the English Crown in the seventeenth century, Genovese stresses the importance of the antebellum proslavery apologists. For both men, southern conservatism is rooted in republican traditions of American thought. Southern conservatives, Genovese argued, give only qualified support to property rights and the market, which they hold subject to social constraints. In Genovese's view, the slaveholders saw clearly the revolutionary impact of bourgeois social relations in dissolving familial and communal ties and making the marketplace the "arbiter of moral and social life." "Southerners objected not to a market economy, but to the transformation of that economy into the essence of society itself," Genovese wrote. "They objected, that is, to the transformation of all spiritual and moral values into commodities."[9] The ostensible value of the southern conservative tradition lies in this anticapitalist perspective, but the true target of Genovese's social criticism is what he considers the excessive individualism fostered by the capitalist system. The admirable Christian doctrine of the equality of all souls has been perverted, he argued, "into an ignoble dream of personal liberation, whether in its radical-democratic, communist, or free-market form." Although then an unbeliever, Genovese admitted to having "long accepted the essentials of the doctrines of original sin and human depravity." [10] In *A Consuming Fire: The Fall of the Confederacy in the Mind of the White Christian South* (1998), Genovese argues that southern ministers and theologians saw that political liberalism, egalitarianism, and social radicalism, resulting in "family disintegration (divorce, promiscuity, prostitution) and unemployment, poverty, and social disorder," were linked to the lapse from religious orthodoxy. [11]

Indeed, Genovese's attention to the historical role of religion, despite his historical materialism, is striking. This scholarly sensitivity has been reflected in his personal life. In December 1995, Elizabeth Fox-Genovese converted to Roman Catholicism; he subsequently returned to the church. [12] Genovese's analysis of Afro-Christianity in *Roll, Jordan, Roll* was central to his interpretation of the resistance and accommodation that defined slaves' life in the Old South. Genovese derived chapter titles and epigraphs from the Bible; a quote from Revelation ended the book. ("Given my own biases, I was dragged kicking and screaming to that vantage point," he observed in an interview with Boyd Cathey published in 1985.) Genovese now argues that Protestant Christianity was fundamental to the Old South. He arrived at this thesis, revealingly, through his reading of twentieth-century southern conservatives, notably the Agrarians (particularly Allen Tate), Richard Weaver, and Bradford. "One of the things that has amazed me is that I've worked on these Antebellum Southerners now for a long, long time," he told Cathey, "but it wasn't until I started to go back and reread the conservative interpretation and defenses of Southern tradition that the full force of that hit me, the force of what it might mean." [13]

The burden of Genovese's exploration of southern conservatism is, following Richard Weaver, to outline a "social bond individualism" that delicately balances a commitment to political freedom and equality with a strong center of social authority. Southern conservatives, he argued, uphold a "Christian individualism," as opposed to the bourgeois individualism descended from the Renaissance and French Enlightenment. At the core of Genovese's version of the conservative tradition is this essential Weaverian faith in a rooted individualism. Southern conservatives, he claimed, condemn "an individualism torn loose from family, community, and civic responsibility—an individualism that has metamorphosed into egocentrism, personal irresponsibility, and a loss of civic discipline." Christian individualism as opposed to radical individualism, Genovese argues, is based on the presumption that personality matures when in a community that demands loyalty and responsibility. "It is an individualism," Genovese declared, "that emphatically rejects visions of personal liberation—of a New Man and New Woman liberated from the constraints of those rules and prejudices necessary to community life." [14]

Such a conception of individualism is the centerpiece of a southern republicanism skeptical of mass democracy; respectful of community wisdom, tradition, and prejudice; and wary of centralized power, whether in the centralized government or corporate bureaucracies. Citizens of such a republic accept "natural, necessary, and proper" hierarchy and stratification, while rejecting "artificially promoted aristocracies and elites." This southern republicanism, Genovese asserts emphatically, must make a complete break with white supremacy, which, he argues, contemporary southern conservatives are attempting to do.[15] The defense of segregation, Genovese declared, though based on valid principle, led to a "moral and political quagmire": "In defining their communities, conservatives long spoke as if blacks were an unwelcome foreign presence rather than of the marrow."[16]

Genovese's attempt to rehabilitate the southern master class as well as his recent embrace of southern conservatism, both projects informed by the work of Weaver and Bradford, have been met with both fascination and consternation by academic historians and observers on the left, many of whom viewed Genovese's previous scholarship as a model of materialist historical analysis. Genovese's portrayal of the "southern tradition" as an embodiment of organicism and order, much along the lines of neo-Agrarians and paleoconservatives, and his seeming belief that it can be distinguished from the tradition of white supremacy reflected a shift, some believed, from socioeconomic to intellectual analysis (which, ironically, recapitulated that of the broader Agrarian tradition). Labor historian Alex Lichtenstein, for example, argues that "without a firm basis in historical materialism, Genovese's account of southern conservative thought has become rudderless, and as a result drifts perilously close to apologia."[17] "Genovese appears to have squandered the original boldness of his thinking by abandoning its initial Marxian impulse," Lichtenstein continued, "and thus detaching the anti-bourgeois, anti-market virtues of the southern hostility to modernity from their source in the defense of a slave society." There is little in the southern tradition's critique of modern alienation, exploitation, and disintegration caused by market societies that cannot be found on the left, Lichtenstein declares. Moreover, southern conservatism is, he argues, indelibly and undeniably implicated in the history of slavery and racial oppression. The social basis and intellectual rationale of southern conservatism, Lichtenstein holds, was and remains racial hierarchy.[18] Why should this be an attractive tradition for the Left or for anyone in America, particularly when socialists have long arrived at the same conclusions about bourgeois social relations?

Lichtenstein believes that Genovese seeks a position from which to attack both right-wing liberal defenders of the market and the "personal liberationists" of the Left, whom he has long despised. But his attempt, Lichtenstein suggests, necessarily leads Genovese to diminish the vital role that race and racial oppression have played in forming southern conservatism, forcing him to "retreat to a rather essentialist account of southern thought, a view which suggests that its values emanate from a free-floating Southern 'culture' disconnected from the region's politics or political economy."[19] The historian David L. Chappell, a student of Genovese's, has reached opposite conclusions about Genovese's project. Chappell argues that Genovese's need to rigorously rearticulate the thought of the southern master class is derived from his "mania for consistency" and "intellectual coherence," which compels him to seek out a real and historically effective opposition to bourgeois capitalism in the past but at the same time examine the flaws and deficiencies of any such historical tradition with an unblinking eye and unrelenting analysis.[20] "His history of *the* anticapitalist tradition of America—the one that, although it was defeated in war, gave capitalism a harder run for its money than any other anticapitalist tradition in America—could help the left . . . regain some intellectual and political bearings," Chappell writes.[21] Genovese does not ignore the centrality of slavery to the southern tradition, Chappell argues. Reviewing *The Southern Tradition*, he claims that Genovese "is much franker about the association of conservatism with slavery than most conservatives today." Genovese's book "chides conservatives for their unwillingness to recognize how much their tradition owes to its original grounding in bonded labor."[22]

Lichtenstein and Chappell are both correct. Genovese's analysis of the southern tradition is shaped by the neo-Agrarian tendency to "essentialize" the South as the embodiment of Christian orthodoxy and Western civilization. And yet it is quite possible to read Genovese as a penetrating, if sympathetic, critic of southern conservatism. Some of the outlines of Genovese's and Fox-Genovese's interpretation of the master class are sketched in Genovese's recent work. In *The Slaveholders' Dilemma*, Genovese stressed that the master class found much to criticize in the feudal ideal of medieval society, despite a general admiration for it. Southern slaveholders embraced the organic social relations, the chivalric ideals, the constitutionalism, and the Christian sentiment that they perceived in the Middle Ages but disdained the era's tendencies to ignorance, violence, and despotism, as well as its sheer material backwardness.[23] The slaveholders embraced material progress even as they sought to preserve elements of prebourgeois social relations through the slave-based social order they created. They pursued an "alternate route to modernity"—one that would not uproot the social hierarchy and lead to excessive freedom (and thus radical egalitarianism, demagoguery, and finally social disarray followed by despotism).[24] "The South, virtually alone," Genovese wrote, "stood for progress and modernity without the horrible evils that plagued the bourgeois societies."[25]

However, the southern slave-based social order was, ultimately, untenable, and perceptive southern slaveholders recognized this dilemma. Freedom and liberalization were necessary to economic progress, but liberty would inevitably expand and be claimed by the laboring class, thus leading to the radical egalitarianism and social disarray that southerners feared would necessarily follow. However, were southerners to reject progress and the freedom it required, their region would stagnate and fall under the control of the industrializing North. The slaveholders' choice lay between freedom and progress (and subsequent chaos and social strife) or the slave order and an end to progress (and subsequent economic decline).[26] The southern slave-owning class emerges as tragic in Genovese's work, because they saw clearly the moral deficiencies and evils of the emerging market society in the North and were determined to stand against it, yet they saw that emerging modern commitments to freedom and justice—commitments they did not share—would doom their own alternative slave-based society. Their only option was to reject modernity as a whole, a repudiation they could not and would not make.

Genovese unflinchingly declares slavery to be at the heart of the southern order. Many contemporary southern traditionalists—when defending the public display of the Confederate battle flag or re-arguing the causes of the Civil War—ignore or dismiss the role of slavery in the Confederacy. (The rebel flag symbolizes southern pride and identity; the war was fought for states' rights and regional sovereignty.) As David Chappell notes, Genovese's work explicitly rejects this tendency. The proslavery argument, Genovese observed in *The Slaveholders' Dilemma*, was the "pillar" of the southern "worldview." The slaveholders' formula for change was "progress through freedom based on slavery"; the slave system, in antebellum theorist Thomas Dew's assessment, promised "republican liberties for the propertied, security for the propertyless, and stability for the state and society."[27]

"Virtually all Southern spokesmen, clerical and lay, readily acknowledged that the South was fighting to uphold slavery," Genovese declared at the beginning of *A Consuming Fire*.[28] This latter work is an elegant commentary on the southern slaveholders' inability to see the evil of slavery—their unwillingness to interpret the "consuming fire" of civil war and the catastrophic defeat of the Confederacy as God's just verdict on the peculiar institution. In the book, Genovese details the extended but ineffective effort by southern ministers and theologians to reform the institution of slavery from within. Southern ministers, Genovese argues, defended slavery not on the basis of black racial inferiority (theological orthodoxy was the "strongest bulwark against scientific racism") but rather by appealing to Scripture.[29] Southern ministers enjoined slaveholders to live up to their Christian responsibilities as masters; blacks should be treated humanely, educated, and their families recognized and preserved.[30] Yet, to have truly reformed slavery along the lines that ministers discerned in the Bible would have essentially transformed the institution beyond recognition and deprived slaveholders of many of its material advantages.[31] The ministers failed in their mission of reform.

Southern ministers tended to interpret the Confederate defeat as God's punishment for southerners' failings as masters and not as a judgment on slavery itself.[32] (Genovese also seems to see the war as God's judgment, although he is somewhat ambiguous himself as to whether the war was a judgment on slavery or merely on the mistreatment of slaves.)[33] Genovese is critical of the southern religious establishment, however, for its acquiescence to segregation and its embrace of racism after the war. He emphasizes the antebellum theologians' rejection of racism, and he attributes the postwar religious adoption of "racial-imperialist ideology" to a decline in orthodoxy and an embrace of Yankee values: "Indeed, in essential respects, the Southern embrace of imperialism represented a substitute for—and a betrayal of—the ideals and visions of the proslavery worldview, although it was tailor-made for a New South bent on continuing the racial subordination of blacks."[34] Although Genovese's argument is a sly jab at theological liberalism, which, he argues, bolsters "political reaction," it highlights, for a southern audience, the fact that southern elites, owing to expediency and self-interest, did not fulfill the moral obligations to blacks that they themselves outlined. Few ministers were able or willing to provide moral justifications for white supremacy or racism. "The proslavery divines may be criticized severely for theological error, but they cannot fairly be accused of bad faith, much less hypocrisy, in their scriptural defense of slavery," Genovese argues. "The same cannot be said for their successors' efforts to defend postbellum segregation."[35]

Genovese's turn toward the southern conservatism he sees rooted in the antebellum master class not only continues his long-held disdain for the ethical and social vision of bourgeois individualism but also reflects an embrace of biblically held absolutes and moral traditions. Although Chappell argues that Genovese is still a historical

materialist and will, in the end, refuse to be "taken in" by conservatism, Alex Lichtenstein's claim that Genovese has turned his attention
from the material forces shaping society to abstract and essential abstractions has some merit.[36] Nevertheless, despite his admiration for
the southern master class and his affinity for the social organicism of
the neo-Agrarians, Genovese is unrelenting in his reminder to southern conservatives that their worldview was historically rooted in the
justification of slavery and that their ancestors were guilty of acqui-
escing to large-scale racial discrimination and white supremacy.

Wendell Berry upholds an organic vision of society, but one rooted
in ecology rather than in patriarchy. The belief that industrial capitalism and Western notions of progress subvert an organic and healthy
social order lies at the heart of his social criticism. He is also a practical
agrarian, operating a subsistence farm above the Kentucky River near
Port Royal, a small settlement in Henry County, Kentucky, about
forty miles northeast of Louisville and close to the border with Indiana. "Real agrarianism begins with practical farming and involves
itself with practical solutions to the problems of farming," he declares.
His social and cultural criticism is rooted in Henry County, where he
was born in 1934 and grew up. As a boy, Berry observed the fracturing
of this tight-knit farming community in the wake of World War II. In
the late 1930s, Port Royal was a town of 100–125 people with eight to
ten small businesses and its own doctor: "These people worked hard,
and without any modern conveniences or labor savers. They had no
tractors, no electricity, no refrigerators, no washing machines, no vac-
uum cleaners. Their one luxury was the telephone party line, which
cost fifty cents a month. But their work was in limited quantities; they
did not work at night or away from home; they knew their work, they
knew how to work, and they knew each other."[37] Although Berry lived
in the town of New Castle, where his father practiced law, he still absorbed the rhythms of farm life on visits to his paternal grandfather's
farm, which had been the home of three generations of Berrys. His
father and grandfather possessed a "profound solicitude for the land
and its welfare"; both men "knew that a gully is a wound." His father
fostered a connection between Berry and the land: "He talked and
contrived endlessly to the effect that I should understand the land, not
as a commodity, an inert fact to be taken for granted, but as an ultimate value, enduring and alive, useful and beautiful and mysterious
and formidable and comforting, beneficent and terribly demanding,
worthy of the best of a man's attention and care."[38]
After attending Millersburg Military Institute in Kentucky, Berry
enrolled at the University of Kentucky in Lexington in 1952. There
he began to publish poems and short stories and formed the convic-

tion to be a writer. There, too, he first read *I'll Take My Stand* and learned, from one of his teachers, Robert D. Jacobs, that his writing revealed him to be an "Agrarian." After graduation, Berry married Tanya Amyx, daughter of Clifford Amyx, a professor of art at the University of Kentucky and a former classmate and friend of Richard Weaver's.[39] From 1958 to 1960, Berry studied creative writing under Wallace Stegner at Stanford University, where his classmates included Ernest Gaines and Ken Kesey.[40] After briefly returning to farm in Kentucky in 1960 and 1961, Berry received a Guggenheim award to study in France and Italy. On his return, he accepted a position at the University Heights campus of New York University. In 1964, however, he returned to Kentucky to stay, accepting an appointment at the University of Kentucky, where he taught until 1977 and again from 1987 to 1993 and acquired twelve acres to farm in Henry County.[41]

On returning to Kentucky for the first time, after his fellowship at Stanford, Berry became more deeply committed to exploring his relationship to the land. In the summer of 1961, he used the cabin of his great-uncle Curran Mathews, which was located near the Kentucky River, not far from Port Royal, as a place for reading and writing. The cabin had been a family retreat during his childhood and a place during his adolescence of contemplation and escape. "I began to think of myself as living within rather than upon the life of the place," Berry later wrote. He formed the ambition to "belong fully" to the area.[42] This sense of relation to the land and to one's place is at the heart of Berry's thought, which he has elaborated in several volumes of essays and which informs his poetry, novels, and stories.[43] Although his emphases have changed throughout his career, Berry has elaborated an agrarian and ecological argument built on a set of consistently held core principles. At the heart of his thought is the conviction that healing—both for human beings and communities—comes from reconnection and renewal. The deepest wound, for Berry, is always that produced by disconnection. In the 1960s, for example, he argued that the Vietnam War, which he opposed and protested, revealed the disjuncture between American actions and ideals. Racism, he believed, created a "hidden wound" as much in whites as in blacks, which would only be healed by a rapprochement between the races.[44]

The ultimate division requiring healing is between humans and the environment. This is the sort of reconnection to which Berry aspired at his great-uncle's cabin:

> It is only in a country that is well-known, full of familiar names and places, full of life that is always changing, that the mind goes free of abstractions, and renews itself in the presence of the creation,

that so persistently eludes human comprehension and human law. It is only in the place that one belongs to, intimate and familiar, long watched over, that the details rise up out of the whole and become visible: the hawk stoops into the clearing before one's eyes; the wood drake, aloof and serene in his glorious plumage, swims out of his hiding place.[45]

Berry laid out a set of ecological principles built on the belief that health arises out of the creation of harmonious communities in "Discipline and Hope," an essay published in *A Continuous Harmony: Essays Cultural and Agricultural* (1972). He identified what he considered the roots of contemporary cultural disorder in the usurpation of older standards of quality by the single standard of efficiency. Quoting from *I'll Take My Stand*, Berry urged the nation to turn from the "false god" of the technology-driven, industrial economy and toward harmony with nature, which would be built on a sound agriculture. A healthy agriculture required a stable farm population, which, because it lived on the land, would develop the knowledge and skills required to live in harmony with the earth.[46]

Life is cyclical, Berry argued. All is produced from something that came before and contributes to some other form of life that will come after. Death is merely one element of this natural cycle. Just as wastes returned to the earth serve to fertilize it and continue the cycle, so we must see that the patterns in which we live are ones of both decay and renewal. A linear view of human history evades the responsibility and the necessary disciplines of renewal, such as the recycling of waste into the soil. Waste conceived apart from reuse is a linear concept.

> This implies a profound contempt for correct discipline; it proposes, in the giddy faith of prodigals, that there can be production without fertility, abundance without thrift. We take and we do not give back, and this causes waste. It is a hideous concept, and it is making the world hideous. It is consumption, a wasting disease. And this disease of our material economy becomes also the disease of our spiritual economy, and we have made a shoddy merchandise of our souls.[47]

Berry called for a return to the ancient disciplines of community, founded on marriage—between both men and women but also humans and the earth—and faith in principles.[48] For Berry, one such principle was peace. "If we believe in peace, then we must see that violence makes us infidels," he argued. "When we institute repressions to protect democracy from enemies abroad, we have already damaged it at home. The demands of faith are absolute: we must put all our eggs in one basket; we must burn our bridges." Ultimately, there is only one value, Berry declared: "the life and health of the world."[49]

Ecology informed Berry's religious beliefs. Raised a Southern Baptist, he became estranged from institutional religion over time, identifying with Christianity but feeling organized Christianity to be compromised by worldly concerns and complicit with destructive practices.[50] Modern Christianity has become, he wrote, "the religion of the state and the economic status quo." There is justice, he asserted, to the claim that Christianity has been and continues to be complicit in "the rape and plunder of the world and its traditional cultures."[51] Above all, Christianity, Berry argued, has divorced itself from economic concerns, meaning the effects of the industrial economy but also "the ways by which the human household is situated and maintained within the household of nature." Such a disjunction reflects a deeper dualism, which Berry condemns—that which distinguishes body and soul, materiality and the spirit. In Berry's view, God did not merely infuse the body with a soul; they body and spirit are one unit and together form the soul.[52] The Bible did not condemn the earth; rather, its stewardship was a gift of God to humans. All things, Berry argued, partake of God's being. Daily work is a form of worship; artful craftsmanship, a way to honor God. Organized Christianity's acceptance of the dualism of body and soul, Berry believed, has led to an unbiblical deprecation of work, the material world, and human communities and a misguided focus on the hope of an otherworldy paradise. "Because it has been so exclusively dedicated to incanting anemic souls into Heaven," Berry wrote of modern Christianity, "it has been made the tool of much earthly villainy. It has, for the most part, stood silently by while a predatory economy has ravaged the world, destroyed its natural beauty and health, divided and plundered its human communities and households. It has flown the flag and chanted the slogans of empire."[53]

In *The Unsettling of America: Culture & Agriculture* (1977), Berry sharpened his political analysis and developed his own agrarianism in greater detail. He lambasted industrialized agriculture, or agribusiness, for damaging the land and, by driving Americans from a settled life on it, destroying the possibilities for a healthy agriculture. Modern agriculture, Berry argued, is focused on achieving greater crop yields, whatever the cost to the land. Mechanization and chemical fertilizers promote the erosion of topsoil (basically a nonrenewable resource) by encouraging continuous tillage and row-crop monoculture and reduce the health of the soil that remains.[54] What is worse, this "corporate totalitarianism" drives the knowledgeable, who possess wisdom accumulated over the centuries, from the land, thus creating another nonrenewable resource—wise husbandry. Berry placed the blame on corporations, university agricultural programs, and government agencies, all of which promote the movement toward large-scale mechanized monoculture and away from small, sustainable farms.[55]

For Berry, the solution to this agrarian crisis is a variation of that advocated by the Southern Agrarians in 1930: the promotion of small-scale, nonmechanized farming on as wide a scale as possible. His aim is to preserve both the land and the culture of farming. As with the Agrarians, however, the scope of his analysis lies far beyond crop diversification, the preservation of marginal lands, or the setting of production controls, all of which he advocated in *The Unsettling of America*.[56] The larger crisis lies in a more general disconnection—that between husband and wife, marriage and community, community and the earth, ultimately, body and soul. "Together, these disconnections add up to a condition of critical ill health, which we suffer in common—not just with each other, but with all other creatures," he wrote. "Our economy is based upon this disease. Its aim is to separate us as far as possible from the sources of life (material, social, and spiritual), to put these sources under the control of corporations and specialized professionals, and to sell them to us at the highest profit."[57] The broader American culture, not just agriculture, is sick, and Berry's prescription was the reconnection, through meaningful work, faithful marriage, and small-scale communities, of the body and the earth.[58] "Only by restoring the broken connections can we be healed," Berry declared. "Connection *is* health." It is the agrarian, or yeoman farmer's, tradition that Berry believed carried the secret to this more broadly needed sense of connection.[59] In *The Unsettling of America* and elsewhere, Berry has singled out the Amish as models not only of "Christian agriculture" but also of community. Their religion, he believes, binds humans to nature, and they limit both the growth of institutions and the use of technology.[60]

Berry's subsequent writings elaborate the social vision contained in his earlier essays. He advocates the development of local economies marked by an autonomous and more self-sufficient food economy in which cities foster relationships with small farmers in their exurban landscape as well as by support for all locally owned businesses.[61] Small farmers must own the land: "To renounce the principle of democratic property, which is the only basis of democratic liberty, in exchange for specious notions of efficiency or the economics of the so-called free market is tragic folly." Berry's preferred decentralized economy would require a change in Americans' values and habits and a movement away from being merely "consumptive machines." The American diet, Berry argues, "is at once cheap and luxurious—too cheap to support adequate agricultural land and yet so goofily self-indulgent as to demand, in every season, out-of-season foods produced by earth-destroying machines and chemicals."[62] The maintenance of localized economies, in other words, would require a diminution of consumer freedoms, as would life in the kind of inter-dependent communities that form an essential part of Berry's vision. For Berry, health arises from rootedness and interrelationships. In his preferred community, one's life should be bound with the fates of one's neighbors, one's responsibilities would be manifold, one's sexu-ality would be contained within marriage, and one's options would be circumscribed.[63] As with all communitarian philosophies, Berry's knowingly places limits on human action and freedom; for Berry, it is this interdependence that can promise a true freedom from the dep-redations of commercial culture and the corporate-controlled free-market economy.[64] For individuals, life outside a strong community provides only an illusory freedom and promises a life of spiritual dis-location and unfulfilled labor. The long-term costs for society of such unsettled people are cultural decay and, ultimately, ecological catas-trophe.

Berry acknowledges a "big debt" to *I'll Take My Stand*, although it is evident that his influences are wide-ranging. He began read-ing environmentalist writers early in the 1960s, having read, among others, Marston Bates, *The Forest and the Sea* (1960), as well as Henry David Thoreau by that point. He acknowledges a debt to Wallace Stegner's work and his Stanford seminar. He drew on the countercul-ture, reading and benefiting from the *Whole Earth Catalog* and devel-oping a friendship with poet Gary Snyder, who was greatly influenced by Eastern religious beliefs. And he has been shaped by various agri-cultural reformers, including Wes Jackson of the Land Institute of Salina, Kansas. In the late 1970s, he was briefly a contributing editor at Rodale Press, publisher of *Organic Gardening*.[65] But Berry read the Agrarian symposium while in college and still professes an admira-tion for it, particularly the statement of principles. Like many other undergraduates in the 1950s, he also read Robert Penn Warren and Cleanth Brooks's *Understanding Poetry*, which influenced him. While in college, he and a friend traveled to Gambier, Ohio, to meet John Crowe Ransom; he also met Warren, Andrew Nelson Lytle, and Allen Tate. He particularly admired Tate, with whom he corresponded.[66] All the same, while consonant with the ideas contained in *I'll Take My Stand*, Berry's agrarianism is more sustained and thoroughgoing than that of the Southern Agrarians and, in certain ways, fundamentally different.

Berry considers himself a Kentuckian or "border-stater," but not a southerner. "I was astonished when I realized that people up North thought I was a southerner," he recalls. "I didn't think of myself that way." Although growing up with a "certain prejudice for the Confederacy," he does not, so far as he knows, have any ancestors who fought in the Civil War. The local memory of the Confederacy, moreover, was decidedly ambivalent. As biographer Andrew Angyal observed, World War II is the watershed in Berry's fiction, not the Civil War. Those who currently bandy about secession bemuse Berry. "Well, you know, the South is the headquarters of so much stuff I'd like to secede from, that I think maybe they ought to secede from the South," he observes of current secessionists with a laugh. Moreover, he does not consider southerners to be particularly adept agriculturalists. They exhausted much of the land in the South. Berry points to the Midwest as a better example of balanced agriculture; it is the Amish who are, for him, a "truly exemplary people." [67]

Although his family had black servants and had, on both sides, owned slaves in the past, Berry early questioned segregation. He organized a debate on the issue in high school, which aroused much consternation. He argued that segregation was wrong. Racism, he argued in his 1970 memoir of race relations, *The Hidden Wound*, is an illness. In the book he attempted to elucidate "the continuing crisis of my life, the crisis of racial awareness — the sense of being doomed by my history to be, if not always a racist, then a man always limited by the inheritance of racism, condemned to be always conscious of the necessity *not* to be a racist, to be always dealing deliberately with the reflexes of racism that are embedded in my mind as deeply at least as the language I speak." In the book, he recounted his close friendship as a boy with Nick Watkins, a black hand on his grandfather's farm. It was Nick who taught him many of the pleasures of work and leisure on a farm. Blacks, Berry argued, following a suggestion by Allen Tate in "The Profession of Letters in the South," published in *The Virginia Quarterly Review* in 1935, because forced to work on the land, gained the wisdom of the soil in a way whites did not.[68] In the book, Berry portrayed blacks as the worthy and spiritually whole poor, who, despite their poverty, possessed the soul absent from whites, with their "artificial" and "flimsy" culture. Blacks possessed the "knowledge for the lack of which we are incomplete and in pain," Berry wrote.[69] "A certain strain of my agrarianism," Berry still claims, "which I think is a very pure kind of agrarianism, came from blacks, and their sense of the importance of land, of the landscape, of the household economy, of independence, of longing and fantasizing, dreaming of what they'd do if they had land. I think that sank deep into me." [70]

The Agrarians, Berry argued in *A Continuous Harmony*, had "a tendency to love the land, not for its life, but for its historical associations." Unlike the Agrarians, Berry did not look to history or ethnicity for the validation of values or for identity. Rather, he found healing in attachment to place. Berry escaped the trap of nostalgia and never suffered under the enervating rebuke of history because, unlike the Agrarians, he was an ecologist. "So long as we think of ourselves as African Americans or European Americans or Asian Americans, we will never settle anywhere," Berry wrote in *Sex, Economy, Freedom, and Community* (1993). "For an authentic community is made less in reference to who we are than to where we are." He does not farm as a European American or American or Kentuckian but "only as a person belonging to the place itself." The history of his people or region is less important than a healthy relation to the land. "If I am to use it well and live on it authentically, I cannot do so by knowing where my ancestors came from (which, except for one great-grandfather, I do not know and probably never can know); I can do so only by knowing where I am, what the nature of the place permits me to do here, and who and what are here with me."[71]

In the end, Berry's ecologically oriented agrarianism preserves more of the Southern Agrarians' radical conservatism than does Weaver's politics of order or the patriarchal organicism espoused by Bradford and Thomas Fleming. The latter thinkers shared none of Ransom's, Tate's, or Warren's modernist questioning of religious orthodoxy, nor, as they sought allies on the probusiness right, did they pay much more than lip service to the Agrarians' anti-industrialism. Like Berry and the Agrarians, they believed that modern America is experiencing a moral crisis, but, like the Agrarians' intellectual rivals, the New Humanists, they simply affirmed a set of moral absolutes and did not concern themselves with the sociological question of how those values may be made real in America.

When writing of his ideal of a "defensible" society, Berry's words are consonant with the old, isolationist Right. A defensible country, he argued, is independent. It "can live, if it has to, independent of foreign supplies and of long distance transport within its own boundaries. It must also rest upon the broadest possible base of economic prosperity, not just in the sense of a money economy, but in the sense of properties, materials, and practical skills. Most important of all, it must be generally loved and competently cared for by its own people, who, individually, identify their own interest with the interest of their neighbors and of the country (the land) itself."[72] In part, Berry's conservatism constitutes an alternative view of what the modern American Right, established in response to modernism in the 1920s, might have (but never could have) become: socially conservative but tolerant; respectful, if critical, of countercultures; skeptical of big government programs but ready to criticize corporate power as well; opposed both to military adventurism abroad and militarism at home; opposed to an emerging global economic order but seeking economic decentralization domestically as well. Berry's attention is relentlessly focused on "home economics" and the need for Americans to bolster independent farmers and locally owned businesses in their hometowns across the nation. This decentralist politics leads to his own community and the efforts of his own family. He and his brother farm; both of his children farm for a living. His daughter started a farmers' market in New Castle. His son grows food for markets in Louisville and for a community-supported agricultural operation. "My own kids are at stake in this, my grandchildren," Berry says. "And so, of course, I'm pulling as hard as I can for them, doing everything I can to support this effort."[73] In this, like the Southern Agrarians, Berry represents less a southern conservative tradition than a broader strain of American radical conservatism, one oriented to community and organic social relations and born of opposition to the inhuman scale, deadening routinization, bland homogenization, and economic centralization of the modern industrial order.

The evolution of the tradition of Southern Agrarianism from a species of radical conservatism to a type of traditionalist conservatism is exceedingly complex, entailing, as it does, attention to two large stories. One is the story of how a group of contrarian poets and academics, who came by cultural criticism as an avocation, engaged their region's history. Allen Tate and Donald Davidson, in particular, were consumed by the southern past, at least spiritually and intellectually. This group, which so proudly announced a dedication to tradition (and the willingess to take their stand in this tradition), stumbled when the emotional and social costs of being true to the past and seeking to construct themselves in the image of the past proved impossible for some members. The past can be ravenous, Tate discovered; nostalgia can lead to narcissism. Simple loyalty to the past, Robert Penn Warren argued, is insufficient if one aspires to morally responsible action in the modern world.

The second story is an intellectual tale and concerns how a set of ideas is remembered, or how a discourse is interpreted and reinterpreted over time. In a larger sense, it is about how American conservative thought and the Right developed in the twentieth century. Donald Davidson and neo-Agrarian followers such as Richard Weaver and M. E. Bradford did not share Tate's ambivalence toward the southern past or the moral qualms about racism and segregation publicly expressed by Warren. Their defense of the South led them to a defensive particularism: Davidson defended the healthy American provinces against the corrupt metropolitan core in the 1930s; both he and Bradford clung to a politics of southern identity in an age of uncertainty. All three of these figures and others in their literary and conservative circles became increasingly opposed to the federal government's growing power and to the liberal policymakers who seemed to control the government. Davidson and Weaver gravitated to a political Right that was, by 1945, defined by its antistatism.

Yet it was not simply that Davidson and other conservatives found common ground in the 1940s. Davidson and Weaver transmuted their southern particularism into a symbolic rereading of the South and southern history. Eager to ally with the conservative political coalition developed most effectively by William F. Buckley Jr. and the *National Review* in the 1950s, Davidson and Weaver recast themselves as southern traditionalists, and they envisioned the South as a last bastion of social order and moral absolutes in an overwhelmingly liberal nation. In 1930, the Twelve Southerners had worried about both cultural modernism and social and economic modernization. Postwar conservatives, by contrast, welcomed modernization for the most part, even as they continued to attack the values of modernism. Neo-Agrarians did not engage modernist ideas or seek to reconcile traditional social patterns with economic change so much as affirm Christian belief and reconcile economic individualism and a limited federal state with strong sources of social authority. The firmly ordered society, one in which authority was respected, which many postwar traditionalists upheld, was to be achieved through the reassertion of tradition, values, and moral absolutes and not by any attempt to restrain material progress or socioeconomic change. Davidson and Weaver (and later Bradford) identified with the conservative coalition because they felt it was doing the vital work of resisting the influence and values of progressives (if not necessarily rolling back progress itself).

Davidson and his neo-Agrarian followers have been fated to occupy a somewhat marginal role within the national conservative movement, even as the South has become an important bulwark in Republican presidential politics. The question of whether it was Buckley and his coalition—focused, at root, on gaining power within the Republican Party and then in government—or right-wing populists exemplified by Alabama governor George C. Wallace and the New Right of the 1970s who were more responsible for the national ascendancy of conservative politicians after 1980 should be the subject of much debate. It is certainly true that the conservative movement has been riven by a fairly continual hostility between the populist and grass-roots wing, rooted in provincial hostility to a cosmopolitan and corporate-dominated nation, and a more pragmatic, business-oriented, and state-centered establishment. Buckley and his allies chose to paper over this split as best as possible and to redescribe it as a less threatening and less intractable ideological split between libertarians and traditionalists. Whether because of the lingering associations with segregation and racism or because of this deeper split on the right, the contemporary legatees of Agrarianism—the paleoconservatives and neo-Agrarians gathered around such organs as *Chronicles* and *Southern Partisan*—form a vocal but minor adjunct to the contemporary conservative movement.

The evolution of the Agrarian tradition, then, is two stories, one about history and one about ideology. The stories are complex, shaped as they are by the intersection of history, community, and progress. The contrasting figures of Eugene Genovese and Wendell Berry provide an appropriate concluding commentary on this tradition. Writing, in a sense, from within the neo-Agrarian viewpoint, Genovese reveals the extent to which Agrarianism is now seen as a moral and political position defined by its opposition to radical individualism. The South and southernness have become the symbolic touchstone for these thinkers, yet Genovese's work is a sharp reminder of the problematic role that race occupies in this body of conservative thought.

Genovese and Bradford, as well as other neo-Agrarians, tend to place the Agrarians in a tradition of antistatist political thought. Yet the Agrarians were not political thinkers; they were cultural critics, concerned above all with the ravages committed on communities by the forces of progress. In certain, limited ways, *I'll Take My Stand* resonates most clearly with contemporary communitarians or with the late Christopher Lasch, an idiosyncratic critic of progress. The stubborn core of *I'll Take My Stand* was a call to resist progress, to remember the superiority of inherited ways of life and to prevent their destruction. The contemporary critic who best embodies this central aim is Berry, someone not closely identified with neo-Agrarian political thinkers and someone who, despite being an Agrarian sympathizer, eschews any particular identification with the South or the southern past. Berry's cultural criticism retains the original Agrarian impulse to preserve and strengthen the inherited community, but he roots his effort in an ecological philosophy founded on ideals of harmony, marriage, and connection and not in an appeal to history. Berry is at once profoundly conservative in his views on marriage, sexuality, and community and radical in his condemnation of modern agribusiness, the military establishment, and global capitalism. Although he is certainly not devoid of a sense of history, Berry's ability to retain a radical conservatism even as it has faded in the conservative mainstream and in the Agrarian tradition is testimony, perhaps, to the limits of history in social and cultural analysis. In the end, different Agrarians looked into the mirror of the past and saw different things, learning different and, at times, contradictory, lessons. The historical evolution of the Agrarian tradition reveals history's rebuke to be inspiring but also ambiguous, a clarion call to defend past achievements but one that vouchsafes no clear explanation of how to do this in a world that changes and grows more complex every day.

Introduction

1. Maddocks, "In Tennessee," 10, 13; Havard and Sullivan, *Band of Prophets*, 9.

2. Twelve Southerners, *I'll Take My Stand*, xi, xlii–xliii, 330–32, 335; Donald Davidson, "At Bread Loaf: 1938 (To the Graduating Class)," unpublished manuscript, pp. 5–6, folder 1, box 22, Donald Davidson Papers, Special Collections and University Archives, Heard Library, Vanderbilt University, Nashville, Tennessee. On the vogue of anthologies in the 1920s, see Susman, *Culture as History*, 114.

3. Twelve Southerners, *I'll Take My Stand*, xlvii–xlviii, xl–xliii, 1, 282. Ten of the twelve contributors to *I'll Take My Stand* had been associated with Vanderbilt at one time or another: Ransom, Davidson, and John Donald Wade taught in the English Department; Tate, Robert Penn Warren, Andrew Nelson Lytle, and Henry Blue Kline were former students; Frank L. Owsley and Herman Clarence Nixon taught in the History Department; and Lyle Lanier taught in the Psychology Department. The two remaining contributors were acquaintances of Tate: Stark Young, an established critic in New York; and John Gould Fletcher, an expatriate southern poet.

4. "Can Democracy Survive in a World of Technology?," 64; Lyle Lanier to Robert Penn Warren, 30 Mar. 1980, folder 748, box 38, Robert Penn Warren Papers, Beinecke Rare Book and Manuscript Library, Yale University, New Haven, Connecticut.

5. Havard and Sullivan, *Band of Prophets*, 162–63, 180.

6. Ibid., 170, 182–83, 186.

7. Ibid., 188, 180.

8. See Genovese, *Slaveholders' Dilemma.*

9. Richard Gray analyzes the idea of the South as a "structuring principle" in southern culture and literature, one characterized by alternately populist or patriarchal pastoral modes. He links the Agrarians to antebellum southern theorists but argues that they were forced, of necessity, to reinvent southern myths owing to the forces of modernism and modernization changing the South in the 1920s. The leading Agrarians had to "will themselves into being Southerners." In this sense, *I'll Take My Stand* was an "edgy, splendidly rebarbarative, and even moving book: an argument for the South, certainly, but also an account, however veiled, of personal crisis." Gray, *Writing the South*, xiv, 158. See also Gray, *Literature of Memory.* Fred Hobson is concerned primarily with acute southern self-consciousness and the need felt by many southern writers to explain their region. He places the Agrarians within this context, focusing particularly on Donald Davidson and the neo-Agrarian Richard M. Weaver. Hobson, *Tell about the South.* Richard H. King provides a psychoanalytically informed study of southern intellectual life between 1930 and 1955, seeking the hidden meanings and impulses in southern writers' images and symbols of their region. He identifies the family, particularly the father and grandfather, as the crucial image and the family romance as the model of southern discourse. For King, the Agrarians give only a more sophisticated version of this traditional romance, avoiding critical interrogation of their culture and producing, in *I'll Take My Stand*, a work that is "flat and hysterical," polemical and self-serving, and lacking any complex thought about the South. King, *Southern Renaissance*, esp. 53. There

are other relevant histories: Conkin, *Southern Agrarians*, is a good introduction to the Southern Agrarians and contains many insightful remarks but is not carefully documented and marred by occasional factual errors and thus should be used with care. The 1961 dissertation of Virginia J. Rock provides a pioneering but still useful and thorough narrative of the origins of Agrarianism. Rock, "Making and Meaning of *I'll Take My Stand.*" See also Rock, "They Took Their Stand." Early book-length studies also include Stewart, *Burden of Time*, a leisurely and elegant account of the Agrarian circle, part history, part literary criticism; and Karanikas, *Tillers of a Myth*, a comprehensive, but essentially thin, history of the Agrarians shaped by the author's antagonism to their thought.

10. In *The War Within*, Daniel Joseph Singal treated the South as a microcosm in which to examine the larger cultural transition from Victorian to modernist thought. The Agrarians, Singal argued, were paradoxical figures perched on the cusp of changing cultural paradigms. Ransom, Tate, and Davidson were "modernists by the skin of their teeth," internally divided between Victorian instincts and modernist ideas. The construction of the Agrarian myth enabled them to overcome the "anguish of cultural transition." Allen Tate, one of the most tortured modernist intellectuals that a historian is likely to find either north *or* south, became, then, the epitome of Agrarianism. Singal, *War Within*, 3–10, 111–13, 201, 232. Michael O'Brien's *The Idea of the American South* was a contribution to the "historiography of Southern self-consciousness." The "South" is not an empirical reality but a product of romantic social theory, O'Brien insisted. The Agrarians provided O'Brien with a study in the intellectual persistence of this lingering romantic impulse—even in such otherwise modernist minds as those of the Agrarians. For O'Brien, too, Agrarianism, as a twentieth-century adaptation of the idea of the South, was a product of the intellectual needs of a group of southern thinkers. O'Brien sees modernism as a critical engagement of the romantic tradition, which, he argues, combined a sociology of community and a psychology of alienation. His larger aim is to use southern intellectual history as a ground from which to launch a reevaluation of romanticism, which he sees as a rich and fecund discourse and the source of much Anglo-American social and literary thought. O'Brien, *Idea of the American South*, xxi–xxii, xxiv–xxv, 27, 160, 221, 224. For a broader analysis of romanticism, see O'Brien, *Rethinking the South*, chap. 2, esp. 39–45, 162–66, 176–78. O'Brien views Singal's definition of modernism and Victorianism as both distorted and too simple, arguing that Singal praises southern intellectuals who embraced his own politics and deprecates those who chose a more apolitical stance. O'Brien, *Rethinking the South*, 172–75. Both Singal's and O'Brien's studies sought to explicate the spiritual and social roots of Agrarianism in southern culture. Singal was interested in the dissonance between Victorianism and modernism in the South, O'Brien in the way in which southerners used the idea of the South, which, he believes, essentially transmuted romantic notions into a southern idiom, to integrate both their personal lives and their society. By contrast, this study does not focus on the particular psychic needs of the Agrarians but on the ideas that these needs led them to articulate. This is not to deny the deep split between modernism and romanticism among the Agrarians or the complexities presented by modernism; modernist schisms arguably accounted for the ultimate failure of Agrarianism as a viable social, even intellectual, movement. But it is to take seriously the Agrarians' social theory, their appeal over the years to both southerners and nonsoutherners alike, and the paradoxical evolution of their tradition.

11. Kreyling, *Inventing Southern Literature*, xii, 6–7, 13–14, 34.

12. O'Brien, *Rethinking the South*, 168; Louis D. Rubin Jr., introduction to Torchbook Edition (1962) in Twelve Southerners, *I'll Take My Stand*, xxviii.

13. Rubin, *Faraway Country*, 159. Rubin reiterated the point at a 1980 Agrarian symposium at Vanderbilt. *I'll Take My Stand*, he declared, is important primarily as a *"literary work."* Rubin, *"I'll Take My Stand: The Literary Tradition,"* in Havard and Sullivan, *Band of Prophets*, 141.

14. Simpson, Olney, and Gulledge, *The "Southern Review" and Modern Literature*, 7.

15. Holman, "Summary," 161–63. Rock's dissertation on the Agrarians, a basic source for many later interpretations, helped shape this view of Agrarianism as a myth. Rock, "Making and Meaning of *I'll Take My Stand*."

16. See, for example, Pells, *Radical Visions and American Dreams*, 103–5. This is beginning to change, however. Lewis Perry, following Singal, treats the Agrarians within the context of modernist thought in his recent survey of American intellectual history. Perry, *Intellectual Life in America*, 338. The Agrarians appear as the extreme right-wing end of the anti-industrial spectrum of the 1930s and are represented by John Crowe Ransom's contribution to *I'll Take My Stand*, in the second edition of David A. Hollinger and Charles Capper's college reader in intellectual history. Hollinger and Capper, *American Intellectual Tradition*, 2:214–26.

17. George H. Nash provides a brief treatment of Richard M. Weaver, which is careful to emphasize his southernness but focuses on his influential conservative writings. Nash, *Conservative Intellectual Movement in America*, 36–43, 203–6. Two recent biographies notably unsuccessful in tracing the evolution of Weaver's ideas are Young, *Richard M. Weaver*, and Scotchie, *Barbarians in the Saddle*. The neo-Agrarians themselves are very attentive to Weaver's roots in Agrarianism but, owing to their own imperatives, necessarily distort the transition from Agrarianism to conservatism. See, for example, Bradford, "Agrarianism of Richard Weaver."

18. An interesting exception is Allan Carlson, who seeks to place the Agrarians in a tradition of rural decentralism that he identifies as the "new agrarian mind"—thinkers "at once socially conservative and economically radical." Carlson discusses a wide variety of thinkers, many of whom seem to have more affinities to mainstream and progressive agricultural reform thought than to Southern Agrarianism. Indeed, he treats only two Agrarians, Andrew Nelson Lytle and Frank L. Owsley, as well as an Agrarian ally, Troy Cauley, in depth. Carlson's analysis is shaped by his conviction that the state and American culture threaten the American family; decentralized, religiously based rural communities offer the best hope for its survival. He cites social groups such as the Amish—founded on religious traditionalism—as exemplars of his ideal and is curiously focused on the issue of fertility rates in America. In the end, he seriously distorts the Agrarians' views by exaggerating some features of their thought and ignoring others. Carlson, *New Agrarian Mind*.

19. See, for example, several of the essays in an anniversary symposium edited by Clyde N. Wilson, Fifteen Southerners, *Why the South Will Survive*. For the essence of M. E. Bradford's social thought and interpretation of Agrarianism, see Bradford, *Remembering Who We Are*, *Reactionary Imperative*, and *Against the Barbarians and Other Reflections on Familiar Themes*. For Eugene D. Genovese's interpretation of southern conservatism, see Genovese, *Southern Tradition* and *Southern Front*. Conservative interpretations of Agrarianism in this vein are also likely to be found in the conservative journal *Chronicles*, a magazine of cultural criticism edited by Thomas Fleming and published by

the Rockford Institute in Rockford, Illinois.

20. Malvasi, *Unregenerate South*. An illuminating perspective on Mark G. Malvasi's viewpoint can be found in Malvasi, "Choosing Southernness," 28–33.

21. Gleason, "Identifying Identity," 914, 918, 923–26, 928.

22. Caroline [Gordon] Tate to Lincoln Kirstein, [Oct. 1931], "Tate, Allen and Caroline, 1929–31, I," *Hound and Horn* Correspondence, Ra–Tz, *Hound and Horn* Papers, Beinecke Rare Book and Manuscript Library, Yale University, New Haven, Connecticut. On Caroline Gordon, see Waldron, *Close Connections*.

23. Purdy, *Fugitive's Reunion*, 208–9.

24. Ibid., 210.

25. Twelve Southerners, *I'll Take My Stand*, 19.

Chapter One

1. Smith, *So Good a Cause*, 197–98.

2. Cowan, *Fugitive Group*, 4, 14–15, 18.

3. Farrell, "Poetry as a Way of Life," 316–17; Tate, "*The Fugitive*, 1922–1925: A Personal Recollection Twenty Years After," in Tate, *Memoirs and Opinions*, 31–32.

4. Farrell, "Reminiscences," 786–87; Watkins, Hiers, and Weaks, *Talking with Robert Penn Warren*, 237–38; Robert Penn Warren, "A Reminiscence," in Egerton, *Nashville*, 217; Wood, "On Native Soil," 182. A favorite amusement of the "brethren," their spouses, and visitors was to play elaborate games of charades, in which the group would split up, choose words or phrases, and act them out, perhaps even dressing in costumes. Jonza, *Underground Stream*, 131–32. Robert Penn Warren, in addition to spending much time with the Ransoms, would visit often with Frank and Harriet Owsley at their camp overlooking the Cumberland River. Warren, "A Reminiscence," in Egerton, *Nashville*, 216.

5. Ayers, *Promise of the New South*, 20, 24–25, 55.

6. Doyle, *Nashville in the New South*,

xiv, 19–20, 42, 45, 63, 82–83, 183, 201, 205–8, 212, 233, 235; Doyle, *Nashville since the 1920s*, 5, 30–35.

7. Ayers, *Promise of the New South*, 20–21, 105. See also Gaston, *New South Creed*.

8. Ayers, *Promise of the New South*, 113; Doyle, *Nashville in the New South*, 215–16. On "public work" in the South, see Hall et al., *Like a Family*, 44–113.

9. Williamson, *Crucible of Race*, 115, 180–81, 249, 253–54. For an argument linking segregation with the process of modernization, see Cell, *Highest Stage of White Supremacy*. See also Rabinowitz, *Race Relations in the Urban South*.

10. Williamson, *Crucible of Race*, 6–7, 312, 316–17, 478, 481–82.

11. Ibid., 7, 459, 482. On the "savage ideal," see Cash, *Mind of the South*, 61–102.

12. Conkin, *Gone with the Ivy*, 10, 12–19.

13. Ibid., 17, 19, 21.

14. Doyle, *Nashville in the New South*, 201–3; Conkin, *Gone with the Ivy*, 149–84, 223, 229–30; Conkin, *Southern Agrarians*, 3–4.

15. Farrell, "Poetry as a Way of Life," 319; Wood, "On Native Soil," 179.

16. Cowan, *Fugitive Group*, 37–38; Conkin, *Gone with the Ivy*, 315; Thomas Daniel Young, introduction to Davidson, *Tennessee*, 1:xvi.

17. Knickerbocker, "Up from the South," 177, 176. Ransom had originally submitted the essay to the *Nation*, where it was rejected by Carl Van Doren. O'Brien, *Idea of the American South*, 123.

18. Ransom, "The South—Old or New?," 139.

19. John Crowe Ransom to Allen Tate, 3 and 13 Apr. 1927, in Young and Core, *Selected Letters*, 173. "I am delighted with your idea of a book on the Old South," John Crowe Ransom wrote to Allen Tate, pointing out, however, that there was "so little in Southern literature to point the principle." Ibid. By this time Ransom seems to have already given the talk

at Sewanee's EQB club that was the kernel of his later essay in *I'll Take My Stand*. He wrote Tate: "I've got out an article somewhat in this field, though rather emulsified into pap for popular consumption." Ibid. In this letter Ransom used some of the same phrasing that appeared in the 1928 *Sewanee Review* essay.

20. Donald Davidson to Tate, 4 Mar. 1927, in Fain and Young, *Literary Correspondence*; Davidson to John Gould Fletcher, 21 Mar. [1927], folder 8, box 1, Donald Davidson Papers, Special Collections and University Archives, Heard Library, Vanderbilt University, Nashville, Tennessee. This letter is dated by Donald Davidson 1926, but it has been established that on the same day Davidson wrote another letter to Tate and misdated it to Tate in the same way. In any case Davidson seems to be discussing the Tate proposal for a literary symposium, a proposal not made until 1927. The misdating, which seems to be a slip of the pen on Davidson's part, has caused some confusion for historians in the past. See Singal, *War Within*, 398 n. 5. For Davidson's enthusiasm in reacting to Tate's proposal, see Davidson to Tate, 21 Mar. [1927], in Fain and Young, *Literary Correspondence*, 196.

21. In February, Davidson wrote Tate, who was overseas on a Guggenheim fellowship, of Ransom's, John Donald Wade's, and his own efforts to "get up a symposium on Southern matters, but without success so far." Davidson to Tate, 5 Feb. 1929, in Fain and Young, *Literary Correspondence*, 221.

22. Young, *Gentleman in a Dustcoat*, 213.

23. All quotes are taken from Twelve Southerners, *I'll Take My Stand*, and are indicated by page numbers enclosed within parentheses.

24. Don H. Doyle mentions the pall of smoke in Nashville in the 1920s. Doyle, *Nashville since the 1920s*, 5.

25. Tate found writing the essay to be agonizing and was unsatisfied with the result. Tate to Davidson, 27 July 1930, folder 47, box 10, Davidson Papers. The progress of the essay, which Tate began five different times, can be traced in Tate to Davidson, 5 July, 18 July, 27 July, and 1 Aug. 1930, folders 47–48, box 10, ibid.

26. Conkin, *Gone with the Ivy*, 330.

27. On the cultural criticism of the Young American critics, see Blake, *Beloved Community*.

Chapter Two

1. Squires, *Allen Tate*, 15, 17–18; Allen Tate, "A Lost Traveller's Dream," in Tate, *Memoirs and Opinions*, 7.

2. Tate, "A Lost Traveller's Dream," 8–9; Squires, *Allen Tate*, 14.

3. Squires, *Allen Tate*, 14–15; Tate, "A Lost Traveller's Dream," 6–8, 20–21. The encounter between Allen Tate and his mother was described by Andrew Lytle in an interview with Ann Waldron on 1 Dec. 1983. Waldron, *Close Connections*, 61.

4. Squires, *Allen Tate*, 18; Young and Sarcone, *Lytle-Tate Letters*, xiii–xiv.

5. Conkin, *Southern Agrarians*, 43; Rubin, *Wary Fugitives*, 88. Allen Tate to Davidson, [8 June 1924], 17 Dec. [1924], in Fain and Young, *Literary Correspondence*, 120, 132.

6. Malcolm Cowley, "Two Winters with Allen Tate and Hart Crane," in Squires, *Allen Tate and His Work*, 27–28; Bak, *Malcolm Cowley*, 329; and Jonza, *Underground Stream*, 42.

7. Robert Penn Warren had attempted suicide, somewhat half-heartedly, in May. The reasons for Warren's action are unclear, but he was plagued by vision problems—his eyesight was always defective in one eye—and possibly feared the loss of his sight and the ability to be a poet. For a discussion of this, see chapter 7.

8. Waldron, *Close Connections*, 31–32, 38–40; Jonza, *Underground Stream*, 44–45.

9. Tate to Hart Crane, 4 Apr. 1923, cited in Hammer, *Hart Crane and Allen Tate*, 61; Tate to Davidson, 16 Feb. 1925, folder 29, box 10, Donald

Davidson Papers, Special Collections and University Archives, Heard Library, Vanderbilt University, Nashville, Tennessee; Tate to Davidson, 26 Nov. 1925, in Fain and Young, *Literary Correspondence*, 147. "I can never forget you all," Tate wrote Davidson. "But really I shall never return to Nashville; so you must come up here when you can." Tate to Davidson, 17 Dec. 1924, quoted in O'Brien, *Idea of the American South*, 137.

10. Tate to Malcolm Cowley, 29 Aug. 1928, Malcolm Cowley Papers, Newberry Library, Chicago, Illinois; *Nashville Tennessean*, 20 Apr. 1924.

11. Tate to Davidson, 8 July 1925, in Fain and Young, *Literary Correspondence*, 142; Tate, "One Escape from the Dilemma," 35; Tate to Cowley, 19 Nov. 1926, Cowley Papers. After learning that T. S. Eliot had complimented his poetry, Tate wrote Davidson: "I feel like putting a record on the gramophone." Tate to Davidson, 31 July 1923, folder 9, box 10, Davidson Papers. For T. S. Eliot's critical theory, see Eliot, *Sacred Wood*; Schwartz, *Matrix of Modernism*; and Shusterman, *T. S. Eliot and the Philosophy of Criticism*.

12. Huff, *Allen Tate and the Catholic Revival*, 12–18; Quinlan, *Walker Percy*, 14, 36. On Tate's conversion, see Huff, *Allen Tate and the Catholic Revival*, 23, 79; Dunaway, *Exiles and Fugitives*, 2; Brinkmeyer, *Three Catholic Writers of the Modern South*, 61–63.

13. Huff, *Allen Tate and the Catholic Revival*, 25–26, 9–10, 29, 73–77; Gleason, *Contending with Modernity*, 105–6, 116–18; Hitchcock, "Postmortem on a Rebirth," 217.

14. Gleason, *Contending with Modernity*, 121, 118–23.

15. Tate to Davidson, 18 Feb. 1929, in Fain and Young, *Literary Correspondence*, 223; Huff, *Allen Tate and the Catholic Revival*, 47; O'Brien, *Idea of the American South*, 141–43. Tate's father was an Episcopalian and, later in his life, a Robert C. Ingersoll Free Thinker. His mother's father was a lapsed Catholic and mother a Calvin-

ist. She sent Tate to a Presbyterian Sunday school but also enrolled him for a time in a Catholic school. Brinkmeyer, *Three Catholic Writers of the Modern South*, 5–6; Huff, *Allen Tate and the Catholic Revival*, 32.

16. Tate to Cowley, 15 Apr. 1929, Cowley Papers. On the dating of the "Ode," see Hammer, *Hart Crane and Allen Tate*, 240 n. 6. Louis Rubin suggested that the poem was begun in 1925–26. Rubin, *Wary Fugitives*, 99. As early as February 1926, Robert Penn Warren expressed a desire to see Tate's "Confederate morgue piece." Robert Penn Warren to Tate, 6 Feb. 1926, folder 28, box 44, Allen Tate Papers, Manuscript Division, Department of Rare Books and Special Collections, Princeton University Library, Princeton University, Princeton, New Jersey.

17. Tate, "Narcissus as Narcissus," 111–13.

18. Tate revised the "Ode" several times. The original version, which appears in Tate, *Mr. Pope and Other Poems*, is used here. Parenthetical numbers refer to pages from this edition.

19. Tate to John Gould Fletcher, 24 Dec. 1927, John Gould Fletcher Papers, Special Collections Division, University of Arkansas Libraries, University of Arkansas, Fayetteville, Arkansas.

20. Young and Inge, *Donald Davidson*, 18–20; Winchell, *Where No Flag Flies*, 7; Louise Davis, "He Clings to Enduring Values," *Nashville Tennessean Magazine*, 4 Sept. 1949, 6–8. A copy of this article is contained in folder 11, box 35, Davidson Papers; Fain, *Spyglass*, 200; Donald Davidson to Louis Rubin, 10 May 1955, folder 47, box 2, Davidson Papers. For Donald Davidson's relationship to his grandmother, see Davidson to Stark Young, 29 Sept. 1952, folder 33, box 2, Davidson Papers; Inge, "Donald Davidson's Notes for an Autobiography," in Winchell, *Vanderbilt Tradition*, 201.

21. Young and Inge, *Donald Davidson*, 21–23; Davis, "He Clings to Enduring Values," 7.

22. Davis, "He Clings to Enduring Values," 8; Young and Inge, *Donald Davidson*, 13, 27–28, 32–33; Winchell, *Where No Flag Flies*, 47; Walter Sullivan, "Strange Children: Caroline Gordon and Allen Tate," in Berry, *Home Ground*, 125. Theresa Davidson, although always deferring to her husband, was accomplished in her own right. After her marriage she received a law degree and a Ph.D. in classics from Vanderbilt University, becoming an associate editor of a massive translation of Roman law. She taught at both Ward-Belmont and Vanderbilt universities. Davis, "He Clings to Enduring Values," 8.

23. Fain, *Spyglass*, xi, xiv–xv. In March 1928, afraid of losing Davidson, the publisher syndicated his book page to two other southern papers. After syndication Davidson reached a wider audience in Tennessee as well as in Mississippi, Arkansas, Louisiana, Georgia, and Kentucky. In addition, his weekly book column was syndicated in the *Miami News*. Ibid., xii.

24. Alexander, *Here the Country Lies*, xii, 151, 154–55. See also Pells, *Radical Visions and American Dreams*, 96–150.

25. Alexander, *Here the Country Lies*, 4.

26. Dorman, *Revolt of the Provinces*, 107, 9–24; Alexander, *Here the Country Lies*, 179.

27. Wilson, *Baptized in Blood*, 1, 3–6.

28. Ibid., 5, 9–11, 79, 82–83.

29. Davidson, "Artist as Southerner," 781–82.

30. Fain, *Spyglass*, 4. On Davidson's early New South views, see O'Brien, *Idea of the American South*, 188, and Singal, *War Within*, 220.

31. Davidson to Fletcher, 21 Mar. 1926, folder 8, box 1, Davidson Papers; Davidson to R. N. Linscott, 9 Apr. 1927, folder 9, ibid. In letters to his publisher when the poem was reissued in 1938, Davidson commented further on the autobiographical intentions of the work. The poem is "biographical, personal, reflective, semi-lyrical," he wrote in 1938. Davidson to R. N.

Linscott, 28 Apr. 1938, folder 39, ibid. "It is an attempt at the statement of a living tradition. . . . It is a definition of a man, not a dream about the past," he observed. Davidson to Linscott, 21 Apr. 1938, folder 38, ibid.

32. On the symbolism of "Fire on Belmont Street," see Young and Inge, *Donald Davidson*, 88–90.

33. Quotations followed by page numbers in parentheses are taken from Davidson, *Lee in the Mountains*. Quotations from "Resurrection" are from the 1927 edition of the poem.

34. Young and Inge, *Donald Davidson*, 93. As Langdon Hammer observed, Davidson's visceral language, with repeated approving references to the bullets through which these men communicated, comprises a "rude fantasy of racial power," marked by a "quest for a premodern, local, and heroic idiom, a phallic language of 'long rifles.'" Hammer, *Hart Crane and Allen Tate*, 81.

35. Jordan, "Donald Davidson's 'Creed of Memory,'" 304. I am indebted to Jordan's dissertation, particularly chapter 6, "*The Tall Men*, Davidson's Response to the Waste Land Theme," for an understanding of the religious themes in this work. For a useful treatment of *The Tall Men*, see Young and Inge, *Donald Davidson*, 62–91. A contrasting reading of the sections on religion is found in ibid., 81–86.

36. Davidson to Linscott, 9 Apr. 1927, folder 9, box 1, Davidson Papers.

37. Davidson, *Tall Men*, 110.

38. Tate to Davidson, 14 May 1926, in Fain and Young, *Literary Correspondence*, 167; Davidson to Tate, 15 Aug. 1926, in ibid., 178.

39. Tate to Davidson, 29 Dec. 1929, 5 Jan. 1927, in ibid., 181–83.

40. Davidson to Tate, 21 Jan. 1927, 15 Feb. 1927, in ibid., 185–87. Langdon Hammer said of Davidson's reading of the "Ode": "Even sixty years later, Tate's poem has not received a reading as severe and probing as Davidson's wounded, almost lyrical remarks." Hammer, *Hart Crane and Allen Tate*, 83.

41. O'Brien, *Idea of the American South*, 140.

42. John Crowe Ransom to Allen Tate, 3 and 13 Apr. 1927, in Young and Core, *Selected Letters*, 173.

43. See, for example, his review of William Dodd's *Lincoln or Lee* on 6 June 1928, and of biographies of Mary Todd Lincoln and Varina Howell Davis on 20 June 1928.

44. Waldron, *Close Connections*, 57–58, 61; Tate to Davidson, 17 July 1927, folder 38, box 10, Davidson Papers; Tate to Fletcher, 20 July 1927, Fletcher Papers.

45. Fain, ed., *Spyglass*, 201–2.

46. Tate to Davidson, 10 Aug. 1929, in Fain and Young, *Literary Correspondence*, 229–30; Tate to Lytle, 31 July 1929, in Young and Sarcone, *Lytle-Tate Letters*, 34. See also Tate to Fletcher, 31 July 1929, Fletcher Papers.

47. Davidson to Tate, 26 Oct. 1929, in Fain and Young, *Literary Correspondence*, 237; Tate to Davidson, 9 Nov. 1929, in ibid., 240.

48. Ransom to Tate, 5 Jan. 1930, in Young and Core, *Selected Letters*, 189; Davidson to Tate, 29 Dec. 1929, in Fain and Young, *Literary Correspondence*, 247.

49. Rock, "Making and Meaning of *I'll Take My Stand*," 243–44, 249–51; Conkin, *Southern Agrarians*, 69. "I have never in my life been more deeply impressed with the dilatoriness and indecision of the academic mind," Ransom declared, commenting on the delays in the symposium. See Ransom to Tate, [15 Feb. 1930], in Young and Core, *Selected Letters*, 197–98. The editors dated this letter 15 Mar. 1930, but, following Virginia Rock and based on a discussion of a potential contract for the book, it seems more accurate to date it 15 Feb. 1930. See Rock, "Making and Meaning of *I'll Take My Stand*," 244 n. 1. Eventually, only Stringfellow Barr, a professor of history at the University of Virginia, was excluded from the symposium because of reservations about the proposed statement of principles. Conkin, *Southern Agrarians*, 62.

50. Hoeveler, *New Humanism*, 8–

12, 24–27; Foerster, *Humanism and America*; Craven, "Seward Collins and the Traditionalists," 7, 12–13, 17–19, 33.

51. Hoeveler, *New Humanism*, 33 n. 6, 34–35; Foerster, *American Criticism*, 244.

52. Matthew Arnold, "The Study of Poetry" (1880), in Arnold, *English Literature and Irish Politics*, 163; Hoeveler, *New Humanism*, 64, 59.

53. Ibid., 132.

54. Davidson to Ransom, 5 July 1929, folder 12, box 1, Davidson Papers; Munson, *Dilemma of the Liberated*.

55. Tate to Fletcher, 19 Oct. 1928, Fletcher Papers.

56. Tate to Davidson, 18 Feb. 1929, in Fain and Young, *Literary Correspondence*, 223–24.

57. Tate to William S. Knickerbocker, 13 Feb. 1930, William S. Knickerbocker Papers, Rare Book and Manuscript Library, Columbia University, New York City; Tate, "Fallacy of Humanism," 234.

58. Tate, "Fallacy of Humanism," 238–40.

59. Ransom to Tate, 4 July 1929, in Young and Core, *Selected Letters*, 180; Ransom to Davidson, n.d., folder 36, box 8, Davidson Papers.

60. Tate, "Fallacy of Humanism," 253–54.

61. Ibid., 254–55. Robert Dupree traced the derivation of Tate's language in the essay to Oswald Spengler. Tate was arguing, in Dupree's interpretation, for the existence of a temporal mode of knowing, made accessible through symbols or figures in art or religion, that the empirical mind missed. This was a style of argument akin to that of Tate as a Catholic critic in the 1940s. Dupree, *Allen Tate and the Augustinian Imagination*, 26–30.

62. Young and Core, *Selected Letters*, 24; Young, *Gentleman in a Dustcoat*, 1–9, 11, 40; Cowan, *Fugitive Group*, 13.

63. Quinlan, *John Crowe Ransom's Secular Faith*, xiv, 45–46; Conkin, *Southern Agrarians*, 54; Young, *Gentleman in a Dustcoat*, 271; Ransom, *God*

without Thunder, 81. My understanding of Ransom's religious views are based in large part on Quinlan's excellent monograph. Thomas Daniel Young recounts that Ransom for a time in the 1930s returned to regular attendance at Methodist Church services, even teaching Sunday school, focusing on specific passages much in the manner of his English courses at Vanderbilt. After his students challenged him on his unwillingness to recite the Apostle's Creed, owing, Ransom admitted, to his lack of belief in the Trinity, Ransom quietly withdrew from Sunday school teaching as soon as convenient and shortly thereafter broke off his new Sunday habit of attending services. Young, *Gentleman in a Dustcoat*, 271–72.

64. Ransom, *God without Thunder*, 29, 5, 97.

65. Ransom to Tate, 4 July 1929, in Young and Core, *Selected Letters*, 180–81. Tate agreed with Ransom's assessment, writing to Andrew Nelson Lytle of his own Humanism essay in relation to Ransom's views of the South. (Ransom had revised his *Sewanee Review* essay and published it as "The South Defends Its Heritage" in *Harper's*): "It is nowhere so fine as John's, and it doesn't touch the political and social question, but it argues for much the same views from a more general position." Tate to Andrew Nelson Lytle, 16 June 1929, in Young and Sarcone, *Lytle-Tate Letters*, 33.

66. Tate to Ransom, 27 July 1929, folder 43, box 10, Davidson Papers.

67. O'Brien, *Idea of the American South*, 144.

68. Tate to Ransom, 27 July 1929, folder 43, box 10, Davidson Papers.

69. Twelve Southerners, *I'll Take My Stand*, 162.

70. Ransom's admiration for Tate's essay and agreement with him is expressed in Ransom to Davidson, n.d., folder 36, box 8, Davidson Papers. This letter was written to Davidson after Tate's 27 July 1929 letter to Ransom.

71. John Crowe Ransom, "Humanists and Schoolmasters," typescript,

pp. 6–7, 9, folder 27, box 36, Tate Papers.

72. *Nashville Tennessean*, 9 Mar. 1930.

73. Rock, "Making and Meaning of *I'll Take My Stand*," 247–49; Ransom to Tate, 5 Jan. 1930, in Young and Core, *Selected Letters*, 189; Tate to Davidson, 9 Feb. 1930, cited in Rock, "Making and Meaning of *I'll Take My Stand*," 247; O'Brien, *Idea of the American South*, 147.

74. "Articles of an Agrarian Reform," typescript, p. 7, folder 6, box 5, Richmond Croom Beatty Papers, Special Collections and University Archives, Heard Library, Vanderbilt University, Nashville, Tennessee. Cf. Twelve Southerners, *I'll Take My Stand*, xliv.

75. Twelve Southerners, *I'll Take My Stand*, xliv, 42.

76. Ibid., 168; Ransom, *God without Thunder*, 116.

77. Tate to Bandler, n.d., "Tate, Allen and Caroline, 1929–31, I," *Hound and Horn* Correspondence Ra–Tz, *Hound and Horn* Papers; Tate to C. Hartley Grattan, 19 Feb. 1930, copy, ibid.; Tate to Bandler, 7 Feb. 1930, ibid.

78. Beatty, "Personal Memoir of the Agrarians," 12–13.

Chapter Three

1. Allen Tate to Andrew Nelson Lytle, 31 July 1929, in Young and Sarcone, *Lytle-Tate Letters*, 34; Tate to John Crowe Ransom, 27 July 1929, folder 43, box 10, Donald Davidson Papers, Special Collections and University Archives, Heard Library, Vanderbilt University, Nashville, Tennessee; Tate to Donald Davidson, 9 Nov. 1929, in Fain and Young, *Literary Correspondence*, 241.

2. "I think that the title, 'I'll Take My Stand,' is the god-damnedest thing I ever heard of; for the love of God block it if you can," Robert Penn Warren blustered to Allen Tate from England. "Wade must be an idiot, and certainly all the rest are if they submit to it." Robert Penn Warren to Allen Tate, 19 May 1930, Allen Tate Papers,

Manuscript Division, Department of Rare Books and Special Collections, University Library, Princeton University, Princeton, New Jersey. For exchanges among the contributors on the title, see Warren to Davidson, 25 June 1930, folder 17, box 12, Davidson Papers; Lytle to Davidson, 1 Aug. 1930, folder 8, box 7, ibid.; Lytle to Tate, [Spring 1930], [June 1930], in Young and Sarcone, *Lytle-Tate Letters*, 38–39, 40; Davidson to Tate, "Saturday," n.d., box 18, folder 2, Tate Papers; Tate to Davidson, 7 Sept. 1930, in Fain and Young, *Literary Correspondence*, 254–55; and the letters contained in app. B, Fain and Young, *Literary Correspondence*, 406–8. See also Rock, "Making and Meaning of *I'll Take My Stand*," 251–62; Conkin, *Southern Agrarians*, 70–72; and Young, *Gentleman in a Dustcoat*, 213–15.

3. Tate to the Contributors to the Southern Symposium, 24 July 1930, in Fain and Young, *Literary Correspondence*, 406; Twelve Southerners, *I'll Take My Stand*, 155.

4. Tate to Davidson, 7 Sept. 1930, in Fain and Young, *Literary Correspondence*, 255.

5. *New York Times*, 15 Feb. 1931; Johnson, "South Faces Itself," 157; *Macon Telegraph*, 24 Sept. 1930; *Buffalo News*, 13 Dec. 1930. Numerous clippings relating to *I'll Take My Stand* are collected in folders 1–4, box 35, Davidson Papers.

6. Knickerbocker, "Back to the Hand," 468; *Dallas News*, 21 Dec. 1930; Hesseltine, "Look Away, Dixie," 98, 101.

7. *Chattanooga News*, 6 Dec. 1930.

8. Smith, "Dilemma of Agrarianism," 226, 224–25.

9. Couch, "Reflections on the Southern Tradition," 291–92.

10. Tate to Davidson, 10 Aug. 1929, in Fain and Young, *Literary Correspondence*, 230; Tate to Ransom, 27 July 1929, folder 43, box 10, Davidson Papers. Tate reiterated his fundamental objection to Humanism in a response to a Humanist critic: "The only condition under which the Humanistic values (doctrines)

can be realized is an actual center of life religiously and morally consistent with them. Until this center is found, and not eclectically pieced together at the surface, Humanism is an attempt to do mechanically—that is, naturalistically—what should be done morally." Tate, "Same Fallacy of Humanism," 33.

11. Wilson, "Tennessee Agrarians," 280.

12. Tate to Edmund Wilson, [late July 1931], in Young and Sarcone, *Lytle-Tate Letters*, 367–68. See also Tate to Lytle, 28 July 1931, in ibid., 47.

13. "Memorandum of Organization," 22 Nov. 1930, folder 11, box 19, Davidson Papers; Young, *Gentleman in a Dustcoat*, 217.

14. Young, *Gentleman in a Dustcoat*, 217–27.

15. Ibid., 217–22, 224.

16. Ibid., 238, 225–26; Twelve Southerners, *I'll Take My Stand*, xlv; John Crowe Ransom, "Land!," typescript, 1:14–18; 2:8, 17; 4:9, folder 12, box 3, John Crowe Ransom Papers, Special Collections and University Archives, Heard Library, Vanderbilt University, Nashville, Tennessee. (The typescript is divided into sections, each of which is separately paginated.) For John Crowe Ransom's economic thought, see, in addition to "Land!": Ransom, "State and the Land"; Ransom, "Shall We Complete the Trade?"; Ransom, "Happy Farmers"; Ransom, "A Capitol for the New Deal." See also O'Brien, *Idea of the American South*, 127–29, 134–35, Singal, *War Within*, 217–18; and Young, *Gentleman in a Dustcoat*, 238–42, 248–49.

17. Ransom, "Land!," 3:16–17, 23, 29; 4:9–10, 13–15, 18–19, 31, 33; Ransom, "Happy Farmers," 533–35.

18. Tate to Bernard Bandler, n.d., quoted in Greenbaum, *Hound and Horn*, 135.

19. Tate to Davidson, 10 Dec. 1932, in Fain and Young, *Literary Correspondence*, 279–80.

20. [Bandler] to Tate, 10 Nov. 1931, "Tate, Allen and Caroline, 1929–31, I," *Hound and Horn* Correspondence,

Ra–Tz, *Hound and Horn* Papers, Beinecke Rare Book and Manuscript
Library, Yale University, New Haven,
Connecticut. Kirstein referred to a
planned symposium entitled "'Ol Brer
Ransom and his Friends." [Kirstein]
to Tate, 21 Aug. 1931, ibid.

21. Greenbaum, *Hound and Horn*,
127, 137, 126, 150–58.

22. Editorial Notes, *American Review* 1 (April 1933): 123–26; Young,
Gentleman in a Dustcoat, 251–52;
Memorandum, n.d., pp. 1–2, folder 29,
box 19, Davidson Papers. The memorandum is identified at the top as
"Composed by the Nashville group,
about the time of Collins' visit."

23. Diggins, *Mussolini and Fascism*,
211. For Tate's rejection of fascism and
the distancing of himself from Seward
Collins, see Tate, "Fascism and the
Southern Agrarians." On Collins,
see Craven, "Seward Collins and the
Traditionalists," and Stone, "Seward
Collins and the *American Review*."

24. Huff, *Allen Tate and the Catholic
Revival*, 52–61; McCarraher, "Ameri-
can Gothic," 7–8, 10–16. On the
various efforts to form a decentralist
intellectual movement in the 1930s,
involving the Agrarians and the Dis-
tributists, see O'Brien, *Idea of the
American South*, 156–57; Shapiro,
"American Distributists and the New
Deal"; Shapiro, "Decentralist Intel-
lectuals and the New Deal," 938–57;
Shapiro, "American Conservative
Intellectuals," 370–80; and Shapiro,
"Catholic Agrarian Thought and the
New Deal," 583–99.

25. Young, *Gentleman in a Dustcoat*,
252; Lytle, "Backwoods Progression,"
411–16; Lytle, "John Taylor," 96,
432–34, 439.

26. Owsley, "Pillars of Agrarianism," 533, 537–39, 541, 543–44, 547.

27. Gilbert and Brown, "Alternative
Land Reform Proposals in the 1930s,"
356, 360–63, 366; Virginia Rock, "The
Twelve Southerners: Biographical
Essays," in Twelve Southerners, *I'll
Take My Stand*, 390; Fite, *Cotton Fields
No More*, 146–47.

28. For the Agrarians' involvement
with Herbert Agar in particular, see

Leverette and Shi, "Herbert Agar and
Free America," 189–206.

29. Tate to Bishop, 7 Apr. 1933, in
Young and Hindle, *Republic of Letters*,
77; Tate to Eugene F. Saxton, 17 Nov.
1933, in Fain and Young, *Literary
Correspondence*, 409.

30. Agar and Tate, *Who Owns
America?*; O'Brien, *Idea of the Ameri-
can South*, 156–57; "Minutes," Con-
vention of the Committee for the
Alliance of Agrarians and Distributist
Groups, 4–5 June 1936, Nashville,
Tennessee, typescript, folder 1, box
15, Andrew Nelson Lytle Papers,
Special Collections and University
Archives, Heard Library, Vanderbilt
University, Nashville, Tennessee.
The eight Agrarians who attended
the convention and contributed to
Who Owns America? were John Crowe
Ransom, Allen Tate, Donald David-
son, Andrew Nelson Lytle, Frank
Owsley, Robert Penn Warren, Lyle
Lanier, and John Donald Wade. On
Ralph Borsodi, see Issel, "Ralph Bor-
sodi and the Agrarian Response to
Modern America," and Leverette and
Shi, "Agrarianism for Commuters."
For useful sketches of Borsodi and
Herbert Agar, see Carlson, *New
Agrarian Mind*, chaps. 3 and 6.

31. Tate to Fletcher, 3 Dec. 1930,
John Gould Fletcher Papers, Special
Collections Division, University of
Arkansas Libraries, University of Arkansas, Fayetteville, Arkansas. Tate
indicated in the same letter that he did
not shrink from the implications of
his rhetorical call for violence: "I'm
afraid that most of our colleagues
imagine they are writing pleasant
essays on the old South; if they are
they are deceiving themselves — or
rather if they imagine this, they had
better leave us quickly." Ibid.

32. Tate to Bishop, [early June
1931], in Young and Hindle, *Republic of
Letters*, 34.

33. Tate to R. P. Blackmur, 18 Dec.
1933, quoted in Greenbaum, *Hound
and Horn*, 157; Tate, "Regionalism and
Sectionalism," 160–61, 159.

34. Davidson to Tate, 23 Jan. 1933,
in Fain and Young, *Literary Correspon-*

dence, 282; Davidson, "Sectionalism in the United States," 579; Tate to Davidson, 5 Feb. 1933, folder 51, box 10, Davidson Papers; Tate to Lincoln Kirstein, 6 Feb. 1933, "Tate, Allen and Caroline 1933–34, III," *Hound and Horn* Correspondence, *Hound and Horn* Papers.

35. Tate to Davidson, 5 Feb. 1933, folder 51, box 10, Davidson Papers; Tate to Blackmur, 18 Apr. 1934, folder 11, box 8, R. P. Blackmur Papers, Manuscript Division, Department of Rare Books and Special Collections, Princeton University Library, Princeton University, Princeton, New Jersey. See also Tate to Blackmur, 12 Dec. 1935, ibid.

36. Lowell, "Visiting the Tates," in Squires, *Allen Tate and His Work*, 34.

37. Waldron, *Close Connections*, 122, 125–28; Cowley, "Meriwether Connection," 54, 53.

38. Cowley, *Exile's Return*, 7, 11, 29. Contemporary southern literary scholars have treated Cowley respectfully and sympathetically. Lewis P. Simpson argued that in *Exile's Return* Cowley had crafted a myth of the "lost generation," which revolved around a "poetics of exile." Simpson, *Brazen Face of History*, 139.

39. Jonza, *Underground Stream*, 134–35; Sullivan, *Allen Tate*, 38; Waldron, *Close Connections*, 128; Tate to Caroline Gordon, 10 May 1954, 20 May 1954, folder 9, box 37, Caroline Gordon Papers, Manuscript Division, Department of Rare Books and Special Collections, Princeton University Library, Princeton University, Princeton, New Jersey. "Whenever Caroline 'went Meriwether,' it always drove Allen mad," observed Caroline Gordon's biographer Ann Waldron, whether in 1933 or in 1945, the time of the Tates' first divorce. Waldron, *Close Connections*, 233. Gordon to Katherine Anne Porter, 6 Oct. 1945, quoted in Waldron, *Close Connections*, 238–39. Tate always claimed that it was Caroline's inability to forget his initial infidelity that led to the deterioration of their relationship. On the breakup of their marriage, see Waldron, *Close*

Connections, 239, 243, 324–25, 332, 336–51.

40. Waldron, *Close Connections*, 71; Tate to Lytle, 1 Apr. 1929, in Young and Sarcone, *Lytle-Tate Letters*, 21.

41. Waldron, *Close Connections*, 100; Kreyling, *Figures of the Hero in Southern Narrative*, 111; Tate to Lytle, 16 July 1931, in Young and Sarcone, *Lytle-Tate Letters*, 46.

42. Squires, *Allen Tate*, 131–33; unpublished biography of Robert E. Lee, typescript, pp. 17, 20–21, 22–27, folder 6, box 2, Tate Papers; Tate to Bishop, 11 Feb. 1932, in Young and Hindle, *Republic of Letters*, 52. John Peale Bishop urged Tate to finish the biography even if it lapsed into autobiography. Bishop to Tate, [19–26 Oct. 1932], in Young and Hindle, *Republic of Letters*, 65. See also Squires, *Allen Tate*, 128. As early as 1931, Tate had, for no clear reason, written up his own "Genealogical Statement of Reasons for Entering the Symposium" and distributed it to his fellow Agrarians. Singal, *War Within*, 255.

43. Waldron, *Close Connections*, 29; Tate to Ellen Glasgow, 31 May 1933, quoted in Squires, *Allen Tate*, 129.

44. Waldron, *Close Connections*, 132; Tate to Warren, n.d., letter fragment, box 70, folder 1383, Robert Penn Warren Papers, Beinecke Rare Book and Manuscript Library, Yale University, New Haven, Connecticut. To Bishop he wrote that the issue resolved itself into a "simple problem that I could not solve": "The discrepancy between the outward significance and the private was so enormous that I decided that I could not handle the material in any form at all, without faking the significance or the material. . . . I feel a great release of spirit, but for the moment at least a good deal of sheer exhaustion." Tate to Bishop, 30 Oct. 1933, in Young and Hindle, *Republic of Letters*, 84–85. In explaining the origins of his novel *The Fathers* in an interview with Michael Millgate published in 1961, Tate traced it to his earlier ancestry book, which was to show the mingling of his father's and mother's family. "I couldn't write it

as history," Tate said. "So I decided to do just one side of the book that I'd originally planned." Millgate, "Interview with Allen Tate," 28.

45. Tate, "New Provincialism," 272.

46. All quotations are taken from Tate, *The Fathers*, as indicated in parentheses. The novel was shaped by Tate's private obsessions: Posey has an invalid mother whom he cannot escape; Lacy associates sexuality with his mother's undergarments. If the Buchan plantation shares the name of one in Tate's own family background, the Posey family hails from Washington, D.C., where Tate spent much time as a youth with his mother's family. Lewis P. Simpson has suggested further that, like the Poseys, Tate believed he had family relations who were black. Simpson, *Fable of the Southern Writer*, 37.

47. John Crowe Ransom to Allen Tate, 17 Sept. 1936, in Young and Core, *Selected Letters*, 217.

48. Gallagher, "History of Literary Criticism," 133; Graff, *Professing Literature*, 240; Young, *Gentleman in a Dustcoat*, 272–73, 287, 289–90. Tate led a public campaign to keep Ransom at Vanderbilt University, chiding the university for allowing such a distinguished man of letters to leave the South and orchestrating much national pressure from the literary community. Vanderbilt undergraduates Randall Jarrell and Peter Taylor were among the leaders of a student effort to retain Ransom. See Young, *Gentleman in a Dustcoat*, 273–88.

49. Graff, *Professing Literature*, 19–20, 55, 81–82, 85, 121; Abrams, "Transformation of English Studies," 106; Russo, "Tranquilized Poem," 219–20.

50. Leitch, *American Literary Criticism*, xii, 26–27; Jancovich, *Cultural Politics of the New Criticism*, 9, 14; King, "South and Cultural Criticism," 700; Gallagher, "History of Literary Criticism," 134, 136–38; Abrams, "Transformation of English Studies," 109; Graff, *Literature against Itself*, 141–42.

51. Schwartz, *Creating Faulkner's*

Reputation, 6, 125–26; Leitch, *American Literary Criticism*, 24–25; Graff, *Professing Literature*, 152, 157–58; Abrams, "Transformation of English Studies," 108.

52. Ransom to Tate, 11 Mar. 1937, in Young and Core, *Selected Letters*, 221; Graff, *Professing Literature*, 145–46; Gallagher, "History of Literary Criticism," 135–36.

53. Bové, *Mastering Discourse*, 115; Gallagher, "History of Literary Criticism," 134–35; Graff, *Professing Literature*, 145–46, 148–52, 190–91; Russo, "Tranquilized Poem," 198–99, 219–20; Jancovich, *Cultural Politics of the New Criticism*, 3–5, 130, 138; Crews, *Critics Bear It Away*, xv; Graff, *Literature against Itself*, 133, 140–41; Leitch, *American Literary Criticism*, 25–26; Abrams, "Transformation of English Studies," 108–9. On the New Critics' role in the professionalization of literary study, see also Wilson, "Criticism, Inc." For a contemporary critique of the conservatism of the New Critics, see Davis, "New Criticism and the Democratic Tradition."

54. Jancovich, *Cultural Politics of the New Criticism*, 69, 27, 30, 80, 137–38; Bové, *Mastering Discourse*, 115, 130, 141–42. See also Walter Kalaidgian, "Marketing Modern Poetry and the Southern Public Sphere," in Dettmar and Watt, *Marketing Modernism*, 297–319.

55. Ransom, *World's Body*, 140–41, 43; Ransom, *New Criticism*, 205. For the best study of Ransom's evolving religious views over the course of his life, see Quinlan, *John Crowe Ransom's Secular Faith*.

56. Ransom, *New Criticism*, 79, 100–101.

57. Ibid., 42–43, 219–20, 280–81, 302–3, 327–29; Ransom, *World's Body*, x–xi, 293.

58. Ransom, *World's Body*, 210–11.

59. Southard, "Religious Poetry of Robert Penn Warren," 674–75; Adorno, "Theses upon Art and Religion Today," 677–78; Ransom, "Art and the Human Economy," 684–86.

60. Ransom, "Art and the Human Economy," 685–87.

61. "Symposium: The Agrarians Today," 14–15.

62. Tate, "Traditionist Looks at Liberalism," 734.

63. Allen Tate, "What Is a Traditional Society?," in Tate, *Essays of Four Decades*, 547, 556.

64. Tate, "Traditionist Looks at Liberalism," 738, 741.

65. Allen Tate, "The Symbolic Imagination: The Mirrors of Dante," in Tate, *Essays of Four Decades*, 429, 427–28, 442; Allen Tate, "The Angelic Imagination: Poe as God," in ibid., 411–12, 422. On Tate's Catholic criticism in general, see Huff, *Allen Tate and the Catholic Revival*, 72–99, esp. 79–83, 86–89, 96–98; Meiners, *Last Alternatives*, 33–58; and Dupree, *Allen Tate and the Augustinian Imagination*, chap. 2. For an important statement of the New Criticism by Tate, see Tate, "Miss Emily and the Bibliographer."

66. Rubin, *Wary Fugitives*, 302.

Chapter Four

1. Donald Davidson, "The Center That Holds," in Smith, *So Good a Cause*, 220, 222.

2. For an interesting assessment of the therapeutic and quasi-religious tendencies present in recent academic work on collective memory, as well as its affinity for identity politics, see Klein, "On the Emergence of *Memory* in Historical Discourse," 127–50, esp. 138–45. Memory, Klein argues, has been a "therapeutic alternative to historical discourse." Ibid., 145. For a discussion of the therapeutic dimensions of collective memory informed explicitly by psychoanalytical theory and focused on southern letters, see King, *Southern Renaissance*, chap. 1, esp. 16–19.

3. Allen Tate to Bernard Bandler, 24 Feb. 1932, quoted in O'Brien, *Idea of the American South*, 191.

4. Davidson, *Lee in the Mountains*, 91.

5. Donald Davidson to Tate, 26 May 1936, folder 3, box 18, Allen Tate Papers, Manuscript Division,

Department of Rare Books and Special Collections, Princeton University Library, Princeton University, Princeton, New Jersey; David A. Hollinger, "Ethnic Diversity, Cosmopolitanism, and the Emergence of the American Liberal Intelligentsia," in Hollinger, *In the American Province*, 56–73; Cooney, *Rise of the New York Intellectuals*, 165, 244–46.

6. Fain, *Spyglass*, 31, 221–22.

7. O'Brien, *Idea of the American South*, 187, 194, 190–91, 153; Singal, *War Within*, 231. As early as 1926, Davidson confided to Jesse Wills, a friend and fellow Fugitive poet, that he felt inferior when around his English Department colleagues Ransom and Walter Clyde Curry, a major Chaucer scholar. Jesse Wills to Tate, 15 Mar. 1926, folder 4, box 46, Tate Papers; Conkin, *Southern Agrarians*, 7.

8. Andrew Nelson Lytle to Tate, [Spring 1930], in Young and Sarcone, *Lytle-Tate Letters*, 41; Tate to John Gould Fletcher, 3 Dec. 1930, John Gould Fletcher Papers, Special Collections Division, University of Arkansas Libraries, University of Arkansas, Fayetteville, Arkansas; Davidson to Tate, 19 Dec. 1931, folder 2, box 18, Tate Papers; John Crowe Ransom to Tate, 3 Jan. [1932], folder 27, box 36, Tate Papers; Ransom to Tate, 25 Oct. [1932], in Young and Core, *Selected Letters*, 209.

9. O'Brien, *Idea of the American South*, 189, 192, 194; Winchell, *Where No Flag Flies*, 150–51; Davidson to Tate, 14 Apr. 1931, 22 Feb. 1932, 5 Apr. 1933, folder 2, box 18, Tate Papers.

10. Robert Penn Warren to Tate and Caroline Gordon, [Nov. 1932], folder 28, box 44, Tate Papers; Lyle Lanier to Tate, 20 Nov. 1929, folder 8, box 27, ibid.

11. O'Brien, *Idea of the American South*, 191; Davidson to Tate, 19 Feb. 1933, folder 2, box 18, Tate Papers; Davidson to Warren, 21 Oct. 1936, *Southern Review* Papers, Beinecke Rare Book and Manuscript Library, Yale University, New Haven, Connecticut. Much later, in 1947, he

observed to Warren ruefully, "I seem to be in another line, going another way, but I don't know how I got there, since I have simply stayed put, or so I thought." Davidson to Warren, 28 Feb. 1947, folder 399, box 21, Robert Penn Warren Papers, Beinecke Rare Book and Manuscript Library, Yale University, New Haven, Connecticut.

12. Tate to Davidson, 27 Mar. 1936, in Fain and Young, *Literary Correspondence*, 298–99. Davidson responded in a familiar note of self-pity, expressing his hope that Tate would not have to undergo the strains he and his family had for the last five years. Tate, who for several years had attempted to support his family as an independent writer, was, in turn, mystified by Davidson's response. "There must be something extraordinary in your life in the past five years," he wrote Davidson. "From any ordinary point of view my life is far more difficult, more harassed and insecure, than yours." Davidson to Tate, 9 Apr. 1936, in ibid., 299; Tate to Davidson, 16 Apr. 1936, folder 54, box 10, Donald Davidson Papers, Special Collections and University Archives, Heard Library, Vanderbilt University, Nashville, Tennessee.

13. Young and Inge, *Donald Davidson*, 99; Ransom to Tate, 29 Mar. 1939, in Young and Core, *Selected Letters*, 257.

14. Rubin, *Wary Fugitives*, 147–51, 154, 140; Singal, *War Within*, 220; Hobson, *Tell about the South*, 230; Conkin, *Gone with the Ivy*, 329; O'Brien, *Idea of the American South*, 209, 185, 206–7.

15. Davidson to Fletcher, 17 Mar. 1935, folder 27, box 1, Davidson Papers.

16. Donald Davidson, "The Gardens of John Donald Wade," in Davidson, *Selected Essays and Other Writings of John Donald Wade*, 1; O'Brien, *Idea of the American South*, 194–95.

17. Unpublished memorial oration, p. 10, folder 7, box 22, Davidson Papers; Davidson to Seward Collins, 18 Mar. 1933, folder 112, box 4, Seward Collins Papers, Beinecke Rare Book and Manuscript Library, Yale University, New Haven, Connecticut.

18. Davidson, "Where Regionalism and Sectionalism Meet," 24–25; Davidson to John Donald Wade, 3 Mar. 1934, folder 24, box 1, Davidson Papers.

19. Davidson, *Attack on Leviathan*, 11, 216–18.

20. Davidson, "*I'll Take My Stand*," 319; Davidson, *Attack on Leviathan*, 124–28.

21. Davidson, *Attack on Leviathan*, 161, 163, 11–12.

22. Davidson, "Sectionalism in the United States," 570.

23. Ibid., 570, 577–78, 574.

24. Ibid., 579, 584, 588–89. In the version of the essay reprinted in *Attack on Leviathan*, Davidson also suggested that national political parties served as a useful check on sectionalism. Davidson, *Attack on Leviathan*, 106. Cf. John Randolph, who declared manufacturers to be "citizens of no place or any place." Gray, *Writing the South*, 28.

25. Davidson, *Attack on Leviathan*, 131, 135.

26. Ibid., 138–41.

27. Davidson, "Gulliver with Hay Fever," 153, 170.

28. Ibid., 161, 169.

29. Davidson, *Attack on Leviathan*, 142.

30. Ibid.

31. Ibid., 143–45, 147.

32. Ibid., 283–84, 261–65, 309.

33. Davidson to Wade, 3 Mar. 1934, folder 24, box 1, Davidson Papers.

34. Davidson, "Preface to Decision," 407.

35. Ibid., 407. See also Davidson, "Gulliver with Hay Fever," 164.

36. Davidson, "Mr. Cash and the Proto-Dorian South," in Davidson, *Still Rebels, Still Yankees*, 207–8.

37. Ibid., 209.

38. Ibid., 210–11.

39. Davidson, "Preface to Decision," 395.

40. Ibid., 395–96.

41. Alexander, *Here the Country Lies*, 196. When approached by John Farrar, Davidson was eager to do the volume, for he had been working with Tennessee historical materials off and on since 1929. Davidson to John Farrar, 21 Mar. 1940, folder 1, box 2, Davidson Papers; Davidson to Ferris Greenslet, 28 Apr. 1940, folder 1, box 2, Davidson Papers; Davidson to Ransom, 5 July 1929, folder 12, box 1, Davidson Papers; Davidson to Tate, 14 Apr. 1931, folder 2, box 8, Tate Papers.

42. Davidson, *Lee in the Mountains*, 136–37.

43. Davidson, *Tennessee*, 1:80, 86.

44. Ibid., 2:112.

45. Ibid., 148.

46. Ibid., 223, 333. As he explained to a correspondent in 1948, Davidson believed that the states should have had more power in the administration of the Tennessee Valley Authority and scorned the suggestion that the TVA would be some sort of agent of moral reform for the inhabitants of the Tennessee Valley. Donald Davidson to Harvey Broome, 25 Apr. 1948, copy, folder 22, box 2, Davidson Papers. "To me, the fundamental principle is that the government can and often should act as a restraining mechanism upon private and corporate behavior; but government, once entrusted with sweeping power, *never* ultimately can be expected to exercise *self*-restraint," Davidson wrote to Brainard Cheney with regard to the TVA. Davidson to Brainard Cheney, 28 May 1948, folder 16, box 4, Brainard Cheney Papers, Special Collections and University Archives, Heard Library, Vanderbilt University, Nashville, Tennessee.

47. Davidson, *Tennessee*, 276–77, 282–83, 285.

48. Ibid., 251, 256, 259, 237–38.

49. Tate, *Memoirs and Opinions*, 37–38.

50. Louise Davis, "He Clings to Enduring Values," *Nashville Tennessean Magazine*, 4 Sept. 1949, 6, 8. This article can be found in folder 11, box 35, Davidson Papers.

Chapter Five

1. Schulman, *From Cotton Belt to Sunbelt*, 3, 5–6; Wright, *Old South, New South*, 8–9.

2. Wright, *Old South, New South*, 198–236; Schulman, *From Cotton Belt to Sunbelt*, vii–viii, 21–31.

3. Schulman, *From Cotton Belt to Sunbelt*, 15–20; Fite, *Cotton Fields No More*, 129–48.

4. Daniel, "Transformation of the Rural South"; Daniel, *Breaking the Land*.

5. Morton Sosna, "More Important than the Civil War?: The Impact of World War II on the South," in Cobb and Wilson, *Perspectives on the American South*.

6. Bartley, *New South*, 2, 11; Boles, *South through Time*, 452–53, 455; Grantham, *South in Modern America*, 172–75; Schulman, *From Cotton Belt to Sunbelt*, 82, 102–3; Fite, *Cotton Fields No More*, 168–69.

7. Ransom, "Art and the Human Economy," 687; Donald Davidson to Tate, 3 Oct. 1945, in Fain and Young, *Literary Correspondence*, 344; Davidson to Robert Penn Warren, 29 Oct. 1946, folder 399, box 21, Robert Penn Warren Papers, Beinecke Rare Book and Manuscript Library, Yale University, New Haven, Connecticut.

8. "Symposium: The Agrarians Today," 27, 31; Purdy, *Fugitives' Reunion*, 206; Owsley, "Pillars of Agrarianism," 529–47.

9. "Symposium: Agrarians Today," 28–29. On Allen Tate's conversion, see Brinkmeyer, *Three Catholic Writers of the Modern South*, 61. Allen Tate reiterated his view of Agrarian idolatry in a letter to Davidson: "We were trying to find a religion in the secular, historical experience as such." Tate to Davidson, 14 Jan. 1953, in Fain and Young, *Literary Correspondence*, 370. At the 1956 Fugitives' reunion, Tate stated that he thought Agrarianism was "religious humanism." Purdy, *Fugitives' Reunion*, 207. Tate claimed in a later interview that Agrarianism was a statement of the "permanent values of Western society." Millgate, "Interview with Allen Tate," 32.

10. Cleanth Brooks, Letter to the Editor, *Shenandoah* 3 (Autumn 1952): 45–46.

11. Nash, *Conservative Intellectual Movement in America*, xvi. For a succinct version of George H. Nash's argument, updated through the early Reagan years, see Nash, "Historical Roots of Contemporary American Conservatism," 297–303. See also Gottfried, *Conservative Movement*; Himmelstein, *To the Right*; Judis, *William F. Buckley, Jr.*; Blumenthal, *The Rise of the Counter-Establishment*; and Dionne, *Why Americans Hate Politics*. On the explicit fusionism of the *National Review*, see Judis, *William F. Buckley, Jr.*, 118–19.

12. See, for example, Nash's treatment of the success of fusionism, in which there is no clear explanation why the conservative movement suddenly seemed to lose interest in its inveterate intramural combat in the early 1960s. Nash, *Conservative Intellectual Movement in America*, 180–85.

13. Rothbard, "Huntington on Conservatism," 787.

14. Wills, *Confessions of a Conservative*, 33.

15. "The Magazine's Credenda," *National Review*, 19 Nov. 1955, 6.

16. Himmelstein, *To the Right*, 62, 25.

17. Davidson, *Southern Writers in the Modern World*, 145.

18. Fred Siegel, "Conservatism," in Foner and Garraty, *Reader's Companion to American History*, 221–22.

19. Dumenil, *Modern Temper*, 4–7, 12–13, 26–28, 201–49 passim.

20. Shawn Lay, "Introduction: The Second Invisible Empire," in Lay, *Invisible Empire in the West*, 6, 8–9; Lay, *Hooded Knights on the Niagara*, 6; Moore, *Citizen Klansmen*, xii, 1–2, 7; Dumenil, *Modern Temper*, 236, 239; Coben, *Rebellion against Victorianism*, 136–37.

21. Coben, *Rebellion against Victorianism*, 140–42; Leonard J. Moore, "Historical Interpretations of the 1920s Klan: The Traditional View and Recent Revisions," in Lay, *In-visible Empire in the West*, 19, 24, 30, 33; Shawn Lay, "Conclusion: Toward a New Historical Appraisal of the Ku Klux Klan of the 1920s," in Lay, *Invisible Empire in the West*, 220; Moore, *Citizen Klansmen*, 19–22. Moore, "Historical Interpretations of the 1920s Klan," and Lay, *Hooded Knights of the Niagara*, 177–91, provide historiographical essays on the second Klan. Important revisionist works not previously cited include Goldberg, *Hooded Empire*; Cocoltchos, "Invisible Government and the Viable Community"; Gerlach, *Blazing Crosses in Zion*; Horowitz, "Klansman as Outsider," 12–20; Jenkins, *Steel Valley Klan*; and Blee, *Woman of the Klan*. A historian who challenges the revisionist account is Nancy MacLean in *Behind the Mask of Chivalry*.

22. Moore, *Citizen Klansmen*, 22, Coben, *Rebellion against Victorianism*, 138, 142.

23. Moore, "Good Old-Fashioned New Social History," 557, 560–61.

24. Ribuffo, *Old Christian Right*, xvii, 15, 18; Rudolph, "American Liberty League," 19–33.

25. Brinkley, *Voices of Protest*, xi–xii, 144, 154.

26. Rothbard, "Life in the Old Right," 15–18; Nash, *Conservative Intellectual Movement in America*, 24.

27. Doenecke, "Origins and Outcome," 17–18; Powers, *Not without Honor*, 164; Doenecke, *Not to the Swift*, 24–25; Kauffman, *America First!*, 191.

28. Doenecke, "Origins and Outcome," 18; Diamond, *Roads to Dominion*, 24; Doenecke, *Not to the Swift*, 10, 239–40; Rothbard, "Life in the Old Right," 19; Nash, *Conservative Intellectual Movement in America*, 123–28. See also Radosh, *Prophets on the Right*.

29. Wilson, "Theory of Conservatism," 34, 42.

30. LeRoy, "New Conservatism," 270; Haiman, "New Look at the New Conservatism," 444; MacDonald, "Revival of Conservative Thought," 67, 77–78, 80.

31. On Dwight Macdonald, see Sumner, *Dwight Macdonald and the "Politics" Circle*. On Lewis Mumford,

see Blake, *Beloved Community*. For brief discussions of Hannah Arendt, see McClay, *Masterless*, 213–23; and Pells, *Liberal Mind in a Conservative Age*, 83–96. For postwar culture in general, see McClay, *Masterless*, and Graebner, *Age of Doubt*.

32. Schlesinger, "Not Left, Not Right, but a Vital Center," 47; Schlesinger, *Vital Center*, 3–5. John P. Diggins refers to Schlesinger's "existential liberalism" in *Up from Communism*, 418. On liberal intellectuals in the 1950s, see Pells, *Liberal Mind in a Conservative Age*, 183–261. For a good discussion of liberal interest in conservative thought in the immediate postwar years, see Nash, *Conservative Intellectual Movement in America*, 132–40.

33. Niebuhr, *Children of Light and the Children of Darkness*, 16–17.

34. Schwartz, *Creating Faulkner's Reputation*, 3–5, 28–32, 140–41, 200–203; David A. Hollinger, "The Canon and Its Keepers: Modernism and Mid-Twentieth-Century American Intellectuals," in Hollinger, *In the American Province*, 74–91; Spender, "Beyond Liberalism," 191–92. On the New York Intellectuals' campaign against popular culture, see Teres, *Renewing the American Left*, chap. 7.

35. Hitchcock, "Postmortem on a Rebirth," 211, 216, 219; Gleason, *Contending with Modernity*, 106–8, 114–15, 163–64, 297; Huff, *Allen Tate and the Catholic Revival*, 27–29. A good memoir reflecting the activist commitment fostered by the Catholic Revival is Brien, "Catholic Revival Revisited."

36. Hitchcock, "Postmortem on a Rebirth," 215, 217; Gleason, *Contending with Modernity*, 163–64; Allitt, *Catholic Converts*, 317; Huff, *Allen Tate and the Catholic Revival*, 79.

37. Gleason, *Contending with Modernity*, 118, 267, 298; Nash, *Conservative Intellectual Movement in America*, 63; Allitt, *Catholic Intellectuals and Conservative Politics in America*, 7–8.

38. Nash, *Conservative Intellectual Movement in America*, 68; Allitt, *Catholic Intellectuals and Conservative Politics*, 55–57. On the Burkean

revival in general, see Nash, *Conservative Intellectual Movement in America*, 163–66.

39. Viereck, "But—I'm a Conservative!," 538–39, 541–43, 538. Irving Babbitt was "one of the greatest influences on my entire life," Viereck confessed to Russell Kirk. Peter Viereck to Russell Kirk, 8 Nov. 1954, Russell Kirk Papers, in possession of Russell Kirk estate, Mecosta, Michigan. See in general Hénault, *Peter Viereck*.

40. Rossiter, *Conservatism in America*, 66; "Where Are the American Conservatives?," 61; Reichley, "Young Conservatives at Old Harvard," 14.

41. Kristol, "Old Truths and the New Conservatism," 365; Aaron, "Conservatism, Old and New," 99–100, 109; Niebuhr, "Liberalism," 12–13.

42. Davis, "New Criticism and the Democratic Tradition," 10–11.

43. Hartz, *Liberal Tradition in America*. Others who pointed to the dependence of conservative thought on aristocracy or the lack of a conservative tradition in the United States included Himmelfarb, "Prophets of the New Conservatism," 79–80; Aaron, "Conservatism, Old and New," 101–2; Walter, "Conservatism Recrudescent," 522; Crick, "Strange Quest for an American Conservatism," 363; Freund, "New American Conservatism and European Conservatism," 16; McKitrick, "'Conservatism' Today," 51–52; Strout, "Liberalism, Conservatism, and the Babel of Tongues," 106; Fogelman, "New Conservatism and American Values," 26; and Auerbach, *Conservative Illusion*, 2–4, 69–71, 73, 87. John Higham's early discussion of the "consensus school" is Higham, "Cult of the 'American Consensus.'"

44. Stoke, "Outlook for American Conservatism," 266; Brown, "Democracy, the New Conservatism, and the Liberal Tradition in America," 8–9; Schlesinger, "New Conservatism," 12; Trilling, *Liberal Imagination*, vii.

45. Judis, *William F. Buckley, Jr.*, 21–22, 25–28, 46–89; Buckley, *God and Man at Yale*.

46. Chambers, *Witness*, 10, 17, 16.

47. For a useful distinction between liberal and countersubversive anti-Communists, see Powers, *Not without Honor*, 199, 214.

48. Nash, *Conservative Intellectual Movement in America*, 112–17, 146–48.

49. Ibid., 91–98, 145–47, 148–49, 158–59; Judis, *William F. Buckley, Jr.*, 115–16, 121–24, 129–30, 146–47. An excellent analysis of the evolution from radicalism to conservatism of Max Eastman, John Dos Passos, Will Herberg, and James Burnham is Diggins, *Up from Communism.*

50. Nash, *Conservative Intellectual Movement in America*, 90–91, 95, 258–59.

51. Ibid., 123–28.

52. For discussions of the development of Buckley and the *National Review*'s monitorial role on the right, see Judis, *William F. Buckley, Jr.*, 130, 137–38, 160–61, 173–74, 193–200, and Nash, *Conservative Intellectual Movement in America*, 155–63, 292–93.

53. Meyer, "Collectivism Rebaptized," 559.

54. Nash, *Conservative Intellectual Movement in America*, 367 n. 123; Judis, *William F. Buckley, Jr.*, 104. On the relation between Buckley and the New Conservatives and divisions within the Right in general with regard to this group, see Nash, *Conservative Intellectual Movement in America*, 112–23, 136–37, 155–56; Judis, *William F. Buckley, Jr.*, 96–97.

55. Franklin D. Roosevelt is credited with making the term "liberal," which had generally positive connotations, a widely used term of approbation and, in the process, making "conservative" synonomous with selfishness, greed, and arrogance by Rotunda, *Politics of Language*, 14, 16, 54–61, and Green, *Shaping Political Consciousness*, 119–63. Herbert Hoover and Senator Robert A. Taft were not finally reconciled to the conservative label until 1948. Green, *Shaping Political Consciousness*, 113, 224.

56. "Publisher's Statement," *National Review*, 19 Nov. 1955, 5; "The Magazine's Credenda," ibid., 6.

57. Buckley, *Up from Liberalism*, 125–26.

58. Ibid., 119, 123.

59. Buckley, *God and Man at Yale*, 185.

60. Kendall, rev. of Weaver, *Ideas Have Consequences*, 260–61.

61. Kendall, "Three on the Line," 180.

62. Nash, *Conservative Intellectual Movement in America*, 119–20. Nash indicates that Kendall may have written part of *McCarthy and His Enemies*. Ibid. Kendall, *Conservative Affirmation*, 74–75.

63. Kendall to Wilson, 4 Aug. 1960, "K 1958–61," box 2, Francis G. Wilson Papers, Record Series 15-18-24, University Archives, University of Illinois, Urbana, Illinois. See Kendall, "'Open Society' and Its Fallacies," 972–79.

64. Kendall, "Three on the Line," 181.

65. Judis, *William F. Buckley, Jr.*, 138.

66. Buckley, *Up from Liberalism*, 198.

67. See, for example, Frank S. Meyer, "Conservatism," in Meyer, *In Defense of Freedom*, 187–205.

68. Ibid., 34.

69. Ibid., 78, 71, 48.

70. See, for example, ibid., 89–127, 130–32.

71. Ibid., 120.

72. Bozell, "Freedom or Virtue?," 186.

73. Ibid., 182–83, 185.

74. "American Scholar Forum," 86–87, 100; Nash, *Conservative Intellectual Movement in America*, 151.

75. Kirk, "American Conservative Character," 256, 249, 250; Kirk, "Dissolution of Liberalism," 375; Kirk, *Conservative Mind: From Burke to Santayana*, 2d ed., 441–42; "Conservative vs. Liberal—A Debate," 11; Kirk, *Program for Conservatives*, 23.

76. Kirk, *Confessions of a Bohemian Tory*, 5–6, 8–10; Kirk, *Decadence and Renewal in the Higher Learning*, xviii; Kirk, *Sword of the Imagination*, 3, 4, 7.

77. Kirk, *Confessions of a Bohemian Tory*, 3–4.

78. Kirk, *Sword of the Imagination,*
42–49; Kirk, *Confessions of a Bohemian Tory,* 13–19; Russell Kirk to
William C. McCann, 5 Feb., 3 Mar.
1941, box 6, Russell Kirk Papers,
Clarke Historical Library, Central
Michigan University, Mount Pleasant,
Michigan. For Kirk's memories of his
time in the South, see Kirk, *Sword
of the Imagination,* 50–54. For examples of Kirk's interest in southern
issues, see Russell Kirk to William C.
McCann, Jan. 15, Jan 25, April 14,
1941, box 6, Kirk Papers, Clarke
Library.

79. Kirk, *Sword of the Imagination,*
34; Nash, *Conservative Intellectual
Movement in America,* 70–71; Kirk to
McCann, 4 Mar., 2 Nov. 1942, box
6, Kirk Papers, Clarke Library. Kirk
supported Robert Taft's bid for the
1952 Republican presidential nomination. Kirk, *Sword of the Imagination,*
140–41.

80. Kirk, *Confessions of a Bohemian Tory,* 14, 19, 22–23; Kirk, *Sword
of the Imagination,* 14. During this
period, Kirk made the acquaintance
of Richard Weaver, who lectured at
a literary club Kirk helped organize.
Kirk, *Sword of the Imagination,* 80–82,
172.

81. Kirk, *Confessions of a Bohemian
Tory,* 27, 23–24; Nash, *Conservative
Intellectual Movement in America,* 72.

82. Nash, *Conservative Intellectual
Movement,* 74–76; Rusher, *Rise of the
Right,* 28–29; Regnery, "Russell Kirk
and the Making of the Conservative Mind," 345. The conservative
sociologist Robert Nisbet wrote to
Kirk that the book had broken "the
cake of intellectual opposition to the
conservative tradition in the United
States." Nash, *Conservative Intellectual Movement in America,* 73–74. The
book received favorable reviews from
New Conservatives. See Rossiter, rev.
of Kirk, *Conservative Mind;* Hecksher, "Toward a New Conservatism";
Viereck, "Conservatism vs. Smugness"; Hallowell, rev. of Russell Kirk,
Conservative Mind.

83. Kirk, *Program for Conservatives,* 50.

84. Kirk, *Conservative Mind,* 195.
All references to *The Conservative
Mind* are from the original 1953 edition previously cited, unless otherwise
noted.

85. Ibid., 61; Crick, "Strange Quest
for an American Conservatism," 372.

86. Kirk, *Conservative Mind,* 7–
8, 426–27; Kirk, "York and Social
Boredom," 664, 667.

87. Kirk, "St. Andrews," 369; Kirk,
Confessions of a Bohemian Tory, 5, 27–
28; Kirk, "New Towns and Rotting
Houses in Fife," 36.

88. Kirk, "Broken Cake of British
Custom," 331; Kirk, *Confessions of a
Bohemian Tory,* 29–30.

89. Kirk, *Conservative Mind,* 363,
420. Kirk also cited the work of
Richard M. Weaver. Ibid., 420. Kirk,
Sword of the Imagination, 173; Kirk to
Brainard Cheney, 29 Aug. 1954, folder
43, box 6, Brainard Cheney Papers,
Special Collections and University
Archives, Heard Library, Vanderbilt
University, Nashville, Tennessee;
Cheney to Kirk, 7 Sept. 1955, Russell
Kirk Papers, Russell Kirk Center,
Mecosta, Michigan; Davidson to
Tate, 24 Oct. 1955, folder 4, box 18,
Allen Tate Papers, Manuscript Divi-
sion, Department of Rare Books and
Special Collections, Princeton Uni-
versity Library, Princeton University,
Princeton, New Jersey; Kirk, *Sword
of the Imagination,* 178; Davidson to
Kirk, 10 June 1955, 19 Jan. 1957, Kirk
Papers, Mecosta; "The Revolving
Bookstand: Neglected Books," *American Scholar* 25 (Autumn 1956): 486.
Kirk wrote of Davidson three times
in his *National Review* column. Kirk,
"Davidson against Leviathan," 498.
"Let me express my personal admiration for you, in the position you
have been taking and the wonderfully
pertinent, wise, and telling writing
that you have been doing," Davidson wrote Kirk in August 1954. "You
will never realize how much you are
doing to sustain people—some of
whom I know—who, without such
strokes and counters as you have been
giving, would have despaired of the
possibility either of offense or defense

against what has been happening to us." Davidson to Russell Kirk, 31 Aug. 1954, Kirk Papers, Mecosta.

90. "Symposium: Agrarians Today," 20, 18–19, 15–16.

91. Donald Davidson, "Why the Modern South Has a Great Literature," in Davidson, *Still Rebels, Still Yankees*, 172.

92. Davidson to Cleanth Brooks, 17 Feb. 1957, folder 68, box 3, Cleanth Brooks Papers, Beinecke Rare Book and Manuscript Library, Yale University, New Haven, Connecticut; Young and Inge, *Donald Davidson*, 144; O'Brien, *Idea of the American South*, 200.

93. Davidson, *Southern Writers in the Modern World*, 6, 28–30.

94. Ibid., 36–37.

95. Davidson to Richard Weaver, 25 Mar. 1949, folder 3, box 1, Richard M. Weaver Papers, Special Collections and University Archives, Heard Library, Vanderbilt University, Nashville, Tennessee; Richard Weaver, "Agrarianism in Exile," typescript, back of p. 9, ibid.; Purdy, *Fugitives' Reunion*, 93, 199; Cowan, "Fugitive Poets in Relation to the South," 6; Davidson, *Southern Writers in the Modern World*, 40.

96. See, for example, Stewart, "Relation between Fugitives and Agrarians," 56; Rock, "Making and Meaning of *I'll Take My Stand*," 206; Connelly, "Vanderbilt Agrarians," 32; Stewart, *Burden of Time*, 114–19; Montgomery, "Bells for John Stewart's Burden," 172; Rock, "Fugitive-Agrarians in Response to Social Change," 174; Hobson, *Serpent in Eden*, 150–51; Hobson, *Tell about the South*, 208; Gray, *Literature of Memory*, 41; Young, "From Fugitives to Agrarians," 420; Havard, "Politics of *I'll Take My Stand*," 765; King, *Southern Renaissance*, 15; Young, *Waking Their Neighbors Up*, 3–4; Charles P. Roland, "The South and the Agrarians," in Havard and Sullivan, *Band of Prophets*, 38; Conkin, *Southern Agrarians*, 32; Huff, "Donald Davidson and 'America's Other Lost Generation,'" 227. Louis Rubin notes the effect of

the Scopes trial on Davidson but also his oddly mild reactions to it. Rubin, *Wary Fugitives*, 154–55. Daniel Joseph Singal comments on the misperception of the Scopes trial in *War Within*, 200–201. Richard Gray provides a nuanced analysis of the trial's role in instigating Agrarianism in *Writing the South*, 125–26.

97. Virginia J. Rock notes that at a 1968 gathering of the Agrarians in Dallas, Texas, John Crowe Ransom, Allen Tate, Andrew Nelson Lytle, and Robert Penn Warren dismissed the effects of the Scopes trial at the time in shaping their defense of the South. Rock, "They Took Their Stand," 292–93 n. 197.

98. See the section "The Breaking Mould" in "The Tall Men" in Davidson, *Lee in the Mountains*, 120–26.

99. *Nashville Tennessean*, 6 Sept. 1925; ibid., 7 June 1925. For examples of Davidson's relatively liberal sentiments at the time, see ibid., 1 Feb. 1925, for a commendation of Howard Odum's *Journal of Social Forces*; ibid., 12 Apr., 26 July 1925, 16 Jan. 1927, for approving references to the *New Republic;* and ibid., 18 Oct. 1925, for his disappointment at a disparaging comment on Tennessee in the *Nation*, "which might be a considerable liberal influence" otherwise. Davidson later remarked that poets convey the power of religious myth better than fundamentalists: "The dogmas of the fundamentalist . . . have thinned out the religious tradition, have cheapened and made trivial its great figures and originally grand conceptions. At this point the poet enters as the restorer of a lost grandeur." Ibid., 25 Sept. 1927.

100. Two famous Tate essays on this theme are "Profession of Letters in the South," 161–76, and "Southern Mode of the Imagination," 9–23. As Richard H. King observed, with regard to Tate's boosting of the idea of a southern renaissance, "It understates the case considerably to say that the Agrarians rated their own literary and cultural achievement quite highly." King, "South and Cultural Criti-

cism," 702. For an insightful critique (and refutation) of Tate's thesis, see O'Brien, *Rethinking the South*, chap. 7, esp. 157–58, 162–71, 176–78.

101. Allitt, *Catholic Converts*, 313; Herbert Marshall McLuhan, "The Southern Quality," in Tate, *Southern Vanguard*, 104, 107; Marshall McLuhan to Tate, 11 June 1945, folder 6, box 29, Tate Papers.

102. McLuhan, "Southern Quality," 112. See also ibid., 107–8.

103. McLuhan to Tate, 10 Aug. 1945, folder 6, box 29, Tate Papers; McLuhan, "Southern Quality," 100.

104. McLuhan, "Southern Quality," 114. See also McLuhan to Tate, 24 Aug., 13 Sept. 1945, folder 6, box 29, Tate Papers.

105. Cheney, "What Endures in the South?," 409–10.

106. Kirk, *Program for Conservatives*, 296.

107. Viereck, "Rootless 'Roots,'" 219.

Chapter Six

1. Miller, *Emigrants and Exiles*, 6.

2. Ibid., vii.

3. Sullivan, *In Praise of Blood Sports and Other Essays*, 28.

4. In preparing a forthcoming biography of Richard Weaver, Ted J. Smith III has assembled many sources on Weaver, including much correspondence. On the misconception that Weaver was reclusive and hermitlike, see Smith, introduction to Smith, *In Defense of Tradition*, xiii–xx.

5. Nash, *Conservative Intellectual Movement in America*, 36–42; Nash, "Historical Roots of Contemporary American Conservatism," 297; Himmelstein, *To the Right*, 50; Forrest McDonald, "Conservatism," in Greene, *Encyclopedia of American Political History*, 1:366; "In Memoriam: Richard M. Weaver," 2.

6. Biographical information on Richard Weaver can be found in some of the documents collected by Gerald Thomas Goodnight in his dissertation, "Rhetoric and Culture," 669–75; also see ibid., 467–68; Smith, introduction to Smith, *In Defense of Tradition*, xvii, xxv; Ted J. Smith III, "How *Ideas Have Consequences* Came to Be Written," in Smith, *Steps toward Restoration*, 6–7; Young, *Richard M. Weaver*, 1–4, 15–18; Weaver, "Up from Liberalism," 21–32; Nash, *Conservative Intellectual Movement in America*, 37–39; and Duffy and Jacobi, *Politics of Rhetoric*, 2–6. For Polly Weaver Beaton's comments, see Duffy and Jacobi, *Politics of Rhetoric*, 5. On Weaver's mother's family, see Amyx, "Weaver the Liberal," 102. A biography of Weaver currently being written by Ted J. Smith III, a communications professor, promises to surpass those available.

7. She wrote this the year before Weaver's death. Goodnight, "Rhetoric and Culture," 467.

8. Weaver mentions taking motor trips with his mother in Weaver to Russell Kirk, 15 Feb. 1958, 2 June 1959, Russell Kirk Papers, in possession of Russell Kirk estate, Mecosta, Michigan.

9. Mark Ashin, "A Tribute to Richard Weaver," *Chicago Maroon*, 5 Apr. 1963, 3. A copy of this may be found in the "Weaver, Richard M." file, box 28, General Correspondence, William F. Buckley Jr. Papers, Manuscripts and Archives, Sterling Memorial Library, Yale University, New Haven, Connecticut. Smith, introduction to Smith, *In Defense of Tradition*, xviii; Young, *Richard M. Weaver*, 167; Kendall, "How to Read Richard Weaver," 81 n. 20; Russell Kirk, "Foreword," in Weaver, *Visions of Order*, viii; Ebbitt, "Richard M. Weaver, Teacher of Rhetoric," 415. See also Wilma R. Ebbitt, "Richard Weaver: Friend and Colleague," in Smith, *Steps toward Restoration*.

10. Amyx, "Weaver the Liberal," 104–6; Weaver, "Up from Liberalism," 21–23; Goodnight, "Rhetoric and Culture," 674–75, 752–53; Young, *Richard M. Weaver*, 23, 31–33; Smith, "How *Ideas Have Consequences* Came to Be Written," 10–11. Richard Weaver and Clifford Amyx's comment on *I'll Take My Stand* is in *Kentucky Kernel*, 7 Aug. 1931. On

Weaver's extracurricular activities, see "Richard Weaver Wins Peace Prize," *Lexington Leader,* 24 May 1929, clipping, Alumni/Student File, University of Kentucky Archives, University of Kentucky, Lexington, Kentucky; "U.K. Students Join League for Industrial Democracy," *Louisville Courier-Journal,* 20 Mar. 1929, clipping, Liberal Club folder, Departmental File, University of Kentucky Archives; "Pamphlet Outlines Aims and Principals of Liberal Club, New Organization at U.K.," clipping, [Mar.–Apr. 1929], Liberal Club folder, Departmental File, University of Kentucky Archives. (Weaver denied that the Liberal Club was affiliated with the League for Industrial Democracy. "Liberal Club Independent," *Lexington Herald,* 10 Nov. 1929, clipping, Liberal Club folder, Departmental File, University of Kentucky Archives) *Kentucky Kernel,* 1 Apr. 1932, 1; "Harlan Trip Planned by U.K. Liberal Club," *Lexington Herald,* 3 Apr, 1932, clipping, Herndon Evans Collection, University of Kentucky Special Collections, University of Kentucky, Lexington; "Rap Action of Liberal Club," *Lexington Herald,* 8 Apr. 1932, Liberal Club folder, Departmental File, University of Kentucky Archives; "University Club Draws Fire from Harlan," *Lexington Herald,* 6 Apr. 1932, Liberal Club folder, Departmental File, University of Kentucky Archives.

11. Weaver, "Revolt against Humanism," 73, 36–39.

12. Ibid., 77, 79–81.

13. Weaver, "Up from Liberalism," 23. The essay was written in 1953 although only published in an apparently revised form in the winter of 1958–59. Weaver to Kirk, 27 July 1958, Kirk Papers, Mecosta.

14. Weaver, "Up from Liberalism," 24; Weaver to John Randolph, 26 Jan. 1939, quoted in Smith, "How *Ideas Have Consequences* Came to Be Written," 11. Weaver's use of religious imagery to describe his turn toward Agrarianism is evident early: he described a "kind of religious conver-

sion" to the "Church of Agrarianism" in a letter to John Randolph. See Weaver to Randolph, 20 Jan. 1942, quoted in Smith, "How *Ideas Have Consequences* Came to Be Written," 11.

15. Goodnight, "Rhetoric and Culture," 669, 675.

16. Cleanth Brooks to Kendall Beaton, 13 May 1963, folder 320, box 15, Brooks Papers; Brooks to Robert Hamlin, 9 Sept. 1966, ibid.

17. Weaver, *Southern Tradition at Bay,* 223–24, 47–48.

18. Ibid., 224, 229. Weaver mentions revising the dissertation in an undated letter to Brooks that seems to have been written sometime in 1943–44. Weaver to Brooks, n.d., folder 320, box 15, Brooks Papers. Weaver revised the dissertation in 1944–45. William Terry Couch of the University of North Carolina Press had agreed to publish it. However, Couch left North Carolina to become director of the University of Chicago Press in September 1945. Couch was unable to publish the work at Chicago, and his successor at North Carolina rejected the manuscript. Smith, "How *Ideas Have Consequences* Came to Be Written," 16, 18–19. See also George Core and M. E. Bradford, preface to Weaver, *Southern Tradition at Bay,* 12.

19. Weaver, *Southern Tradition at Bay,* 111; Weaver, "Older Religiousness of the South," 237–38.

20. Weaver, *Southern Tradition at Bay,* 56, 59; Weaver, "Aspects of the Southern Philosophy," 6; Weaver, "Up from Liberalism," 28.

21. Weaver, *Southern Tradition at Bay,* 393–94; Weaver to Randolph, 16 Jan. 1945, 24 Aug. 1945, quoted in Smith, "How *Ideas Have Consequences* Came to Be Written," 17–18. The epilogue to *Southern Tradition at Bay* was written in 1945. Smith, "How *Ideas Have Consequences* Came to Be Written," 16.

22. Weaver to Brooks, 30 Mar. 1944, 27 May 1944, 2 May 1957, folder 320, box 15, Brooks Papers. On Weaver's position at North Carolina State, see Weaver to Brooks, n.d., ibid.

23. Dzuback, *Robert M. Hutchins*, ix; Rubin, *Making of Middlebrow Culture*, 186–97; McNeill, *Hutchins' University*, 34–40, 68–69.

24. *One in Spirit*, 85, 88; McNeill, *Hutchins' University*, 141–43; Young, *Richard M. Weaver*, 156. For Weaver's teaching award, see Scotchie, *Vision of Richard Weaver*, 9.

25. Weaver, "Up from Liberalism," 29–30.

26. Weaver turned his attention to chivalry periodically throughout the 1940s and 1950s. See Weaver, "Southern Chivalry and Total War," 267–78; Weaver, *Ideas Have Consequences*, 175–76, and Weaver, *Visions of Order*, 92–112.

27. Weaver, *Ideas Have Consequences*, 175; Young, *Richard M. Weaver*, 167.

28. Weaver to Brooks, 31 May 1948, folder 320, box 15, Brooks Papers; Smith, "How *Ideas Have Consequences* Came to Be Written," 19–20, 23–25; Smith, introduction to Smith, *In Defense of Tradition*, xxxv. The editorial process of the manuscript can be tracked in Fred Wieck to Brooks, 14 Dec. 1946, folder 320, box 15, Brooks Papers; Weaver to Brooks, 13 Jan., 1 May, 24 May, 12 July 1947, Brooks Papers.

29. Weaver to Brooks, 28 Jan. 1948, folder 320, box 15, Brooks Papers. The reviewers' comments can be found on the back of the 1984 paper edition of the book from University of Chicago Press and in a full-page advertisement in the *New York Herald Tribune Weekly Book Review*, Feb. 29, 1948, 17. Weaver felt the title to be "hopelessly banal." Smith, "How *Ideas Have Consequences* Came to Be Written," 27.

30. Weaver to Brooks, 31 May 1948, folder 320, box 15, Brooks Papers; Nash, *Conservative Intellectual Movement in America*, 41–42. Weaver's chairman, Crane, was irritated with the book, convinced that it drew unflattering attention to the University of Chicago's English department. Weaver to Brooks, 31 May 1948, folder 320, box 15, Brooks Papers.

31. Weaver, *Ideas Have Consequences*, 1–3. Cf. Marshall McLuhan on Perry Miller's analysis of Puritanism: "Two things most important for an understanding of the quarrel between North and South are not shown by Miller: first, the violent European opposition of the humanist to the dialectical mind in the sixteenth and seventeenth centuries; and, second, the age-old quarrel between these minds in fifth century Athens, twelfth century France, and fourteenth century Italy. This is not the place to provide such an historical picture. But were the New England mind as capable of perceiving its own roots in the dialectics of Abelard and Ockham (striving to settle the problems of metaphysics, theology, and politics as though they were problems in logic) as the South has been able to feel and to focus its own forensic tradition of Ciceronian humanism, then some qualifying modesty might have gotten into the dispute a lot earlier." Herbert Marshall McLuhan, "The Southern Quality," in Tate, *Southern Vanguard*, 107. Weaver's indebtedness to another essay by McLuhan is expressed in Weaver to Brooks, 20 Mar. 1944, folder 320, box 15, Brooks Papers.

32. Weaver, *Ideas Have Consequences*, 3–6, 2, 16.

33. Smith, "How *Ideas Have Consequences* Came to Be Written," 17–18, 22.

34. Weaver, "Humanism in an Age of Science," 17–18.

35. Weaver, "Up from Liberalism," 30; Weaver, *Southern Tradition at Bay*, 215.

36. Weaver, *Ideas Have Consequences*, 18, 19.

37. Ibid., 21–22. See Niebuhr, *Children of Light and the Children of Darkness*.

38. Weaver, *Ideas Have Consequences*, 64–65, 31–32.

39. Ibid., 102–3, 29. Anticipating some of the contemporary critic Neil Postman's arguments about the detrimental effect of television on logical context, Weaver condemned the randomness of radio, which broke down any sense of hierarchy. Cf. Postman, *Amusing Ourselves to Death*.

40. Weaver, *Ideas Have Consequences*, 113, 116, 126–28.

41. Ibid., 133, 172, 148, 170–72, 175, 177–80.

42. Nisbet, *Conservatism*, 67; Weaver, *Ethics of Rhetoric*, 173.

43. Richard M. Weaver, "Rhetorical Strategies of the Conservative Cause: Address at the University of Wisconsin," 26 Apr. 1959, in Goodnight, "Rhetoric and Culture," 585.

44. Weaver to Randolph, 27 Dec. 1942, quoted in Smith, "How *Ideas Have Consequences* Came to Be Written," 17; Weaver to Brooks, 30 Mar. 1944, 22 Nov. 1946, folder 320, box 15, Brooks Papers; Weaver, "Up from Liberalism," 32.

45. Weaver to Brooks, 8 May 1955, folder 320, box 15, Brooks Papers; Gottfried, *Conservative Movement*, 119; Ted J. Smith, preface to Richard M. Weaver, *Visions of Order: The Cultural Crisis of Our Time* (1964; reprint, Bryn Mawr: Intercollegiate Studies Institute, 1995), xii; Young, *Richard M. Weaver*, 175. George H. Nash noted that the Volker Fund supported some traditionalist scholarship. Nash, *Conservative Intellectual Movement in America*, 182–83. For Weaver's involvement with the Intercollegiate Society of Individualists, see Goodnight, "Rhetoric and Culture," 431.

46. Weaver, "Agrarianism in Exile," 588–89, 592, 605.

47. Ibid., 597–98, 602.

48. Donald Davidson to Weaver, 25 Mar. 1949, folder 3, box 1, Richard Weaver Papers, Special Collections and University Archives, Heard Library, Vanderbilt University, Nashville, Tennessee.

49. "Notes on 'Agrarianism in Exile,' " 7, 5, included with Davidson to Weaver, 25 Mar. 1949, folder 3, box 1, Weaver Papers. "If we had kept up a continuous fight on the scale we used in the early 1930's," Davidson wrote Weaver, "I can see no reason why we could not have gained at least a foothold, despite the Roosevelt administration, the war, etc. If we had done so, then the Thurmond

movement of 1948 would have had a broader base and perhaps better leadership." Davidson to Weaver, 25 Mar. 1949, ibid.

50. Weaver, "Agrarianism in Exile," 602, 605. Revealingly, Davidson approved this aspect of Weaver's argument: "Your point about the 'Humanists' is excellent. You are right in our emphasis on the theistic aspects of agrarian doctrine." "Notes on 'Agrarianism in Exile,' " 9.

51. James Burnham to Buckley, 23 Oct. 1957, "Inter-Office Memos, 1955–1957" folder, box 2, General Correspondence, Buckley Papers; Burnham to Editor, 24 Nov. 1957, ibid.

52. Meyer, "Richard M. Weaver: An Appreciation," 243–44, 247. On Frank S. Meyer, see Nash, *Conservative Intellectual Movement in America*, 98; Wills, *Confessions of a Conservative*, 38–48. Meyer was also suspicious of James Burnham, who, along with Willmoore Kendall, had worked for the Central Intelligence Agency; Meyer seriously considered the notion that Burnham might be running the *National Review* for the CIA. Ibid., 46.

53. See, for example, Meyer, *What Is Conservatism?*, 3–9; Frank S. Meyer, "Conservatism," in Goldwin, *Left, Right, and Center*, 5–8.

54. Meyer, *In Defense of Freedom*, 92–93, 133.

55. Richard M. Weaver, "Education and the Individual," in Weaver, *Life without Prejudice and Other Essays*, 62, 64. For similar arguments, see a lecture delivered by Weaver at Holy Name College in Washington, D.C., "Conservatism and Liberalism," 15 Oct. 1960, pp. 10–11, folder 6, box 2, Weaver Papers.

56. Weaver, *Ideas Have Consequences*, 181.

57. Weaver, "Two Types of Individualism," 122.

58. Weaver, *Visions of Order*, 16, 12, 18. On the writing of *Visions of Order*, see Smith, preface to the 1995 Intercollegiate Studies Institute's reprint of *Visions of Order*, xii–xiii.

59. Weaver to Brooks, 4 Dec.

1953, 10 Sept. 1954, folder 320, box 15, Brooks Papers. The nature of Weaver and Kendall's planned project is unknown. Kendall, "How to Read Richard Weaver," 78, 81. Weaver and Kendall may well have become acquainted before the 1950s. Kendall and Cleanth Brooks were good friends, having been on the faculty together at Louisiana State University, where Kendall was an instructor from 1937 through 1940, and Yale University. On their friendship, see Winchell, *Cleanth Brooks and the Rise of Modern Criticism*, 134–36, 261–62, 286, 304–5. Brooks said of Kendall: "I may have helped push him to the right, but I didn't mean to push him quite so far" (261).

60. Weaver, *Visions of Order*, 23–24, 26. Cf. Weaver on radicalism: "The constant warfare which it wages against anything that has *status* in the world, or against all the individual, particular, unique existences of the world which do not fit into a rationalistic pattern, is but a mask for the denial of substance. If one benighted class of men begins by assuming that whatever is, is right, they [radicals] begin by assuming that whatever is, is wrong." Weaver, "Up from Liberalism," 26.

61. Weaver, *Visions of Order*, 41.

62. Richard M. Weaver, "The Role of Education in Shaping Our Society," 25 Oct. 1961, in Goodnight, "Rhetoric and Culture," 629; Richard M. Weaver, "Conservatism and Libertarianism," in Weaver, *Life without Prejudice*, 164. For Weaver's strictures on "anarchic individualism," see Weaver, "Two Types of American Individualism," and Weaver, "Anatomy of Freedom," 444, his review of Frank S. Meyer's *In Defense of Freedom*.

63. "Segregation and Democracy," 5; Meyer, "In the Great Tradition," 527; Nash, *Conservative Intellectual Movement*, 200, 202.

64. "Why the South Must Prevail," 149; Bozell, "Open Question," 209; "A Clarification," *National Review*,

7 Sept. 1957, 199; Judis, *William F. Buckley, Jr.*, 138–39.

65. Buckley, *Up from Liberalism*, 125, 128.

66. Judis, *William F. Buckley, Jr.*, 192–93, 283–87. Senator Barry Goldwater, in a similar way, expressed his moral opposition to Barnett's action but supported Mississippi's right to block James Meredith's admission to the University of Mississippi. Goldberg, *Barry Goldwater*, 154.

67. William F. Buckley Jr.'s campaign was in part a move against the liberal Republican John V. Lindsay and in part a quixotic stunt suited to Buckley's personality. Buckley's central issues were a residency requirement for welfare and a rejection of a police civilian review board. He stressed the rising black crime rate in his speeches and was frequently accused of racism by his opponents. Buckley succeeded in winning 13 percent of the vote, doing best among middle- and upper-middle-class ethnic suburban voters. Judis, *William F. Buckley, Jr.*, 237–38, 244, 255–56.

68. Goldberg, *Barry Goldwater*, 140, 154, 197, 232.

69. Weaver to Buckley, 31 Oct. 1962, "Weaver, Prof. R. M." folder, box 23, General Correspondence, Buckley Papers. In 1961 Weaver had written that he found the *National Review* indispensable on integration issues. Weaver to Buckley, 9 Mar. 1961, "Weaver, Richard M." folder, box 17, ibid.

70. Weaver, *Southern Tradition at Bay*, 55, 52, 169, 266.

71. Weaver, "Integration Is Communization," 67–68. Paul Gottfried claims that Weaver participated in white Citizens' Councils, but he does not cite a source for this claim. Gottfried, *Conservative Movement*, 28. Weaver did attend a meeting of the officers of the pro-segregation Tennessee Federation for Constitutional Government at Donald Davidson's home in November 1955, as indicated in contemporary correspondence and

the recollection of Jack Kershaw, a member of the federation. I am indebted to Ted W. Smith III for this information.

72. Richard M. Weaver, "The South and the American Union," in Rubin and Kilpatrick, *Lasting South*, 65–66; Weaver to Kirk, 15 Feb. 1958, Kirk Papers, Mecosta.

73. Weaver, *Visions of Order*, 21, 15, 14.

74. Ibid., 6.

75. Ibid., 7–8.

76. "Address of Dr. Richard M. Weaver, Chicago University," to a family meeting, 10 Aug. 1950, in Goodnight, "Rhetoric and Culture," 471.

Chapter Seven

1. Robert Penn Warren, "A Reminiscence," in Egerton, *Nashville*, 206–7; Watkins, Hiers, and Weeks, *Talking with Robert Penn Warren*, 290.

2. Robert Penn Warren, *The Legacy of the Civil War: Meditations on the Centennial*, in Warren, *Robert Penn Warren Reader*, 304.

3. Warren, *All the King's Men*, 436.

4. Wood, "On Native Soil," 182, 183. "Donald Davidson was a racist whose name was never spoken in our home," declared Robert Penn Warren's daughter, Rosanna, in a 1993 interview with Mark Royden Winchell. Winchell, *Where No Flag Flies*, 298.

5. Warren, *Jefferson Davis Gets His Citizenship Back*, 15–20; Watkins, *Then and Now*, 18–19, 32–33, 52–53; Watkins, Hiers, and Weaks, *Talking with Robert Penn Warren*, 250–51; Warren, *Portrait of a Father*, 26–27, 36, 39–41; Blotner, *Robert Penn Warren*, 6–7, 9, 24–26, 119–20, 144–45.

6. Watkins, Hiers, and Weaks, *Talking with Robert Penn Warren*, 124, 2; Watkins, *Then and Now*, 27–28, 35–37, 42–45; Warren, *Portrait of a Father*, 24–25, 43, 48–50; Bohner, *Robert Penn Warren*, 11; Warren, *Jefferson Davis Gets His Citizenship Back*, 1; Blotner, *Robert Penn Warren*, 11–12, 14–15, 17. According to Joseph Blotner, both

Warren's paternal great-grandfather and grandfather fought at Shiloh (13).

7. Watkins, Hiers, and Weaks, *Talking with Robert Penn Warren*, 375, 251–52; Warren, "Reminiscence," 205; Bohner, *Robert Penn Warren*, 9; Watkins, *Then and Now*, 54–55; Blotner, *Robert Penn Warren*, 30, 50–51.

8. Blotner, *Robert Penn Warren*, 43–52. The exact reasons for Robert Penn Warren's attempted suicide are difficult to discern. Warren's travails can be traced in Jesse Wills to Allen Tate, 22 May 1924, 22 June 1924, folder 4, box 46, Allen Tate Papers, Manuscript Division, Department of Rare Books and Special Collections, Princeton University Library, Princeton University, Princeton, New Jersey; Lyle Lanier to Tate, 18 Mar. 1924, 19 Apr. 1924, folder 8, box 27, Tate Papers; Robert Penn Warren to Tate, "Wednesday" [May 1924], 21 Mar. 1924, folder 28, box 44, Tate Papers; Donald Davidson to Tate, 21 May 1924, box 18, folder 1, Tate Papers; Tate to Davidson, 24 May 1924, 26 May [1924], box 10, folder 23, Donald Davidson Papers, Special Collections and University Archives, Heard Library, Vanderbilt University, Nashville, Tennessee. See also Singal, *War Within*, 342–44. Allen Tate's initial vehement reaction to the news of Warren's attempted suicide ("I am MAD—mad as hell") is revealing of his own emotional distance from Nashville. He pictured Warren as a sensitive soul crushed by Philistines: "God! I wish I were there. I am sure that I am the only person who doesn't look on Red as a merely interesting monstrosity mostly to be avoided," he wrote Donald Davidson. Tate continued, "He has a peculiar nature, to be sure, but it is a nature quite susceptible of definition. His spiritual loneliness and his thirst for companionship and genuine affection are back of this; he's in a social order where men are afraid to love each other." He dismissed Warren's own explanation for his action, assigning the cause instead to Warren's having

been "beaten down so constantly and brutally." "I get so goddam mad I can't breathe," Tate raged. Tate to Davidson, 24 May 1924, folder 23, box 10, Davidson Papers. Two days later, he wrote Davidson again, asking him to discount the "vehemence" of the previous letter. Tate to Davidson, 26 May [1924], Davidson Papers. Warren claimed later in life that the attempt resulted from his fear of blindness. Farrell, "Poetry as a Way of Life," 322. Mark Royden Winchell argued that the attempt was due to Warren's sensitive nature, his falling behind in his academic work, and his unrequited love for Chink Nichol. Winchell, *Cleanth Brooks and the Rise of Modern Criticism*, 26, 49.

9. Warren to Tate, 16 Nov. 1978, folder 10, box 9, Additional Correspondence, Tate Papers; Warren, "Reminiscence," 206; Watkins, Hiers, and Weaks, *Talking with Robert Penn Warren*, 288.

10. Watkins, Hiers, and Weaks, *Talking with Robert Penn Warren*, 361; Warren to Tate, 16 Nov. 1978, folder 10, box 9, Additional Correspondence, Tate Papers.

11. Warren, "Reminiscence," 213; Watkins, Hiers, and Weaks, *Talking with Robert Penn Warren*, 272. For Warren's tenure at Louisiana State University and *Southern Review*, see Cutrer, *Parnassus on the Mississippi*. Lewis P. Simpson includes an interesting discussion of Warren's relation to the South and to Baton Rouge, the home of Louisiana State University, in Simpson, *Fable of the Southern Writer*, 132–54. Warren confessed to Simpson that he felt an exile (138).

12. Warren, *John Brown*.

13. Friar and Brinnin, *Modern Poetry*, 542–43.

14. For my general understanding of Warren's existentialist outlook and literary themes, I have relied on Justus, *Achievement of Robert Penn Warren*; Bohner, *Robert Penn Warren*; Casper, *Robert Penn Warren*; Watkins, *Then and Now*; Clark, *American Vision of Robert Penn Warren*; Thomas L. Connelly, "Robert Penn Warren

as Historian," in Edgar, *Southern Renascence Man*; and the chapter on Warren in Singal, *War Within*. For a succinct assessment of Warren's characteristic themes, see King, *Southern Renaissance*, 232.

15. Bohner, *Robert Penn Warren*, 125. Warren used "definition" obsessively in his fiction and poetry of the 1940s and 1950s, Robert Lowell observed. Robert Lowell, Review of Robert Penn Warren, *Brother to Dragons*, in Grimshaw, *Robert Penn Warren's* Brother to Dragons, 165.

16. Warren, "Knowledge and the Image of Man," 187.

17. Roper, *C. Vann Woodward*, 132, 130; Bohner, *Robert Penn Warren*, 9; C. Vann Woodward to author, 22 Sept. 1997 (in author's possession); Walker, *Robert Penn Warren*, 253.

18. All references followed by page numbers in parentheses are taken from Warren, *All the King's Men*. See also ibid., 45.

19. Robert Penn Warren, "Introduction to the Modern Library Edition of *All the King's Men*," in Warren, *Robert Penn Warren Reader*, 228.

20. Warren, "Introduction to the Modern Library Edition of *All the King's Men*," 227.

21. Blotner, *Robert Penn Warren*, 125–26, 145, 156, 242–43, 249, 251–60; Winchell, *Cleanth Brooks and the Rise of Modern Criticism*, 130–31, 257.

22. For an essay that relates the end of Warren's period of "drought" in lyric poetry to his second marriage, see Miller, "Faith in Good Works," 58.

23. James, *Writings, 1902–1910*, 538–39.

24. Warren, "John Crowe Ransom," 94–96, 99; Watkins, Hiers, and Weaks, *Talking with Robert Penn Warren*, 382.

25. Warren, "*Nostromo*," 377. Cf. William James's use, in *Pragmatism* (1907), of a similar metaphor in which water is the "world of sensible facts" and air the "world of abstract ideas": "We are like fishes swimming in the sea of sense, bounded above by the superior element, but unable to breathe

it pure or penetrate it. We get our oxygen from it, however, we touch it incessantly, now in this part, now in that, and every time we touch it, we are reflected back into the water with our course re-determined and re-energized. The abstract ideas of which the air consists are indispensable for life, but irrespirable by themselves, as it were, and only active in their re-directing function. All similes are halting, but this one rather takes my fancy. It shows how something, not sufficient for life in itself, may never-theless be an effective determinant of life elsewhere." James, *Writings, 1902–1910,* 541.

26. Warren, *Brother to Dragons,* xii.

27. Ibid., ix–xii. Boynton Merrill Jr., *Jefferson's Nephews: A Frontier Tragedy* (Princeton: Princeton University Press, 1976), covers the historical background to the incident, which Warren modified in small ways, and is excerpted in Grimshaw, *Robert Penn Warren's* Brother to Dragons, 283–94.

28. Justus, *Achievement of Robert Penn Warren,* 61. Warren visited Rocky Hill, the ruins of the Lewis's home, twice with his father, in 1946 and 1951. Blotner, *Robert Penn Warren,* 284.

29. Quotations taken from Warren, *Brother to Dragons.*

30. Warren, *All the King's Men,* 188–89. See Bohner, *Robert Penn Warren,* 74–77.

31. Watkins, Hiers, and Weaks, *Talking with Robert Penn Warren,* 43.

32. Mooney, *Ghost-Dance Religion,* xi–xii.

33. Kehoe, *Ghost Dance,* 14–15, 17–19, 21–24.

34. Mooney, *Ghost-Dance Religion,* v–vi, ix.

35. Ibid., 1.

36. Ibid., 22–23.

37. Kehoe, *Ghost Dance,* 3, 5; Mooney, *Ghost-Dance Religion,* 14.

38. Kehoe, *Ghost Dance,* 8, 36; Mooney, *Ghost-Dance Religion,* 18.

39. Kehoe, *Ghost Dance,* 8.

40. Ibid., 32–35, 39, 113–21; Wallace, *Death and Rebirth of the Seneca.*

41. Fox, *Reinhold Niebuhr,* 245; Niebuhr, *Irony of American History,* 133, vii–viii, 5, 37, 156.

42. Woodward, *Burden of South-ern History,* 5, 16–21; Woodward to author, 22 Sept. 1997 (in author's possession).

43. Donald Davidson, "Some Day, in Old Charleston," in Davidson, *Still Rebels, Still Yankees,* 223.

44. Egerton, *Speak Now against the Day,* 68–69. Davidson recalled the incident in Davidson to Caroline Gordon, 21 Jan. 1953, folder 34, box 2, Davidson Papers. Tate declared that Mabry's critical distance from the Agrarians derived from his re-bellion against his father's tobacco business—"and," he wrote, "this too influences him in his humanitarian sensibility about negroes and the underdog." Tate to Lincoln Kirstein, 5 Feb. 1933, "Tate, Allen and Caro-line 1933–34, III" folder, *Hound and Horn* Correspondence, *Hound and Horn* Papers, Beinecke Rare Book and Manuscript Library, Yale University, New Haven Connecticut. Tate sig-naled Tom Mabry his willingness to meet with James Weldon Johnson and Langston Hughes outside the South. Winchell, *Where No Flag Flies,* 190–91.

45. Warren to Tate and Gordon, [Nov. 1932], Tate Papers; Watkins, Hiers, and Weaks, *Talking with Robert Penn Warren,* 159; Reddick, "Whose Ordeal?," 9. Warren recalled that his undergraduate roommates brought black students from Fisk to Vanderbilt to talk in the 1920s. In his senior year, he roomed with Saville T. Clark, a left-leaning student who befriended some Fisk students and had them to the room to discuss their conflicts with the Fisk administration. The landlady was scandalized; Warren considered the meeting an "eye-opener." Warren, "Reminiscence," 211; Blotner, *Robert Penn Warren,* 54–55. He remembered, too, that his father placed a high value on being respect-ful to blacks when he was boy, barring the use of the term "nigger" from the Warren home, for example. Warren, *Portrait of a Father,* 14–15.

46. O'Brien, *Idea of the American South*, 17.

47. Tate to Kirstein, 10 May 1933, "Tate, Allen and Caroline 1933–34, III" folder, *Hound and Horn* Correspondence, *Hound and Horn* Papers. The letter is reprinted in Greenbaum, *Hound and Horn*, 145–47.

48. Warren, *Band of Angels*, 186.

49. Winchell, *Where No Flag Flies*, 290; Davidson to W. T. Couch, 13 Oct. 1948, folder 22, box 2, Davidson Papers; O'Brien, *Idea of the American South*, 208; Warren, *Who Speaks for the Negro?*, 127. Davidson was angered by the *Brown* decision, writing in his diary: "U.S. Supreme Court handed down 9–0 decision against segregation—9 justices against how many million white folks in South and elsewhere! A black day. More black days to come. All foreseen, not for that reason either welcome or tolerable." Winchell, *Where No Flag Flies*, 282.

50. Bartley, *Rise of Massive Resistance*, 100, 121–22; McMillen, *Citizens' Council*, 109–10; Doyle, *Nashville since the 1920s*, 237. Davidson alluded to the Tennessee organization's connection to the larger Federation for Constitutional Government in Davidson to John Donald Wade, 4 Aug. 1955, folder 48, box 2, Davidson Papers.

51. Davidson to Wade, 4 Aug. 1955, folder 48, box 2, Davidson Papers; Davidson to Louis D. Rubin Jr., 2 Sept. 1955, ibid.

52. Davidson to Floyd C. Watkins, 11 June 1956, folder 50, box 2, Davidson Papers; Davidson to Stark Young, 29 Sept. 1952, folder 33, ibid.

53. *Tyranny at Oak Ridge*, 15. Davidson's claim of responsibility for the pamphlet's contents is on p. 3. The pamphlet can be found in folder 3, box 39, Davidson Papers.

54. Graham, *Crisis in Print*, 82, 82 n. 42, 91–92, 104–6; McMillen, *Citizens' Council*, 110–11, 309; Bartley, *Rise of Massive Resistance*, 14, 99. On the black community and the process of desegregation in Nashville, see Pride and Woodard, *Burden of Busing*.

55. Graham, *Crisis in Print*, 93,

99, 99 n. 12, 103; McMillen, *Citizens' Council*, 108; Muse, *Ten Years of Prelude*, 97–98; Pride and Woodard, *Burden of Busing*, 56; Davidson to Thomas J. B. Walsh, 2 Sept. 1956, folder 50, box 2, Davidson Papers. See also Winchell, *Where No Flag Flies*, 292–95.

56. Davidson, "New South and the Conservative Tradition," 141–42.

57. Ibid., 143–44.

58. Weaver, "Integration Is Communization," 67–68.

59. Davidson to Warren, 22 Aug. 1958, folder 400, box 21, Robert Penn Warren Papers, Beinecke Rare Book and Manuscript Library, Yale University, New Haven, Connecticut; Tate to Warren, 5 Oct. 1960, folder 1376, box 70, ibid.; Warren to Donald R. Ellegood, 3 Jan. 1956, folder 400, box 21, ibid. Tate wrote to Davidson that, after talking with Ransom, they both agreed they would feel uncomfortable in an integrated South. "It would not be my world: I would not know how to conduct myself." But he saw integration as inevitable. "Since desegregation is coming, I believe that the proper course is for the South to take it over, enforce it slowly, and to accomplish it with order and dignity." He expressed support for black rights but disapproval for the actions of the Supreme Court. "Whether we like it or not, the Negro has got to have the vote, and let the chips fall where they may." Tate to Davidson, 19 Oct. 1962, folder 5, box 11, Davidson Papers. Ransom, too, accepted, and supported, desegregation. Ransom to Warren, 14 Apr. 1955, in Young and Core, *Selected Letters*, 375. In the 1060s, after the Tennessee Federation for Constitutional Government was defunct, Davidson helped establish a local chapter of the White Citizens' Council. Winchell, *Where No Flag Flies*, 352.

60. Prothro, "A Southerner's View of a Southerner's Book," 46.

61. Warren, *Segregation*, 3, 8. Davidson expressed his opinion of Warren's thesis in the book to him directly: "You were badly off the beam,

both as to facts and your interpretation of facts, since there is no 'inner conflict' of the sort you attempt to define—and certainly no 'guilt complex'—I can't imagine how you ever developed such an interpretation." Davidson to Warren, 12 Jan. 1958, folder 400, box 21, Warren Papers. In his diary, Davidson referred to Warren's work as his "horrible little book on Segregation": "Red 'interviewing' himself—an egotistical spectacle one wouldn't have expected of hardboiled Red. He joins the 'enemy,' pretty much; debates with his 'conscience' in public; and makes money out of it!" Winchell, *Where No Flag Flies*, 297.

62. Warren, *Segregation*, 32, 64, 65; Reddick, "Whose Ordeal?," 9.

63. Warren, *Segregation*, 55–56, 22–23.

64. Warren, *Brother to Dragons*, 215; Warren, *Legacy of the Civil War*, 284. It is worth noting that Richard M. Weaver was critical of *The Legacy of the Civil War*, arguing that antebellum southern culture was a "paradigmatic ideal" and finding Warren insufficiently appreciative of the war's tragedy: "What was lost was a transcendent idea of community, and a kind of integrity of the personality." Weaver, "Altered Stand," 389.

65. Warren, *Who Speaks for the Negro?*, 17.

66. Ibid., 36, 52–58, 266. See also Warren, "Malcolm X," 161–71.

67. Warren, *Who Speaks for the Negro?*, 413–15, 406–8; "On Civil Disobedience and the Algerian War," 477–78; "Faces of Change," 84A–84B; *Newsweek*, 5 July 1965, 2. For the 1965 incident at the University of Mississippi, see Blotner, *Robert Penn Warren*, 359–60.

68. Warren, *Who Speaks for the Negro?*, 334, 345–46, 348–50. Tate, too, shared Warren's admiration for Ellison. "When the smoke of battle begins to clear," he wrote Warren after reading the book, "he will be there as the authentic culture-hero." Tate to Warren, 8 June 1965, folder 1377, box 70, Warren Papers.

69. Warren, "Episode in the Dime Store," 654–56; Warren, "Faulkner," 510.

Chapter Eight

1. Clyde N. Wilson, telephone interview by author, 6 July 1998 (notes in author's possession). For an influential popular analysis of the declining South, see Egerton, *Americanization of Dixie*. A more recent analysis of the South's status in the United States is Applebome, *Dixie Rising*.

2. Bartley, *New South*, 18–19; Boles, *South through Time*, 455–57, 463–69; Grantham, *South in Modern America*, 261, 265–68; Schulman, *From Cotton Belt to Sunbelt*, 102. The classic account of the impact of air-conditioning on the South is Arsenault, "End of the Long Hot Summer."

3. Bartley, *New South*, 123, 126–27, 134, 146; Grantham, *South in Modern America*, 261; Fite, *Cotton Fields No More*, 207; Cooper and Terrill, *American South*, 738, 740.

4. Black and Black, *Vital South*, 217; Weisbrot, *Freedom Bound*, 6–7; Boles, *South through Time*, 491, 504; Franklin and Moss, *From Slavery to Freedom*, 525, 528; Grantham, *South in Modern America*, 286–87.

5. Cooper, and Terrill, *American South*, 720; Diamond, *Roads to Dominion*, 62, 64; Jonathan Rieder, "The Rise of the 'Silent Majority,'" in Fraser and Gerstle, *Rise and Fall of the New Deal Order*, 254.

6. Bartley, *New South*, 383, 397, 411; Black and Black, *Vital South*, 4, 218, 325–26; Grantham, *South in Modern America*, 302–3. On realignment in the South generally, see Black and Black, *Vital South*. On George Wallace more generally, see Carter, *From George Wallace to Newt Gingrich*, and Carter, *Politics of Rage*.

7. Fifteen Southerners, *Why the South Will Survive*, vii; Wilson interview. Ronald Reagan appointed David B. Sentelle to the United States Court of Appeals for the District of Columbia in 1987. As one of the judges on the panel overseeing appointment of independent counsels,

Sentelle was instrumental in the appointment of Kenneth Starr to investigate President Bill Clinton. Critics charge that Sentelle was influenced by North Carolina senator Lauch Faircloth, a Republican opponent of Clinton's.

8. Fifteen Southerners, *Why the South Will Survive*, 1.

9. Ibid., 61, 63.

10. Ibid., 61–65.

11. Ibid., 20, 35, 2.

12. One thinks also of *The Dukes of Hazzard*, a network television series of the late 1970s in which the male leads raced across the backroads of a southern rural county in a car emblazoned with the Confederate battle flag.

13. Fifteen Southerners, *Why the South Will Survive*, 45–46, 49.

14. Ibid., 53–54.

15. Ibid., 8, 81–90, 100–103.

16. Ibid., 170, 168–69.

17. Ibid., 171–75, 178, 194, 179, 183.

18. Ibid., 222, 229.

19. King, "South and Cultural Criticism," 705. John Shelton Reed identified the 1979 Columbia meeting as a key organizing event for this group of intellectuals. John Shelton Reed, telephone interview by author, 11 June 1998 (notes in possession of author).

20. Thomas Fleming, the cantankerous and independent editor of *Chronicles*, bridles at the very notion of a coherent intellectual circle. Thomas Fleming to author, 18 Nov. 1998 (in author's possession).

21. Louis D. Rubin Jr.'s study of Ransom, Allen Tate, Donald Davidson, and Robert Penn Warren, *The Wary Fugitives*, is the best literary study of Agrarianism. Louise Cowan's early study of the Fugitive group is still important. Cowan, *Fugitive Group*. Thomas Daniel Young has written the best scholarly biography of Ransom as well as producing an annotated bibliography of Ransom's writings. Young, *Gentleman in a Dustcoat*; Young, *John Crowe Ransom: An Annotated Bibliography*. In collaboration, he has written a brief literary

biography of Davidson as well as compiled a bibliography (with M. Thomas Inge); brought out a selection of Ransom's letters (with George Core); and coedited collections of the correspondence between Davidson and Tate, Andrew Nelson Lytle and Tate, and Tate and John Peale Bishop. Young and Inge, *Donald Davidson*; Young and Inge, *Donald Davidson: An Essay and a Bibliography*; Young and Core, *Selected Letters*; Fain and Young, *Literary Correspondence*; Young and Sarcone, *Lytle-Tate Letters*; Young and Hindle, *Republic of Letters*. M. E. Bradford and Core brought out an edition of Weaver's doctoral dissertation as *The Southern Tradition at Bay*.

22. Bové, *Mastering Discourse*, 116.

23. Simpson, *Fable of the Southern Writer*, 117. On Tate's role in southern literary studies, see Simpson, *Brazen Face of History*, 67. In *Fable of the Southern Writer*, Simpson declared that he, increasingly, sees Tate as central to the cultural history of the South. Simpson, *Fable of the Southern Writer*, 26.

24. Kreyling, *Inventing Southern Literature*, 41.

25. Rubin, *Gallery of Southerners*, 215, xii; Rubin, "Southern Martial Tradition," 289.

26. See, for example, Rubin, "Southern Martial Tradition," 289–92.

27. Louis D. Rubin Jr., "General Longstreet and Me; Or: Refighting the Civil War," unpublished typescript, p. 2 (in author's possession); Rubin, *Mockingbird in the Gum Tree*, 246, 252–53, 260–61; biography of Louis D. Rubin Jr., on "http://www.ncwriters.org/lrubin"; Louis D. Rubin Jr. occasionally worked on copy desks in Wilmington, Delaware, and for the *Baltimore Sun*. Rubin, "General Longstreet and Me," 6. Woodward served on Rubin's doctoral committee. Rubin, "General Longstreet and Me," 8.

28. Rubin, "Gathering of Fugitives," 660; Louis D. Rubin Jr. to Allen Tate, 12 Dec. 1957, folder 71, box 37, Allen Tate Papers, Manuscript

Division, Department of Rare Books and Special Collections, Princeton University Library, Princeton University, Princeton, New Jersey.

29. Rubin, *Faraway Country*, 159, 5.

30. Rubin, *Wary Fugitives*, 222, 224–27.

31. Ibid., 228.

32. See, for example, Louis D. Rubin Jr., "Southern Literature: The Historical Image," in Rubin and Jacobs, *South*, 37; Rubin, *Faraway Country*, 7–9, 14–15; Rubin, *Curious Death of the Novel*, 135–37; Rubin, *Writer in the South*, 107–8, 113.

33. Rubin, *Wary Fugitives*, 74; Walter Sullivan, "Southern Writers in Spiritual Exile," in Simpson, Olney, and Gulledge, *"Southern Review" and Modern Literature*, 108; Winchell, "Whole Horse," 2. For Walter Sullivan's argument concerning the southern renascence, see Sullivan, *Requiem for the Renascence*, and Walter Sullivan, "The Southern Renaissance and the Joycean Aesthetic," in Core, *Southern Fiction Today*.

34. Simpson, *Brazen Face of History*, 71, 72–79, 238, 242–43, 255.

35. See, for example, Rubin's denial that the Old South possessed a superior moral structure to modernity in Core, *Southern Fiction Today*, 44–45. Also see Rubin, *Curious Death of the Novel*, 277–78.

36. O'Brien, "Last Theologians," 405, 408.

37. Rubin, "General Longstreet and Me," 8–9; Rubin to author, 27 July 2000. Davidson avidly supported James J. Kilpatrick's endeavors. Davidson and the Tennessee Federation for Constitutional Government championed the cause of interposition—the idea that a state has the right to interpose itself between an unjust and unconstitutional federal law and its own citizens, thus nullifying the federal law. In a short assessment of Kilpatrick's *The Sovereign States* (1957), perhaps written for the publisher, Davidson praised Kilpatrick: "His great distinction—and his great service as a patriot and thinker—is that he has lifted an ex-

ceedingly dangerous sectional quarrel into its proper and inescapable historical perspective and underlined its truly national meaning." Donald Davidson, "A Comment on James Jackson Kilpatrick's The Sovereign States," folder 4, box 37, Donald Davidson Papers, University Archives and Special Collections, Heard Library, Vanderbilt University, Nashville, Tennessee. Kilpatrick's writings are treated in Nash, *Conservative Intellectual Movement in America*, 200–202. For several years, Rubin wrote a weekly book column for the *Richmond News-Leader*, beginning in 1950. Rubin, "General Longstreet and Me," 6.

38. Rubin, "General Longstreet and Me," 9; Rubin to Robert Penn Warren, 12 Sept. 1956, folder 1197, box 60, Robert Penn Warren Papers, Beinecke Rare Book and Manuscript Library, Yale University, New Haven, Connecticut; Rubin to Tate, 1 Mar. 1974, Additional Correspondence, folder 17, box 7, Tate Papers. See also Rubin to Warren, 5 Oct. 1956, folder 1197, box 60, Warren Papers.

39. Rubin and Kilpatrick, *Lasting South*, ix; Louis D. Rubin Jr., "An Image of the South," in ibid., 1–6, 10, 12.

40. Rubin and Jacobs, *South*, 15; Rubin, *Curious Death of the Novel*, 134, 137; Core, *Southern Fiction Today*, 47.

41. Wilson interview; Cartwright, "Southern Discomfort," 222.

42. Wilson interview; Reed interview; John Shelton Reed, "Taking a Stand," typescript version of article originally published in *News and Observer* (in author's possession). "Taking a Stand" was reprinted as "On the Agrarians' *I'll Take My Stand*," in Perkins, *Books of Passage*.

43. Reed interview; John Shelton Reed to author, 11 Nov. 1998 (e-mail; copy in author's possession). John Shelton Reed had a 2-S student deferment until 1968, when such deferments were canceled, at which point he was too old for the draft. Reed to author, 11 Nov. 1998. Clyde Wilson held a similarly ambivalent view of

the Vietnam War, disliking what he perceived as the "anti-Americanism" of the antiwar protesters but believing that the United States should "win or get out." Although married and having a child, Wilson was classified as 1-A but never called up. Clyde Wilson to author, 16 Nov. 1998 (in author's possession).

44. Reed interview; Wilson interview; Wilson to author, 16 Nov. 1998.

45. Thomas Fleming, interview by author, 21 July 1998 (tape in possession of author); Fleming, "Return of the Alien," 10–13; Fleming, "My Old Man," 16–17.

46. Reed interview; Wilson interview; Fleming interview; Smith, *So Good a Cause*, xiii. For Fleming's experiences at the Archibald Rutledge Academy, see Fleming, "It Takes a Village," 12, and Fleming, "Loser in a Lawn Chair," 13. Details concerning early issues of the *Southern Partisan* can be found on a Web page on southern neo-Confederate movements run by Ed Sebesta under the pseudonym "Crawfish." See "http://www.anet-dfw.com/~crawfsh/Reed.html."

47. Fleming interview; Smith, *So Good a Cause*, xii; Applebome, *Dixie Rising*, 120–21.

48. Fleming interview. For information on Fleming's tenure at *Chronicles*, see "http://www.anet-dfw.com/~crawfsh/[RockfordBackground].htm."

49. Wilhelmsen, "Melvin E. Bradford," 3; Thomas H. Landess, "The Education of Mel Bradford: The Vanderbilt Years," in Wilson, *Defender of Southern Conservatism*, 7–9, 15; James McClellan, "Walking the Levee with Mel Bradford," in Wilson, *Defender of Southern Conservatism*, 41; Bradford, "M. E. Bradford," 242; Winchell, "Paleoconservative Imagination," 20; Cartwright, "Southern Discomfort," 222.

50. Bradford, *Remembering Who We Are*, xii.

51. See, for example, Lewis P.

Simpson's comment in Lewis P. Simpson, "Introduction: A Certain Continuity," in Simpson, Olney, and Gulledge, *The "Southern Review" and Modern Literature*, 14.

52. McAllister, *Revolt against Modernity*, 17–21; Winchell, "Extended Family," 201. Richard Weaver was also at LSU at the time, but it is difficult to know if he knew Voegelin personally. For the influence of Eric Voegelin's *New Science of Politics* on Weaver, see Weaver, *Visions of Order*, chap. 7.

53. This summary of gnosticism is taken from Eliade, *Encyclopedia of Modern Religion*, 5:566–80; Cross, *Oxford Dictionary of the Christian Church*, 683–85; Craig, *Routledge Encyclopedia of Philosophy*, 83–85; and *New Catholic Encyclopedia*, 523–28.

54. Voegelin, *New Science of Politics*, 107–9, 122.

55. Ibid., 111–13, 117–19, 122–24, 126–27, 163. For a brief sketch of Voegelin's thought, see McAllister, *Revolt against Modernity*, 21–24; and Nash, *Conservative Intellectual Movement in America*, 49–50.

56. Landess, "Education of Mel Bradford," 16; Bradford, *Remembering Who We Are*, 61; Judis, "Conservative Wars," 16; "M. E. Bradford: An Appreciation," 8, 12.

57. Bradford, *Remembering Who We Are*, xi; Bradford, *Generations of the Faithful Heart*, 18.

58. Bradford, *Remembering Who We Are*, 21; Bradford, *Generations of the Faithful Heart*, 117; Bradford, *Reactionary Imperative*, 10.

59. Bradford, *Better Guide Than Reason*, 208–9. For an analysis of the school of republican revisionist historians, see Rodgers, "Republicanism," 11–38.

60. Bradford, *Better Guide Than Reason*, xviii, 7, 35.

61. Bradford, *Remembering Who We Are*, 13; Bradford, *Reactionary Imperative*, 141, 123–24, 128.

62. Bradford, *Reactionary Imperative*, 129.

63. Ibid., 59; Bradford, *Generations of the Faithful Heart*, 75.

64. The letter is quoted by Simpson in Simpson, "Story of M. E. Bradford," 103. Simpson found such talk disconcerting at the time, which from the context of his article seems to be 1969–70. Bradford's attitude, Simpson believed, "implied a developing tendency by Bradford to take Davidson's advice about the duty of the Southern writer more literally than Davidson himself did." Ibid.

65. Bradford, "Dividing the House," 10–11, 21 n. 12, 15–17, 19, 23 n. 68; Bradford, *Better Guide Than Reason*, 44, 215, 56 n. 36; Bradford, *Remembering Who We Are*, 144, 146–53; Bradford, *Reactionary Imperative*, 222–25, 227 n. 18; Bradford, *Against the Barbarians*, 231, 237–40, 245.

66. Simpson, "Story of M. E. Bradford," 103; Bradford, *Remembering Who We Are*, 15–16, 24, 74, 76; Bradford, *Reactionary Imperative*, 116, 118.

67. Bradford, *Reactionary Imperative*, 119, 121. The brackets are Bradford's own.

68. Ibid., 129.

69. Bradford, *Remembering Who We Are*, xii, 66, 95, 103; Bradford, *Against the Barbarians*, 71.

70. Fleming, *Politics of Human Nature*, vii, 58; Fleming interview.

71. Fleming, *Politics of Human Nature*, 5–6, 9, 11, 24, 102.

72. Ibid., 231.

73. Ibid., 70, 93–94, 113–15, 117–19, 188, 218.

74. Ibid., 130.

75. Ibid., vii; Fleming interview.

76. Fleming, *Politics of Human Nature*, 155, 159–60, 175, 162–81.

77. Ibid., 187–88, 231; Fleming, "It Takes a Village," 13.

78. Fleming interview; Fleming, *Politics of Human Nature*, 23; Fleming, "Letter from Zagreb," 37; Thomas Fleming, "Old Rights and the New Right," in Whitaker, *New Right Papers*, 183, 189–90; Fleming, "Further Reflections on Violence," 14; Fleming, "Revolution to Save the World," 11.

79. "*Partisan* Conversation: Samuel Francis," 36.

80. Samuel T. Francis, "Message from MARs: The Social Politics of the New Right," in Whitaker, *New Right Papers*, 65–71.

81. See Francis, *Power and History*.

82. Francis, "Secret of the Twentieth Century," 32–33. For a brief statement of Francis's views on managerialism, see Francis, "Force and Idea," 26.

83. Francis, "Nationalism, Old and New," 20–21; Francis, "Principalities and Powers," 10–11.

84. Fleming interview; Simpson, "Four Years Later, Buchanan's Advisers, Not His Words, Draw Cries of Extremism," A16; Francis, "From Household to Nation," 16.

85. Francis, "New Shape of American Politics," 31; Francis, "Revolt of the 300-Pound Beefy Guys," 32; Francis, "New Majority?," 33. For Samuel Francis's assessment of Pat Buchanan's campaigns, see Francis, "Buchanan Revolution, Part I"; Francis, "Buchanan Revolution, Part II"; Francis, "From Household to Nation"; Francis, "Buchanan Victory"; and Francis, "Beyond Conservatism." "*Chronicles* has been to me, in the last ten years, what *National Review* was in the very early 1960's, with this difference: *Chronicles* repeatedly comes to my defense," Pat Buchanan declared in a 2000 preelection interview published in *Chronicles*. Kauffman, "'I'm Liberated; Free at Last!,'" 17.

86. Fleming interview; Clyde Wilson, "As a City upon a Hill," in *Immigration and the American Identity*, 29–30, 34; Fleming, "Real American Dilemma," 8, 10–11.

87. Francis, "Principalities and Powers," 11; Francis, "Story of the Days to Come," 9–10; Fleming, "Broken Promise of American Life," 17.

88. Thomas Fleming, "A Not So Wonderful Life," in *Immigration and the American Identity*, 152.

89. Fleming, "Real American Dilemma," 9; Fleming, "It's Stupid, the Economy," 12–13; Fleming, "In the Time of the Breaking of Nations,"

10–12; Fleming, "Caliban in the Classroom," 11.

90. Fleming, "White Like Me," 10–12. For Fleming's deprecation of racialist thinking, see Fleming, "X2K."

91. Fleming, "Empire's Tattoo," 10, 12. *Chronicles* has adopted a generally antagonistic attitude toward Martin Luther King Jr. In this same article, Fleming characterizes King as a "leftist demagogue who turned an honorable movement for civil rights into a social and political revolution that betrayed his own people while undermining all that was best in the old bourgeois order." He continues: "In his dissolute private life, in his Marxist anti-American principles, in the social destruction he inflicted upon both black and white communities, Martin Luther King, Jr., is the perfect symbol of the new American regime that makes slaves of all of us. . . . Today, the first political holiday of the year honors the man who, while accomplishing nothing, still stands as a symbol representing the destruction of our Constitution, the nationalization of our schools, and the extinction of our political liberty." Ibid., 12. See also Pappas, "Doctor in Spite of Himself"; Pappas, "Houdini of Time"; and Gottfried, "Martin Luther King, Jr., as Conservative Hero."

92. Francis, "A Curriculum of Inclusion," in *Immigration and the American Identity*, 144; Francis, "Forty Years Later," 10–11; Francis, "Prospects for Racial and Cultural Survival," 4.

93. Francis, "Prospects for Racial and Cultural Survival," 1, 4–6.

94. Ibid., 6–7. In a January 1999 *Chronicles* piece, Francis pointed to talk of "*reconquista*" among Hispanic activists as a sign of chronic ethnic conflict in the future. Future conflict in American politics, he argued, would be between those who want the nation to persist and "those who want it to vanish, either into the transnational haze of the New World Order or into the racial-national frag-

ments that can manipulate and exploit its shell." Francis, "Nation within Nations," 22–23.

95. Fleming interview.

96. Bradford, "Sacrilege and Cupidity," 40; Bradford, "Faulkner, James Baldwin, and the South," 431–32, 441 n. 1. For a defense of prejudice by Richard Weaver, see Weaver, "Life without Prejudice," 4–9.

97. Bradford, "Faulkner, James Baldwin, and the South," 442 n. 4, 433.

98. Ibid., 436, 437–38.

99. "*Time on the Cross:* Debate," 341. For Bradford's review of Robert W. Fogel's successor volume, *Without Consent or Contract: The Rise and Fall of American Slavery*, see Bradford, "All We Could Want to Know." In it he identified what he considered the moral flaw of slavery: "What finally *was* wrong with the peculiar institution was its denial that all of us live to become morally responsible, insofar as we are able, and can come to practice that providentially intended responsibility only to the degree that we are free" (41).

100. Bradford, *Remembering Who We Are*, 51; Bradford, *Reactionary Imperative*, 97. The logic of Bradford's prescriptive political philosophy left him few intellectual resources with which to adapt to or promote change. This tendency to make history into fate, was, in fact, a debilitating barrier to any effective theory of social change, as Richard H. King has argued. "When Southern conservatives are true to their social and cultural vision, they land in a political dead-end," King observed. "Their political theory—or lack of one—allows them no way to preserve the local or regional society they treasure or to bring it back into line with their traditions." He concluded, "Southern conservatives will the ends but not the means." King, "Anti-Modernists All!," 198.

101. To trace the paleoconservative-neoconservative split in the conservative movement, see Judis, "Conservative Wars"; Judis, "Conservative Crackup," 30–42; Dorrien, *Neo-*

conservative Mind, 341–49; Gerson, *Neoconservative Vision*, 311–15; Diamond, *Roads to Dominion*, 279–88; Frum, *Dead Right*, 133–35; and Gottfried, *Conservative Movement*, 85, 88–92, 144–45. Paleoconservative criticisms of the conservative movement can be found in "The State of Conservatism."

102. The controversy can be traced in *New York Times*, 19 Sept. 1981, 1; *New York Times*, 24 Sept. 1981, B10; Hall, "Bradford's Boosters," D1, D10; Hall, "Bradford Speaks Out," B1, B6; Hall, "Amazing Endowment Scramble," L1, L5–L6; *New York Times*, 14 Nov. 1981, 48. For George F. Will's comments, see Will, "Shrill Assault on Mr. Lincoln," C7. For Bradford's response, see Bradford, "It's George Will Who's Being Shrill," A13. Eric Foner suggested the importance of Bradford's control over federal funds for the humanities in "Lincoln, Bradford, and the Conservatives," 25. Journalist David Frum downplayed Irving Kristol's role in blocking Bradford, citing the Heritage Foundation's Edwin Feulner's claim to have played a much greater role in the affair. Frum, *What's Right*, 62. Paul Gottfried, a regular contributor to *Chronicles*, noted that the Heritage Foundation received more than half its operating budget from neoconservative sources in 1981. Gottfried, "And What Isn't . . . ," 33.

103. Judis, "Conservative Wars," 15–16.

104. Fleming interview; Dorrien, *Neoconservative Mind*, 346–47; Gerson, *Neoconservative Vision*, 311–12; Diamond, *Roads to Dominion*, 284; Gottfried, *Conservative Movement*, 144–45; Lind, *Up from Conservatism*, 226. The Richard John Neuhaus quote from *First Things* 1 (March 1990) is quoted in Dorrien, *Neoconservative Mind*, 347. According to Fleming, Richard John Neuhaus promised to one day "cut you off at the knees," a stance for which Fleming professed a grim respect. Fleming interview.

105. Francis, "Rise and Fall of a Paleoconservative at the *Washington*

Times (Part I)," 35–37; Francis, "Rise and Fall of a Paleoconservative at the *Washington Times* (Part II)," 43–45; *Chronicles* 20 (March 1996): 5; *Chronicles* 20 (July 1996): 4–5. See also D'Souza, *End of Racism*, 387–89.

106. Fleming interview; Fleming, "New Fusionism"; "Conservative Movement, R.I.P.," 20–21; Wilson interview; Gottfried, *Conservative Movement*, 146–48. For Rothbard's sympathies for the Old Right, see Rothbard, "Life in the Old Right," 15–19.

107. For Fleming's reportage from Serbia, see Fleming, "Ghosts in the Graveyard." See also Fleming, "Letter from Zagreb"; Fleming, "Sarajevo Today, Chicago Tomorrow"; Fleming, "Hanging with Our Friends"; and *Chronicles* 19 (Feb. 1995): 5–6. On northern Italy, see Fleming, "Divorce Italian Style"; Fleming, "League of Their Own"; Fleming, "Letter from Italy"; and Fleming, "Cabbages and Worms."

108. Fleming interview; Applebome, *Dixie Rising*, 118, 143; "Hill Leaves Stillman to Run League of the South," *Tuscaloosa News*, 7 July 1999, quoted on "http://www.dixienet.org/press_quotes/inthepress.html"; Cartwright, "Southern Discomfort," 224, 230, 232. Michael Hill and Thomas Fleming, "New Dixie Manifesto—States Rights' Will Rise Again," *Washington Post*, 29 Oct. 1995. The manifesto is available on the League of the South Web site. See "http://www.dixienet.org/slpapers/washpost.html." The "Declaration of Southern Cultural Independence" is available on "http://www.dixienet.org/ls-homepg/declaration.html."

109. Francis, "Secessionist Fantasies," 11; Francis, "Infantile Disorder," 32.

110. Deaton, "*Partisan* Conversation: John Shelton Reed," 31; Reed, *Whistling Dixie*, 19, 78; Reed, *Kicking Back*, 42. For John Shelton Reed's other writings on the South, see Reed, *Enduring South*; Reed, *Southerners*; and Reed, *My Tears Spoiled My Aim*.

111. Reed, *Whistling Dixie*, 22–23,

169; Reed, *Kicking Back*, 42; Applebome, "Could the Old South Be
Resurrected?," B11.

112. Reed, *Whistling Dixie*, 178.

113. Fifteen Southerners, *Why the
South Will Survive*, 24, 23.

114. Ibid., 25–26.

115. Ibid., 24.

116. Ibid., 27.

117. MacIntyre, *After Virtue*, 33–34.

118. Ibid., 156.

119. Bradford, *Remembering Who We
Are*, xii, 65, 72, 85–87.

120. Ibid., 86.

121. Bradford, "Prophetic Voice
of Donald Davidson," 29; Bradford,
Generations of the Faithful Heart, 117,
127, 131–33; Bradford, "Aeschylus in
Nashville," 52. Bradford completed
much research but had finished only
one chapter of the biography at his
death. Winchell, *Where No Flag
Flies*, ix.

122. Bradford, "Donald Davidson
and the Calculus of Memory," 17.

123. Lasch, *True and Only Heaven*,
83.

124. Fifteen Southerners, *Why the
South Will Survive*, 224–25; Lytle,
Wake for the Living, 205–6.

Epilogue

1. Genovese, *Southern Front*, 17, 22,
289; Roper, "Marxing through Geor-
gia," 78–79; Radosh, "Interview with
Eugene Genovese," 34; Novick, *That
Noble Dream*, 419, 432–33; Phelps,
"What He Knew and When," 41.

2. Novick, *That Noble Dream*, 432–
35, 447; Wiener, "Radical Historians
and the Crisis in American History,"
416, 422.

3. Roper, "Marxing through
Georgia," 79, 83; Genovese, *Politi-
cal Economy of Slavery*; Meier and
Rudwick, *Black History and the His-
torical Profession*, 260–61. A useful
discussion of *The Political Economy
of Slavery* was distributed on the
H-Net listserv: James W. Oberly,
Review of Eugene D. Genovese, *The
Political Economy of Slavery*, posted
H-Rural, Oct. 1995; Jeffrey Reed,
posted H-Rural, Oct. 1995; Eugene D.
Genovese, "Response to Criticism

of *The Political Economy of Slavery*,"
posted H-Rural Dec. 1995; and
Oberly and Reed, Rejoinders, posted
H-Rural, Oct. 1995.

4. Meier and Rudwick, *Black History and the Historical Profession*,
262–65; Genovese, *Roll, Jordan, Roll*;
Davis, "Southern Comfort," 43,
44; and Fredrickson, "Conservative
Mind," 276.

5. [Cathey], "Partisan Conversation," 36; Genovese, *Slaveholders'
Dilemma*, xvi.

6. Hall, "Bradford Speaks Out,"
36; Genovese, *Slaveholders' Dilemma*,
v. On Eugene D. Genovese's friendship with M. E. Bradford, see also
the appreciation by Elizabeth Fox
Genovese and him appearing in
"M. E. Bradford: An Appreciation,"
10. Genovese rejects the conservative
label in Genovese, *Southern Tradition*, x. In a 1985 interview, however,
Genovese labeled himself both a
"real conservative" and a Marxist.
[Cathey], "Partisan Conversation," 36.

7. Genovese, *Southern Tradition*,
37; Genovese, *Southern Front*, 13, 14;
Phelps, "What He Knew and When,"
41. "The Question," *Dissent* 41 (Summer 1994): 371–76, is reprinted as
chapter 23 of Genovese, *Southern
Front*.

8. Genovese, *Southern Tradition*,
xiii. The worldview of antebellum
southern educators, Genovese wrote,
"remains defensible, including an
acute critique of the social atomization of modern society and of the
destructive consequences of political
and economic centralization. And
many of those who taught it ranked as
selfless, admirable, dedicated Christians." Genovese, *Southern Front*, 106.

9. Genovese, *Southern Tradition*, 8,
14; Genovese, *Southern Front*, 251, 126.

10. Genovese, *Southern Tradition*,
40; Genovese, *Southern Front*, 151.

11. Genovese, *Consuming Fire*, 87.

12. On Elizabeth Fox-Genovese's
conversion, see Mathewes-Green,
"Interview: The Genoveses Find
God," 56; and "Partisan Conversa-
tion: Elizabeth Fox Genovese," 42–47.
Eugene Genovese's return to the Ro-

man Catholic Church is discussed in Mathewes-Green, "Interview: The Genoveses Find God," 56.

13. [Cathey], "Partisan Conversation," 38.

14. Genovese, *Southern Tradition*, 3, 14; Genovese, *Southern Front*, 124.

15. Genovese, *Southern Tradition*, 29, 27–29, 9; Genovese, *Southern Front*, 240.

16. Genovese, *Southern Tradition*, 87.

17. Lichtenstein, "Right Church, Wrong Pew," 61.

18. Ibid., 62, 63–64.

19. Ibid., 62, 65.

20. Chappell, rev. of Genovese, *Southern Tradition*, 111, 107.

21. Ibid., 111.

22. Ibid., 110.

23. Genovese, *Slaveholders' Dilemma*, 5–6.

24. Ibid., 13, 6–7, 17–18, 37–38.

25. Ibid., 7.

26. Ibid., 7–8, 10–11, 14–20, 48.

27. Ibid., 3, 76, 18.

28. Genovese, *Consuming Fire*, 3.

29. Ibid., 4–5, 9, 81–84 (quote on 84).

30. Ibid., 13–29.

31. Ibid., 105–11, 115–20.

32. Ibid., 54–58, 101.

33. Ibid., 125–27.

34. Ibid., 94.

35. Ibid.

36. Chappell, rev. of Genovese, *Southern Tradition*, 113.

37. Wendell Berry, interview by author, 12 July 1998 (tape in possession of author); Angyal, *Wendell Berry*, xvii; Berry, *Home Economics*, 180, 182. The description of Port Royal in the 1930s is based on Berry's recollection.

38. Berry interview; Berry, *Hidden Wound*, 94–95.

39. Angyal, *Wendell Berry*, xvii, 8, 10; Berry interview. Wendell Berry met Richard Weaver once. Berry interview.

40. For Wallace Stegner's influence on Berry, see Berry, *What Are People For?*, 48–57.

41. Berry interview; Angyal, *Wendell Berry*, xvii–xviii. Berry's farm has increased to about 125 acres.

42. Berry, *Long-Legged House*, 149–50, 114–27.

43. Collections of his essays otherwise not cited here include Berry, *Gift of Good Land;* Berry, *Standing by Words;* Berry, *Another Turn of the Crank.* In addition, an anthology of his essays has appeared: Berry, *Recollected Essays.*

44. Berry, *Long-Legged House*, 68–69; Berry, *Hidden Wound.*

45. Berry, *Long-Legged House*, 160.

46. Berry, *Continuous Harmony*, 86, 93–94, 96, 120–21.

47. Ibid., 144, 139–48.

48. Ibid., 152–57.

49. Ibid., 157, 165.

50. Berry, *What Are People For?*, 96, 101; "Toward a Healthy Community," 912; Berry to author, 14 Apr. 2000 (in author's possession); Berry, *Sex, Economy, Freedom, and Community*, 95–96.

51. Berry, *Sex, Economy, Freedom, and Community*, 114, 94.

52. Ibid., 99, 105–6.

53. Ibid., 96–98, 110–13, 114–15.

54. Berry, *Unsettling of America*, 10; Gregory McNamee, "Wendell Berry and the Politics of Agriculture," in Merchant, *Wendell Berry*, 93.

55. Berry, *Unsettling of America*, 10, 33, 42–45.

56. Ibid., 219–22.

57. Ibid., 137–38.

58. Ibid., 103–4, 108–9, 110. On marriage and sexuality, see ibid., 112–23. For Berry's argument in general, see ibid., 97–140.

59. Ibid., 138, 193.

60. Ibid., 210–17. See also Berry, *Home Economics*, 177–78.

61. Berry, *Sex, Economy, Freedom, and Community*, 15–17, 25–26, 40.

62. Berry, *Home Economics*, 165; Berry, *Unsettling of America*, 74; Berry, *Sex, Economy, Freedom, and Community*, 31.

63. On Berry's notion of community, see Berry, *Sex, Economy, Freedom, and Community*, 117–73.

64. Ibid., 149, 151–52.

65. Berry interview; Berry, *Recollected Essays*, 51; Angyal, *Wendell Berry*, xix.

66. Berry interview.

67. Berry interview; Angyal, *Wendell Berry*, 29. It is interesting to contrast Berry's opinion of secessionists such as those active in the League of the South with Genovese's opinion. Although Genovese is consistently critical of the racism and history of white supremacy in the South and dismisses the possibility of secession, he told reporter Peter Applebome, "I'd vote for it tomorrow if it were a biracial secession. I don't like Yankees. I think we'd be much better off without those people." Applebome, "Could the Old South Be Resurrected?," B11.

68. Berry, *Hidden Wound*, 63, 103–8. See Tate, "Profession of Letters in the South," 168.

69. Berry, *Hidden Wound*, 88, 145.

70. Berry interview.

71. Berry, *Continuous Harmony*, 66; Berry, *Sex, Economy, Freedom, and Community*, 171–72.

72. Berry, *Home Economics*, 103.

73. Berry interview.

BIBLIOGRAPHY

Manuscript Sources
Chicago, Illinois
Newberry Library
  Malcolm Cowley Papers

Fayetteville, Arkansas
Special Collections Division,
University of Arkansas Libraries,
University of Arkansas
  John Gould Fletcher Papers

Mecosta, Michigan
Russell Kirk Center
  Russell Kirk Papers

Mount Pleasant, Michigan
Clarke Historical Library, Central
Michigan University
  Russell Kirk Papers

Nashville, Tennessee
Special Collections and University
Archives, Heard Library, Vanderbilt
University
  Richmond Croom Beatty Papers
  Brainard Cheney Papers
  Donald Davidson Papers
  Andrew Nelson Lytle Papers
  Frank L. Owsley Papers
  John Crowe Ransom Papers
  Richard M. Weaver Papers
  Jesse Wills Papers

New Haven, Connecticut
Beinecke Rare Book and Manuscript
Library, Yale University
  Cleanth Brooks Papers
  Seward Collins Papers
  Hound and Horn Papers
  Southern Review Papers
  Robert Penn Warren Papers
Sterling Memorial Library, Yale
University
  William F. Buckley Jr. Papers

New York, New York
Rare Book and Manuscript Library,

Columbia University
  William S. Knickerbocker Papers

Princeton, New Jersey
Manuscript Division, Department
of Rare Books and Special
Collections, Princeton University
Library, Princeton University
  R. P. Blackmur Papers
  Caroline Gordon Papers
  Allen Tate Papers

Urbana, Illinois
University Archives, University of
Illinois
  Francis G. Wilson Papers

Interviews by Author
Wendell Berry, 12 July 1998
Thomas Fleming, 21 July 1998
Russell Kirk, 28 July 1993
John Shelton Reed (telephone),
  11 June 1998
Clyde Wilson (telephone), 6 July
  1998
C. Vann Woodward, 11 Aug. 1997

Newspaper
Nashville Tennessean, book page,
  1924–30

Unpublished Sources
Cocoltchos, Christopher Nickolas.
  "The Invisible Government and
  the Viable Community: The Ku
  Klux Klan in Orange County,
  California, During the 1920s."
  Ph.D. diss., University of
  California, Los Angeles, 1979.
Craven, Robert Kenton. "Seward
  Collins and the Traditionalists:
  A Study of the *Bookman* and the
  American Review, 1928–1937." Ph.D.
  diss., University of Kansas, 1967.
Goodnight, Gerald Thomas.
  "Rhetoric and Culture: A Critical
  Edition of Richard M. Weaver's

Unpublished Works." Ph.D. diss., University of Kansas, 1978.

Jordan, Michael Merritt. "Donald Davidson's 'Creed of Memory.'" Ph.D. diss., University of Georgia, 1989.

Rock, Virginia J. "The Making and Meaning of I'll Take My Stand: A Study in Utopian Conservatism, 1925-1939." Ph.D. diss., University of Minnesota, 1961.

Shapiro, Edward Stanford. "The American Distributists and the New Deal." Ph.D. diss., Harvard University, 1968.

Weaver, Richard M. "The Revolt against Humanism." M.A. thesis, Vanderbilt University, 1934.

Wilson, Elizabeth Anne. "Criticism, Inc.: A Reconsideration of New Criticism and the Profession, 1930–1955." Ph.D. diss., University of Pennsylvania, 1988.

Published Sources

Aaron, Daniel. "Conservatism, Old and New." *American Quarterly* 6 (Summer 1954): 99–110.

———. *Writers on the Left.* 1961. Reprint, New York: Oxford University Press, 1977.

Abrams, M. H. "The Transformation of English Studies: 1930–1995." *Daedalus* 126 (Winter 1997): 105–31.

Adorno, T. W. "Theses upon Art and Religion Today." *Kenyon Review* 7 (Autumn 1945): 677–82.

Agar, Herbert, and Allen Tate, eds. *Who Owns America?: A New Declaration of Independence.* 1936. Reprint, Wilmington, N.C.: University Press of America, [1983].

Alexander, Charles C. *Here the Country Lies: Nationalism and the Arts in Twentieth-Century America.* Bloomington: Indiana University Press, 1980.

Allitt, Patrick. *Catholic Converts: British and American Intellectuals Turn to Rome.* Ithaca, N.Y.: Cornell University Press, 1997.

———. *Catholic Intellectuals and Conservative Politics in America,* 1950–1985. Ithaca, N.Y.: Cornell University Press, 1993.

"American Scholar Forum: The New Criticism." *American Scholar* 20 (Winter 1950–51): 86–104; (Spring 1951): 218–31.

Amyx, Clifford. "Weaver the Liberal: A Memoir." *Modern Age* 31 (Spring 1987): 101–6.

Angyal, Andrew J. *Wendell Berry.* New York: Twayne, 1995.

Applebome, Peter. "Could the Old South Be Resurrected?" *New York Times,* 7 Mar. 1998, B11.

———. *Dixie Rising: How the South Is Shaping American Values, Politics, and Culture.* New York: Random House, 1996.

Arnold, Matthew. *English Literature and Irish Politics.* Edited by R. H. Super. Ann Arbor: University of Michigan Press, 1973.

Arsenault, Raymond. "The End of the Long Hot Summer: The Air Conditioner and Southern Culture." *Journal of Southern History* 50 (Nov. 1984): 597–628.

Auerbach, M. Morton. *The Conservative Illusion.* New York: Columbia University Press, 1959.

Ayers, Edward L. *The Promise of the New South: Life after Reconstruction.* New York: Oxford University Press, 1992.

Bak, Hans. *Malcolm Cowley: The Formative Years.* Athens: University of Georgia Press, 1993.

Bartley, Numan V. *The New South, 1945–1980.* Baton Rouge: Louisiana State University Press, 1995.

———. *The Rise of Massive Resistance: Race and Politics in the South during the 1950's.* Baton Rouge: Louisiana State University Press, 1969.

Beatty, Richmond Croom. "A Personal Memoir of the Agrarians." *Shenandoah* 3 (Summer 1952): 11–13.

Berman, William C. *America's Right Turn: From Nixon to Bush.* Baltimore: Johns Hopkins University Press, 1994.

Berry, J. Bill, ed. *Home Ground: Southern Autobiography.* Columbia: University of Missouri Press, 1991.

Berry, Wendell. *Another Turn of the Crank*. Washington, D.C.: Counterpoint, 1995.

———. *A Continuous Harmony: Essays Cultural and Agricultural*. New York: Harcourt Brace Jovanovich, 1972.

———. *Gift of Good Land: Essays Cultural and Agricultural*. San Francisco: North Point Press, 1981.

———. *The Hidden Wound*. Boston: Houghton Mifflin, 1970.

———. *Home Economics: Fourteen Essays*. New York: North Point Press, 1987.

———. *The Long-Legged House*. New York: Harcourt, Brace & World, 1969.

———. *Recollected Essays, 1965–1980*. New York: North Point Press, 1981.

———. *Sex, Economy, Freedom, and Community*. New York: Pantheon, 1993.

———. *Standing by Words*. San Francisco: North Point, 1983.

———. *The Unsettling of America: Culture and Agriculture*. 1977. Reprint, San Francisco: Sierra Club Books, 1996.

———. *What Are People For?* San Francisco: North Point Press, 1990.

Biel, Steven. *Independent Intellectuals in the United States, 1910–1945*. New York: New York University Press, 1992.

Black, Earl, and Merle Black. *The Vital South: How Presidents Are Elected*. Cambridge: Harvard University Press, 1992.

Blake, Casey Nelson. *Beloved Community: The Cultural Criticism of Randolph Bourne, Van Wyck Brooks, Waldo Frank, and Lewis Mumford*. Chapel Hill: University of North Carolina Press, 1990.

Blee, Kathleen M. *Woman of the Klan: Racism and Gender in the 1920s*. Berkeley: University of California Press, 1991.

Blotner, Joseph. *Robert Penn Warren: A Biography*. New York: Random House, 1997.

Blumenthal, Sidney. *The Rise of the Counter-Establishment: From Conservative Ideology to Political Power*. 1986; New York: Harper & Row, 1988.

Bohner, Charles. *Robert Penn Warren*. Rev. ed. Boston: Twayne, 1981.

Boles, John B. *The South through Time: A History of an American Region*. Englewood Cliffs, N.J.: Prentice-Hall, 1995.

Bové, Paul. *Mastering Discourse: The Politics of Intellectual Culture*. Durham, N.C.: Duke University Press, 1992.

Bozell, L. Brent. "Freedom or Virtue?" *National Review*, 11 Sept. 1962, 181–87, 206.

———. "An Open Question." *National Review*, 7 Sept. 1957, 209.

Bradford, M. E. "Aeschylus in Nashville: 'The Case of Motorman 17: Commitment Proceedings' and the Later Poetry of Donald Davidson." *Southern Literary Journal* 25 (Fall 1992): 52–61.

———. *Against the Barbarians and Other Familiar Themes*. Columbia: University of Missouri Press, 1992.

———. "The Agrarianism of Richard Weaver: Beginnings and Completions." *Modern Age* 14 (Summer–Fall 1970): 249–56.

———. "All We Could Want to Know." *National Review*, 31 Dec. 1989, 39–41.

———. *A Better Guide Than Reason: Federalists and Anti-Federalists*. 1979; New Brunswick, N.J.: Transaction, 1994.

———. "Dividing the House: The Gnosticism of Lincoln's Political Rhetoric." *Modern Age* 23 (Winter 1979): 10–24.

———. "Donald Davidson and the Calculus of Memory." *Chronicles* 18 (May 1994): 16–20.

———. "Faulkner, James Baldwin, and the South." *Georgia Review* 20 (Winter 1966): 431–43.

———. *Generations of the Faithful Heart: On the Literature of the South*. La Salle, Ill.: Sherwood Sugden, 1983.

———. "It's George Will Who's Being Shrill." *Washington Post*, 12 Dec. 1981, A13.

———. "M. E. Bradford." *Modern*

Age 26 (Summer/Fall 1982):
242–44.
———. "The Prophetic Voice of
Donald Davidson." *Chronicles* 16
(May 1992): 29–30.
———. *The Reactionary Imperative:
Essays Literary and Political.* Peru,
Ill.: Sherwood Sugden, 1990.
———. *Remembering Who We Are:
Observations of a Southern
Conservative.* Athens: University of
Georgia Press, 1985.
———. "Sacrilege and Cupidity:
A Plea for Perspective." *Freeman* 16
(Feb. 1966): 38–40.
Brennan, Mary C. *Turning Right in
the Sixties: The Conservative Capture
of the GOP.* Chapel Hill: University
of North Carolina Press, 1995.
Brien, Dolores Elise. "The Catholic
Revival Revisited." *Commonweal,*
21 Dec. 1979, 714–16.
Brinkley, Alan. *Voices of Protest: Huey
Long, Father Coughlin, and the Great
Depression.* New York: Vintage,
1982.
Brinkmeyer, Robert H., Jr. *Three
Catholic Writers of the Modern South.*
Jackson: University Press of
Mississippi, 1985.
Brown, Stuart Gerry. "Democracy,
the New Conservatism, and the
Liberal Tradition in America."
Ethics 66, pt. 1 (Oct. 1955): 1–9.
Buckley, William F., Jr. *God and Man
at Yale: The Superstitions of
"Academic Freedom."* Chicago:
Regnery, 1951.
———. *Up From Liberalism.* New
York: McDowell, Obolensky, 1959.
"Can Democracy Survive in a World
of Technology?" *U.S. News and
World Report,* 18 Aug. 1980, 64–65.
Canfield, Joseph M. "A Steady
Presence." *Modern Age* 39 (Spring
1997): 173–77.
Carlson, Allan. *The New Agrarian
Mind: The Movement toward
Decentralist Thought in Twentieth-
Century America.* New Brunswick,
N.J.: Transaction, 2000.
Carter, Dan T. *From George Wallace to
Newt Gingrich: Race in the
Conservative Counterrevolution,*

1963–1994. Baton Rouge: Louisiana
State University Press, 1996.
———. *The Politics of Rage: George
Wallace, the Origins of the New
Conservatism, and the Transformation
of American Politics.* New York:
Simon & Schuster, 1995.
Cartwright, Gary. "Southern
Discomfort." *Gentlemen's Quarterly*
68 (Nov. 1998): 218–36.
Casper, Leonard. *Robert Penn Warren:
The Dark and Bloody Ground.* New
York: Greenwood, 1960.
[Cathey, Boyd]. "Partisan
Conversation." *Southern Partisan*
(Fall 1985): 35–38.
Cell, John W. *The Highest Stage of
White Supremacy: The Origins of
Segregation in South Africa and the
American South.* Cambridge:
Cambridge University Press, 1982.
Chambers, Whittaker. *Witness.* New
York: Random House, 1952.
Chappell, David L. Review of
Genovese, *Southern Tradition.*
Arkansas Historical Quarterly 55
(Spring 1996): 107–14.
Cheney, Brainard. "What Endures in
the South?" *Modern Age* 2 (Fall
1958): 408–10.
Clark, William Bedford. *The
American Vision of Robert Penn
Warren.* Lexington: University
Press of Kentucky, 1991.
Cobb, James C., and Charles R.
Wilson, eds. *Perspectives on the
American South: An Annual Review
of Society, Politics, and Culture.*
Vol. 4. New York: Gordon and
Breach, 1987.
Coben, Stanley. *Rebellion against
Victorianism: The Impetus for
Cultural Change in 1920s America.*
New York: Oxford University
Press, 1991.
Conkin, Paul. *Gone with the Ivy:
A Biography of Vanderbilt University.*
Knoxville: University of Tennesee
Press, 1985.
———. *The Southern Agrarians.*
Knoxville: University of Tennessee
Press, 1988.
Connelly, Thomas Lawrence. "The
Vanderbilt Agrarians: Time and
Place in Southern Tradition."

Tennessee Historical Quarterly 22 (Mar. 1963): 22–37.

"Conservative Movement, R.I.P." *Chronicles* 15 (May 1991): 18–22.

"Conservatism vs. Liberalism— A Debate." *New York Times Magazine,* 4 Mar. 1956, 11, 58, 60, 62–64.

Cooney, Terry A. *The Rise of the New York Intellectuals: "Partisan Review" and Its Circle.* Madison: University of Wisconsin Press, 1986.

Cooper, William, Jr., and Thomas E. Terrill. *The American South: A History.* 2d ed. New York: McGraw-Hill, 1996.

Core, George, ed. *Southern Fiction Today: Renascence and Beyond.* Athens: University of Georgia Press,1969.

Couch, W. T. "Reflections on the Southern Tradition." *South Atlantic Quarterly* 35 (July 1936): 284–97.

Cowan, Louise. *The Fugitive Group: A Literary History.* Baton Rouge: Louisiana State University Press, 1959.

———. "The Fugitive Poets in Relation to the South." *Shenandoah* 6 (Summer 1955): 3–10.

Cowley, Malcolm. *Exile's Return: A Narrative of Ideas.* New York: Norton, 1934.

———. "The Meriwether Connection." *Southern Review* 1, n.s. (Jan. 1965): 46–56.

Craig, Edward, ed. *Routledge Encyclopedia of Philosophy.* London: Routledge, 1998.

Crews, Frederick. *The Critics Bear It Away: American Fiction and the Academy.* New York: Random House, 1992.

Crick, Bernard. "The Strange Quest for an American Conservatism." *Review of Politics* 17 (July 1955): 359–76.

Cross, F. L., ed. *Oxford Dictionary of the Christian Church.* New York: Oxford University Press, 1997.

Curti, Merle. *The Growth of American Thought.* 2d ed. New York: Harper & Row, 1951.

Cutrer, Thomas W. *Parnassus on the Mississippi: "The Southern Review"*

and the Baton Rouge Literary Community, 1935–1942. Baton Rouge: Louisiana State University Press, 1984.

Daniel, Pete. *Breaking the Land: The Transformation of Cotton, Tobacco, and Rice Cultures since 1800.* Urbana: University of Illinois Press, 1985.

———. "The Transformation of the Rural South, 1930 to the Present." *Agricultural History* 55 (July 1981): 231–48.

Davidson, Donald. "The Artist as Southerner." *Saturday Review of Literature,* 15 May 1926, 781–83.

———. *The Attack on Leviathan: Regionalism and Nationalism in the United States.* Chapel Hill: University of North Carolina Press, 1938.

———. "Gulliver with Hay Fever." *American Review* 9 (Summer 1937): 152–72.

———. "*I'll Take My Stand:* A History." *American Review* 5 (Summer 1935): 301–21.

———. *Lee in the Mountains and Other Poems.* Boston: Houghton Mifflin, 1938.

———. "The New South and the Conservative Tradition." *National Review,* 10 Sept. 1960, 141–46.

———. "Preface to Decision." *Sewanee Review* 53 (1945): 394–412.

———. "Sectionalism in the United States." *Hound and Horn* 6 (July–Sept. 1933): 561–89.

———. *Southern Writers in the Modern World.* Athens: University of Georgia Press, 1958.

———. *Still Rebels, Still Yankees and Other Essays.* Baton Rouge: Louisiana State University Press, 1957.

———. *The Tall Men.* Boston: Houghton Mifflin, 1927.

———. *The Tennessee.* Vol. 1, *The Old River: Frontier to Secession.* 1946. Reprint, Nashville: J. S. Sanders, 1991.

———. *The Tennessee.* Vol. 2, *The New River: Civil War to TVA.* 1948. Reprint, Nashville: J. S. Sanders, 1992.

———. "Where Regionalism and Sectionalism Meet." *Social Forces* 13 (Oct. 1934): 23–31.

———. "The White Spirituals and Their Historian." *Sewanee Review* 51 (Autumn 1943): 589–98.

———, ed. *Selected Essays and Other Writings of John Donald Wade*. Athens: University of Georgia Press, 1966.

Davidson, Eugene. "Richard Malcolm Weaver—Conservative." *Modern Age* 7 (Summer 1963): 226–30.

Davis, David Brion. "Southern Comfort." *New York Review of Books*, 5 Oct. 1995, 43–46.

Davis, Robert Gorham. "The New Criticism and the Democratic Tradition." *American Scholar* 19 (Winter 1949–50): 9–19.

Deaton, Wesley. "Partisan Conversation: John Shelton Reed." *Southern Partisan* (Third Quarter, 1994): 30–32.

Dettmar, Kevin J. H., and Stephen Watt, eds. *Marketing Modernism: Self-Promotion, Canonization, Rereading*. Ann Arbor: University of Michigan Press, 1996.

Diamond, Sara. *Roads to Dominion: Right-Wing Movements and Political Power in the United States*. New York: Guilford Press, 1995.

Diggins, John P. *Mussolini and Fascism: The View from America*. Princeton: Princeton University Press, 1972.

———. *Up from Communism: Conservative Odysseys in American Intellectual History*. New York: Harper & Row, 1975.

Dionne, E. J., Jr. *Why Americans Hate Politics*. New York: Simon & Schuster, 1991.

Doenecke, Justus D. *Not to the Swift: The Old Isolationists in the Cold War Era*. Lewisburg, Pa.: Bucknell University Press, 1979.

———. "Origins and Outcome." *Chronicles* 15 (Dec. 1991): 16–19.

Dorman, Robert L. *Revolt of the Provinces: The Regionalist Movement in America, 1920–1945*. Chapel Hill: University of North Carolina Press, 1993.

Dorrien, Gary. *The Neoconservative Mind: Politics, Culture, and the War of Ideology*. Philadelphia: Temple University Press, 1993.

Doyle, Don H. *Nashville in the New South, 1880–1930*. Knoxville: University of Tennessee Press, 1985.

———. *Nashville since the 1920s*. Knoxville: University of Tennessee Press, 1985.

D'Souza, Dinesh. *The End of Racism: Principles for a Multiracial Society*. New York: Free Press, 1995.

Duffy, Bernard K., and Martin Jacobi. *The Politics of Rhetoric: Richard M. Weaver and the Conservative Tradition*. Westport, Conn.: Greenwood Press, 1993.

Dumenil, Lynn. *The Moden Temper: American Culture and Society in the 1920s*. New York: Hill & Wang, 1995.

Dunaway, John M., ed. *Exiles and Fugitives: The Letters of Jacques and Raïssa Maritain, Allen Tate, and Caroline Gordon*. Baton Rouge: Louisiana State University Press, 1992.

Dupree, Robert S. *Allen Tate and the Augustinian Imagination: A Study of the Poetry*. Baton Rouge: Louisiana State University Press, 1983.

Dzuback, Mary Ann. *Robert M. Hutchins: Portrait of an Educator*. Chicago: University of Chicago Press, 1991.

Ebbitt, Wilma R. "Richard M. Weaver, Teacher of Rhetoric." *Georgia Review* 17 (Winter 1963): 415–18.

Edgar, Walter B., ed. *A Southern Renascence Man: Views of Robert Penn Warren*. Baton Rouge: Louisiana State University Press, 1984.

Edsall, Thomas Byrne, with Mary D. Edsall. *Chain Reaction: The Impact of Race, Rights, and Taxes on American Politics*. New York: Norton, 1992.

Egerton, John. *The Americanization of Dixie: The Southernization of America*. New York: Harper's Magazine Press, 1974.

———. *Nashville: The Faces of Two*

Centuries, 1780–1980. Nashville: PlusMedia, 1979.

———. *Speak Now against the Day: The Generation before the Civil Rights Movement in the South.* New York: Knopf, 1994.

Eliade, Mircea, ed. *Encyclopedia of Modern Religion.* New York: Macmillan, 1987.

Eliot, T. S. *The Sacred Wood: Essays on Poetry and Criticism.* London: Methuen, 1920.

"Faces of Change." *Newsweek,* 7 June 1965, 84A–85.

Fain, John Tyree, ed. *The Spyglass: Views and Reviews, 1924–1930.* Nashville: Vanderbilt University Press, 1963.

Fain, John Tyree, and Thomas Daniel Young, eds. *The Literary Correspondence of Donald Davidson and Allen Tate.* Athens: University of Georgia Press, 1974.

Farrell, David. "Poetry as a Way of Life: An Interview with Robert Penn Warren." *Georgia Review* 36 (Summer 1982): 314–31.

———. "Reminiscences: A Conversation with Robert Penn Warren." *Southern Review* 16 (Oct. 1980): 782–98.

Fifteen Southerners. *Why the South Will Survive.* Edited by Clyde N. Wilson. Athens: University of Georgia Press, 1981.

Fite, Gilbert. *Cotton Fields No More: Southern Agriculture, 1865–1980.* Lexington: University Press of Kentucky, 1984.

Fleming, Thomas. "The Broken Promise of American Life." *Chronicles* 15 (July 1991): 14–18.

———. "Cabbages and Worms." *Chronicles* 21 (Jan. 1997): 8–11.

———. "Caliban in the Classroom." *Chronicles* 19 (Sept. 1995): 10–12.

———. "Divorce Italian Style." *Chronicles* 15 (Jan. 1991): 12–16.

———. "The Emperor's Tattoo." *Chronicles* 24 (May 2000): 10–12.

———. "Further Reflections on Violence." *Chronicles* 14 (Nov. 1990): 12–15.

———. "Ghosts in the Graveyard: The Serbia Question, Again." *Chronicles* 17 (Aug. 1993): 12–20.

———. "Hanging with Our Friends." *Chronicles* 21 (Apr. 1997): 10–13.

———. "In the Time of the Breaking of Nations." *Chronicles* 24 (Jan. 2000): 10–12.

———. "It's Stupid, the Economy: Culture and Immigration." *Chronicles* 19 (July 1995): 10–13.

———. "It Takes a Village." *Chronicles* 22 (Sept. 1998): 10–13.

———. "A League of Their Own." *Chronicles* 17 (Feb. 1993): 12–15.

———. "Letter from Italy: The Italian Revolution." *Chronicles* 18 (Aug. 1994): 38–40.

———. "Letter from Zagreb: Out of the Rubble, a Christian State?" *Chronicles* 18 (Feb. 1994): 35–38.

———. "The Loser in a Lawn Chair." *Chronicles* 14 (Dec. 1990): 12–15.

———. "My Old Man." *Chronicles* 18 (Feb. 1994): 16–17.

———. *The Politics of Human Nature.* New Brunswick, N.J.: Transaction, 1988.

———. "The New Fusionism." *Chronicles* 15 (May 1991): 10–12.

———. "The Real American Dilemma." *Chronicles* 13 (Mar. 1989): 8–11.

———. "Return of the Alien." *Chronicles* 23 (Nov. 1999): 10–13.

———. "A Revolution to Save the World." *Chronicles* 24 (July 2000): 10–12.

———. "Sarajevo Today, Chicago Tomorrow." *Chronicles* 21 (June 1997): 10–13.

———. "White Like Me." *Chronicles* 21 (Nov. 1997): 10–12.

———. "X2K: Aut Christus aut nihil." *Chronicles* 23 (Dec. 1999): 11–12.

Foerster, Norman. *American Criticism: A Study in Literary Theory from Poe to the Present.* Boston: Houghton Mifflin, 1928.

———, ed. *Humanism and America: Essays on the Outlook of Modern Civilisation.* New York: Farrar and Rinehart, 1930.

Fogelman, Edwin. "The New

Conservatism and American
Values." *Southwest Review* 43
(Winter 1958): 18–27.

Foner, Eric. "Lincoln, Bradford, and
the Conservatives." *New York Times*,
13 Feb. 1982, 25.

Foner, Eric, and John A. Garraty, eds.
*The Reader's Companion to American
History.* Boston: Houghton Mifflin,
1991.

Fox, Richard Wightman. *Reinhold
Niebuhr: A Biography.* New York:
Harper & Row, 1985.

Francis, Samuel. "Beyond
Conservatism: The Resistance
Takes Shape." *Chronicles* 24 (Jan.
2000): 20–22.

———. "The Buchanan Revolution,
Part I." *Chronicles* 16 (July 1992):
11–12.

———. "The Buchanan Revolution,
Part II." *Chronicles* 16 (Aug. 1992):
10–11.

———. "The Buchanan Victory."
Chronicles 20 (June 1996): 42–43.

———. "Force and Idea." *Chronicles*
23 (Feb. 1994): 26–27.

———. "Forty Years Later."
Chronicles 18 (May 1994): 10–11.

———. "From Household to Nation:
The Middle American Populism of
Pat Buchanan." *Chronicles* 20 (Mar.
1996): 12–16.

———. "An Infantile Disorder."
Chronicles 22 (Feb. 1998): 31–32.

———. "Nationalism, Old and New."
Chronicles 16 (June 1992): 18–22.

———. "Nations within Nations."
Chronicles 23 (Jan. 1999): 21–23.

———. "A New Majority?" *Chronicles*
24 (June 2000): 32–33.

———. "The New Shape of
American Politics." *Chronicles* 22
(Jan. 1998): 30–31.

———. *Power and History: The
Political Thought of James Burnham.*
Lanham, Md.: University Press of
America, 1984.

———. "Principalities and Powers."
Chronicles 15 (Dec. 1991): 9–11.

———. "Prospects for Racial and
Cultural Survival." *American
Renaissance* 6 (Mar, 1995): 1, 3–7.

———. "Revolt of the 300-Pound
Beefy Guys." *Chronicles* 24 (Feb.
2000): 32–33.

———. "The Rise and Fall of a
Paleoconservative at the *Washington
Times* (Part I)." *Chronicles* 20 (Apr.
1996): 35–37.

———. "The Rise and Fall of a
Paleoconservative at the *Washington
Times* (Part II)." *Chronicles* 20 (May
1996), 43–45.

———. "Secessionist Fantasies."
Chronicles 18 (Aug. 1994): 9–11.

———. "The Secret of the Twentieth
Century." *Chronicles* 14 (Nov.
1990): 31–34.

———. "A Story of the Days to
Come." *Chronicles* 17 (June 1993):
9–11.

Franklin, John Hope, and Alfred A.
Moss, Jr. *From Slavery to Freedom:
A History of African Americans.* 7th
ed. New York: McGraw-Hill, 1998.

Fraser, Steve, and Gary Gerstle, eds.
*The Rise and Fall of the New Deal
Order, 1930–1980.* Princeton:
Princeton University Press, 1989.

Fredrickson, George M. "The
Conservative Mind." *Dissent* 42
(Spring 1995): 276–80.

Freund, Ludwig. "The New
American Conservatism and
European Conservatism." *Ethics* 66,
pt. 1 (Oct. 1955): 10–17.

Friar, Kimon, and John Malcolm
Brinnin, eds. *Modern Poetry:
American and British.* New York:
Appleton-Century-Crofts, 1951.

Frum, David. *Dead Right.* New York:
Basic Books, 1994.

———. *What's Right: The New
Conservative Majority and the
Remaking of America.* New York:
Basic Books, 1996.

Gallagher, Catherine. "The History
of Literary Criticism." *Daedalus* 126
(Winter 1997): 133–53.

Gaston, Paul M. *The New South Creed:
A Study in Southern Mythmaking.*
New York: Knopf, 1970.

Genovese, Eugene D. *A Consuming
Fire: The Fall of the Confederacy in
the Mind of the White Christian
South.* Athens: University of
Georgia Press, 1998.

———. *The Political Economy of*

Slavery: Studies in the Economy and Society of the Slave South. New York: Pantheon, 1965.

———. *Roll, Jordan, Roll: The World the Slaves Made.* New York: Random House, 1974.

———. *The Slaveholders' Dilemma: Freedom and Progress in Southern Conservative Thought, 1820–1860.* Columbia: University of South Carolina Press, 1992.

———. *The Southern Front: History and Politics in the Cultural War.* Columbia: University of Missouri Press, 1995.

———. *The Southern Tradition: The Achievement and Limitations of an American Conservatism.* Cambridge: Harvard University Press, 1994.

Gerlach, Larry R. *Blazing Crosses in Zion: The Ku Klux Klan in Utah.* Logan: Utah State University Press, 1982.

Gerson, Mark. *The Neoconservative Vision: From the Cold War to the Culture Wars.* Lanham, Md.: Madison Books, 1996.

Gilbert, Jess, and Steve Brown. "Alternative Land Reform Proposals in the 1930s: The Nashville Agrarians and the Southern Tenant Farmers' Union." *Agricultural History* 55 (Oct. 1981): 351–69.

Gleason, Philip. *Contending with Modernity: Catholic Higher Education in the Twentieth Century.* New York: Oxford University Press, 1995.

———. "Identifying Identity: A Semantic History." *Journal of American History* 69 (Mar. 1983): 910–31.

Goldberg, Robert Alan. *Barry Goldwater.* New Haven: Yale University Press, 1995.

———. *Hooded Empire: The Ku Klux Klan in Colorado.* Urbana: University of Illinois Press, 1981.

Goldwin, Robert A., ed. *Left, Right, and Center: Essays on Liberalism and Conservatism in the United States.* Chicago: Rand McNally, 1965.

Gottfried, Paul. "And What Isn't. . . ." *Chronicles* 21 (Jan. 1997): 32–33.

———. *The Conservative Movement.* Rev. ed. New York: Twayne, 1993.

———. "Martin Luther King, Jr., as Conservative Hero." *Chronicles* 21 (Apr. 1997): 29–31.

Graebner, William. *The Age of Doubt: American Thought and Culture in the 1940s.* Boston: Twayne, 1991.

Graff, Gerald. *Literature against Itself: Literary Ideas in Modern Society.* Chicago: University of Chicago Press, 1979.

———. *Professing Literature: An Institutional History.* Chicago: University of Chicago Press, 1987.

Graham, Hugh Davis. *Crisis in Print: Desegregation and the Press in Tennessee.* Nashville: Vanderbilt University Press, 1967.

Grantham, Dewey. *The South in Modern America: A Region at Odds.* New York: HarperCollins, 1994.

Gray, Richard. *The Literature of Memory: Modern Writers of the American South.* Baltimore: Johns Hopkins University Press, 1977.

———. *Writing the South: Ideas of an American Region.* Cambridge: Cambridge University Press, 1986.

Green, David. *Shaping Political Consciousness: The Language of Politics in America from McKinley to Reagan.* Ithaca, N.Y.: Cornell University Press, 1987.

Greenbaum, Leonard. *"The Hound and Horn": The History of a Literary Quarterly.* The Hague: Mouton, 1966.

Greene, Jack P., ed. *Encyclopedia of American Political History: Studies of the Principal Movements and Ideas.* 3 vols. New York: Scribner, 1984.

Grimshaw, James A., ed. *Robert Penn Warren's "Brother to Dragons": A Discussion.* Baton Rouge: Louisiana State University Press, 1983.

Haiman, Franklyn S. "A New Look at the New Conservatism." *Bulletin of the American Association of University Professors* 41 (Autumn 1955): 444–53.

Hall, Carla. "The Amazing Endowment Scramble." *Washington Post*, 17 Dec. 1981, L1, L5–L6.

———. "Bradford's Boosters." *Washington Post*, 20 Oct. 1981, D1, D10.

———. "Bradford Speaks Out." *Washington Post*, 28 Oct. 1981, B1, B6.

Hall, Jacquelyn Dowd, James Leloudis, Robert Korstad, Mary Murphy, Lu Ann Jones, and Christopher B. Daly. *Like a Family: The Making of a Cotton Mill World*. Chapel Hill: University of North Carolina Press, 1987.

Hallowell, John H. Review of Russell Kirk, *The Conservative Tradition*. *Journal of Politics* 16 (Feb. 1954): 150–52.

Hamilton, Charles, ed. *Fugitive Essays: Selected Writings of Frank Chodorov*. Indianapolis: Liberty Press, 1980.

Hammer, Langdon. *Hart Crane and Allen Tate: Janus-Faced Modernism*. Princeton: Princeton University Press, 1993.

Hartz, Louis. *The Liberal Tradition in America: An Interpretation of American Political Thought since the Revolution*. New York: Harcourt, Brace, and World, 1955.

Havard, William C. "The Politics of I'll Take My Stand." *Southern Review* 16 (Oct. 1980): 757–75.

Havard, William C., and Walter Sullivan, eds. *A Band of Prophets: The Vanderbilt Agrarians after Fifty Years*. Baton Rouge: Louisiana State University Press, 1982.

Hecksher, August. "Toward a True, Creative Conservatism." *New York Herald Tribune Book Review*, 2 Aug. 1953, 4.

———. "Where Are the American Conservatives?" *Confluence* 2 (Sept. 1953): 54–65.

Hénault, Marie. *Peter Viereck*. New York: Twayne, 1969.

Hesseltine, W. B. "Look Away, Dixie." *Sewanee Review* 39 (Jan.–Mar. 1931): 97–103.

Higham, John. "The Cult of the 'American Consensus': Homogenizing Our History." *Commentary* 27 (Feb. 1959): 93–100.

Himmelfarb, Gertrude. "The Prophets of the New Conservatism: What Curbs for Presumptuous Democratic Man?" *Commentary* 9 (1950): 78–86.

Himmelstein, Jerome L. *To the Right: The Transformation of American Conservatism*. Berkeley: University of California Press, 1990.

Hitchcock, James. "Postmortem on a Rebirth: The Catholic Intellectual Renaissance." *American Scholar* 49 (Spring 1980): 211–25.

Hobson, Fred C., Jr. *Serpent in Eden: H. L. Mencken and the South*. Chapel Hill: University of North Carolina Press, 1974.

———. *Tell about the South: The Southern Rage to Explain*. Baton Rouge: Louisiana State University Press, 1983.

Hodgson, Godfrey. *The World Turned Right Side Up: A History of the Conservative Ascendancy in America*. Boston: Houghton Mifflin, 1996.

Hoeveler, J. David, Jr. *The New Humanism: A Critique of Modern America, 1900–1940*. Charlottesville: University Press of Virginia, 1977.

Hollinger, David A. *In the American Province: Studies in the History and Historiography of Ideas*. Baltimore: Johns Hopkins University Press, 1985.

Hollinger, David A., and Charles Capper, eds. *The American Intellectual Tradition: A Sourcebook*. Vol. 2, *1865 to the Present*. 3d ed. New York: Oxford University Press, 1997.

Holman, C. Hugh. "Summary: The Utility of Myth." *Georgia Review* 11 (Summer 1957): 161–64.

Horowitz, David A. "The Klansman as Outsider: Ethnocultural Solidarity and Antielitism in the Oregon Ku Klux Klan of the 1920s." *Pacific Historical Quarterly* 80 (Jan. 1989): 12–20.

Huff, Peter. *Allen Tate and the Catholic Revival: Trace of the Fugitive Gods*. New York: Paulist Press, 1996.

———. "Donald Davidson and 'America's Other Lost

Generation.'" *Modern Age* 37 (Spring 1995): 226–32.

Immigration and the American Identity: Selections from "Chronicles: A Magazine of American Culture." Rockford, Ill.: Rockford Institute, 1995.

"In Memoriam: Richard M. Weaver." *New Individualist Review* 2 (Spring 1963): 2.

Issel, William H. "Ralph Borsodi and the Agrarian Response to Modern America." *Agricultural History* 41 (Apr. 1967): 155–66.

James, William. *Writings, 1902–1910.* New York: Library of America, 1987.

Jancovich, Mark. *The Cultural Politics of the New Criticism.* Cambridge: Cambridge University Press, 1993.

Jenkins, William D. *Steel Valley Klan: The Ku Klux Klan in Ohio's Mahoning Valley.* Kent, Ohio: Kent State University Press, 1990.

Johnson, Gerald W. "The South Faces Itself." *Virginia Quarterly Review* 7 (Jan. 1931): 152–57.

Jonza, Nancylee Novell. *The Underground Stream: The Life and Art of Caroline Gordon.* Athens: University of Georgia Press, 1995.

Judis, John B. "The Conservative Crackup." *American Prospect* 1 (1990): 30–42.

———. "The Conservative Wars." *New Republic,* 11 and 18 Aug. 1986, 15–18.

———. *William F. Buckley, Jr.: Patron Saint of the Conservatives.* New York: Simon & Schuster, 1988.

Justus, James H. *The Achievement of Robert Penn Warren.* Baton Rouge: Louisiana State University Press, 1981.

Karanikas, Alexander. *Tillers of a Myth: Southern Agrarians as Social and Literary Critics.* Madison: University of Wisconsin Press, 1966.

Kauffman, Bill. *America First!: Its History, Culture, and Politics.* Amherst, N.Y.: Prometheus Books, 1995.

———. "'I'm Liberated; Free at Last!': A Talk with Pat Buchanan." *Chronicles* 24 (Nov. 2000): 13–17.

Kazin, Michael. *The Populist Persuasion: An American History.* New York: Basic Books, 1995.

Kehoe, Alice Beck. *The Ghost Dance: Ethnohistory and Revitalization.* New York: Holt, Rinehart, and Winston, 1989.

Kendall, Willmoore. *The Conservative Affirmation.* Chicago: Regnery, 1963.

———. "How to Read Richard Weaver: Philosopher of 'We the (Virtuous) People.'" *Intercollegiate Review* 2 (Sept. 1965): 77–86.

———. "The 'Open Society' and Its Fallacies." *American Political Science Review* 54 (Dec. 1960): 972–79.

———. Review of Richard Weaver, *Ideas Have Consequences. Journal of Politics* 11 (Feb. 1949): 260–61.

———. "Three on the Line." *National Review,* 31 Aug. 1957, 178–81, 191.

———. *Willmoore Kendall Contra Mundum.* Edited by Nellie D. Kendall. New Rochelle, N.Y.: Arlington House, 1971.

King, Richard H. "Anti-Modernists All!" *Mississippi Quarterly* 44 (Spring 1991): 193–201.

———. "The South and Cultural Criticism." *American Literary History* 1 (Fall 1989): 699–714.

———. *A Southern Renaissance: The Cultural Awakening of the American South, 1930–1955.* New York: Oxford University Press, 1980.

———. "The Vital Center." *Reviews in American History* 24 (June 1996): 232–37.

Kirk, Russell. "The American Conservative Character." *Georgia Review* 8 (Fall 1954): 249–60.

———. "The Broken Cake of British Custom." *Southwest Review* 38 (Autumn 1953): 326–32.

———. *Confessions of a Bohemian Tory: Episodes and Reflections of a Vagrant Career.* New York: Fleet Publishing, 1963.

———. *The Conservative Mind: From Burke to Santayana.* Chicago: Regnery, 1953.

———. *The Conservative Mind: From Burke to Santayana.* 2d ed. Chicago: Regnery, 1954.

———. "Davidson against Leviathan." *National Review,* 18 June 1963, 498.

———. *Decadence and Renewal in the Higher Learning: An Episodic History of American University and College since 1953.* South Bend, Ind.: Gateway Editions, 1978.

———. "The Dissolution of Liberalism." *Commonweal,* 7 Jan. 1955, 374–78.

———. "New Towns and Rotting Houses in Fife." *Southwest Review* 39 (Winter 1954): 35–43.

———. *A Program for Conservatives.* Chicago: Regnery, 1954.

———. "St. Andrews: The Coziest University." *South Atlantic Quarterly* 50 (July 1951): 369–77.

———. *The Sword of the Imagination: Memoirs of a Half-Century of Literary Conflict.* Grand Rapids, Mich.: Eerdmans, 1995.

———. "York and Social Boredom." *Sewanee Review* 61 (Autumn 1953): 665–81.

Klein, Kerwin Lee. "On the Emergence of *Memory* in Historical Discourse." *Representations* 69 (Winter 2000): 127–50.

Knickerbocker, William S. "Back to the Hand." *Saturday Review of Literature,* 20 Dec. 1930, 467–68.

———. "Up from the South." *Western Review* 13 (Spring 1949): 169–78.

Kreyling, Michael. *Figures of the Hero in Southern Narrative.* Baton Rouge: Louisiana State University Press, 1987.

———. *Inventing Southern Literature.* Jackson: University Press of Mississippi, 1998.

Kristol, Irving. "Old Truths and the New Conservatism." *Yale Review* 47 (Mar. 1958): 365–73.

Lasch, Christopher. "The Communitarian Critique of Liberalism." *Soundings* 69 (Spring/Summer 1986): 60–76.

———. *The True and Only Heaven: Progress and Its Critics.* New York: Norton, 1991.

Lay, Shawn, ed. *Hooded Knights on the Niagara: The Ku Klux Klan in Buffalo, New York.* New York: New York University Press, 1995.

———. *The Invisible Empire in the West: Toward a New Historical Appraisal of the Ku Klux Klan of the 1920s.* Urbana: University of Illinois Press, 1992.

Leitch, Vincent B. *American Literary Criticism: From the Thirties to the Eighties.* New York: Columbia University Press, 1988.

LeRoy, Gaylord. "The New Conservatism." *Bulletin of the American Association of University Professors* 41 (Summer 1955): 270–76.

Leverette, William E., Jr., and David E. Shi. "Agrarianism for Commuters." *South Atlantic Quarterly* 79 (Spring 1980): 204–18.

———. "Herbert Agar and *Free America:* A Jeffersonian Alternative to the New Deal." *Journal of American Studies* 16 (Aug. 1982): 189–206.

Lichtenstein, Alex. "Right Church, Wrong Pew: Eugene Genovese and Southern Conservatism." *New Politics* 6 (Summer 1997): 59–68.

Lind, Michael. *Up from Conservatism: Why the Right Is Wrong for America.* New York: Free Press, 1996.

———. "Why Intellectual Conservatism Died." *Dissent* 42 (Winter 1995): 42–47.

Lytle, Andrew. "John Taylor and the Political Economy of Agriculture." *American Review* 3 (Sept. 1934): 432–47; (Oct. 1934): 630–43; 4 (Nov. 1934): 84–99.

———. *A Wake for the Living.* 1975. Reprint, Nashville: J. S. Sanders, 1992.

McAllister, Ted V. *Revolt against Modernity: Leo Strauss, Eric Voegelin, and the Search for a Postliberal Order.* Lawrence: University Press of Kansas, 1996.

McCarraher, Eugene B. "American Gothic: Sacramental Radicalism and the Neo-Medievalist Cultural

Gospel, 1929–1948." *Records of the American Catholic Historical Society of Philadelphia* 105 (Spring–Summer 1995): 3–23.

McClay, Wilfred M. *The Masterless: Self and Society in Modern America.* Chapel Hill: University of North Carolina Press, 1994.

MacDonald, H. Malcolm. "The Revival of Conservative Thought." *Journal of Politics* 19 (Feb. 1957): 66–81.

MacIntyre, Alasdair. *After Virtue: A Study in Moral Theory.* 2d ed. Notre Dame: Notre Dame University Press, 1984.

McKitrick, Eric L. "'Conservatism' Today." *American Scholar* 27 (Winter 1957–58): 49–61.

MacLean, Nancy. *Behind the Mask of Chivalry: The Making of the Second Ku Klux Klan.* New York: Oxford University Press, 1994.

McMillen, Neil R. *The Citizens' Council: Organized Resistance to the Second Reconstruction, 1954–64.* Urbana: University of Illinois Press, 1971.

McNeill, William H. *Hutchins' University: A Memoir of the University of Chicago, 1929–1950.* Chicago: University of Chicago Press, 1991.

Maddocks, Melvin. "In Tennessee: The Last Garden." *Time*, 8 Dec. 1980, 10, 13, 17.

Malvasi, Mark G. "Choosing Southernness: Southern with an Italian Accent." *Southern Partisan* (Fourth Quarter, 1994): 28–33.

———. *The Unregenerate South: The Agrarian Thought of John Crowe Ransom, Allen Tate, and Donald Davidson.* Baton Rouge: Louisiana State University Press, 1997.

Mason, Yvona Kendall, ed. *Oxford Years: The Letters of Willmoore Kendall to His Father.* Bryn Mawr, Pa.: Intercollegiate Studies Institute, 1993.

Mathewes-Green, Frederica. "Interview: The Genoveses Find God." *National Review*, 24 Feb. 1997, 55–57.

"M. E. Bradford: An Appreciation."

Southern Partisan 12 (Fourth Quarter, 1992): 8–13.

Meier, August, and Elliott Rudwick. *Black History and the Historical Profession, 1915–1980.* Urbana: University of Illinois Press, 1986.

Meiners, R. K. *The Last Alternatives: A Study of the Works of Allen Tate.* Denver: Swallow, 1963.

Merchant, Paul, ed. *Wendell Berry.* Lewiston, Idaho: Confluence Press, 1991.

Meyer, Frank S. "Collectivism Rebaptized." *Freeman* 5 (July 1955): 559–62.

———. *In Defense of Freedom and Related Essays.* Indianapolis: Liberty Fund, 1996.

———. "In the Great Tradition." *National Review*, 1 June 1957, 527–28.

———. "Richard M. Weaver: An Appreciation." *Modern Age* 14 (Summer–Fall 1970): 243–48.

———, ed. *What Is Conservatism?* New York: Holt, Rinehart, and Winston, 1964.

Miller, Kerby A. *Emigrants and Exiles: Ireland and the Irish Exodus to North America.* New York: Oxford University Press, 1985.

Miller, Mark D. "Faith in Good Works: The Salvation of Robert Penn Warren." *Mississippi Quarterly* 48 (Winter 1994–95): 57–71.

Millgate, Michael. "An Interview with Allen Tate." *Shenandoah* 12 (Spring 1961): 27–34.

Montgomery, Marion. "Bells for John Stewart's Burden: A Sermon upon the Desirable Death of the 'New Provincialism' Here Typified." *Georgia Review* 20 (Summer 1966): 145–81.

———. *Possum and Other Receits for the Recovery of "Southern" Being.* Athens: University of Georgia Press, 1987.

Mooney, James. *The Ghost-Dance Religion and the Sioux Outbreak of 1890.* Edited by Anthony F. C. Wallace. Chicago: University of Chicago Press, 1965.

Moore, Leonard. *Citizen Klansmen: The Ku Klux Klan in Indiana, 1921–*

1928. Chapel Hill: University of North Carolina Press, 1991.

———. "Good Old-Fashioned New Social History and the Twentieth-Century American Right." *Reviews in American History* 24 (Dec. 1996): 555–73.

Munson, Gorham. *The Dilemma of the Liberated: An Interpretation of Twentieth Century Humanism.* New York: Coward-McCann, 1930.

Muse, Benjamin. *Ten Years of Prelude: The Story of Integration since the Supreme Court's 1954 Decision.* New York: Viking, 1964.

Nash, George H. *The Conservative Intellectual Movement in America: since 1945.* New York: Basic Books, 1976.

———. "The Historical Roots of Contemporary American Criticism." *Modern Age* 26 (Summer/Fall 1982): 297–303.

New Catholic Encyclopedia. New York: McGraw-Hill, 1967.

Niebuhr, Reinhold. *The Children of Light and the Children of Darkness: A Vindication of Democracy and a Critique of Its Traditional Defence.* New York: Scribner's, 1944.

———. *The Irony of American History.* New York: Scribner's, 1952.

———. "Liberalism: Illusions and Realities." *New Republic,* 4 July 1955, 11–13.

Ninkovich, Frank A. "The New Criticism and Cold War America." *Southern Quarterly* 20 (Fall 1981): 1–24.

Nisbet, Robert A. *Conservatism: Dream and Reality.* Minneapolis: University of Minnesota Press, 1986.

Novick, Peter. *That Noble Dream: The "Objectivity Question" and the American Historical Profession.* Cambridge: Cambridge University Press, 1988.

O'Brien, Michael. *The Idea of the American South, 1920–1941.* 1979. Reprint, Baltimore: Johns Hopkins University Press, 1990.

———. "The Last Theologians: Recent Southern Literary Criticism." *Michigan Quarterly Review* 17 (Summer 1978): 404–13.

———. *Rethinking the South: Essays in Intellectual History.* Baltimore: Johns Hopkins University Press, 1988.

"On Civil Disobedience and the Algerian War." *Yale Review* 50 (Mar. 1961): 462–80.

One in Spirit: A Retrospective View of the University of Chicago on the Occasion of Its Centennial. 1973. Reprint, Chicago: University of Chicago Press, 1991.

Owsley, Frank L. "The Pillars of Agrarianism." *American Review* 4 (Mar. 1935): 529–47.

Pappas, Theodore. "A Doctor in Spite of Himself." *Chronicles* 15 (Jan. 1991): 25–29.

———. "A Houdini of Time." *Chronicles* 16 (Nov. 1992): 26–30.

"Partisan Conversation: Elizabeth Fox Genovese." *Southern Partisan* (First Quarter, 1997): 42–47.

"Partisan Conversation: Samuel Francis." *Southern Partisan* (First Quarter, 1996): 34–38.

Pells, Richard H. *The Liberal Mind in a Conservative Age: American Intellectuals in the 1940s and 1950s.* New York: Harper & Row, 1985.

———. *Radical Visions and American Dreams: Culture and Social Thought in the Depression Years.* Middletown, Conn.: Wesleyan University Press, 1973.

Perkins, David, ed. *Book of Passage: Twenty-seven North Carolina Writers on Books That Changed Their Lives.* Asheboro, N.C.: Down Home Press, 1996.

Perry, Lewis. *Intellectual Life in America: A History.* Chicago: University of Chicago Press, 1989.

Phelps, Christopher. "What He Knew and When." *Against the Current* 9 (Nov.–Dec. 1994): 41–42.

Postman, Neil. *Amusing Ourselves to Death: Public Discourse in the Age of Show Business.* New York: Penguin, 1985.

Powers, Richard Gid. *Not without Honor: The History of American*

Anticommunism. New York: Free Press, 1995.

Pride, Richard A., and J. David Woodard. *The Burden of Busing: The Politics of Desegregation in Nashville, Tennessee*. Knoxville: University of Tennessee Press, 1985.

Prothro, James W. "A Southerner's View of a Southerner's Book." *Reporter*, 20 Sept. 1956, 46–47.

Purdy, Rob Roy, ed. *Fugitives' Reunion: Conversations at Vanderbilt, May 3–5, 1956*. Nashville: Vanderbilt University Press, 1959.

Quinlan, Kieran. *John Crowe Ransom's Secular Faith*. Baton Rouge: Louisiana State University Press, 1989.

———. *Walker Percy: The Last Catholic Novelist*. Baton Rouge: Louisiana State University Press, 1996.

Rabinowitz, Howard N. *Race Relations in the Urban South, 1895–1890*. New York: Oxford University Press, 1978.

Radosh, Ronald. "An Interview with Eugene Genovese: The Rise of a Marxist Historian." *Change* 10 (Nov. 1978): 31–35.

———. *Prophets on the Right: Profiles of Conservative Critics of American Globalism*. New York: Simon & Schuster, 1975.

Ransom, John Crowe. "Art and the Human Economy." *Kenyon Review* 7 (Autumn 1945): 683–88.

———. "A Capitol for the New Deal." *American Review* 2 (Dec. 1933): 129–42.

———. *God without Thunder: An Unorthodox Defense of Orthodoxy*. New York: Harcourt, Brace, and Co., 1930.

———. "Happy Farmers." *American Review* 1 (Oct. 1933): 513–35.

———. "Land! An Answer to the Unemployment Problem." *Harper's* 165 (July 1932): 216–24.

———. *New Criticism*. 1941. Reprint, Westport, Conn.: Greenwood Press, 1979.

———. "Shall We Complete the Trade?" *Sewanee Review* 41 (Apr. 1933): 182–90.

———. "The South Defends Its Heritage." *Harper's* 159 (June 1929): 108–18.

———. "The South—Old or New?" *Sewanee Review* 36 (Apr. 1928): 139–47.

———. "The State and the Land." *New Republic*, 17 Feb. 1932, 8–10.

———. *World's Body*. 1938. Reprint, Baton Rouge: Louisiana State University Press, 1968.

Reddick, L. D. "Whose Ordeal?" *New Republic*, 24 Sept. 1956, 9–10.

Reed, John Shelton. *The Enduring South: Subcultural Persistence in Mass Society*. Lexington, Mass.: Lexington Books, 1972.

———. *Kicking Back: Further Dispatches from the South*. Columbia: University of Missouri Press, 1995.

———. *My Tears Spoiled My Aim, and Other Reflections on Southern Culture*. Columbia: University of Missouri Press, 1993.

———. *Southerners: The Social Psychology of Sectionalism*. Chapel Hill: University of North Carolina Press, 1983.

———. *Whistling Dixie: Dispatches from the South*. Columbia: University of Missouri Press, 1990.

Regnery, Henry. "Russell Kirk and the Making of the Conservative Mind." *Modern Age* 21 (Fall 1977): 338–53.

Reichley, James. "Young Conservatives at Old Harvard." *Reporter*, 16 June 1955, 12–16.

"The Revolving Bookstand: Neglected Books." *American Scholar* 25 (Autumn 1956): 472–504.

Ribuffo, Leo P. *The Old Christian Right: The Protestant Far Right from the Great Depression to the Cold War*. Philadelphia: Temple University Press, 1983.

Rock, Virginia. "The Fugitive-Agrarians in Response to Social Change." *Southern Humanities Review* 1 (Summer 1967): 170–81.

———. "They Took Their Stand: The Emergence of the Southern Agrarians." *Prospects* 1 (1975): 205–95.

Rodgers, Daniel T. "Republicanism: The Career of a Concept." *Journal of American History* 79 (June 1992): 11–38.

Roper, John Herbert. *C. Vann Woodward: Southerner.* Athens: University of Georgia Press, 1987.

———. "Marxing through Georgia: Eugene Genovese and Radical Historiography of the Region." *Georgia Historical Quarterly* 80 (Spring 1996): 77–92.

Rossiter, Clinton. *Conservatism in America.* New York: Knopf, 1955.

———. Review of Russell Kirk, *The Conservative Mind. American Political Science Review* 47 (Sept. 1953): 868–70.

Rothbard, Murray N. "Huntington on Conservatism: A Comment." *American Political Science Review* 51 (Sept. 1957): 784–87.

———. "Life in the Old Right." *Chronicles* 18 (Aug. 1994): 15–19.

Rotunda, Ronald D. *The Politics of Language: Liberalism as Word and Symbol.* Iowa City: University of Iowa Press, 1986.

Rubin, Joan Shelley. *The Making of Middlebrow Culture.* Chapel Hill: University of North Carolina Press, 1992.

Rubin, Louis D., Jr. *The Curious Death of the Novel: Essays in American Literature.* Baton Rouge: Louisiana State University Press, 1967.

———. *The Faraway Country: Writers of the Modern South.* Seattle: University of Washington Press, 1963.

———. *A Gallery of Southerners.* Baton Rouge: Louisiana State University Press, 1982.

———. "The Gathering of the Fugitives: A Recollection." *Southern Review* 30 (Autumn 1994): 658–73.

———. *The Mockingbird in the Gum Tree: A Literary Gallimaufry.* Baton Rouge: Louisiana State University Press, 1991.

———. "The Southern Martial Tradition: A Memory." *Southern Cultures* 1 (Winter 1995): 289–92.

———. *The Wary Fugitives: Four Poets and the South.* Baton Rouge:

Louisiana State University Press, 1978.

———. *The Writer in the South: Studies in a Literary Community.* Athens: University of Georgia Press, 1972.

Rubin, Louis D., Jr., and Robert D. Jacobs. *South: Modern Southern Literature in Its Cultural Setting.* Garden City, N.Y.: Dolphin, 1961.

Rubin, Louis D., Jr., and James J. Kilpatrick, eds. *The Lasting South: Fourteen Southerners Look at Their Home.* Chicago: Regnery, 1957.

Rudolph, Frederick. "The American Liberty League, 1934–1940." *American Historical Review* 56 (Oct. 1950): 19–33.

Rusher, William A. *The Rise of the Right.* New York: Morrow, 1984.

Russo, John Paul. "The Tranquilized Poem: The Crisis of the New Criticism in the 1950s." *Texas Studies in Literature and Language* 30 (Summer 1988): 198–229.

Schlesinger, Arthur M., Jr. "The New Conservatism: Politics of Nostalgia." *Reporter,* 16 June 1955, 9–12.

———. "Not Left, Not Right, but a Vital Center." *New York Times Magazine,* 4 Apr. 1948, 7, 44–47.

———. *The Vital Center: The Politics of Freedom.* Boston: Houghton Mifflin, 1949.

Schulman, Bruce J. *From Cotton Belt to Sunbelt: Federal Policy, Economic Development, and the Transformation of the South.* New York: Oxford University Press, 1991.

Schwartz, Lawrence H. *Creating Faulkner's Reputation: The Politics of Modern Literary Criticism.* Knoxville: University of Tennessee Press, 1988.

Schwartz, Sanford. *The Matrix of Modernism: Pound, Eliot, and Early Twentieth-Century Thought.* Princeton: Princeton University Press, 1985.

Scotchie, Joseph. *Barbarians in the Saddle: An Intellectual Biography of Richard M. Weaver.* New Brunswick, N.J.: Transaction, 1997.

———, ed. *The Vision of Richard*

Weaver. New Brunswick, N.J.: Transaction, 1995.

"Segregation and Democracy." *National Review*, 25 Jan. 1956, 5.

Shapiro, Edward S. "American Conservative Intellectuals, the 1930s, and the Crisis of Ideology." *Modern Age* 23 (Fall 1979): 370–80.

———. "Catholic Agrarian Thought and the New Deal." *Catholic Historical Review* 65 (Oct. 1979): 583–99.

———. "Decentralist Intellectuals and the New Deal." *Journal of American History* 58 (Mar. 1972): 938–57.

Shusterman, Richard. *T. S. Eliot and the Philosophy of Criticism.* New York: Columbia University Press, 1988.

Simpson, Glenn R. "Four Years Later, Buchanan's Advisors, Not His Words, Draw Cries of Extremism." *Wall Street Journal*, 22 Feb. 1996, A16.

Simpson, Lewis P. *The Brazen Face of History: Studies in the Literary Consciousness in America.* Baton Rouge: Louisiana State University Press, 1980.

———. *The Fable of the Southern Writer.* Baton Rouge: Louisiana State University Press, 1994.

———. "The Story of M. E. Bradford." *Southern Literary Journal* 26 (Spring 1994): 102–8.

Simpson, Lewis P., James Olney, and Jo Gulledge, eds. *"The Southern Review" and Modern Literature, 1935–1985.* Baton Rouge: Louisiana State University Press, 1988.

Singal, Daniel Joseph. *The War Within: From Victorian to Modernist Thought in the South, 1919–1945.* Chapel Hill: University of North Carolina Press, 1982.

Smith, Henry. "The Dilemma of Agrarianism." *Southwest Review* 19 (Apr. 1934): 215–32.

Smith, Oran P., ed. *So Good a Cause: A Decade of "Southern Partisan."* Columbia, S.C.: Foundation for American Education, 1993.

Smith, Ted J., III. *Steps toward Restoration: The Consequences of*

Richard Weaver's Ideas. Wilmington, Del.: Intercollegiate Studies Institute, 1998.

———, ed. *In Defense of Tradition: Collected Shorter Writings of Richard M. Weaver, 1929–1963.* Indianapolis: Liberty Fund, 2001.

Southard, W. P. "The Religious Poetry of Robert Penn Warren." *Kenyon Review* 7 (Autumn 1945): 653–76.

Spender, Stephen. "Beyond Liberalism." *Commentary* 10 (Aug. 1950): 188–92.

Squires, Radcliffe. *Allen Tate: A Literary Biography.* New York: Pegasus, 1971.

———, ed. *Allen Tate and His Work: Critical Evaluations.* Minneapolis: University of Minnesota Press, 1972.

"The State of Conservatism: A Symposium." *Intercollegiate Review* 21 (Spring 1986): 3–28.

Stewart, John L. *The Burden of Time: The Fugitives and Agrarians: The Nashville Groups of the 1920's and 1930's, and the Writings of John Crowe Ransom, Allen Tate, and Robert Penn Warren.* Princeton: Princeton University Press, 1965.

Stewart, Randall. "The Relation between Fugitives and Agrarians." *Mississippi Quarterly* 13 (Spring 1960): 55–60.

Stoke, Harold W. "The Outlook for American Conservatism." *South Atlantic Quarterly* 41 (July 1942): 266–74.

Stone, Albert E., Jr. "Seward Collins and the American Review: Experiment in Pro-Fascism, 1933–37." *American Quarterly* 12 (Spring 1960): 3–19.

Strout, Cushing. "Liberalism, Conservatism, and the Babel of Tongues." *Partisan Review* 25 (Winter 1958): 101–9.

Sullivan, Walter. *Allen Tate: A Recollection.* Baton Rouge: Louisiana State University Press, 1988.

———. *In Praise of Blood Sports and Other Essays.* Baton Rouge:

Louisiana State University Press,
1990.
———. *Requiem for the Renascence:
The State of Fiction in the Modern
South.* Athens: University of
Georgia Press, 1976.
Sumner, Gregory. *Dwight Macdonald
and the "Politics" Circle: The
Challenge of Cosmopolitan Democracy.*
Ithaca, N.Y.: Cornell University
Press, 1996.
Susman, Warren I. *Culture as History:
The Transformation of American
Society in the Twentieth Century.*
New York: Pantheon, 1984.
"A Symposium: The Agrarians
Today." *Shenandoah* 3 (Summer
1952): 14–33.
Tate, Allen. "Emily Dickinson."
Outlook, 15 Aug. 1928, 621–23.
———. *Essays of Four Decades.*
Chicago: Swallow Press, 1968.
———. "The Fallacy of Humanism."
Hound and Horn 3 (Jan.–March
1930): 234–57.
———. "Fascism and the Southern
Agrarians." *New Republic,* 27 May
1936, 75–76.
———. *The Fathers.* Denver: Swallow,
1960.
———. *Jefferson Davis: His Rise and
Fall: A Biographical Narrative.* New
York: Minton, Balch, & Co., 1929.
———. "Last Days of the Charming
Lady." *Nation,* 28 Oct. 1925,
485–86.
———. *Memoirs and Opinions,
1926–1974.* Chicago: Swallow, 1975.
———. "Miss Emily and the
Bibliographer." *American Scholar*
9 (Autumn 1940): 449–60.
———. *Mr. Pope and Other Poems.*
New York: Minton, Balch, and Co.,
1928.
———. "Narcissus as Narcissus."
Virginia Quarterly Review 14
(Winter 1938): 108–22.
———. "The New Provincialism."
Virginia Quarterly Review 21 (Spring
1945): 262–72.
———. "One Escape from the
Dilemma." *Fugitive* 2 (Apr. 1924):
34–36.
———. "The Profession of Letters in

the South." *Virginia Quarterly
Review* 11 (Apr. 1935): 161–76.
———. *Reactionary Essays on Poetry
and Ideas.* New York: Scribner's,
1936.
———. "Regionalism and
Sectionalism." *New Republic,*
23 Dec. 1931, 158–61.
———. "The Revolt against
Literature." *New Republic,* 9 Feb.
1927, 329–30.
———. "The Same Fallacy of
Humanism: A Reply to Mr. Robert
Shafer." *Bookman* 71 (Mar. 1930):
30–36.
———. "A Southern Mode of the
Imagination: Circa 1918 to the
Present." *Carleton Miscellany*
1 (Winter 1960): 9–23.
———. *Stonewall Jackson: The Good
Soldier.* 1928. Reprint, Nashville:
J. S. Sanders, 1991.
———. "Tiresias." *Nation,* 17 Nov.
1926, 509.
———. "A Traditionist Looks at
Liberalism." *Southern Review*
1 (Spring 1936): 731–44.
———. "What Is a Traditional
Society?" *American Review* 7 (Sept.
1936): 376–87.
———, ed. *A Southern Vanguard: The
John Peale Bishop Memorial Volume.*
New York: Prentice-Hall, 1947.
Teres, Harvey M. *Renewing the
American Left: Politics, Imagination,
and the New York Intellectuals.* New
York: Oxford University Press,
1996.
"*Time on the Cross:* Debate." *National
Review,* 28 Mar. 1975, 340–42, 359.
"Toward a Healthy Community: An
Interview with Wendell Berry."
Christian Century, 15 Oct. 1997, 912.
Trilling, Lionel. *The Liberal
Imagination: Essays on Literature and
Society.* 1950. Reprint, New York:
Anchor, 1953.
Twelve Southerners. *I'll Take My
Stand: The South and the Agrarian
Tradition.* 1930. Reprint, Baton
Rouge: Louisiana State University
Press, 1977.
Tyranny at Oak Ridge. Nashville:
Tennessee Federation for
Constitutional Government, 1956.

Viereck, Peter. "But—I'm a Conservative!" *Atlantic* 165 (Apr. 1940): 538–43.
———. *Conservatism Revisited.* Rev. ed. New York: Free Press, 1962.
———. *Conservatism Revisited: The Revolt against Revolt, 1815–1949.* New York: Scribner's, 1949.
———. "Conservatism vs. Smugness." *Saturday Review,* 3 Oct. 1953, 38–39.
———. "Liberals and Conservatives, 1789–1951." *Antioch Review* 11 (Dec. 1951): 387–96.
———. *Metapolitics: From the Romantics to Hitler.* New York: Knopf, 1941.
———. "The Rootless 'Roots': Defects in the New Conservatism." *Antioch Review* 15 (June 1955): 217–29.
Voegelin, Eric. *The New Science of Politics: An Introduction.* Chicago: University of Chicago Press, 1987.
Waldron, Ann. *Close Connections: Caroline Gordon and the Southern Renaissance.* 1987. Reprint, Knoxville: University of Tennessee Press, 1989.
Walker, Marshall. *Robert Penn Warren: A Vision Earned.* New York: Barnes & Noble, 1979.
Wallace, Anthony F. C. *The Death and Rebirth of the Seneca.* New York: Knopf, 1973.
Walter, E. V. "Conservatism Recrudescent: A Critique." *Partisan Review* 21 (Sept.-Oct. 1954): 512–23.
Warren, Robert Penn. *All the King's Men.* 1946. Reprint, San Diego: Harcourt Brace Jovanovich, 1982.
———. *Band of Angels.* New York: Signet, 1955.
———. *Brother to Dragons: A Tale in Verse and Voices.* New York: Random House, 1953.
———. "Episode in a Dime Store." *Southern Review* 30 (Autumn 1994): 654–57.
———. "Faulkner: The South and the Negro." *Southern Review* 1 (July 1965): 501–29.
———. *Jefferson Davis Gets His Citizenship Back.* Lexington: University Press of Kentucky, 1980.

———. *John Brown: The Making of a Martyr.* 1929. Reprint, Nashville: J. S. Sanders, 1993.
———. "John Crowe Ransom: A Study in Irony." *Virginia Quarterly Review* 11 (Jan. 1935): 92–112.
———. "Knowledge and the Image of Man." *Sewanee Review* 63 (Spring 1955): 182–92.
———. "Malcolm X: Mission and Meaning." *Yale Review* 56 (Dec. 1966): 161–71.
———. "Nostromo." *Sewanee Review* 59 (Summer 1951): 363–91.
———. *Portrait of a Father.* Lexington: University Press of Kentucky, 1988.
———. *A Robert Penn Warren Reader.* New York: Vintage, 1987.
———. *Segregation: The Inner Conflict of the South.* New York: Random House, 1956.
———. *Who Speaks for the Negro?* New York: Random House, 1965.
Watkins, Floyd C. *Then and Now: The Personal Past in the Poetry of Robert Penn Warren.* Lexington: University Press of Kentucky, 1982.
Watkins, Floyd C., John T. Hiers, and Mary Louise Weaks, eds. *Talking with Robert Penn Warren.* Athens: University of Georgia Press, 1990.
Weaver, Richard M. "Agrarianism in Exile." *Sewanee Review* 58 (Autumn 1950): 586–606.
———. "An Altered Stand." *National Review,* 17 June 1961, 389–90.
———. "Anatomy of Freedom." *National Review,* 4 Dec. 1962, 443–44.
———. "Aspects of the Southern Philosophy." *Hopkins Review* 5 (Summer 1952): 5–21.
———. *The Ethics of Rhetoric.* Chicago: Regnery, 1953.
———. "Humanism in an Age of Science." *Intercollegiate Review* 7 (Fall 1970): 11–18.
———. *Ideas Have Consequences.* Chicago: University of Chicago Press, 1948.
———. "Integration Is

Communization." *National Review*,
13 July 1957, 67–68.

———. "Life without Prejudice."
Modern Age 1 (Summer 1957): 4–9.

———. *Life without Prejudice and
Other Essays*. Chicago: Regnery,
1965.

———. "The Older Religiousness in
the South." *Sewanee Review* 51 (Apr.
1943): 237–49.

———. "Southern Chivalry and Total
War." *Sewanee Review* 53 (Apr.
1945): 267–78.

———. *The Southern Tradition at Bay:
A History of Postbellum Thought*.
Edited by George Core and M. E.
Bradford. New Rochelle, N.Y.:
Arlington House, 1968.

———. "Two Types of American
Individualism." *Modern Age*
7 (Spring 1963): 119–34.

———. "Up from Liberalism."
Modern Age 3 (Winter 1958–59):
21–32.

———. *Visions of Order: The Cultural
Crisis of Our Time*. Baton Rouge:
Louisiana State University Press,
1964.

Weisbrot, Robert. *Freedom Bound:
A History of America's Civil Rights
Movement*. New York: Plume, 1991.

Whitaker, Robert W., ed. *The New
Right Papers*. New York: St.
Martin's Press, 1982.

"Why the South Must Prevail."
National Review, 24 Aug. 1957,
148–49.

Wiener, Jonathan M. "Radical
Historians and the Crisis in
American History, 1959–1980."
Journal of American History 76
(Sept. 1989): 399–434.

Wilhelmsen, Frederick D. "Melvin E.
Bradford: Adiós, A Dios . . . ."
Modern Age 36 (Fall 1993): 103–4.

———. "To Recover a Concept and a
Tradition." *Commonweal*, 19 June
1953, 278–79.

Will, George F. "A Shrill Assault on
Mr. Lincoln." *Washington Post*,
29 Nov. 1981, C7.

Williamson, Joel. *The Crucible of Race:
Black-White Relations in the
American South since Emancipation*.

New York: Oxford University
Press, 1984.

Wills, Garry. *Confessions of a
Conservative*. Garden City, N.Y.:
Doubleday, 1979.

Wilson, Charles Reagan. *Baptized in
Blood: The Religion of the Lost Cause,
1864–1920*. Athens: University of
Georgia Press, 1980.

Wilson, Clyde N., ed. *A Defender of
Southern Conservatism: M. E.
Bradford and His Achievements*.
Columbia: University of Missouri
Press, 1999.

Wilson, Edmund. "Tennessee
Agrarians." *New Republic*, 29 July
1931, 279–81.

Wilson, Francis G. "A Theory of
Conservatism." *American Political
Science Review* 35 (Feb. 1941):
29–43.

Winchell, Mark Royden. *Cleanth
Brooks and the Rise of Modern
Criticism*. Charlottesville:
University Press of Virginia, 1996.

———. "An Extended Family."
Southern Review 31 (Apr. 1995):
197–218.

———. "The Paleoconservative
Imagination." *Chronicles* 21 (Apr.
1997): 18–21.

———. *Where No Flag Flies: Donald
Davidson and the Southern Resistance*.
Columbia: University of Missouri
Press, 2000.

———. "The Whole Horse: Walter
Sullivan and the State of Southern
Letters." *Hollins Critic* 27 (Feb.
1990): 1–10.

———, ed. *The Vanderbilt Tradition:
Essays in Honor of Thomas Daniel
Young*. Baton Rouge: Louisiana
State University Press, 1991.

Wood, Edwin Thomas. "On Native
Soil: A Talk with Robert Penn
Warren." *Mississippi Quarterly* 37
(Spring 1984): 179–86.

Woodward, C. Vann. *The Burden of
Southern History*. Baton Rouge:
Louisiana State University Press,
1960.

Wright, Gavin. *Old South, New South:
Revolutions in the Southern Economy
since the Civil War*. Baton Rouge:

Louisiana State University Press, 1996.

Wynn, Dudley. "A Liberal Looks at Tradition." *Virginia Quarterly Review* 12 (Jan. 1936): 59–79.

Young, Fred Douglas. *Richard M. Weaver, 1910–1963: A Life of the Mind.* Columbia: University of Missouri Press, 1995.

Young, Thomas Daniel. "From Fugitives to Agrarians." *Mississippi Quarterly* 33 (Fall 1980): 420–24.

———. *Gentleman in a Dustcoat: A Biography of John Crowe Ransom.* Baton Rouge: Louisiana State University Press, 1976.

———. *John Crowe Ransom: An Annotated Bibliography.* New York: Garland, 1982.

———. *Waking Their Neighbors Up: The Nashville Agrarians Rediscovered.* Athens: University of Georgia Press, 1982.

Young, Thomas Daniel, and George Core, eds. *Selected Letters of John Crowe Ransom.* Baton Rouge: Louisiana State University Press, 1985.

Young, Thomas Daniel, and John J. Hindle, eds. *The Republic of Letters: The Correspondence of John Peale Bishop and Allen Tate.* Lexington: University Press of Kentucky, 1981.

Young, Thomas Daniel, and M. Thomas Inge. *Donald Davidson.* New York: Twayne, 1971.

———. *Donald Davidson: An Essay and a Bibliography.* Nashville: Vanderbilt University Press, 1965.

Young, Thomas Daniel, and Elizabeth Sarcone, eds. *The Lytle-Tate Letters: The Correspondence of Andrew Lytle and Allen Tate.* Jackson: University Press of Mississippi, 1987.